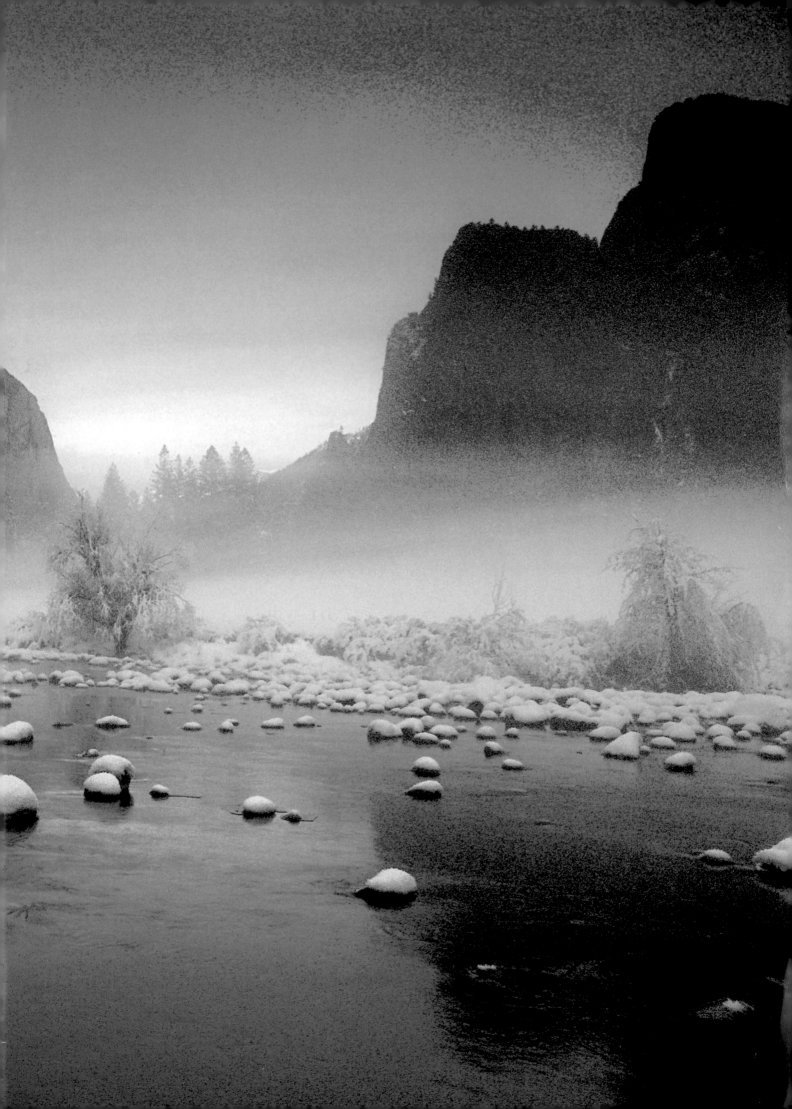

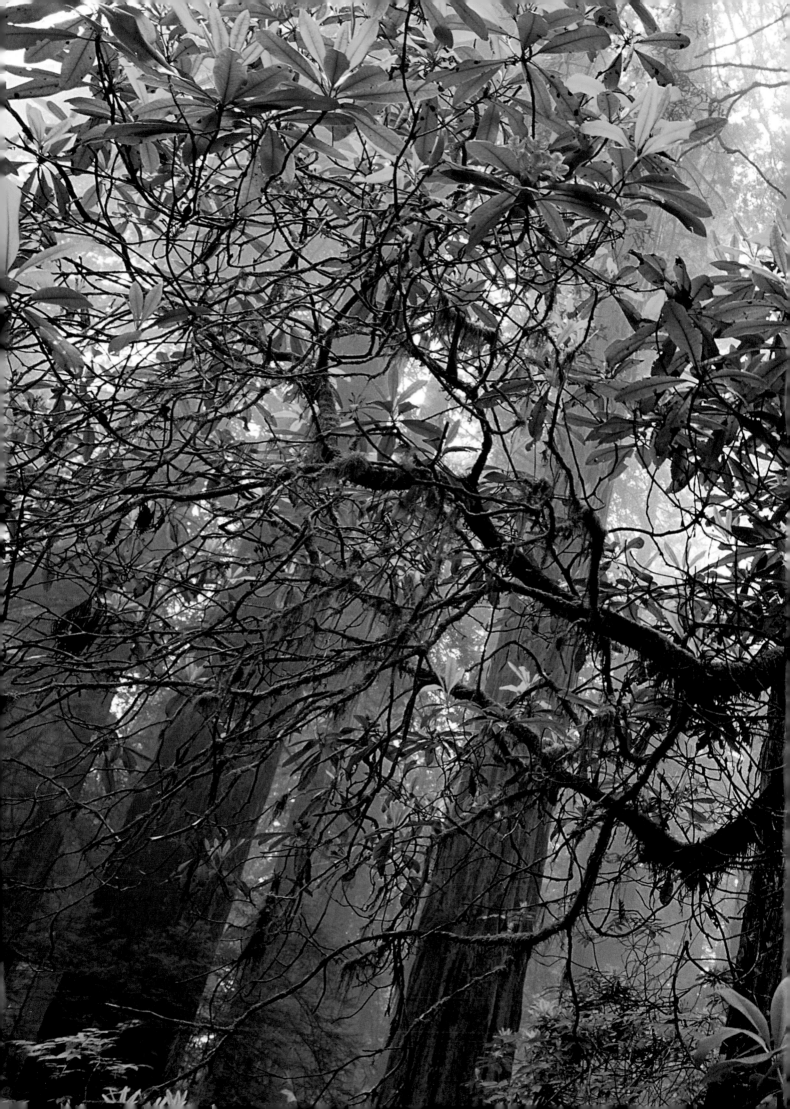

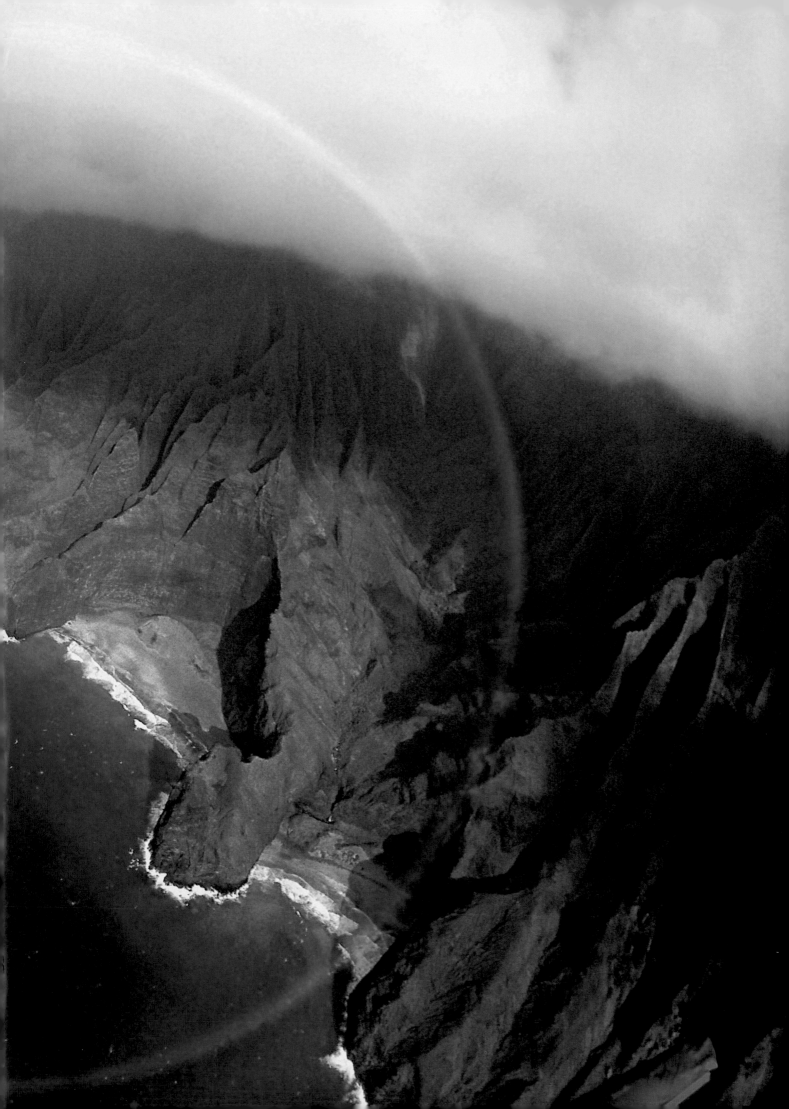

NORTH AMERICA
the beautiful

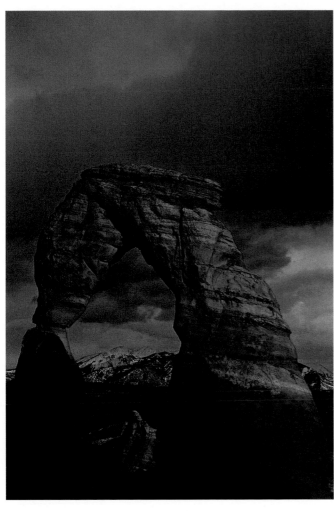

Texts and photographs
Galen Rowell

Graphic design
Luana Gobbo

Editorial coordination
Laura Accomazzo

ISBN 88-544-0108-0

Reprints:
 2 3 4 5 6   10 09 08 07 06

© Photos by Galen Rowell/
Mountain Light Photography

Printed in Indonesia.
Color separations by Fotomec, Turin.

Contents

1 First light over San Francisco and the Golden Gate National Recreation Area, world's largest urban national park.

2–3 A winter sunset turns the face of El Capitan to gold at Gates of the Valley in Yosemite National Park.

4–5 Rising out of the fog along California's North Coast, a cathedral forest of old-growth redwoods reaches skyward out of blooming rhododendrons.

6–7 An extremely rare 360-degree double rainbow frames the richly-colored Na Pali Coast of Kauai Island, Hawaii.

8 Symbolic of the fantastic wind-carved forms of the desert Southwest, Delicate Arch frames a vision of a sandstone spire and the snowy La Sal Mountains of Utah.

9 Alpenglow sets the Sierra Wave afire high over the Owens Valley, America's deepest. Fueled by moist winds from the Pacific Ocean, such lenticular cloud bands form in blue skies on the lee side of California's Sierra Nevada Range.

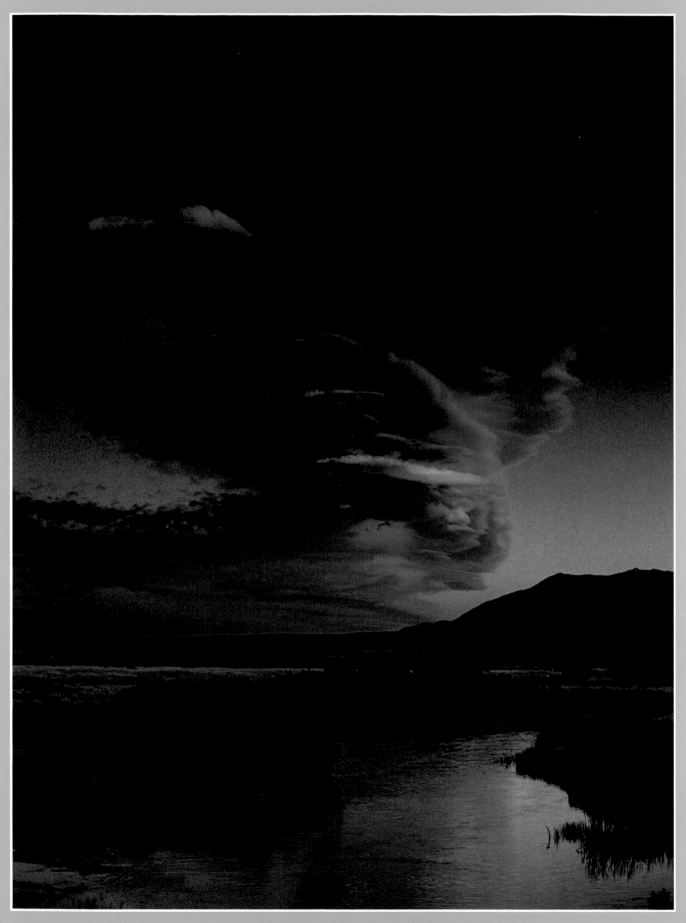

10–11 On a stormy fall evening, the saline, inland sea of Mono Lake adorns the desert of Eastern California with a riot of colors.

12–13 A winter sunrise paints the twisted limbs of an ancient bristlecone pine in California's White Mountains.

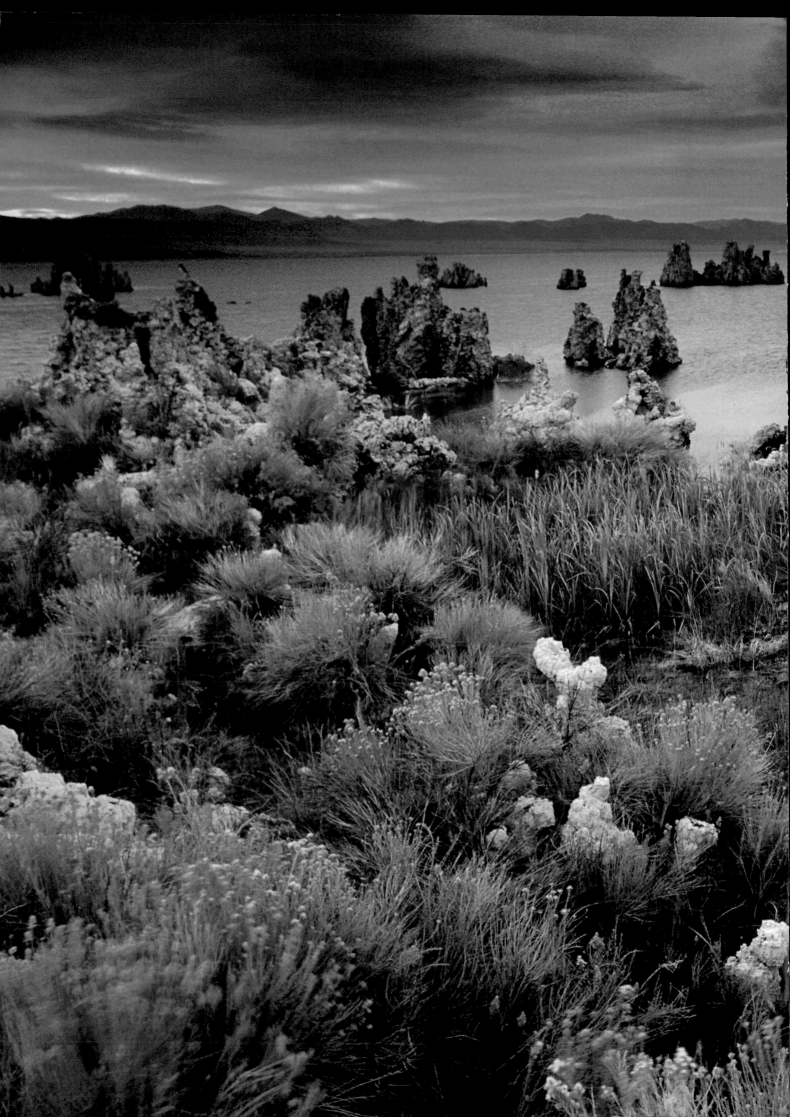

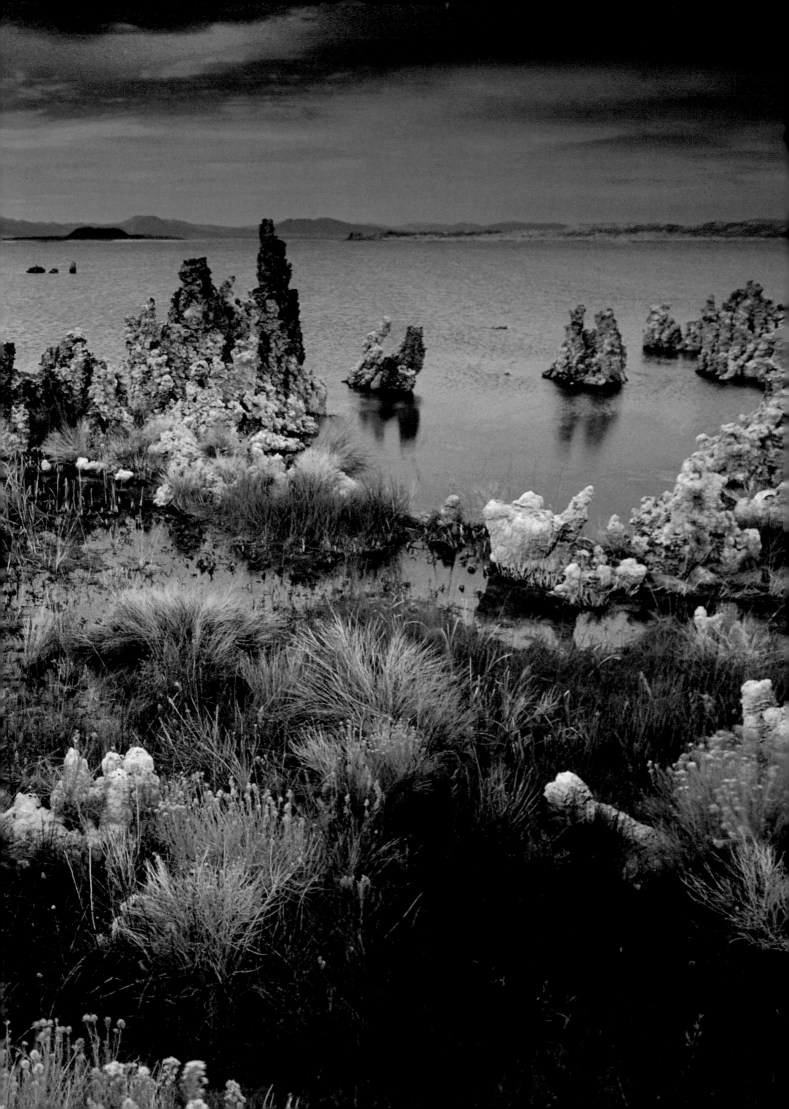

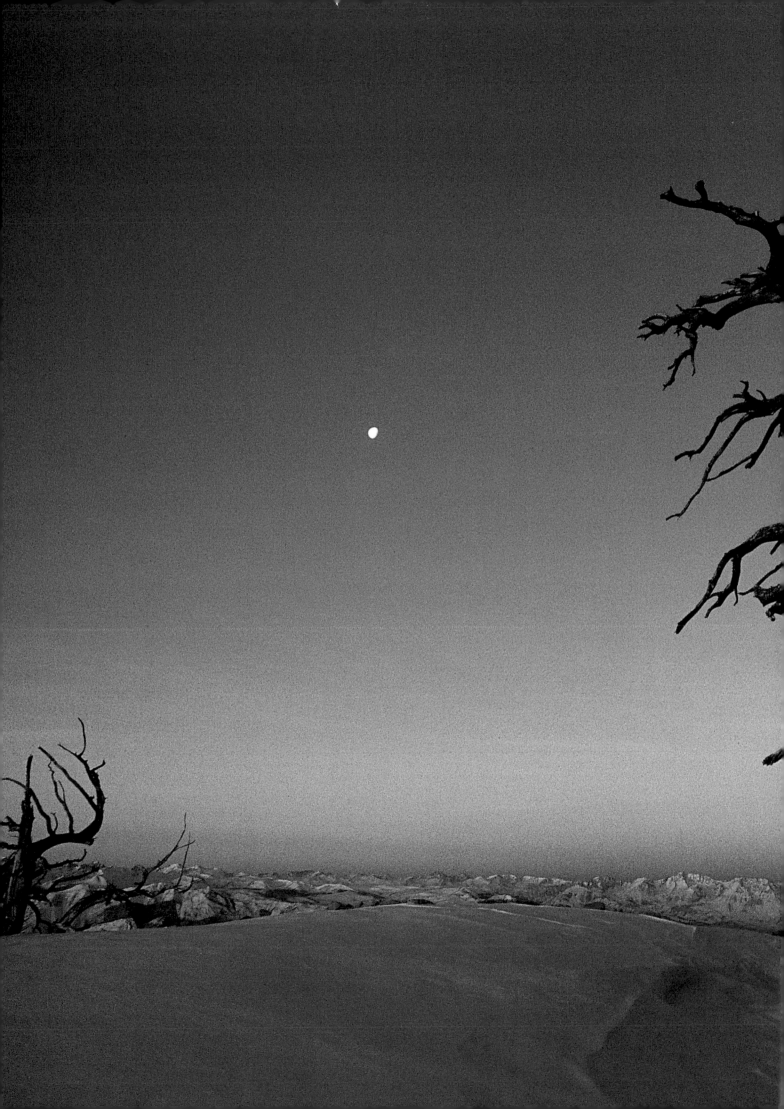

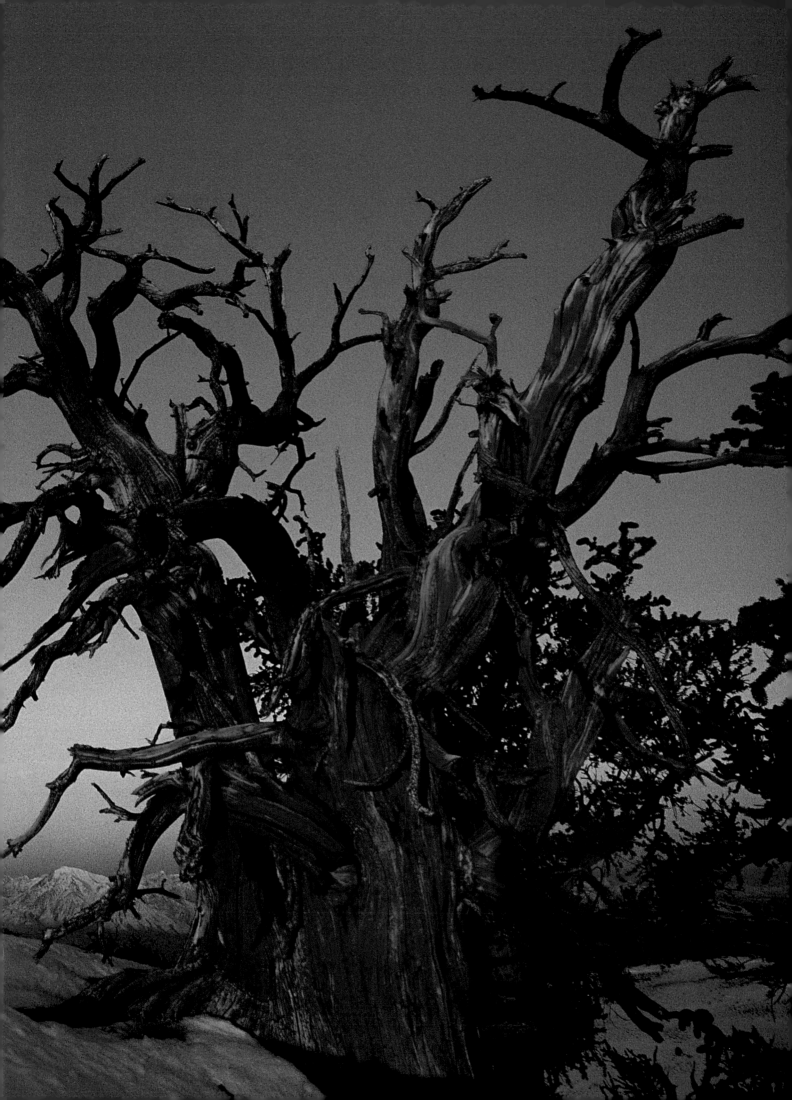

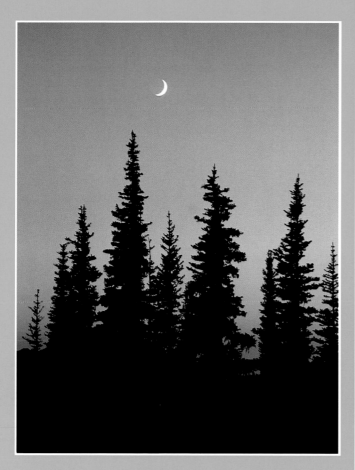

14 A crescent moon hovers over forested Hurricane Ridge on Washington's Olympic Peninsula.

14 A crescent moon hovers over forested Hurricane Ridge on Washington's Olympic Peninsula.

Introduction

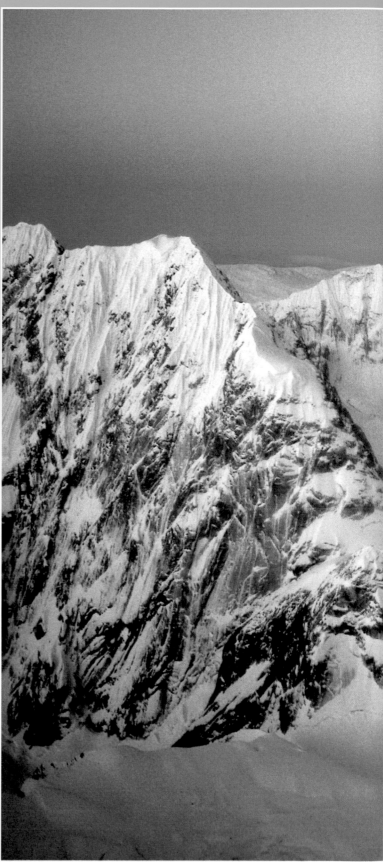

14–15 Like an outsized vision of Yosemite in the Pleistocene, granite walls rise 4,500 feet above Alaska's Ruth Glacier in Denali National Park.

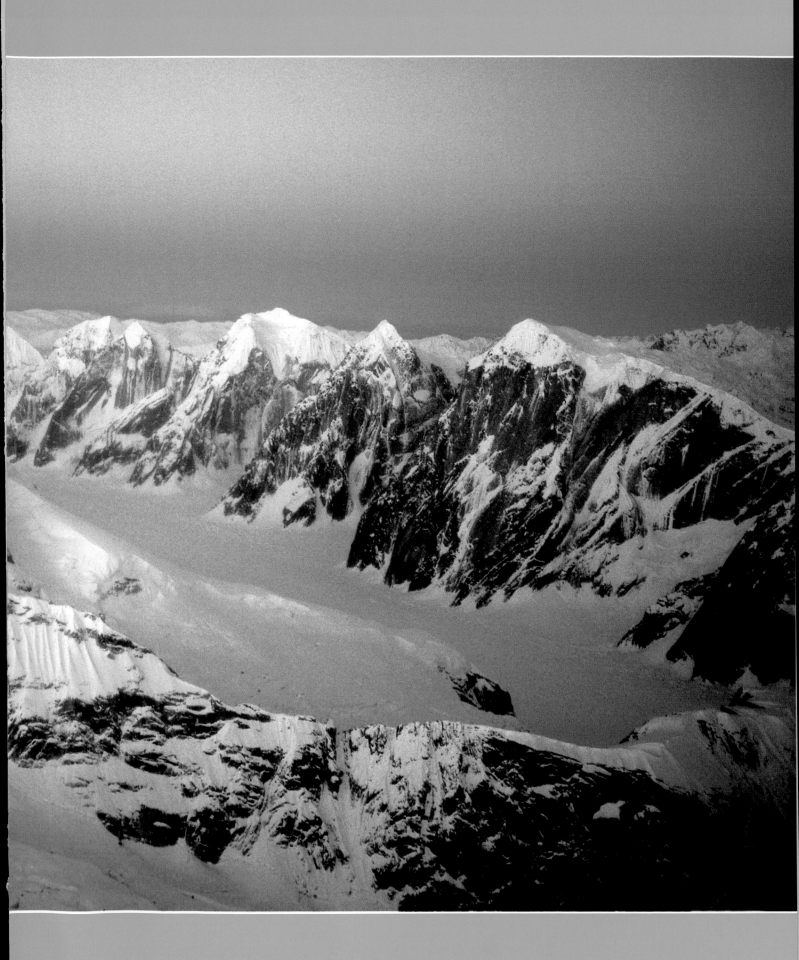

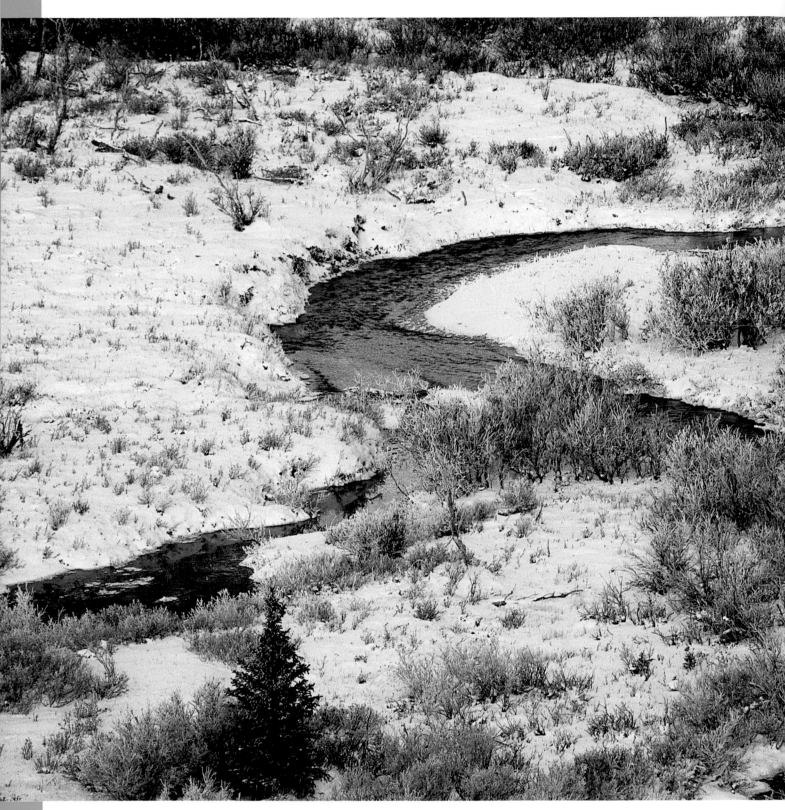

18–19 In Alaska's Denali National Park, the waters of the Savage River reflect an early sunset on a fall afternoon, shortly before they freeze over for the long winter.

19 top August wildflowers line the edge of the Going-to-the-Sun Highway on its way to Logan Pass in Montana's Glacier National Park.

19 bottom A bristlecone pine snag, hewn by eons of winds beneath Wheeler Peak in Nevada's Great Basin National Park, is part of the same grove where the world's oldest known living thing, a 4,900-year-old tree, was found in 1964.

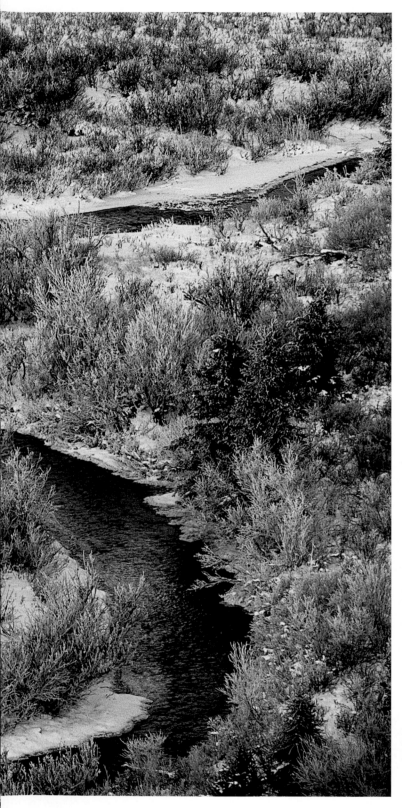

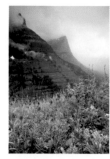

Caribbean, and so much more."

For the most part, I have chosen photographs that match my moments of greatest passion, rather than subjects that geographers have measured as superlatives. Sometimes the concepts overlap, but often the highest mountain or longest river of a region are absent. Due to perception of Central America as a distinct region of its own and space limitations, I opted not to include my considerable coverage of this slender continental ribbon south of Mexico.

Though we tend to think of photographs as only representing what was before the lens at a particular moment, they communicate human intention in the way subjects are selected, composed, and exposed. When the controlled intention of one person's hand and eye becomes consistently recognizable from

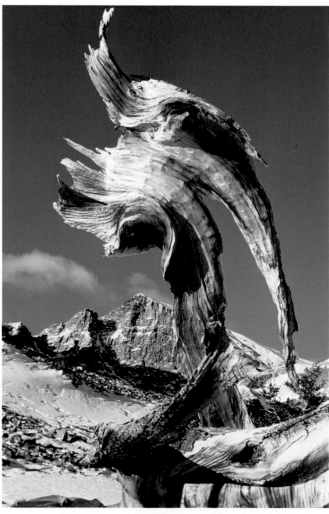

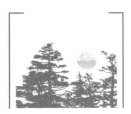

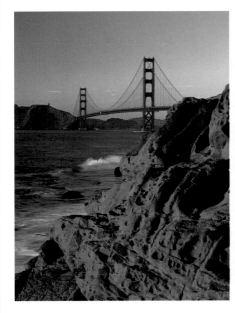

image to image, we call it style. Mine involves moving beyond simple documentation until I begin to feel part of a place physically, mentally, and visually. Only then, after the photograph I'm about to take has become a natural expression of my being and I can visualize how the world before me will appear very differently on film, do I apply my technical photographic skills to create an image.

Nature photographers hold a sacred trust to reproduce no more or less than what was actually before their lenses. No photographs in this book have added subject matter or colors not present at the scene. Where needed, color-neutral graduated filters of my design have been used to control excessive lighting contrasts. No distractions, such as twigs or trash, have been deleted. All animals were photographed in the wild, with the exception of an endangered Florida panther in an Everglades wildlife rehabilitation enclosure. Moments after I clicked the shutter, a second panther jumped me from behind. No wonder I favor the wilds!

20 San Francisco's Golden Gate was named for the sunset colors of its sea cliffs a century before the building of the bridge.

20–21 Coastal California fog veils San Francisco at twilight in this extreme telephoto from the distant Berkeley Hills.

22–23 Walden Pond's abstract reflections of New England fall colors mirror the vision of Henry Thoreau, who lived there in the 1850s and wrote Walden, the original manifesto of American environmental philosophy.

24–25 The barren sands of Mexico's Baja Peninsula ripple beside Magdelena Bay, a key breeding site for gray whales.

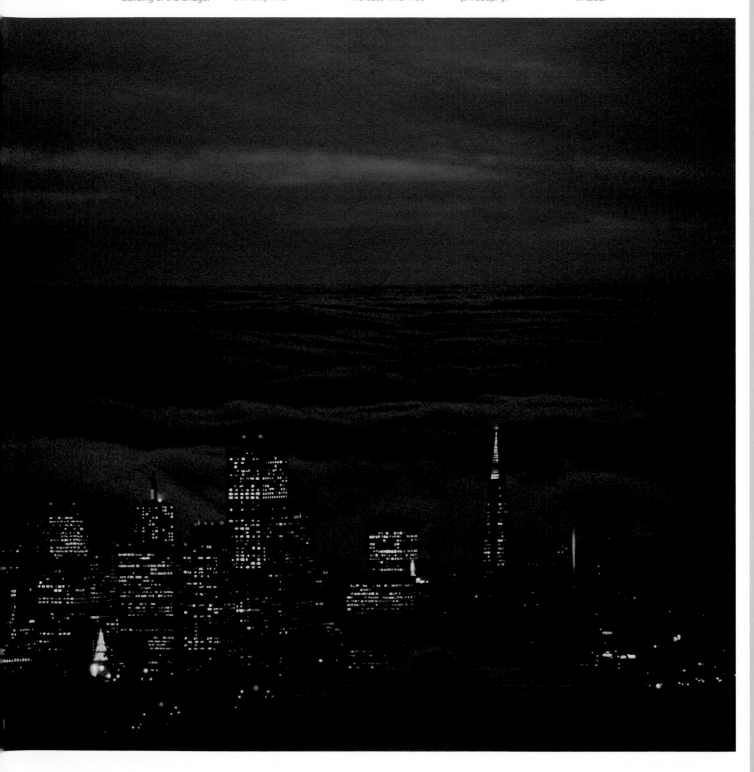

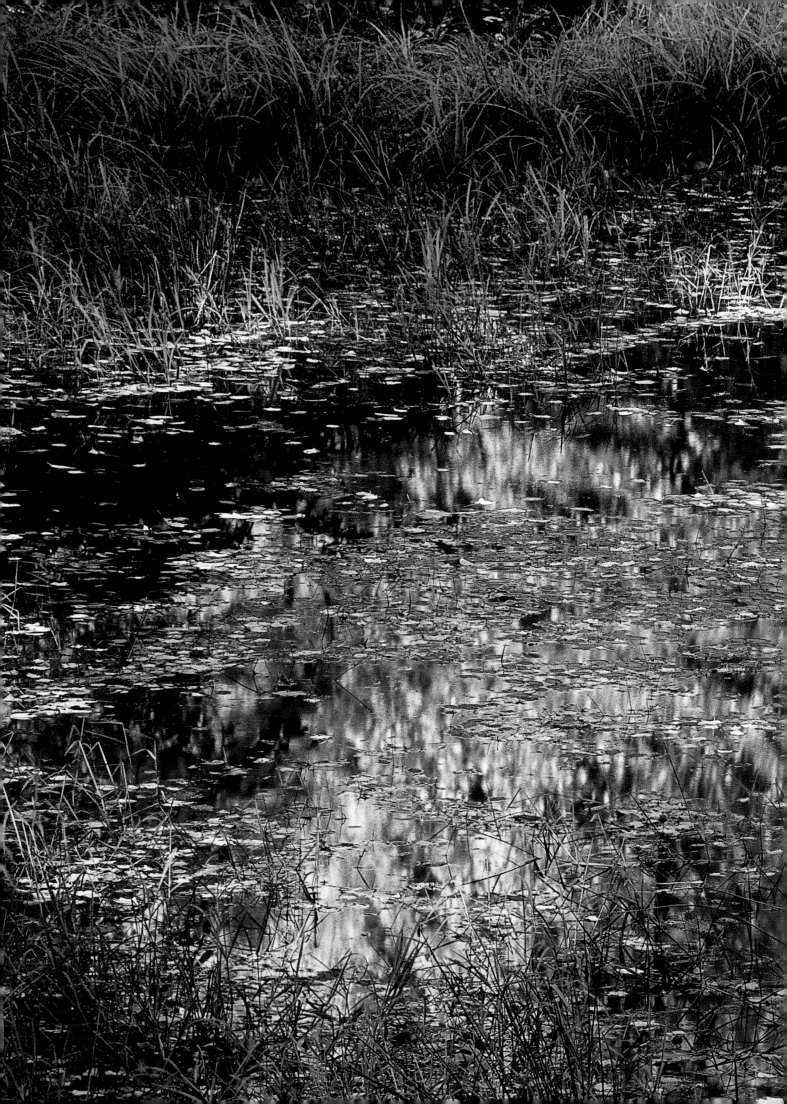

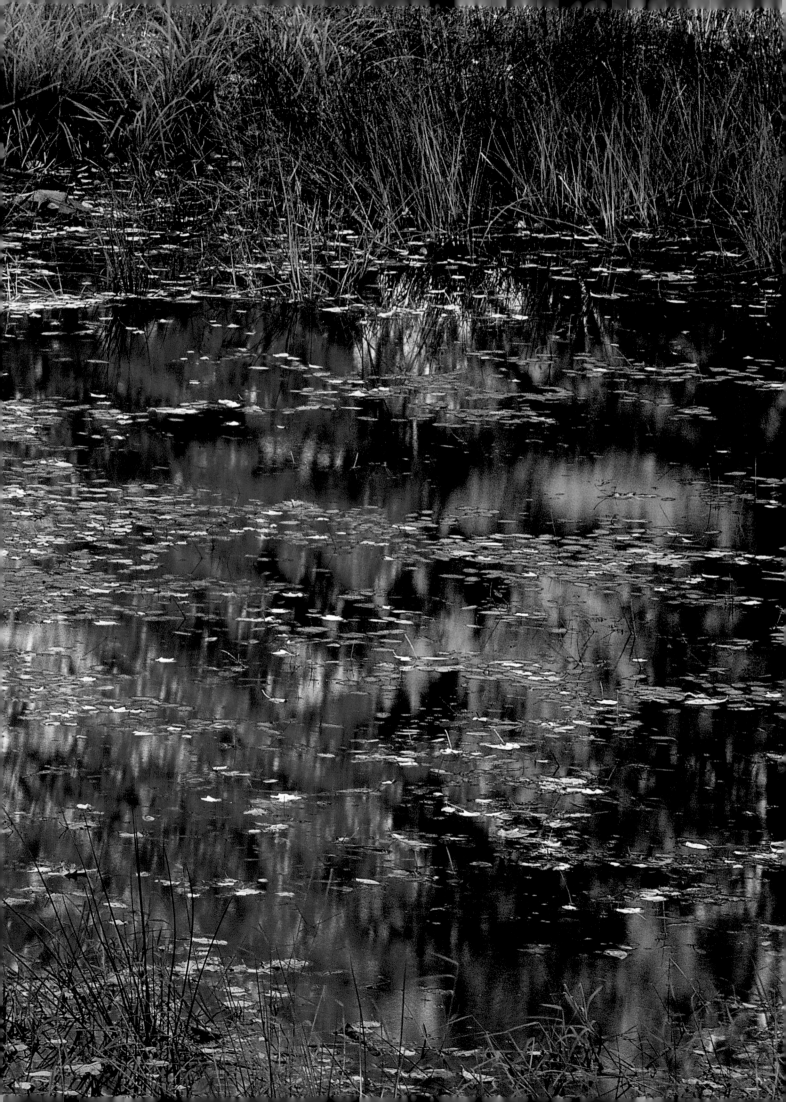

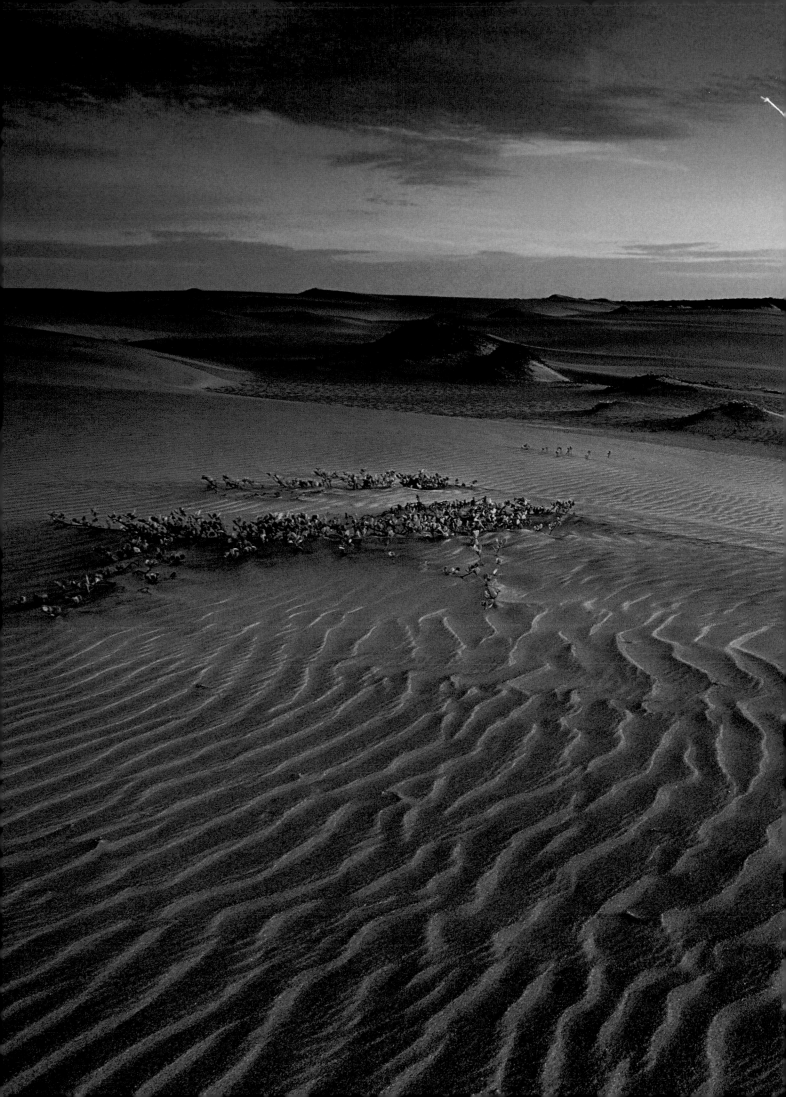

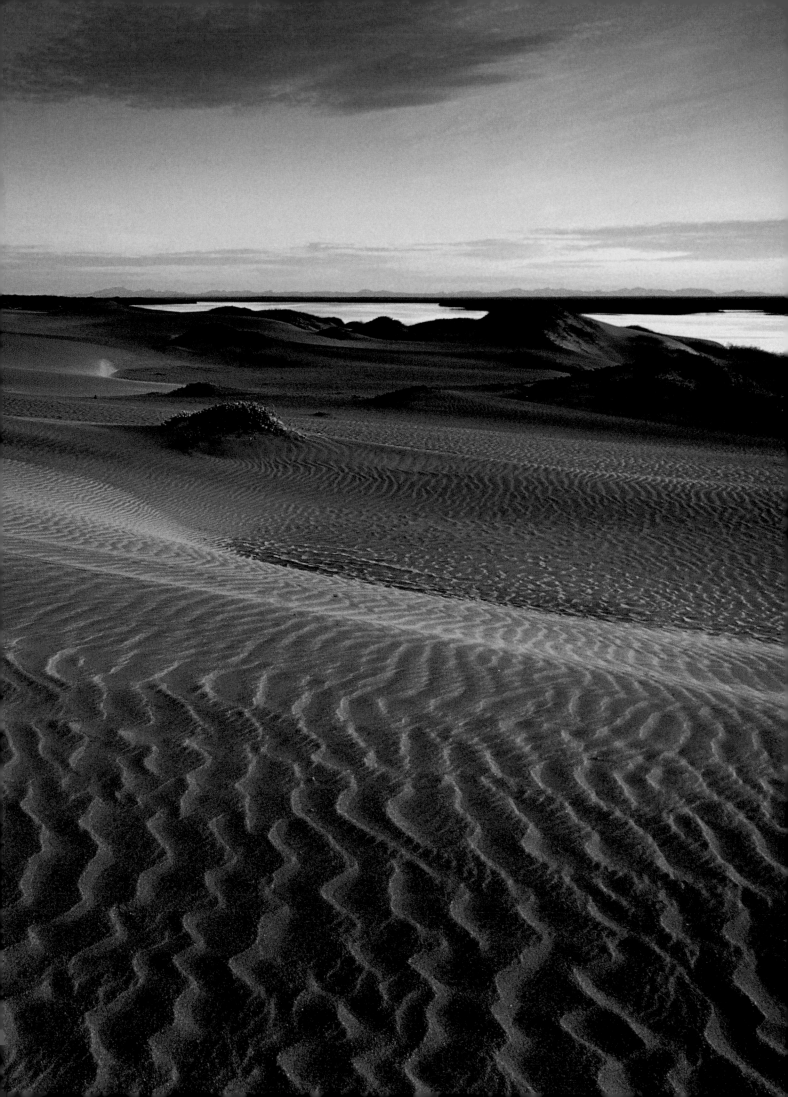

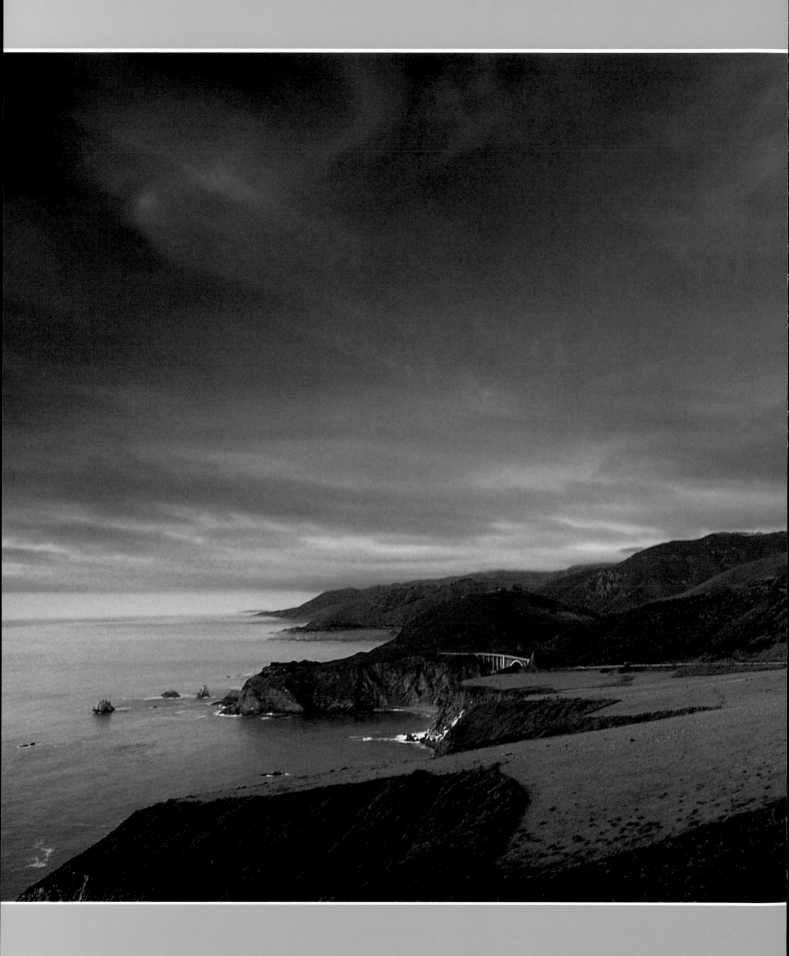

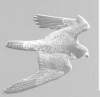

26–27 In the early
spring along the
rugged and wild Big
Sur Coast, an open
field near Bixby
Creek turns vivid
green.

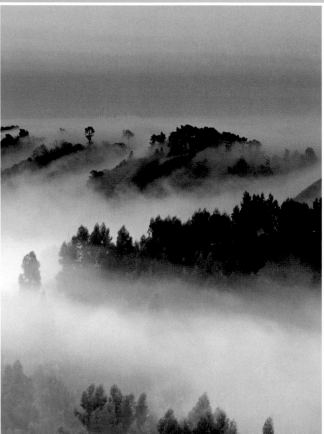

The California
Coast

27 Morning fog rolls
in from the Pacific
Ocean across the
Berkeley Hills on the
east side of San
Francisco Bay.

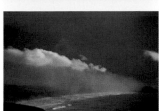

28 top A quiet spring dawn comes to the Big Sur Coast.

28 bottom Winter storm waves crash onto the Great Beach of Point Reyes National Seashore.

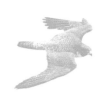

The most interesting natural landscapes are the edges—places where mountains meet skies, meadows meet forests, and rivers part the solid ground beneath our feet. The grandest edges of all are those of continents, where oceans and land have been doing battle over eons.

Among the most beautiful and diverse of the world's edges is the California Coast, traversing a thousand miles of unusually livable climate from the hot sandy surfing meccas of the south to the cool cathedral redwood forests of the north. More than 85 percent of California's 30 million residents have chosen to live within an hour's drive of the crashing waves and shifting sands that appear to define this massive edge, but the true source is below the surface, making itself known every few years in the earthquakes for which California has become rightly famous. Here along the coast, the massive North American and Pacific tectonic plates meet, not in collision, as has caused the Himalaya to rise in Asia, but in a transform boundary that slides horizontally.

I'm reminded of the geologic history of my home coast every time I look out from the Berkeley Hills above San Francisco Bay and see a pointed speck 25 miles out to sea beyond the city. The Farallon Islands, the largest nesting seabird colony in the United States outside of Alaska, are granite spires that perfectly match rocks in the Sierra Nevada, over three hundred miles to the south. The same movement of massive plates along the San Andreas Fault continues south of the border, where Baja California has become broadly separated from the Mexican mainland into a giant peninsula.

Though I'm best known for climbing and exploring the highest places on the planet, I've spent far more time exploring and enjoying the mild coastal wilderness that begins abruptly a block from my home. Here at the crest of the Berkeley Hills is another kind of edge, created by wise local land management, where civilization ends and protected wildlands begin. Several times a week I run out the door before dawn onto dirt trails through forest that lead me along a ridge crest which

normally rises above a blanket of fog that creeps in through the Golden Gate overnight to engulf all the Bay Area cities during the morning hours.

From the dank gray monotony of the fog, I abruptly meet the golden edge of sunlight, announced moments before I emerge into clear air by gold beams coming through the misty forest. From the highest hill, I see the Bay Area much as the first Americans did, looking down upon wildness merging with a sea of mist that hides the cities as it stretches out over the Pacific Ocean. Up here at first light, I'm more likely to see a deer or a coyote than another human being, yet the greater San Francisco Bay Area has over six million residents. Within forty miles of the city, more wildlands have been preserved than in any other metropolitan area of North America. Over two hundred natural preserves have a combined area larger than Yosemite National Park with even greater biodiversity and visitation.

Farther south around Santa Cruz, Monterey, Carmel, and Point Lobos are many more protected areas of coastline. Being anywhere wild in this zone of the central California Coast from Big Sur to Point Reyes on a clear spring morning gets my vote for one of the most pleasurable natural experiences on Earth. Green hills sprinkled with blue lupines and gold poppies—the colors of the University of California—roll inland from rugged headlands that drop into the sea. Trails snake in and out of coastal canyon, meadow, and forest with broad views and a surprise around every bend. The climate, neither too hot nor cold, is a mild winter-wet, summer-dry weather pattern found in only a few sectors of the Mediterranean, Australia, Chile, and South Africa.

In such comfort, I think nothing of heading out on wild trails for long hours wearing just running shorts and a tee shirt—and a camera, of course. The ideal climate has allowed me to perfect systems for hiking, running, or climbing with enough Nikon 35mm camera gear to make top-quality photographs. On a good day, strapping on a camera chest pouch for a solo run seems as normal as tying my shoes, whether for a short loop on trails near my home, seventeen roadless miles of

Mendocino County's Lost Coast, or thirty miles of the Ohlone Wilderness Trail on the east side of San Francisco Bay.

On weekend afternoons, I often head for my favorite path in Marin County, the Coastal Trail that leads through the Golden Gate National Recreation Area (world's largest urban national park) into Mount Tamalpais State Park across sheer open slopes that drop abruptly into the sea. In spring, the green meadows at my feet appear to touch the turquoise waters of Bolinas Lagoon, far below, which lies within the San Andreas Fault. During the famous earthquake of 1906, San Francisco abruptly moved sixteen feet farther south of the Point Reyes Peninsula that extends beyond the lagoon.

Though San Francisco Bay is one of the world's great natural harbors, Spanish galleons failed to notice it for centuries as they sailed along the misty coast. Even Sir Francis Drake, who repaired his ship near Point Reyes in 1579, failed to see the entrance. The bay was finally discovered by Europeans only when the Portola Expedition of 1769 ventured overland from the south. From high hills they observed much of its 400 miles of shoreline and spotted its narrow, mile-wide passage to the sea, later named the Golden Gate. Here the snow-fed waters of the Sacramento and San Joaquin Rivers merge with tidal currents to empty into the Pacific Ocean with a flow that regularly exceeds that of the Amazon.

Much of the central and northern California Coast was initially preserved by its very wildness. The ninety miles of the Big Sur coast were so remote and rugged that the first automobile road wasn't completed until 1937. After environmentalists won a later battle not to widen it into a freeway, the California Coastal Initiative of 1972 prohibited further development along most of the state's remaining wild shores, leaving the primeval forces of surf, headland, and earthquake to battle it out for eternity.

Farther south, protection came too late to preserve much of the coastline from Los Angeles to the Mexican border in a wild state. Resorts, businesses, homes, and highways had forever changed the natural character of the most naturally

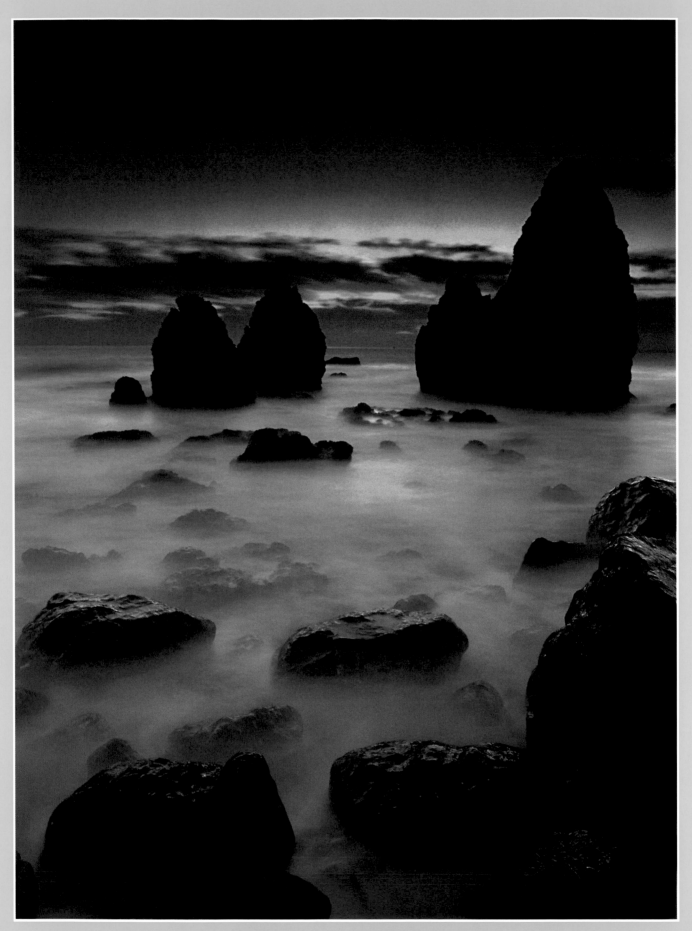

29 Twilight surf is turned into mist by a 10-second exposure as it flows around tall sea stacks at Rodeo Beach in the Marin Headlands of Golden Gate National Recreation Area north of San Francisco. At low tide the sea stacks are surrounded by sand.

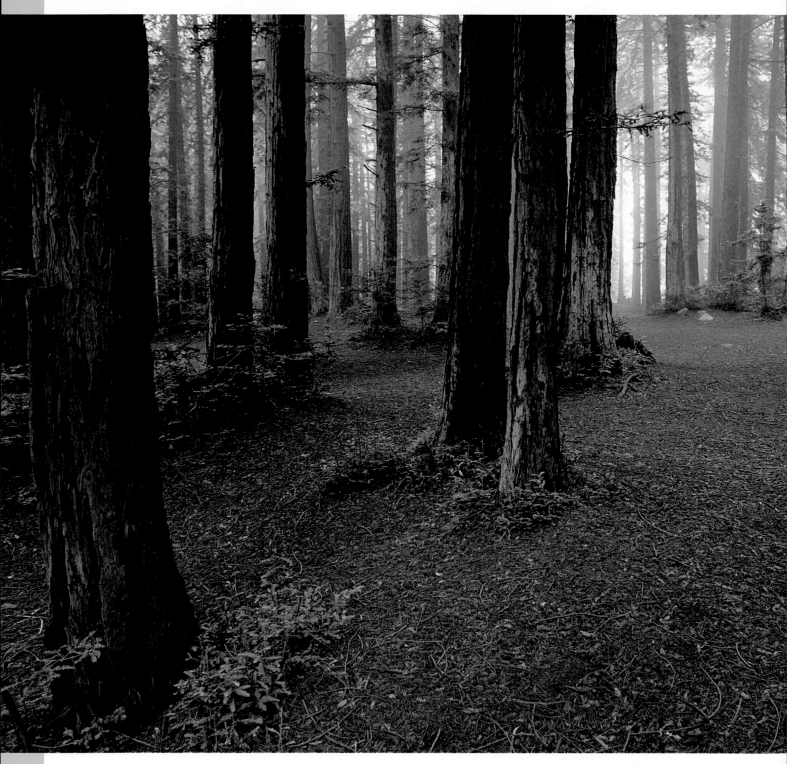

30–31 Morning fog drifts through an open forest of coast redwoods in Redwood Regional Park atop the Oakland Hills above San Francisco Bay.

The second-growth forest stands near the site of two trees reputed to be the world's largest coast redwoods that were cut during the gold rush around 1860.

compelling locations. Small sections of protected coast, such as Torrey Pines near La Jolla, give a clue as to what industrial quagmires, such as the Long Beach harbor in the Los Angeles Basin, must have been like in the not-so-distant past. Small surfer's beaches, tucked away in coves between developed shorelines, also preserve the elemental wildness, if not the isolation, of the natural scene.

One of the most unlikely spots to have a pristine section of coast in the southern half of the state is the major rocket-launching site at Vandenburg Air Force Base. Long closed to the public, these

twenty-plus miles of rugged coastline surrounding Point Arguello remain essentially in their natural state. With special permission to photograph biologists monitoring endangered peregrine falcons, I spent several days camped here, seeing lots of wildlife, but no other human beings.

For combined wild beauty and ease of access, it's hard to beat the Big Sur Coast. It remains among America's most rugged and lonely, broken only by a narrow road, etched into the cliffs like a goat path, that winds its way a hundred miles south from the Monterey Peninsula. The first twenty-six

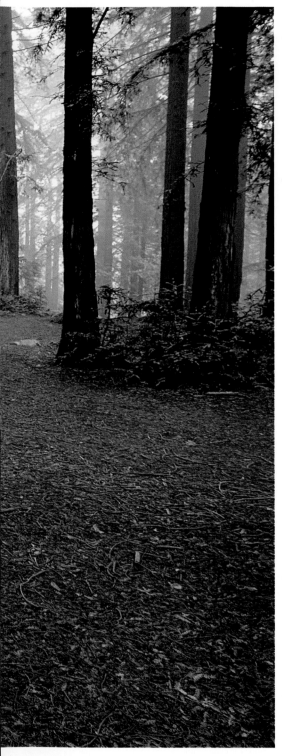

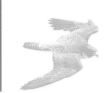

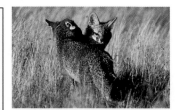

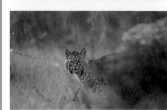

miles have become the course of America's most beautiful marathon, run every spring through literally breathtaking scenery that has far more rugged ups and downs than the standard city courses where speed records are set. To run for hours with a breeze in my face watching waves crash against an endless procession of rugged headlands fading into blue infinity always lures me into spending more time casually exploring trailless parts of the same coast with my camera.

During the months I spent working on a peregrine falcon story for *National Geographic*, I found many secret coves and beaches to which I've returned in the winter when the gray whales are spouting during their annual migration from Mexico to the Arctic; in the early spring when hundreds of elephant seals haul up on a beach unseen from the road many hundred feet above; and a month or two later when the wildflowers are at their height on green hillsides.

During a visit in 1998, I noticed a large bird soaring past the cliffs as I was eating in a restaurant perched on stilts high over the ocean at posh Post Ranch Inn near Pfeiffer Big Sur State Park. As it got closer it grew much larger and I realized that I was seeing a California condor flying in the wild for the first time in my life. North America's largest flying bird has recently been released back into the Big Sur skies after an extensive captive breeding program removed all birds from the wild as the species was on the brink of extinction.

In the far north of California, the Klamath-Siskiyou region has the greatest diversity of conifers of any temperate forests in the world. From misty cathedrals of redwoods filled with pink rhododendrons to stands of Douglas fir, Brewer spruce, and Port Orford cedar, these forests are survivors of a cooler, wetter Pleistocene climate where the flora of the Sierra Nevada, Cascades, and Coast Ranges intersect. On the ground these coastal forests can seem endless, but from high vantage points the checkerboard pattern of clearcutting for timber looks like open wounds on the living face of this landscape. Only a fraction of

the original North Coast forests remain.

What's left of old-growth redwoods is protected here and there by a national park and a few state parks, including my favorite, Del Norte Coast Redwoods, near the Oregon border. Coast redwoods, unlike their fatter cousins, the giant Sequoia of the Sierra Nevada, grow only in the coastal fog belt that can extend up to fifty miles inland within major canyon systems. Far more immortal than the residents of little towns in the valleys below, the old-growth survivors of the redwood forests have already outlived the ancient civilizations of the Mayans and the Romans. Today, just as revenues from international ecotourism to see the remaining forests of these slender, tallest trees in the world are poised to pass income from cutting them down, all too many citizens of the North Coast continue to voice their economic right to make a living by logging.

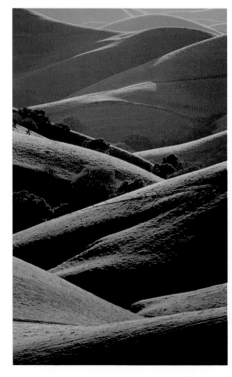

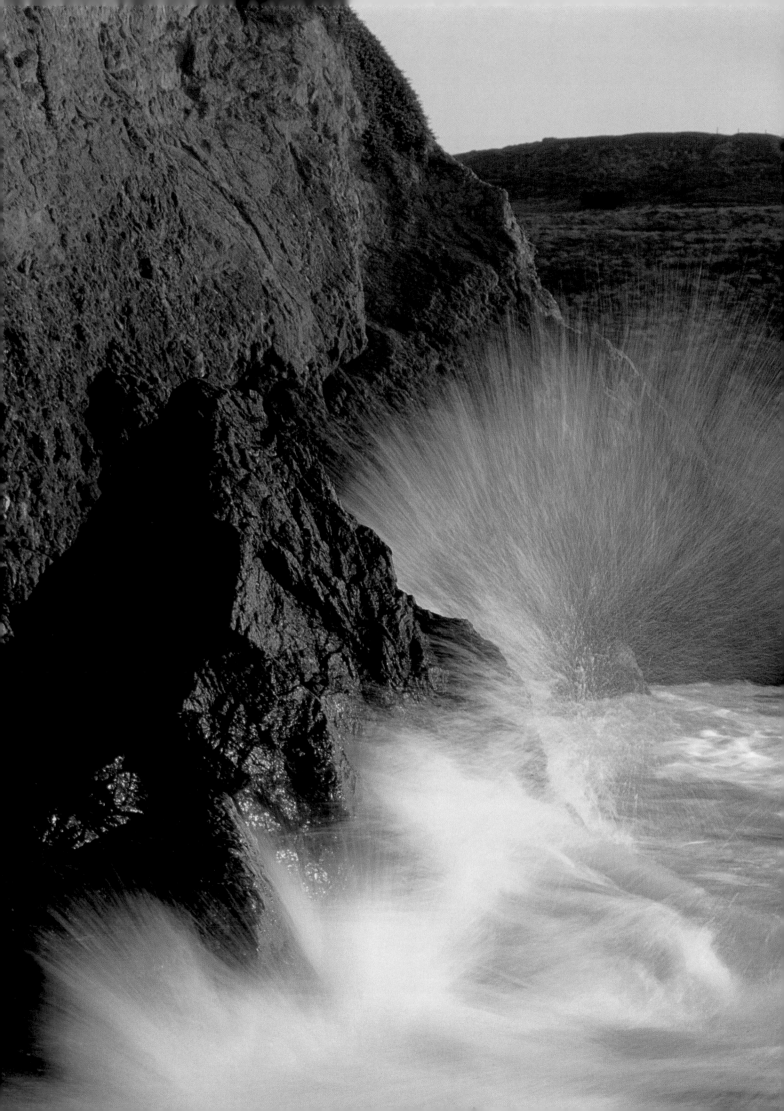

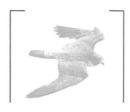

34 Surf crashing against the rugged Marin Headlands in the Golden Gate National Recreation Area north of San Francisco fans out in all directions in this long exposure made in the last moments of sunset on a clear spring evening.

35 The sun sets into a fog bank over the Pacific Ocean behind a Monterey Pine. The lone tree, bent by the wind, sits high on the slopes of Mount Tamalpais near Bolinas Ridge in Mount Tamalpais State Park in Marin County.

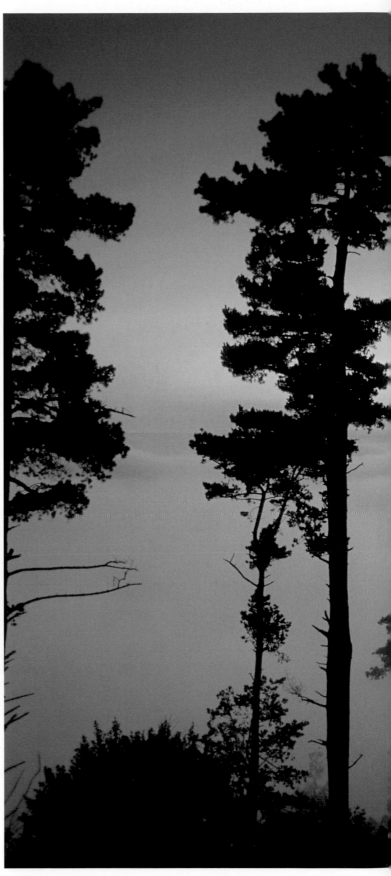

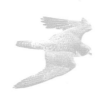

36 top Morning sun breaks into gold beams through Monterey pines in Tilden Regional Park on the crest of the Berkeley Hills, east of San Francisco.

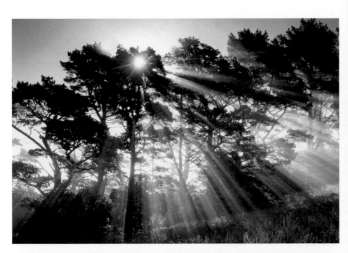

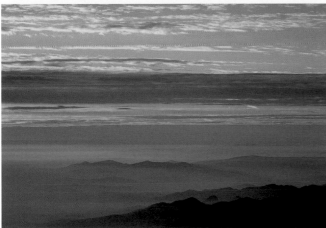

36 bottom Seen from the air at dawn at 7,000 feet over the Santa Clara Valley south of San José, San Francisco Bay is hidden in morning fog with only the receding ridges of the Diablo Range rising up to 4,000 feet to the east of the major cities.

36–37 A fog bank hanging over San Francisco Bay at sunset creeps into a pine forest above Strawberry Canyon in the Berkeley Hills. Dry summers with frequent fog give the San Francisco area a mild Mediterranean climate.

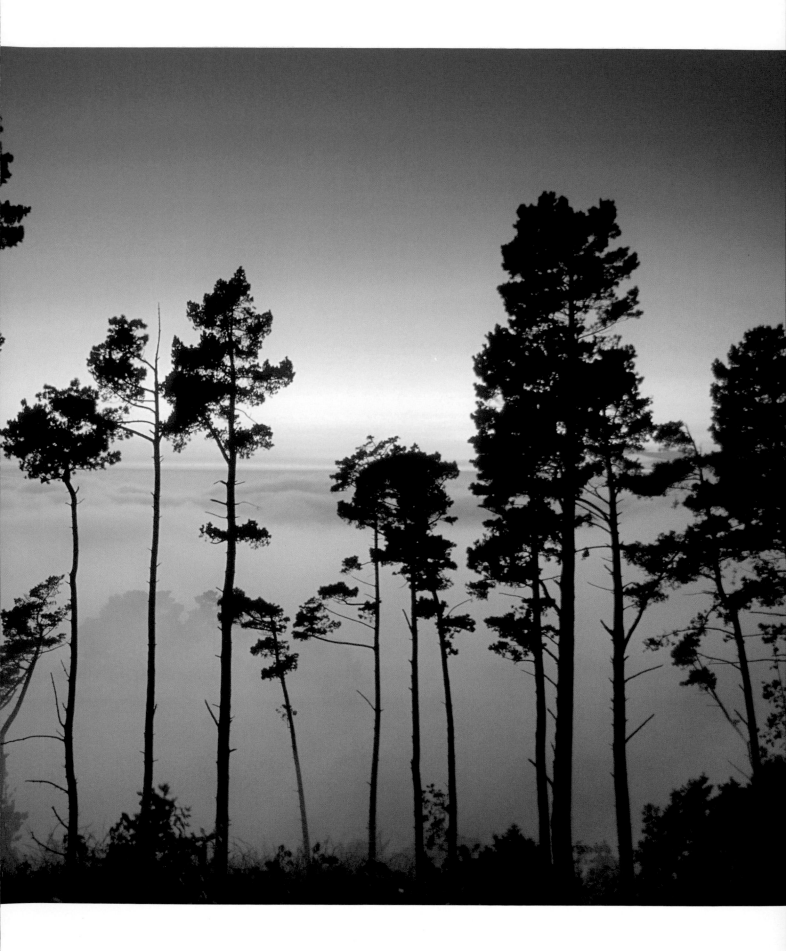

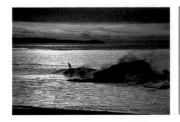

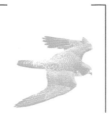

38 top A surfer rides a Malibu wave at dawn off Leo Carillo State Beach along the Malibu coast beneath the Santa Monica Mountains.

38 center Sunrise touches the crest of Marin County's Bolinas Ridge where shadowed mists and sunlit ground frame an ocean vista.

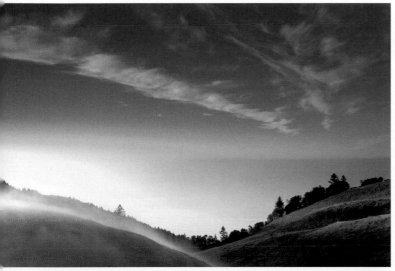

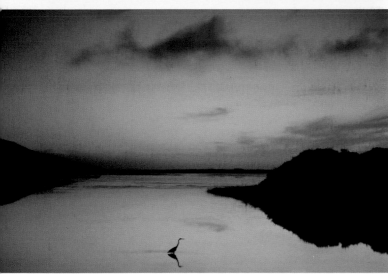

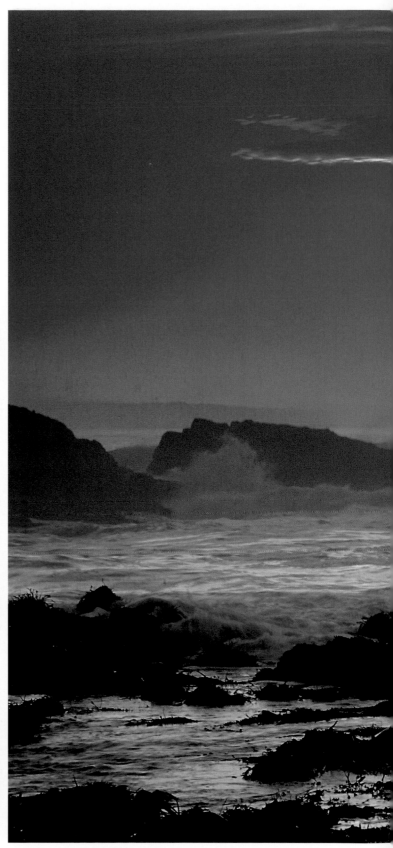

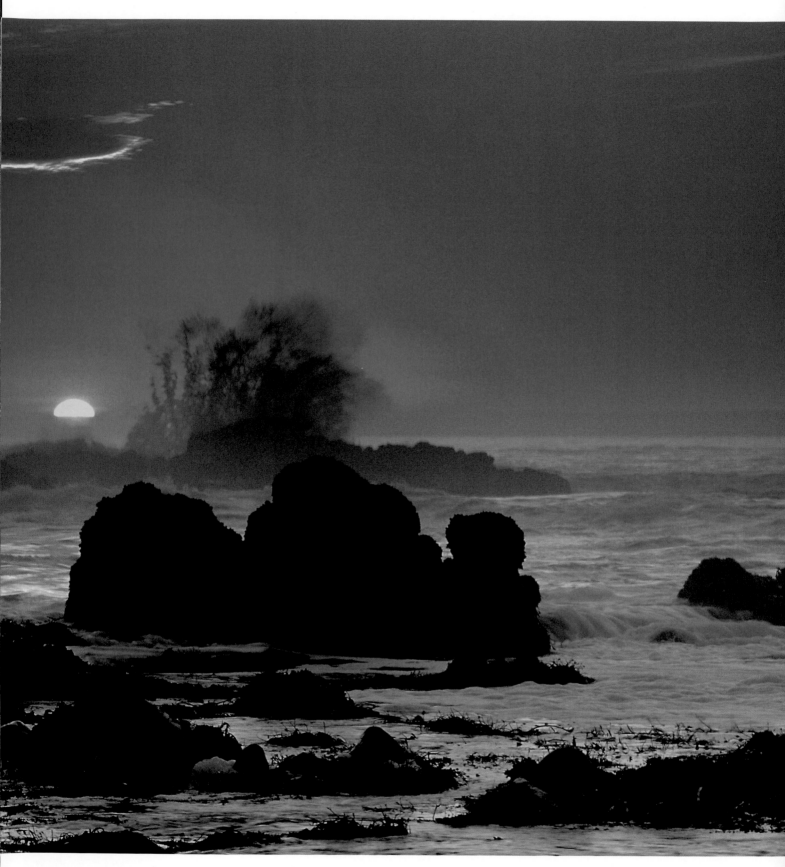

38 bottom A lone egret stands in Rodeo Lagoon at sunset in the Golden Gate National Recreation Area.

38–39 A winter sunset at the end of a storm highlights giant waves at Pescadero State Beach on the San Mateo Coast.

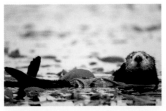

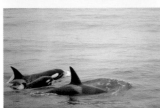

40 top In the teeming waters of Monterey Bay a sea otter (above) floats in a kelp bed, while (below) a pod of resident orcas (killer whales) cruise the more open seas.

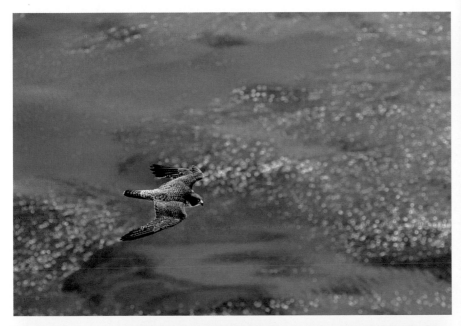

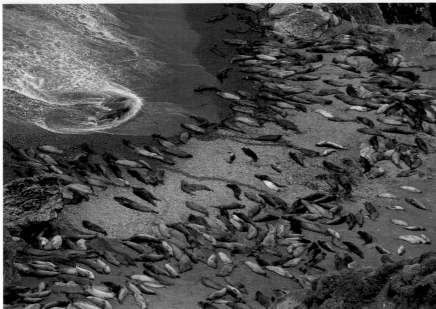

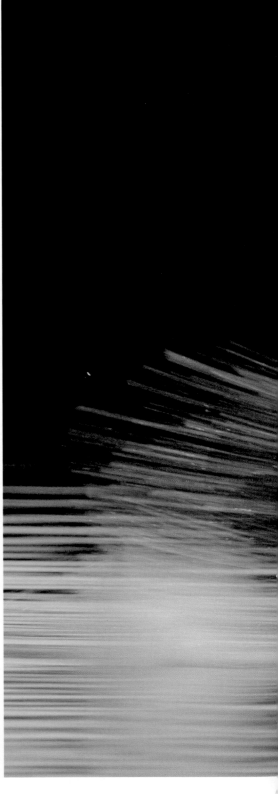

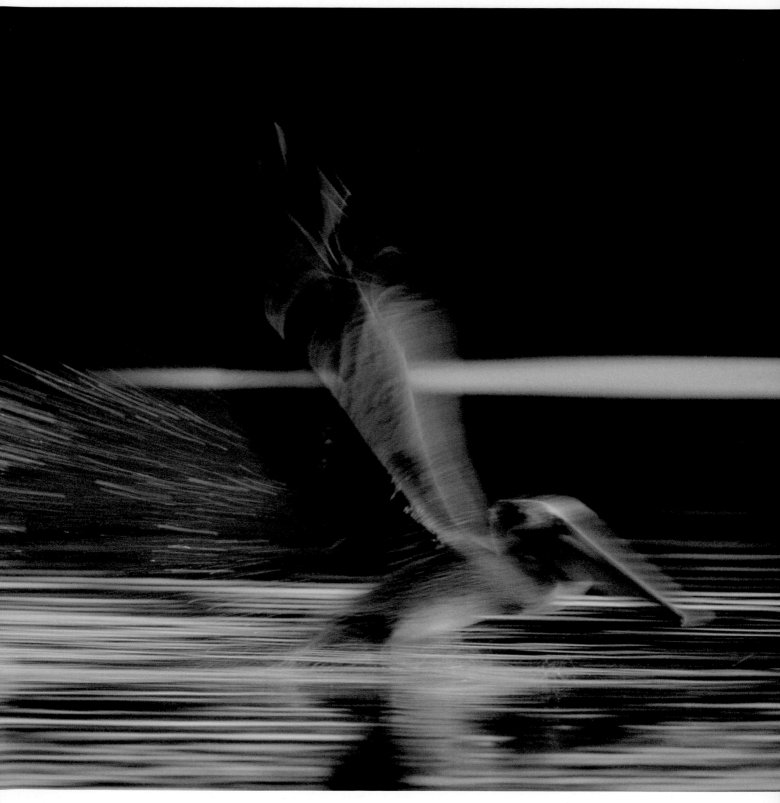

42 *Tule Elk stand profiled against the Pacific Ocean on the Point Reyes Peninsula, north of San Francisco.*

42–43 *Sunset casts a pink glow over Black's Beach at La Jolla on the San Diego Coast.*

40 center *World's fastest bird, the peregrine falcon, cruises over a kelp bed in Avila Bay, south of Big Sur. Officially endangered until recently, peregrines were once reduced to only two known breeding pairs in California by DDT contamination.*

40 bottom *In a cove hidden from view from the Big Sur highway, a colony of elephant seals breed on the mainland after decades of hovering on the brink of extinction.*

40–41 *A brown pelican lands on the tidal waters of Berkeley's Aquatic Park, captured in the blur of a long exposure.*

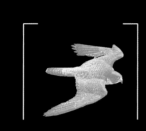

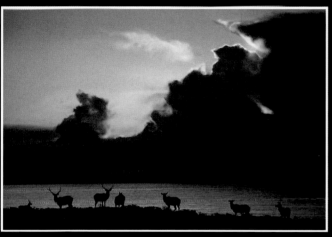

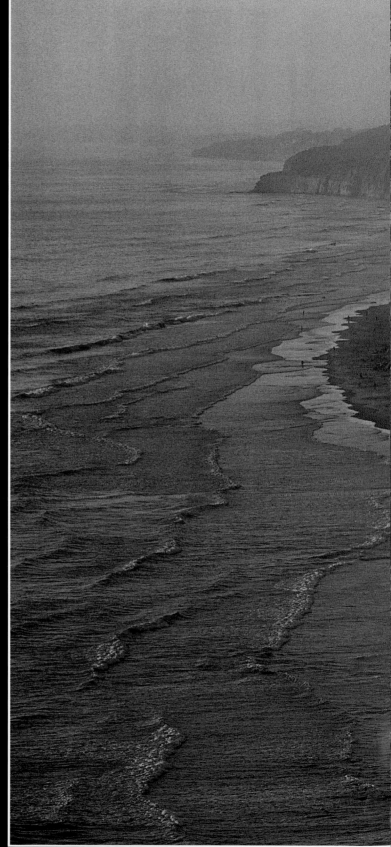

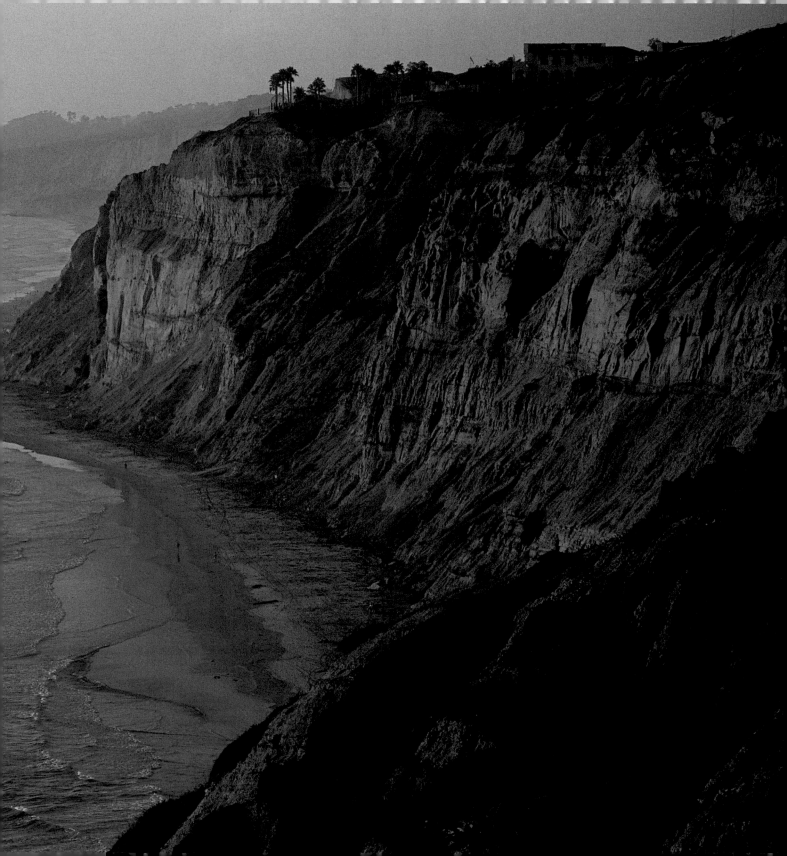

44 *The wild 362-mile Oregon Coast is one of the most legendary scenic drives in North America. A myriad of sea stacks line Bandon Beach lies near its southern end.*

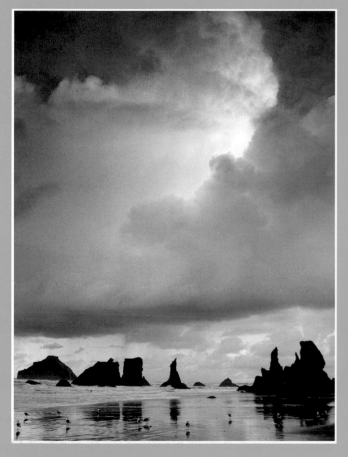

The Pacific Northwest

44–45 A stormy fall sunset profiles a different set of sea stacks along the Oregon Coast's Bandon Beach.

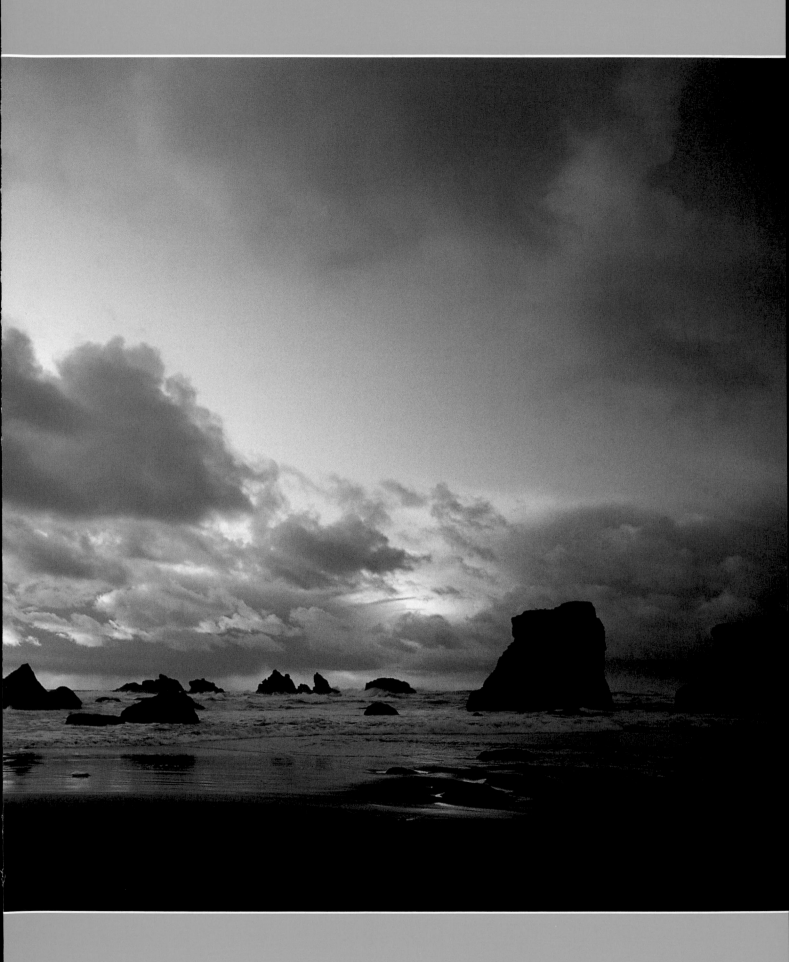

46–47 Famous for its deep blue waters, Oregon's Crater Lake sits in the caldera of an ancient Cascade volcano that blew off its top about 6,500 years ago in an eruption far more violent than any witnessed in North America during historical times. Punctuating the scene like a mini-volcano, the extinct cone of Wizard Island rises well above the 1,900-foot deep waters.

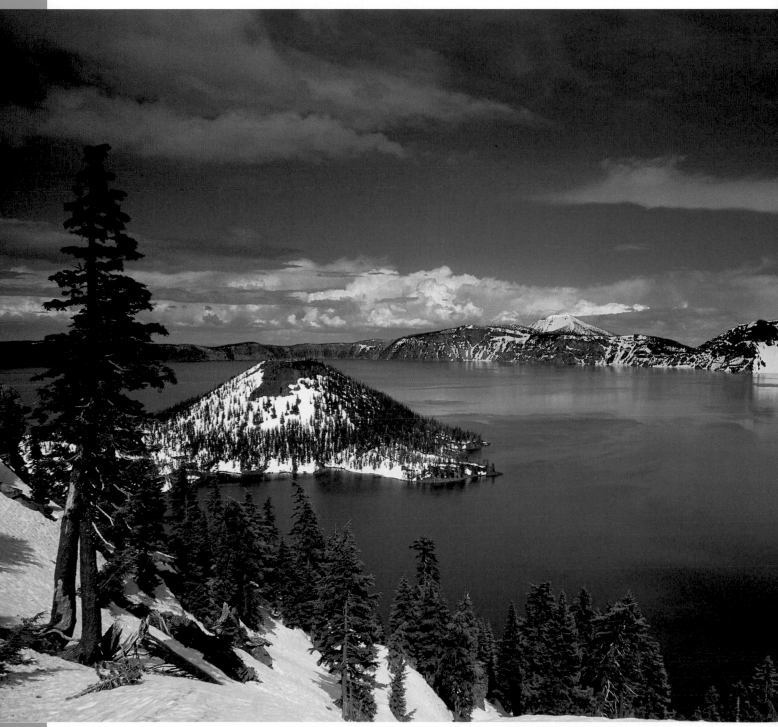

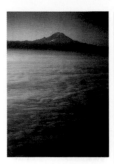

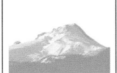

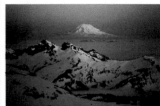

47 left Mount Rainier, highest of the Cascade volcanoes, rises out of the clouds to 14,410 feet within sight of Seattle, Washington.

47 right Seen from a camp on Mount Rainier, Mount Adams rises above the clouds, lit by alpenglow.

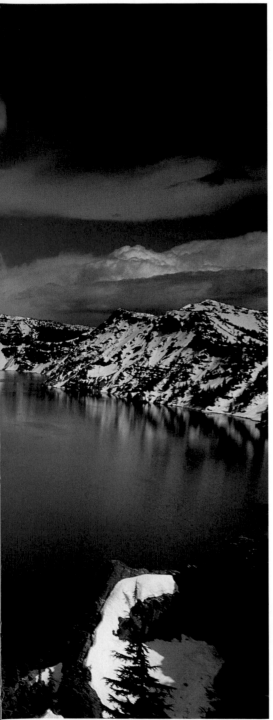

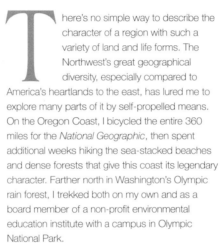

There's no simple way to describe the character of a region with such a variety of land and life forms. The Northwest's great geographical diversity, especially compared to America's heartlands to the east, has lured me to explore many parts of it by self-propelled means. On the Oregon Coast, I bicycled the entire 360 miles for the *National Geographic*, then spent additional weeks hiking the sea-stacked beaches and dense forests that give this coast its legendary character. Farther north in Washington's Olympic rain forest, I trekked both on my own and as a board member of a non-profit environmental education institute with a campus in Olympic National Park.

To reach the highest point in the Cascades, 14,410-foot Mount Rainier, I climbed with fellow teammates training for an expedition to K2. Rainier's 9,000-foot vertical rise and more than thirty glaciers give the peak a distinctly Himalayan appearance, both from a distance as it crowns the Seattle skyline and from up close in the ice world of its upper ramparts rent with crevasses and icefalls.

Despite this monarch of the Northwest's lone appearance in photographs, Mount Rainier is by no means an isolated summit. The Cascade Range stretches two states south into northern California, where another high volcano with fewer glaciers—14,160-foot Mount Shasta—also dominates vast evergreen forests. The long wall of the Cascade Range does an amazing job of stripping away the Northwest's well-known coastal precipitation, setting world records for annual snowfall, first on Mount Rainier, then more recently on Mount Baker. The result is a desert climate for the eastern two-thirds of both Oregon and Washington, despite abundant irrigated fields.

On the sunnier east side of the Cascades, Bend, Oregon, has become a major center of outdoor recreation with easy access to the volcanoes for skiing, hiking, and climbing. Closer to town, some of America's most difficult rock

climbs have been accomplished on the sedimentary cliffs and spires of Smith Rock that rise out of sagebrush. Farther south near Klamath Falls, clouds of hundreds of thousands of snow geese still darken the skies where in 1908, President Theodore Roosevelt set aside the nation's first federal waterfowl refuge in the Lower Klamath Basin.

The Cascade volcanoes owe their creation to molten magma rising near the surface beside a juncture of tectonic plates that have converged and subducted. This Pacific "ring of fire" ends in northern California, where the plates begin sliding horizontally, causing earthquakes rather than volcanoes.

In May 1980, formerly undistinguished Mount St. Helens blew 1,300 feet off its top, causing deaths and massive devastation. On the day of the eruption, my flight to Seattle from San Francisco diverted over the ocean, but on my return I looked down into the giant smoking crater, thankful that I had not had the *National Geographic* assignment of the photographer who died with his camera focused on the exploding mountain.

Another Cascade volcano, absent from maps but posthumously named Mount Mazama by geologists, blew its top off about 6,500 years ago before the eyes of Native Americans, leaving the giant caldera now filled by Crater Lake. While the crater with its 1,900-foot-deep waters of pure indigo has become one of North America's most famous natural wonders, many of the lesser known and more intact volcanoes of the Cascade Range—Mount Bachelor, Mount Jefferson, the Three Sisters, Mount Hood, Mount Adams, Mount Baker—offer better winter skiing and summer hiking opportunities.

Tracing the border between Oregon and Washington, the Columbia River Gorge drains a quarter of a million square miles of the Canadian Rockies and the American Northwest into the sea. When Meriwether Lewis and William Clark followed the Columbia to the Pacific in 1805 after traversing the continent, Clark described, "the grandest and

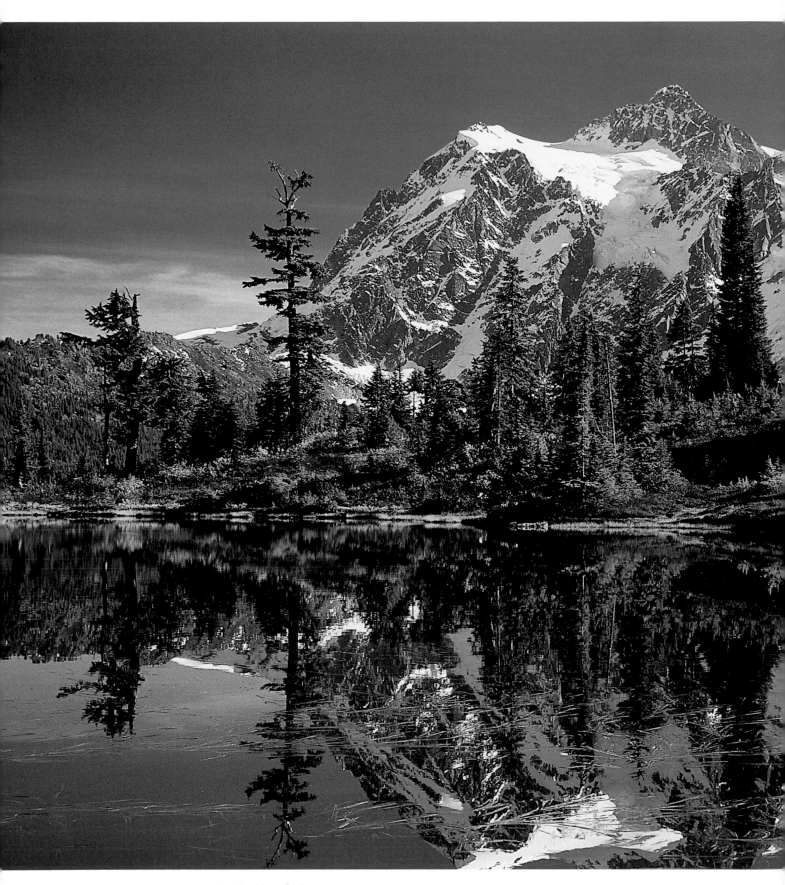

50–51 Mount Shuksan in Washington's North Cascade National Park has been called America's most beautiful mountain, rising like a gothic cathedral veiled in ice over Picture Lake and surrounding evergreen forests laced with fall colors.

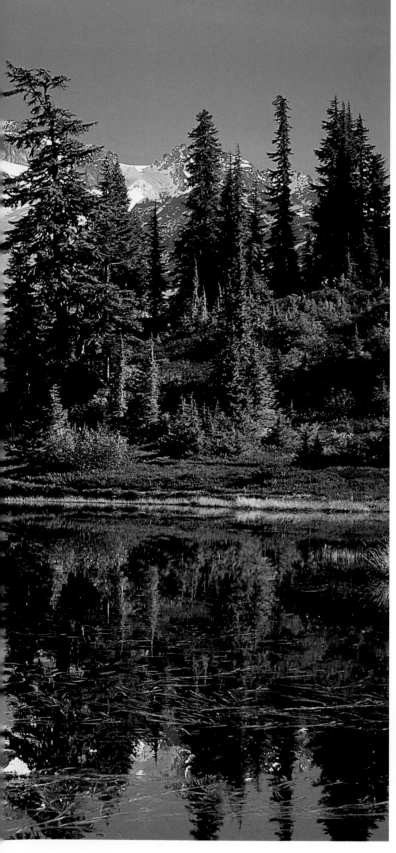

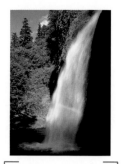

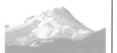

51 top Horsetail Fall casts a faint afternoon rainbow as it parts the lush green vegetation of the Columbia River Gorge.

51 bottom Elowah Fall drops into lush greenery on the floor of the Columbia River Gorge on the Oregon side.

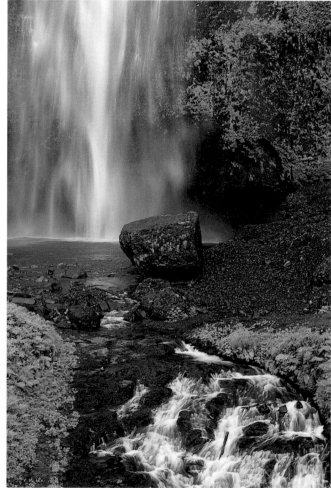

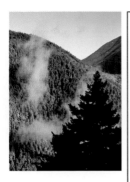

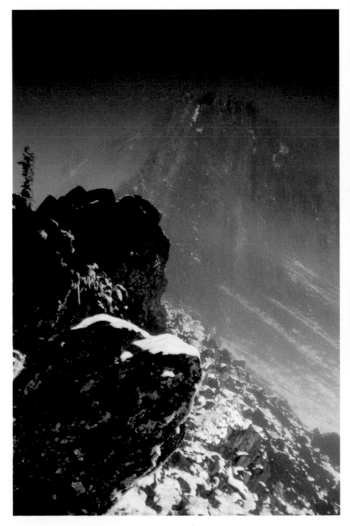

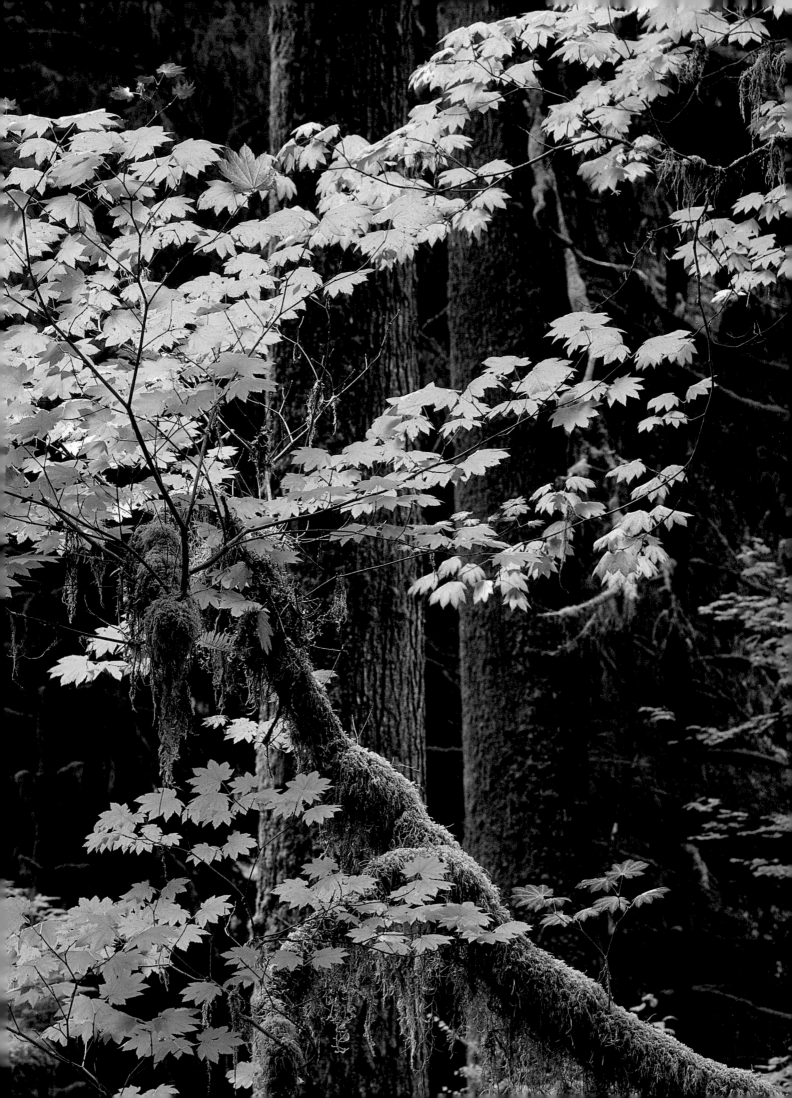

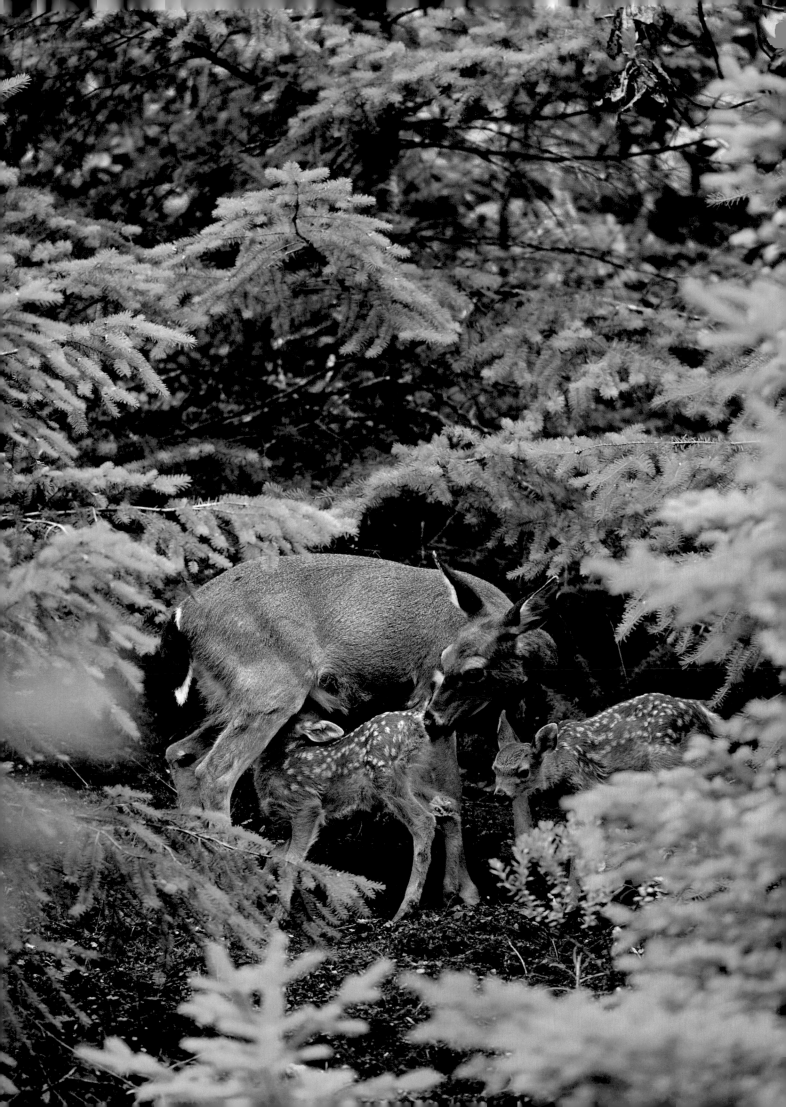

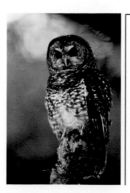

54 A mule deer nurses twin fawns in a forest clearing high in the Siskiyou Mountains of southern Oregon.

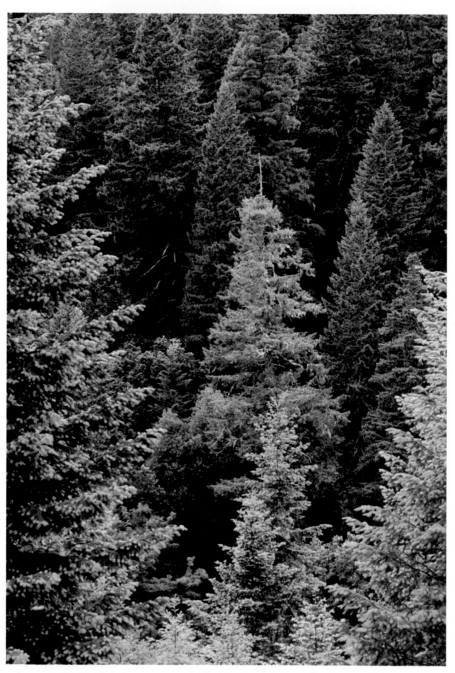

55 top A northern spotted owl perches on a limb deep within an old-growth forest. Threatened with extinction because of the destruction of the old-growth forests that the owls seek out for breeding, these controversial birds are beloved by environmentalists and despised by loggers who have lost their jobs cutting now-protected forest.

55 bottom The world's most diverse conifer forests are in the Klamath and Siskiyou Mountains bordering Southern Oregon and Northern California.

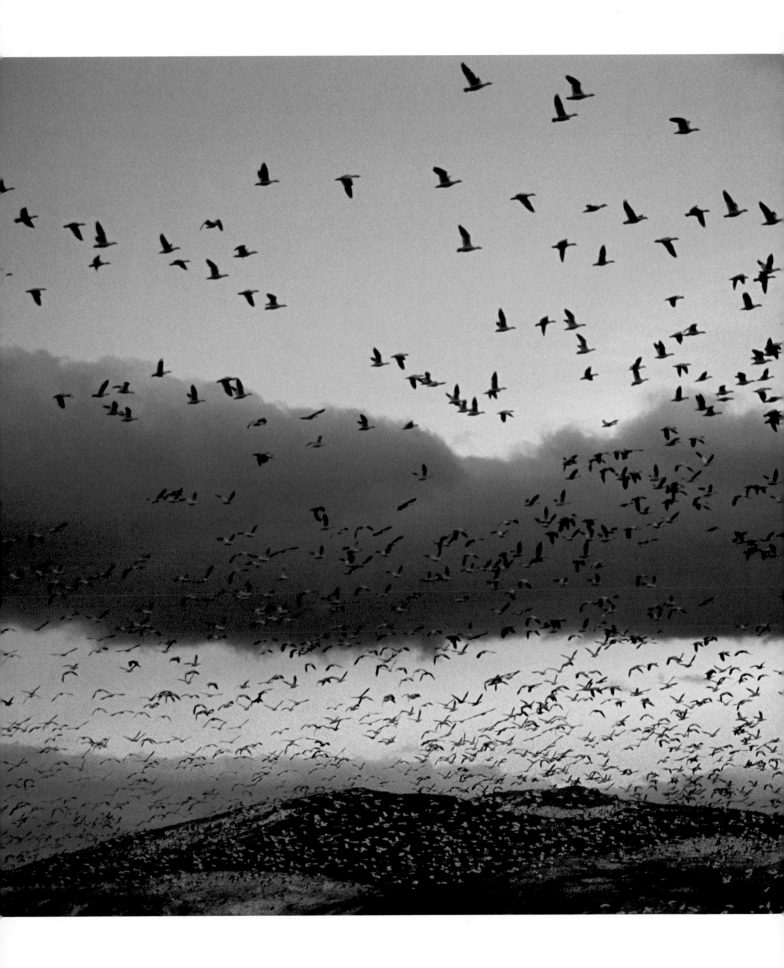

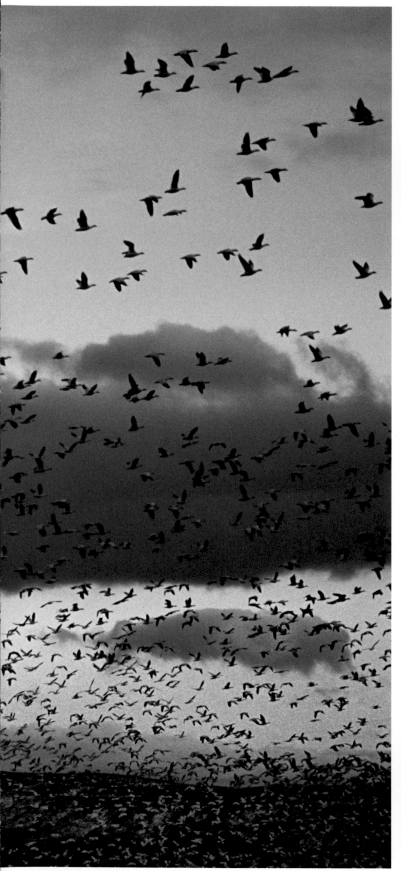

56–57 Tens of thousands of snow geese darken the skies over the Klamath National Wildlife Refuge on a winter evening just south of the California-Oregon border.

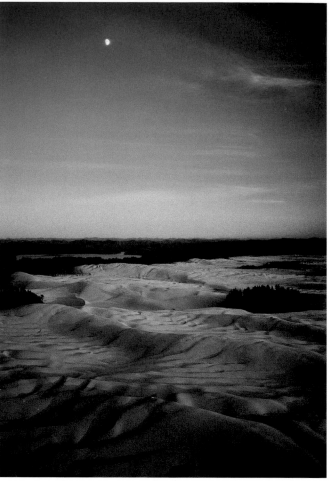

57 top Islands of timber jut out of oceans of sand in the Oregon Dunes along the Oregon Coast near Florence.

57 bottom Smith Rock State Park near Bend in central Oregon is a wonderland of cliffs and spires with a river running through it. The featured rock and clear weather make the park a mecca for rock climbers from around the world.

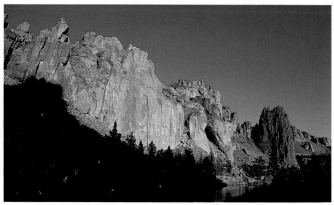

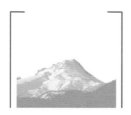

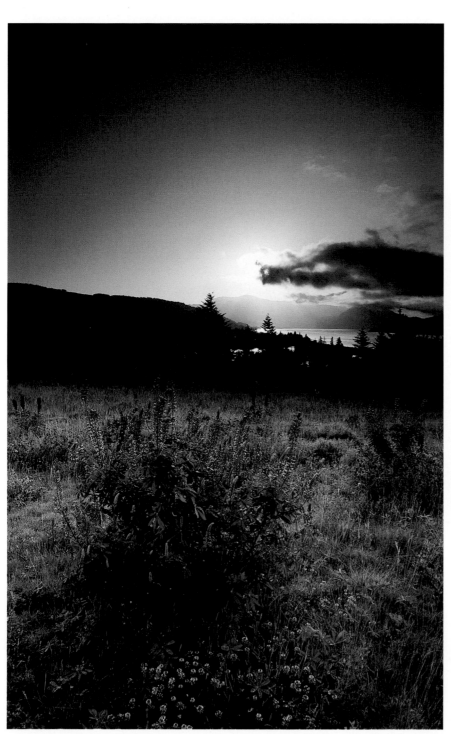

58 left Lupines glow in the morning sun along the Washington shores of the Columbia River.

58 right Draped with ice at just 10,568 feet, Glacier Peak dominates a stormy wilderness area named after it in the Washington Cascades.

59 A meadow beneath Mount Shuksan glistens with frost on a fall morning in the North Cascades. The star effect around the sun is caused by diffraction in the gap between the summits at the moment of sunrise.

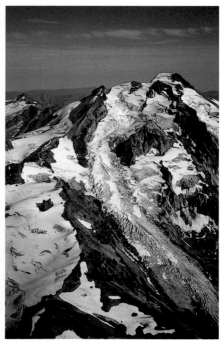

60 The white cone of Mount Baker, seen through fall colors in the North Cascades, holds the North American annual snowfall record of 1,140 inches.

60–61 Maple leaves turn crimson in an old-growth enclave of Hood National Forest in Oregon.

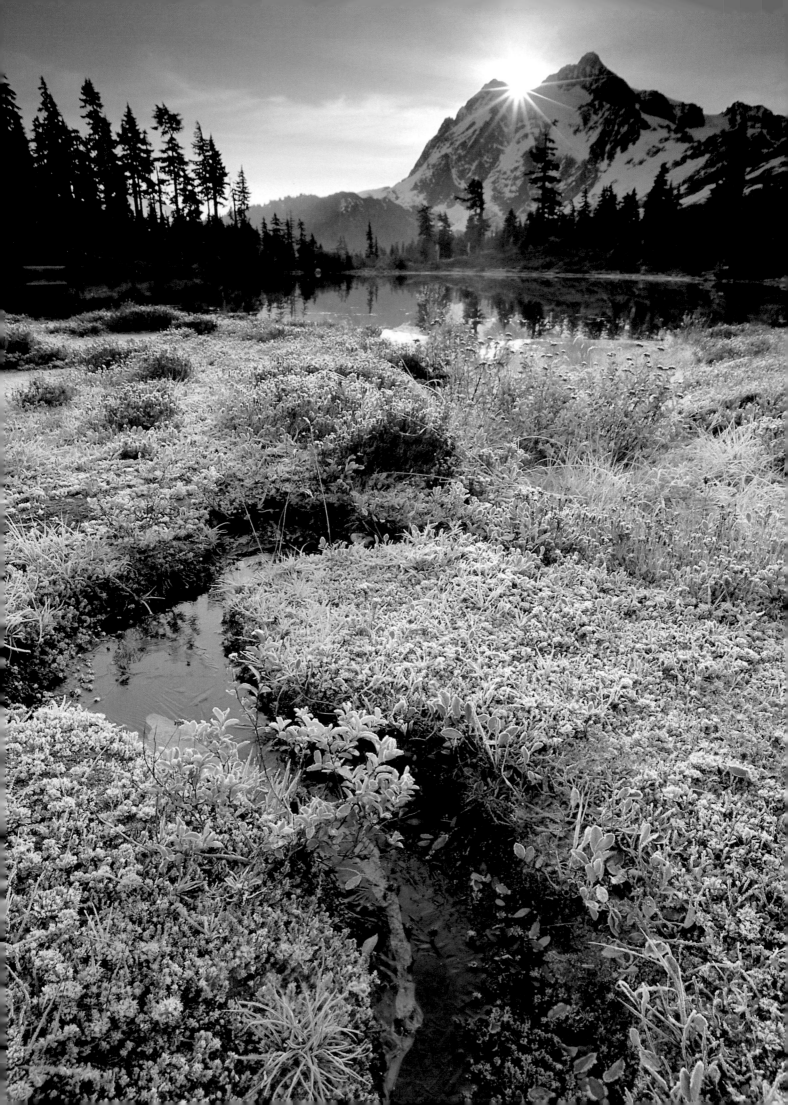

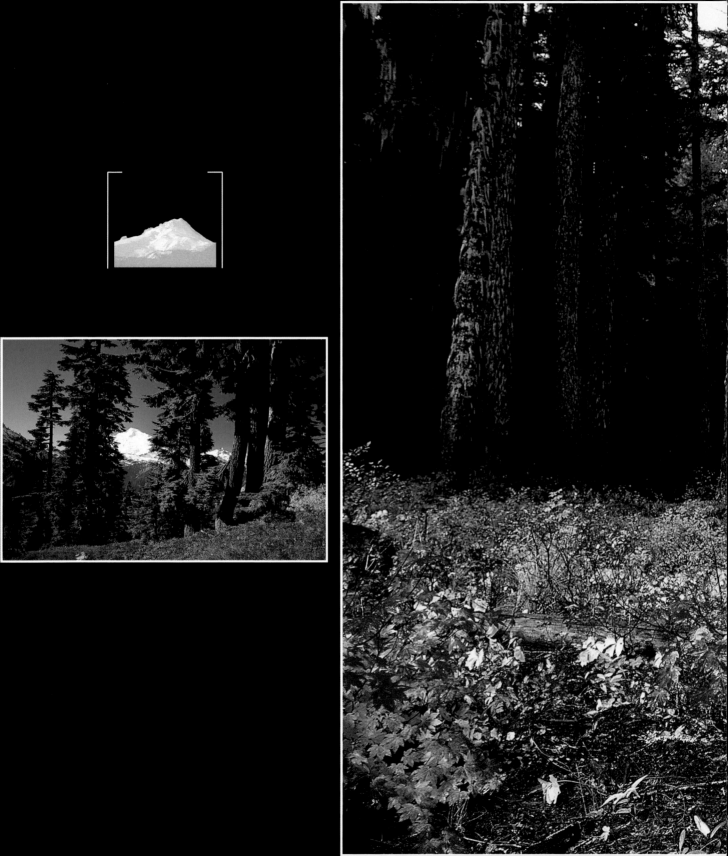

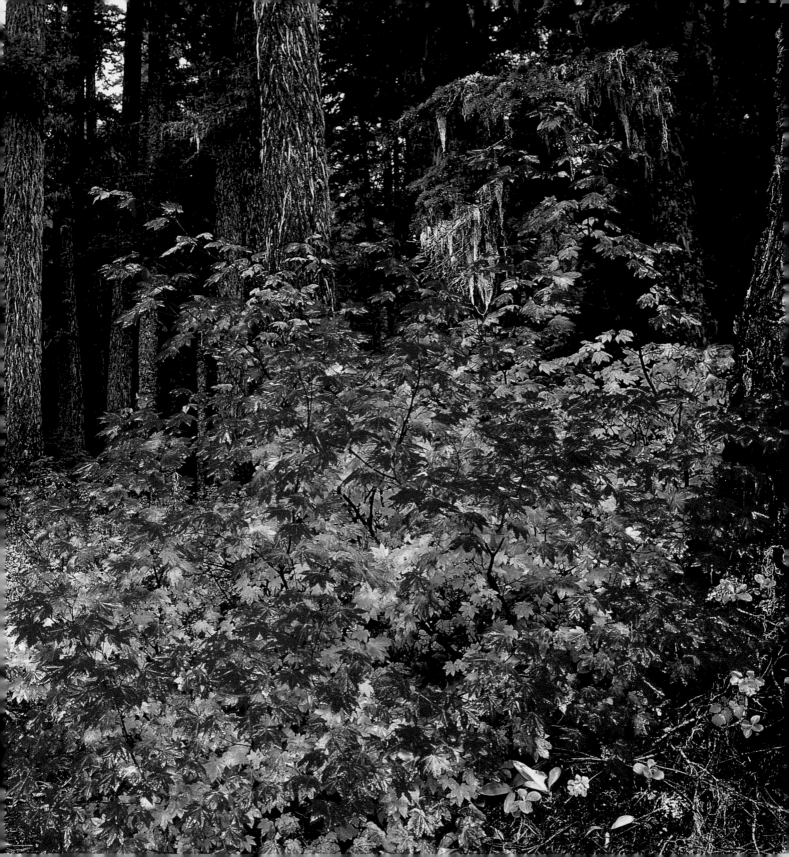

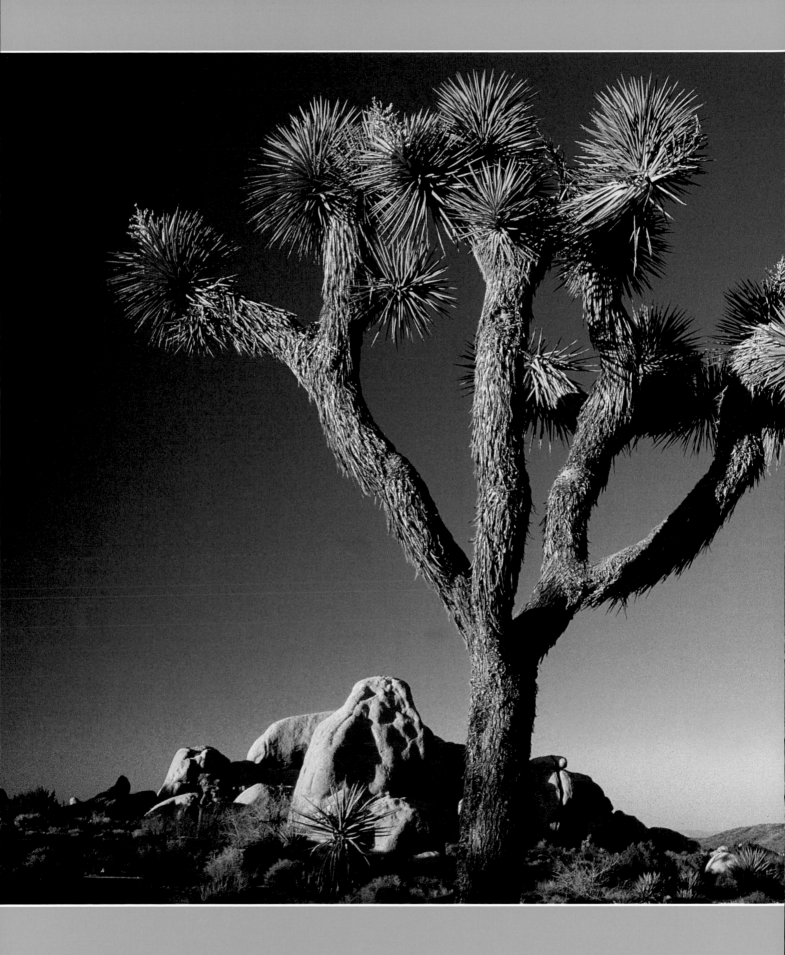

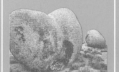

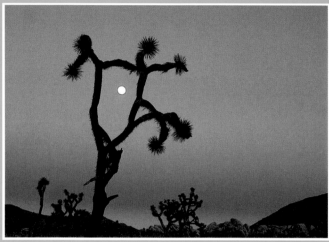

The California Desert

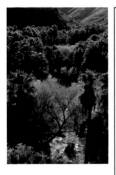

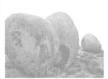

66 top left The resort town of Palm Springs got its name from the native palm oases of Indian Canyon.

66 top right Also close to Palm Springs, cholla cactus grows beneath the Santa Rosa mountains in Deep Canyon.

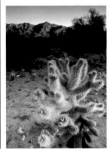

Nearctic biogeographic realm that extends northward across the United States, Canada, Alaska, and Greenland with a strong kinship to the flora of Europe and northern Asia.

The Great Basin, covered directly in Chapter Five, is a relatively cold, high desert that stretches from eastern California across Nevada and Utah into western Colorado. A California example of this realm is the Owens Valley east of the Sierra where high desert sagebrush and mountain mahogany cover slopes that would harbor tall cacti in the Sonoran Desert.

The Mojave Desert is somewhat transitional, yet geographically unique. This smallest of American deserts has fewer cacti, but a great variety of plants and animals. Symbolic of the Mojave is the Joshua Tree, a woody-stemmed type of yucca belonging to the lily family. Fine groves set amidst strangely eroded granite are found in Joshua Tree National Park, an hour's drive from Palm Springs. The park has become a major center of rock climbing, especially in the fall and spring when the weather is relatively cool.

Unlike the other two deserts, the Mojave has California's classic Mediterranean winter-wet, summer-dry weather pattern caused by one of the Earth's most persistent meteorological phenomena—the Pacific High, a high pressure zone that diverts virtually all precipitation away. When it dissipates in early winter, the resulting pulses of rainfall in the Mojave create legendary wildflower displays. The Antelope Valley California Poppy Preserve near Lancaster always has a few fields of flowers in March and April, but after especially heavy rains erupts into an endless carpet rolling from horizon to horizon. Elsewhere at middle elevations in the Mojave, smaller, but incongruously gorgeous fields of aster, blazing star, paintbrush, mariposa lily, mallow, and primrose paint the arid landscape in wet years.

In 1994, Mojave National Preserve was established from 69 Bureau of Land Management areas to have 3.6 million acres of designated wilderness, making it the largest National Park land area in the contiguous forty-eight states. As of this writing, the preserve is compromised by private inholdings, including over 1,000 mining claims and a huge strip of old Sante Fe Pacific Railroad lands opened for commercial development.

At the same time in 1994, the most famous area of the Mojave Desert became a national park. Death Valley, girt by desert peaks against the Nevada border, fits the definition of both the Great Basin and the Mojave Desert, with superlatives all its own. It is the driest and hottest of all North American deserts with a record high of 134°F in the shade and a daily average high of 116°F in July at the Furnace Creek Visitor Center.

Though Death Valley is often characterized by photographs that show its predictable desert sand dunes, I'm more drawn to some of its unique and bolder landforms, such as snowy Telescope Peak rising over 11,000 feet above Badwater at –282 feet, the lowest point in North America. I also love the pastel badlands below Zabriskie Point which are eroded into concentric ridges and narrow canyons of raw earth that flow toward infinity into a central dry wash.

The highest desert peaks in Southern California are on the Los Angeles side of these deserts. Though Mount San Gorgonio at 11,501 feet is the highest, the finest Alpine wilderness in Southern California may be on 10,804-foot Mount San Jacinto around the pine forest and granite cliffs of Tahquitz Rock. The peak's summit rises just above timberline into the southernmost Arctic/Alpine life zone in the United States. Because of an aerial tram a few minutes drive above the resort town of Palm Springs, it's possible to leave hot Sonoran Desert and arrive where winter snows can be ten feet deep at the 8,500-foot level in less than an hour.

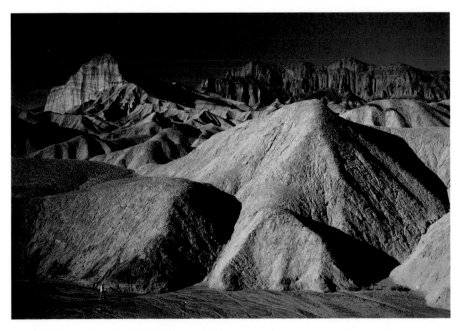

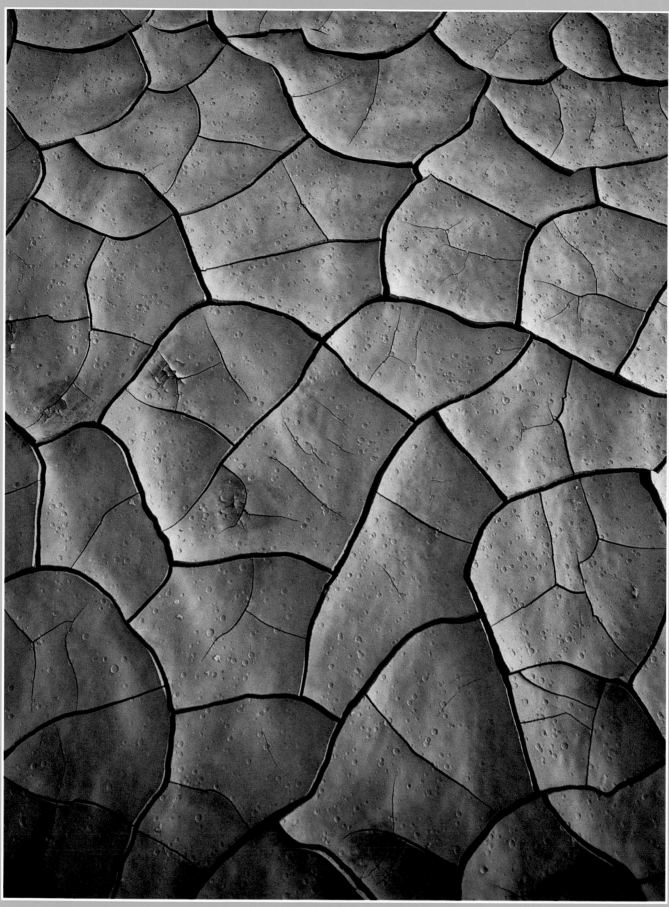

66 bottom The pastel, changing features of Zabriskie Canyon make the short dry wash one of Death Valley's most visited natural sites.

67 The cracked earth of the below-sea-level floor of Death Valley records raindrops that fell months or years before.

68–69 Death Valley's 11,049-foot Telescope Peak is reflected in a pool at Badwater, the continent's lowest point at -282 feet.

70–71 A full moon rises into the earth shadow above the badlands of the Anza-Borrego Desert from Font's Point.

71 Keyes View in Joshua Tree National Park frames snow-capped 10,804-foot Mt. San Jacinto through a pinyon pine.

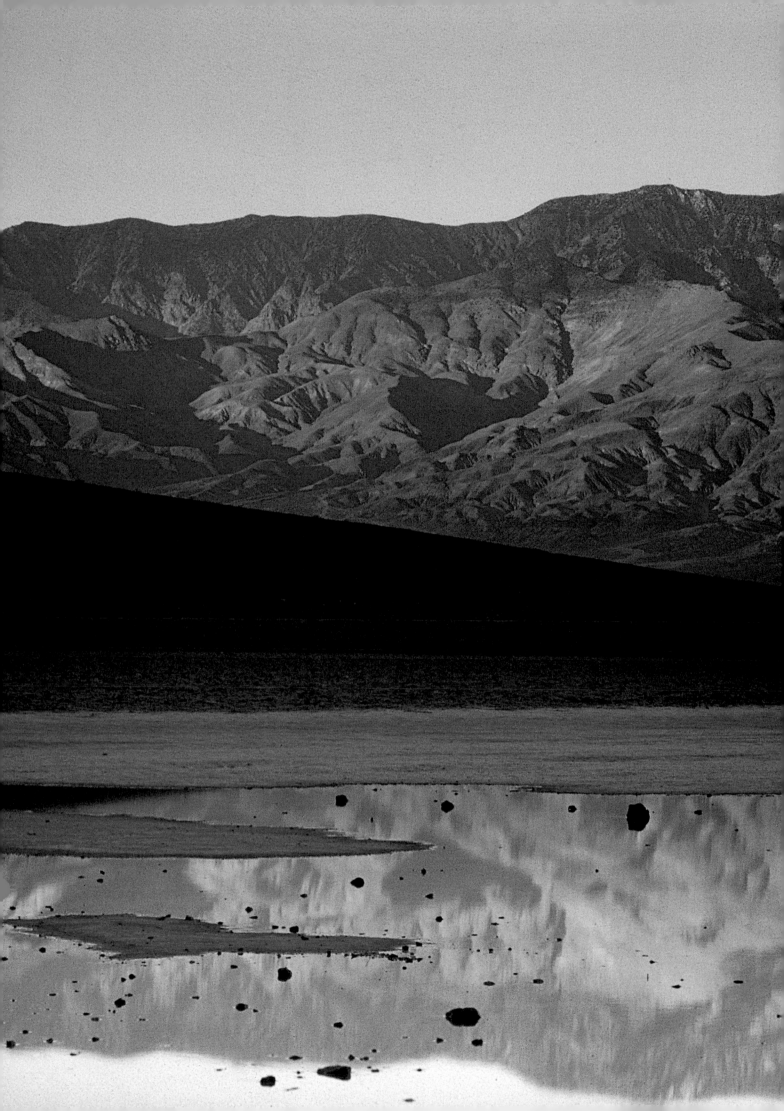

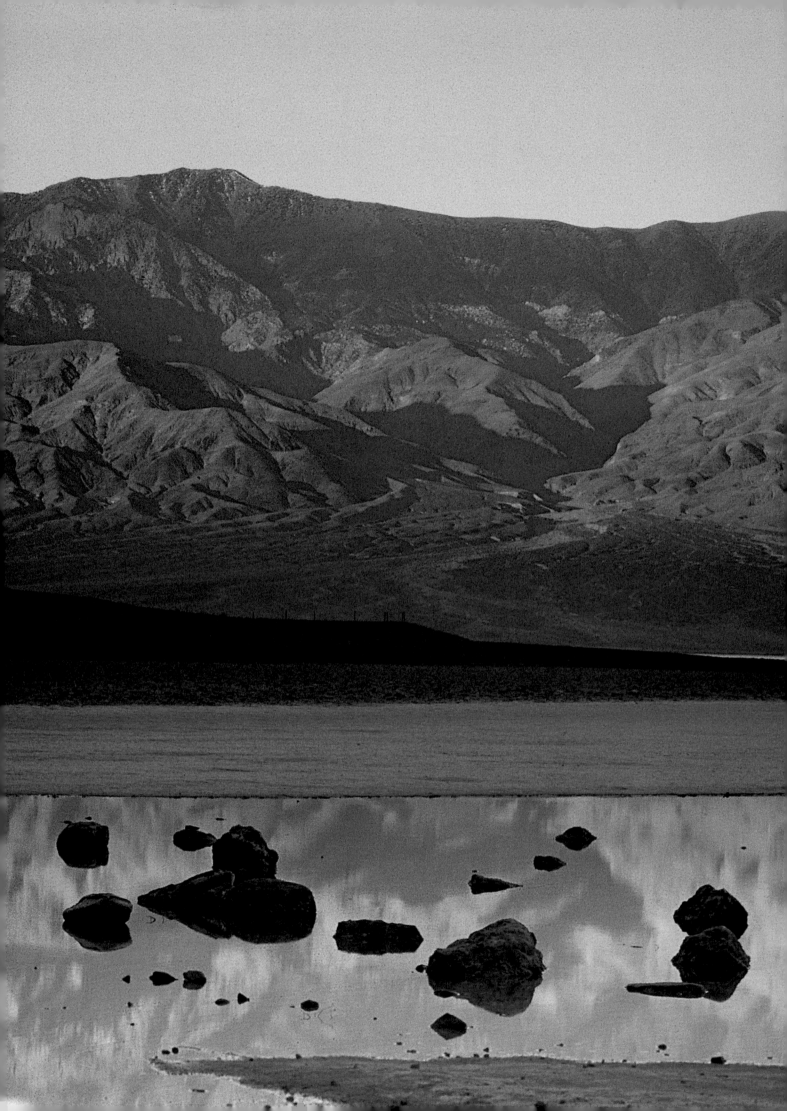

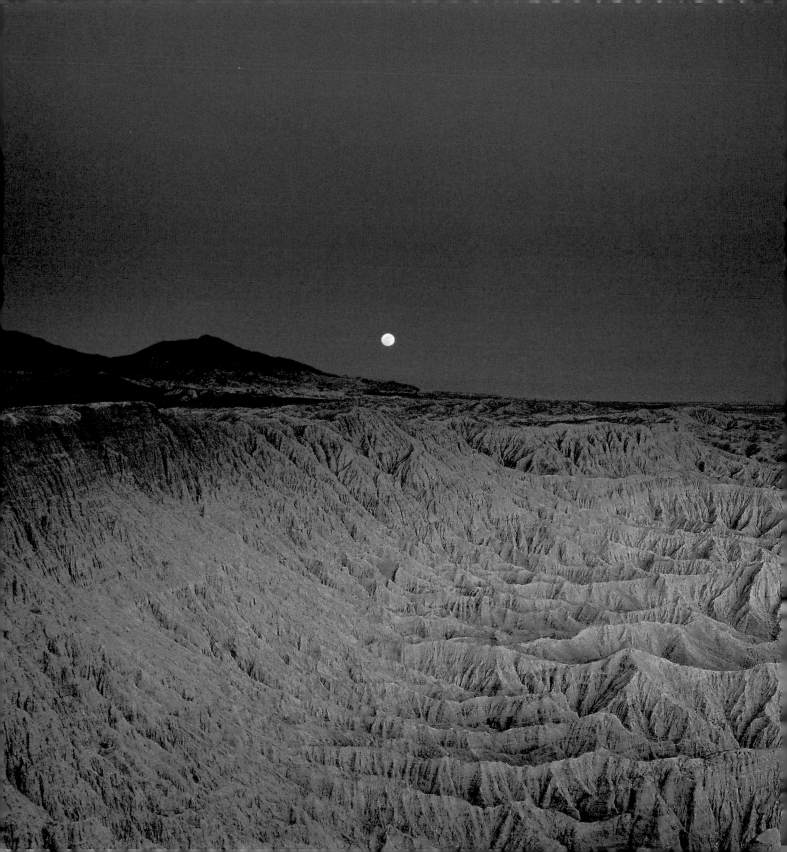

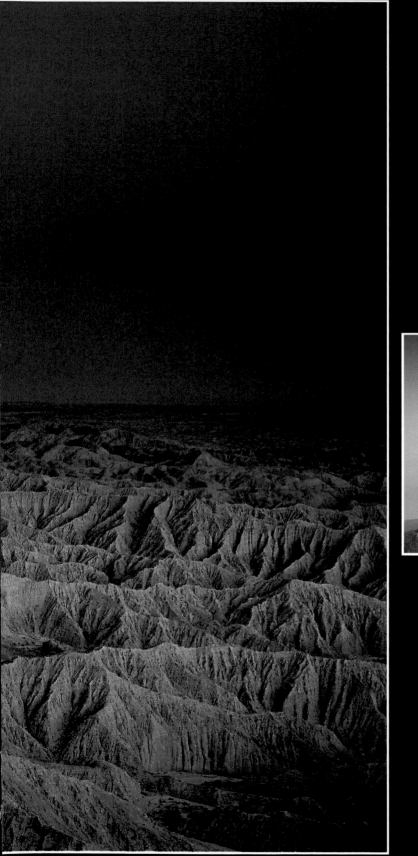

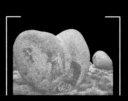

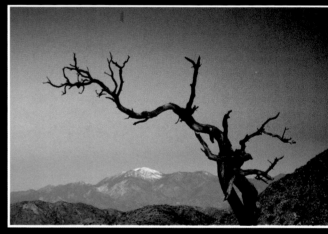

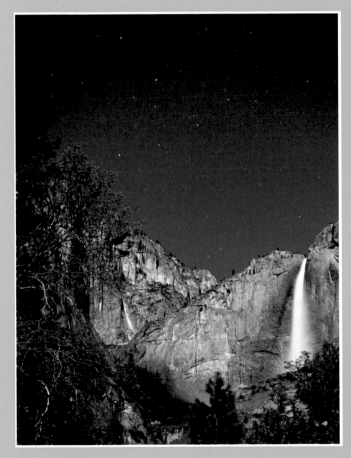

72 Lit by the full moon beneath a starry sky, Yosemite Falls plunge 2,425 feet to the valley floor.

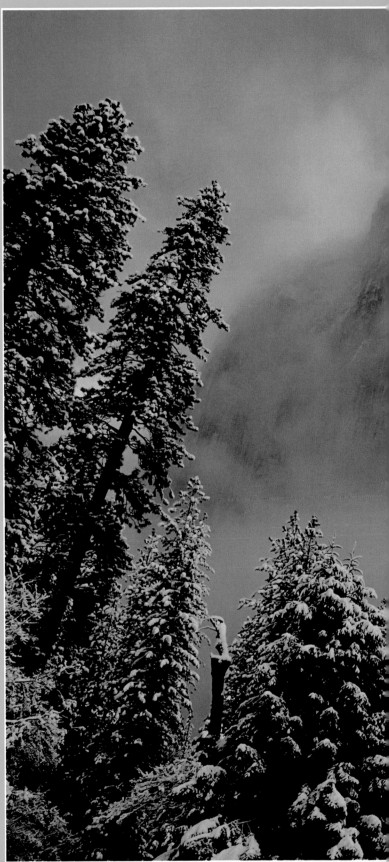

The Sierra Nevada

72–73 A winter storm clearing at dawn veils Yosemite's El Capitan in golden mists.

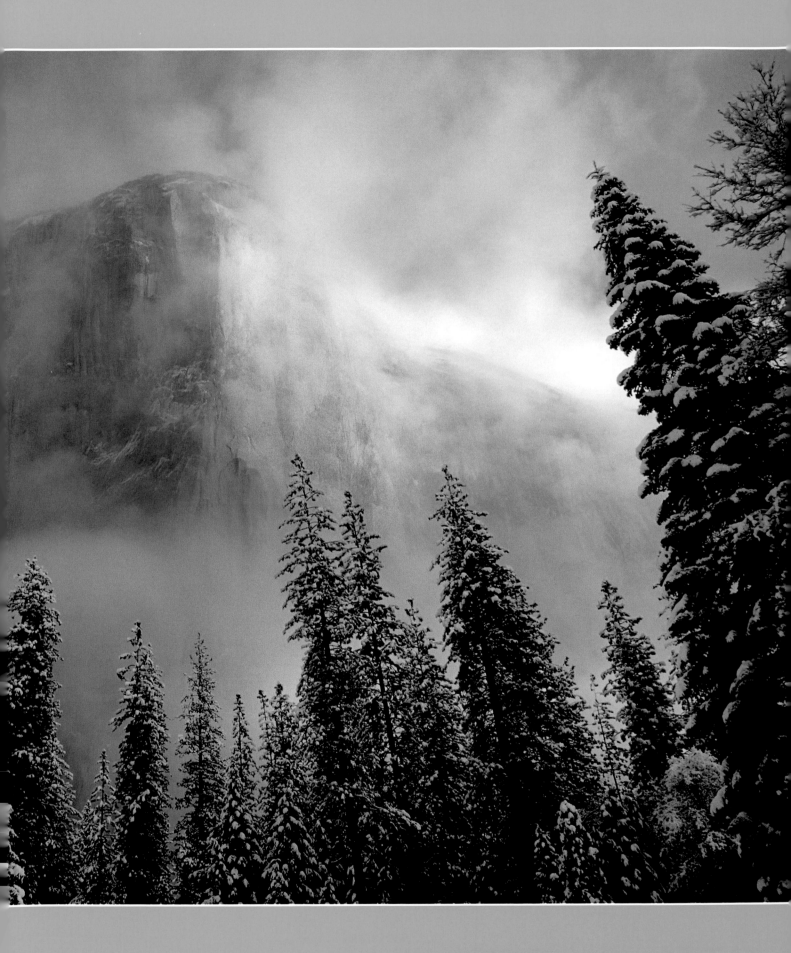

74–75 The fast-flowing waters of the Tuolumne River reflect the golden grasses of the Sierra foothills in this long exposure made just above Clavey Falls. The river originates from glaciers on the highest peaks of Yosemite National Park before plunging through deep canyons to join the San Joaquin River on its way to the sea.

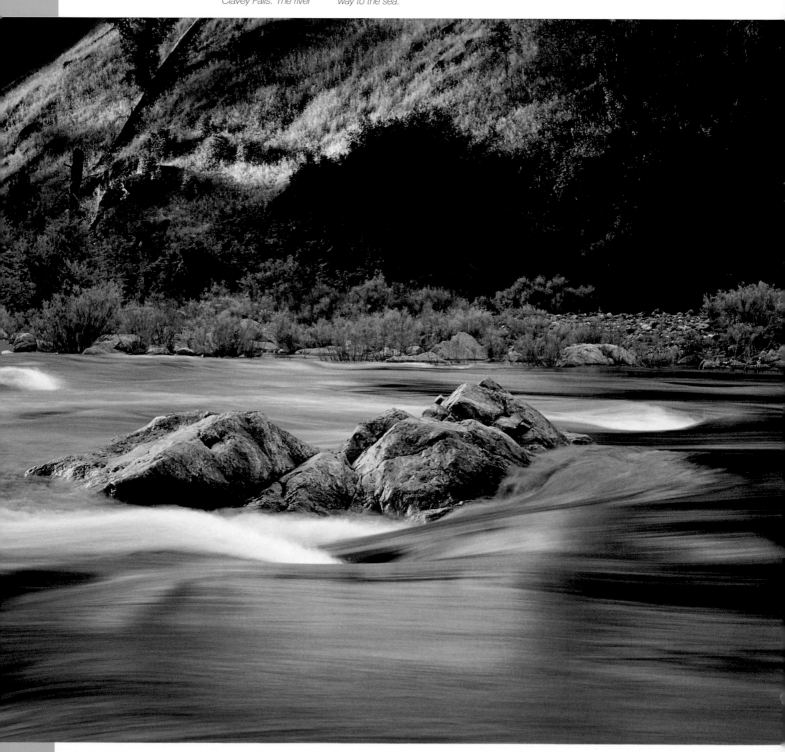

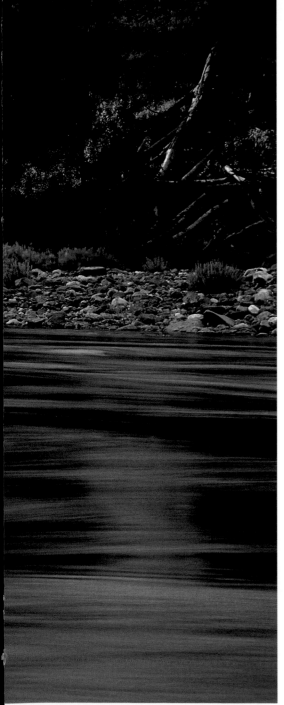

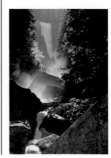

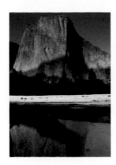

75 left Yosemite's
El Capitan rises 3,000
feet above its reflection
in the Merced River.

75 right Vernal Falls
brings the Merced River
into the valley through
a wild and roadless
canyon.

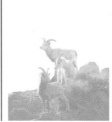

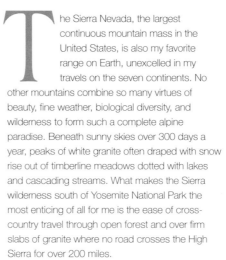

The Sierra Nevada, the largest continuous mountain mass in the United States, is also my favorite range on Earth, unexcelled in my travels on the seven continents. No other mountains combine so many virtues of beauty, fine weather, biological diversity, and wilderness to form such a complete alpine paradise. Beneath sunny skies over 300 days a year, peaks of white granite often draped with snow rise out of timberline meadows dotted with lakes and cascading streams. What makes the Sierra wilderness south of Yosemite National Park the most enticing of all for me is the ease of cross-country travel through open forest and over firm slabs of granite where no road crosses the High Sierra for over 200 miles.

The entire range is over 400 miles long and up to 80 miles wide, extending north well beyond touristy Lake Tahoe's gambling casinos, water sports, and ski resorts. Yosemite Valley is also crowded with over four million tourists a year, most of whom aim their cameras upward at Half Dome, El Capitan, and America's greatest concentration of high waterfalls, then leave the same day, having "done" Yosemite.

Yosemite's reputation of being a dreadfully urbanized national park is not entirely deserved. Politicians, journalists, and television crews lugging heavy cameras on short deadlines rarely venture beyond the seven-square-mile valley floor, overdeveloped before it was added to the park in 1906. They fail to experience the remaining 1200 square miles of national park, of which 94 percent are designated wilderness.

At an American conference on the mountain environment, I shared the podium with the great mountaineer Reinhold Messner, who spoke against commercial development of the world's mountains. When someone asked him why his home mountains, the Alps, were nowhere near as wild and well preserved as those of the American West, Messner simply answered, "You had John Muir."

Had it not been for the efforts of John Muir, America's quintessential conservationist, the High Sierra would not be so wild today. As a teenager, I read several of his books and found My First Summer in the Sierra, about his adventures in 1869, to be the most memorable. Beyond his eloquent descriptions of what he called "the gentle wilderness," I sensed that my own first summer in the Sierra was surprisingly the same, almost a century later.

When I joined my first two-week Sierra Club backcountry outing at the age of ten in 1951, my father brought along his worn first edition of My First Summer. As he read aloud passages that moved him, I enjoyed the poetry of the phrases, but didn't realize their lasting meaning until decades later. Camped amidst a quilted mountainscape of snow, ice, granite, lake, and meadow, it was no coincidence that I had been thinking some of the same thoughts and having some of the same feelings. The motto of those Sierra Club outings was: Life begins at 10,000 feet.

Muir had anticipated his immortality by preserving through his own actions both the physical and the emotional settings in which his writings take place. Other nineteenth century American writers left only words to describe worlds now long gone. Mark Twain's Old West has undergone profound change over the last century, yet John Muir's wild Sierra was still there at my feet on that Sierra Club outing in 1951 as well as on a more recent afternoon in 1999, when I repeated his 1869 solo climb of Cathedral Peak as he had done it, without encountering another human being.

In his later life, John Muir used the power of his fame and the muscle of his prose to help protect the Sierra Nevada for posterity. He founded the Sierra Club, now a major global force for conservation, and was a prime mover in the creation of Yosemite National Park, yet he may have accomplished even more for preservation in just a few days in 1903, when he postponed an extended trip to Asia and Europe to accept an invitation from President Theodore Roosevelt to secretly sneak off on foot and camp together beneath the giant sequoias of

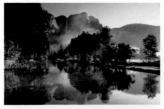

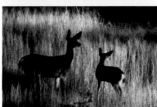

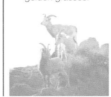

76 top During a spring flood in Yosemite Valley, mists rise over the Merced River.

76 bottom On the Yosemite Valley floor in the fall, a mule deer and fawn gaze through tall golden grasses.

Yosemite. As the "rough rider" president and the veteran mountaineer became kindred spirits around the campfire, Muir talked about the pressing need for forest protection, as well as the need for the trophy-hunting president "to get beyond the boyishness of killing things."

The president, greatly impressed, gave a surprising response: "Muir, I guess you are right." He emerged from the natural cathedral of world's largest living things and promptly delivered a government directive creating national forests continuously from Yosemite to Mount Shasta, four hundred miles to the north. He also promoted the inclusion of Yosemite Valley, then managed with minimal protection by the State of California, into the national park. Thus, as historian Frederick Turner aptly concludes, "Two major figures in American history enacted in microcosm one of the culture's most persistent dreams: creative truancy in the wild heart of the New World." The greatest shift in American environmental policy took place, not in the nation's capital, but in the wilds of the Sierra Nevada.

After Muir's death in 1914, the 211-mile John Muir Trail was constructed near the Sierra crest between Yosemite Valley and the 14,496-foot summit of Mount Whitney, the highest peak in the contiguous United States. It passes through Yosemite, Kings Canyon, and Sequoia National Parks, Devils Postpile National Monument, and three U.S. Forest Service wilderness areas. All of the high peaks of the Sierra above 13,000 feet are south of Yosemite in this southern culmination of the range.

Ever since that first family trip in 1951, the Muir Trail and its environs have lured me back at least once a year. I've hiked the complete trail in summer, run long sections of it, skied its whole length in winter, and made over a hundred first ascents of the faces of surrounding peaks. John Muir, however, never hiked the route of the trail, though he explored many of the areas it now traverses.

The trail was the brainchild of another passionate young mountaineer named Theodore

Solomons, who set out in 1892 to find a route passable for a party using mules to carry loads through the alpine heart of the Sierra. Solomons wanted to experience "a full-length crest-wise journey." Despite the intervening century of progress, his wild vision has survived virtually intact, though with the name of John Muir on the trail of his dreams.

Solomons was probably the first white man to reach the valley at the source of the San Joaquin River and see its wild, unnamed granite domes, sheer spires, and higher metamorphic summits. After three summers of trailbreaking to get a hundred miles south of Yosemite, he entered a broad glaciated landscape surrounded by towering granite peaks. The alpine cul-de-sac seemed so alive with cascading streams and lush flowers that he named the peaks and the valley itself after "the great evolutionists, so at one in their devotion to the sublime in Nature." He called the peaks Darwin, Mendel, Lamarck, Haeckel, Wallace, Fiske, Spencer, and Huxley. Below them lay vast timberline meadows watered by myriad streams descending from canyon walls into a series of lakes below what was later named Muir Pass.

Solomons failed to penetrate the range farther south, veering westward down a difficult canyon that he christened Enchanted Gorge. In 1924, my mother made one of the first traverses of the yet-to-be-completed Muir Trail just after graduating from college. Her party of five mules, four women, three horses, and two men camped in Evolution Valley and looked up at The Hermit, a 12,000-foot sharp granite peak named by Solomons. The next day my mother made the first ascent of The Hermit with the aid of a packer's hemp rope thrown over the summit block. Right up to her death at 94 in 1995, she singled out that summer as the most memorable of her long and happy life.

A few summers later, my wife, Barbara, and I conjured up our own adventure in the spirit of my mother and Theodore Solomons. A packer and six mules dropped food, tents, cameras, tripods, climbing gear, and Barbara's watercolors

at Evolution Lake at 10,800 feet. We walked in with five friends, carrying only day packs. Six more joined us, including Peter Croft a legendary climber known for speed ascents, such as a 4 hour, 22 minute record climb of the face of Yosemite's El Capitan. (The first climb of the face of El Capitan in 1958 required 12 days and nights on the cliff after 18 months of siege climbing with fixed ropes. My own first climb in 1966 took five days, though I managed a 14-hour one-day ascent in 1998.) Thus when Peter casually mentioned the possibility of a one-day grand traverse of the Evolution Peaks and invited me to join him leaving at 4 a.m. the next morning, I had doubts about being up to the task.

By sunrise we had topped Mount Mendel and an hour later, atop Mount Darwin, I caught a photograph of Peter surrounded by a surreal fringe of diffracted sunlight. The jagged ridge to the south was reputed to be unclimbed. Peter led the unroped, exposed traverse, and by 2 P.M. we had traversed seven summits over 13,000 feet and were atop the last of the Evolution Peaks on the Sierra crest. I was glad that the traverse was over because the rough granite had worn through the tips of several of my fingers. Peter's tougher hands were doing fine. He continued over the tops of Mounts Wallace, Fiske, Spencer, and Huxley, off the main Sierra crest, while I descended alone.

As the rest of us were sipping wine before dinner, Peter walked up looking amazingly fresh. He recounted a fine day in the mountains without ropes, pitons, or bivouac gear closer in spirit to John Muir, who celebrated the joy of discovery of new wildness and natural beauty, than of a typical modern climber recounting difficulty ratings.

On our twelfth morning we broke camp and completed a west-east traverse of the Sierra range, ending up in the town of Bishop. On the long drive home, I thought about how thankful I was for Solomons' vision of opening up the timberline wilderness just enough so that "enterprising mountaineers could leave Yosemite Valley with loaded animals to thread their way through the very heart of the High Sierra" a century after his explorations. That vision, as well as Muir's and my own, is alive and well today.

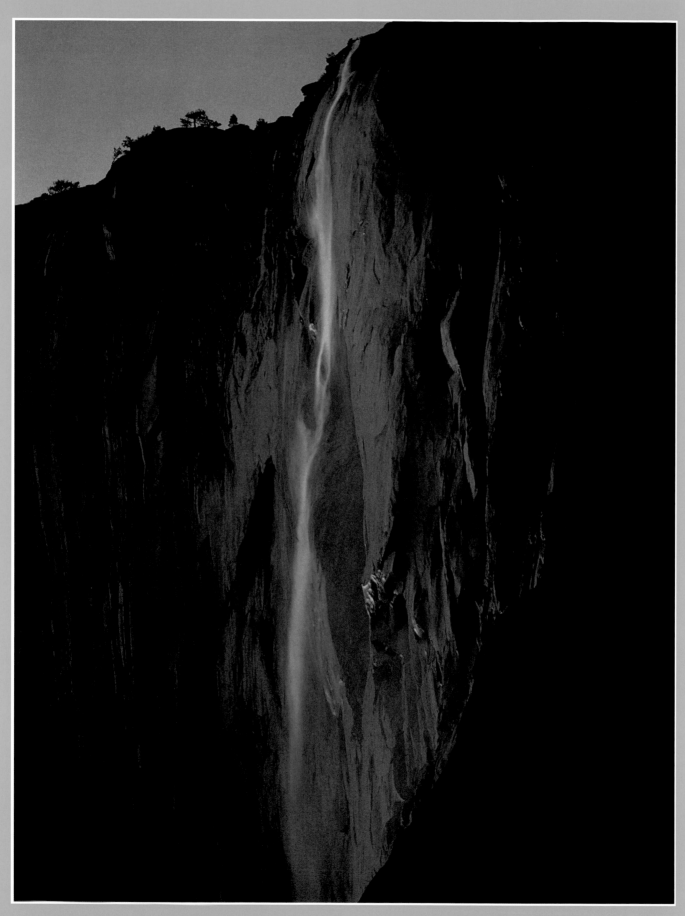

77 Last light on
Horsetail Fall singles
out water falling
over the east face
of Yosemite's El
Capitan, moments
after the cliff behind
has fallen into
shadow. The rare
aligning of the sun
at just the right
point on the horizon
to light only the
waterfall at sunset
occurs once a year
in mid-February,
often when it is too
cloudy for the last
sunlight or too cold
for the waterfall to
flow.

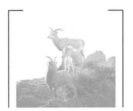

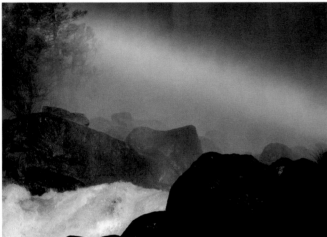

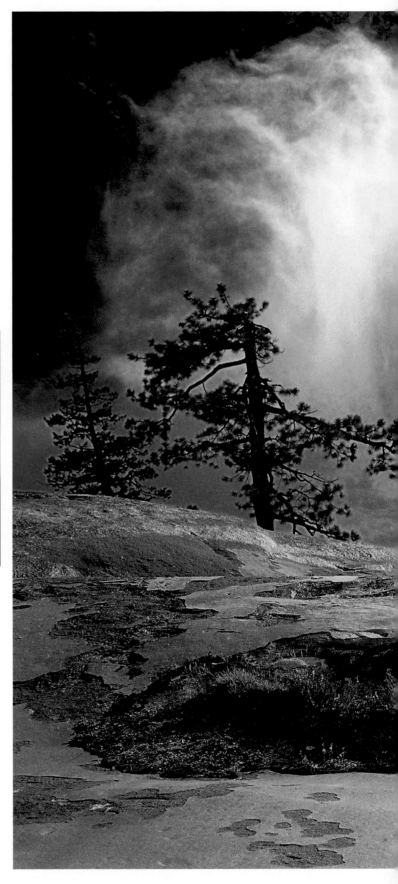

78 An intense rainbow hovers in the spray of Lower Yosemite Fall just above glistening boulders and raging waters during heavy spring snow melt. Summer visitors to Yosemite Valley rarely see the rainbow here because the flow of the creek is too low.

78–79 Mist below Waterwheel Falls in the Grand Canyon of the Tuolumne River sprouts a profusion of wildflowers on a granite ledge. The spectacular canyon is only accessible by trail in the high country of Yosemite National Park.

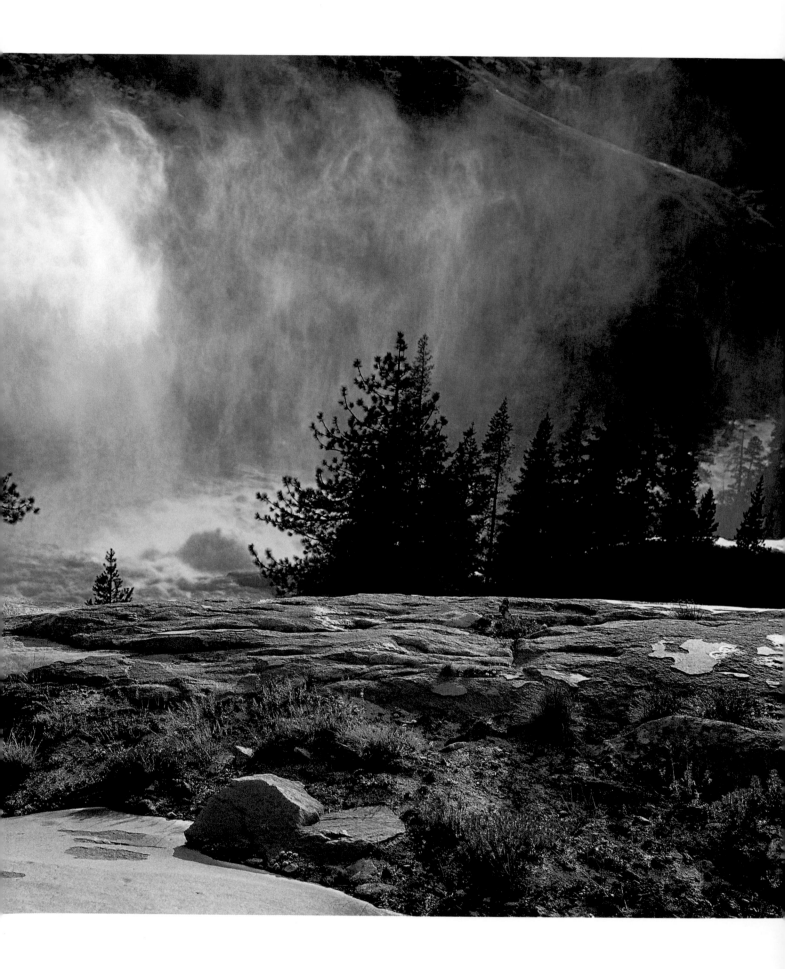

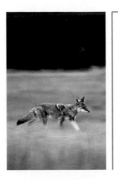

80 top A mountain coyote trots across a Yosemite meadow on a fall morning. Smaller than a wolf, these wild canines generally hunt small game and avoid humans, but many Yosemite coyotes have become habituated to people and vehicles.

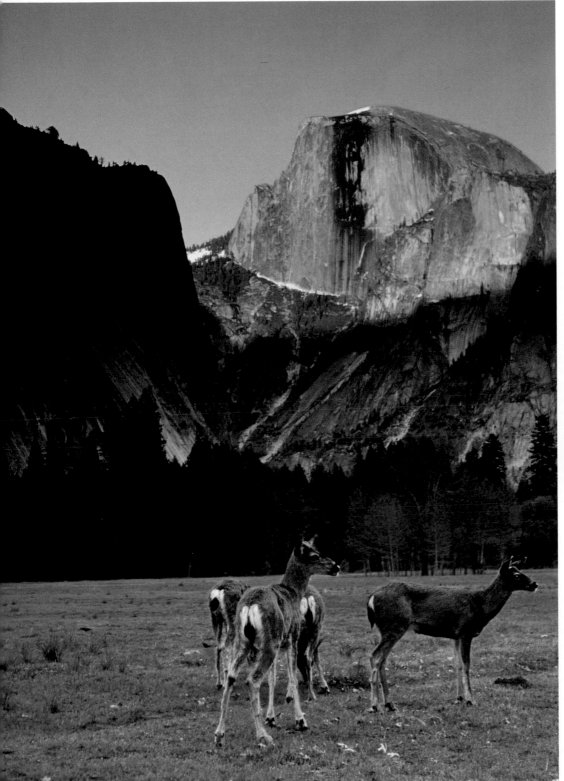

80 bottom left Almost 5,000 feet below Half Dome in last light, mule deer graze the verdant floor of Yosemite Valley.

80 bottom right Less than 100 endangered Sierra bighorn sheep survive, rarely seen in the backcountry of Yosemite.

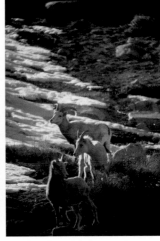

81 Seen from a remote ledge called the Diving Board, the incredibly sheer 2,000-foot Northwest Face of Half Dome turns gold at sunset. The first climb during the summer of 1957 required five days and four nights on the face.

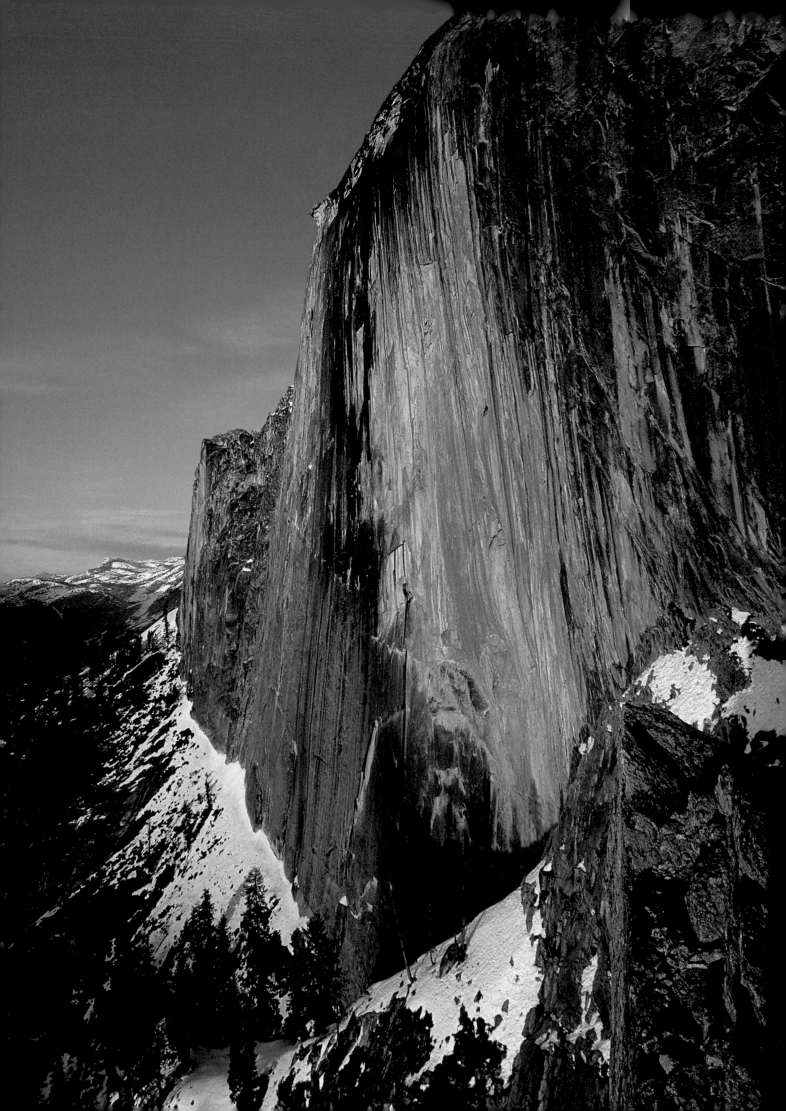

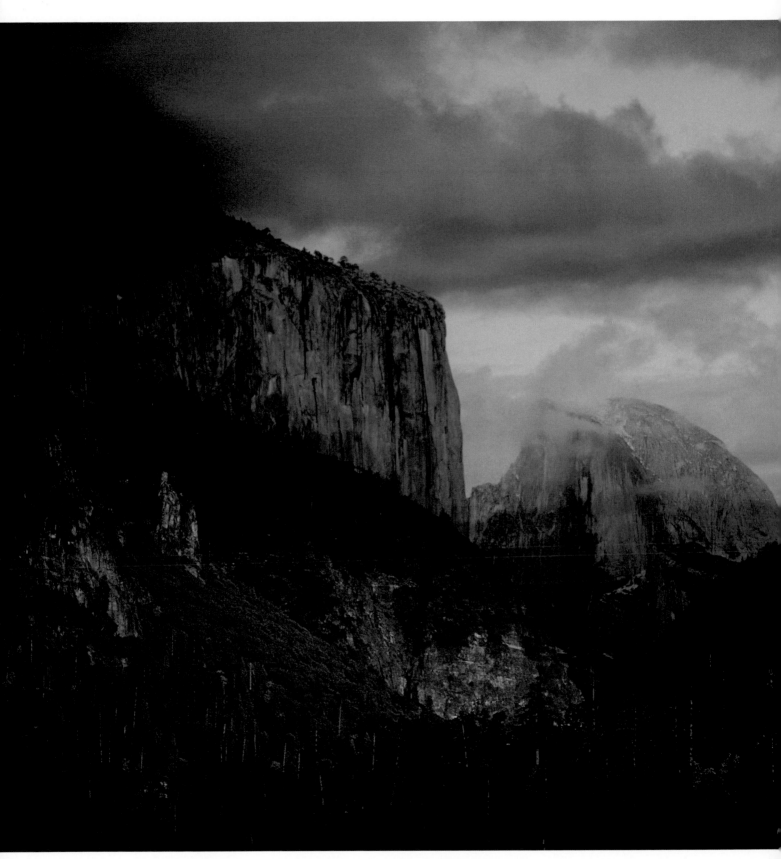

82–83 A telephoto view brings Yosemite's icons—Half Dome and El Capitan—together on an exceptionally clear evening after a ten-day November storm. Seven miles more distant, Half Dome takes on a bluish cast.

83 top The continuously overhanging 1,200-foot face of Leaning Tower graces a winter vista of the first chamber of Yosemite Valley.

83 bottom Fiery mists rising into a Yosemite sunset reflect in the waters of the Merced River, while snowy boulders take on the blue cast of the sky overhead. The intense orange glow during the clearing of a winter storm lasted only minutes.

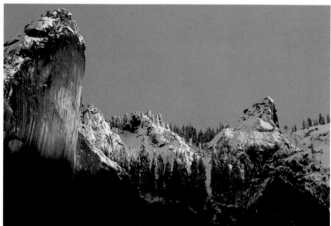

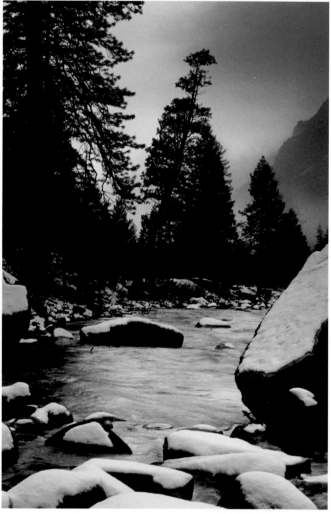

85 top As if hewn by a sculptor, the windblown roots of a fallen whitebark pine cradle a granite boulder lifted from the timberline earth of the High Sierra.

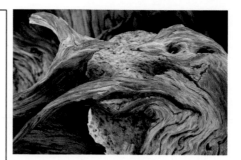

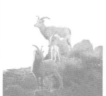

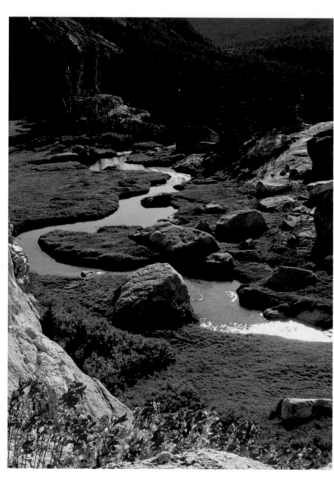

85 bottom right Lit by reflection from a snowfield in the Ansel Adams Wilderness, a dead whitebark pine glows against dark shadows as if lit from within.

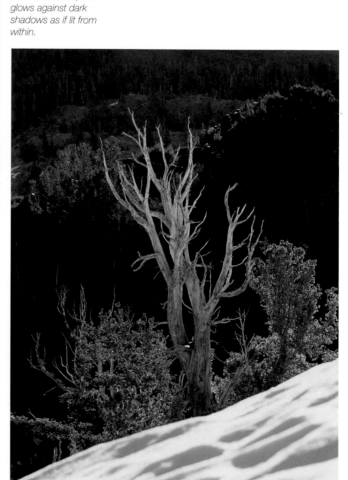

84 A stormy sunset over Tuolumne Meadows mimics the brief summer bloom of pink owl's clover in Yosemite's largest subalpine meadow.

85 bottom left On the flanks of Yosemite's Mt. Conness, a hanging meadow at timberline glistens in morning light at 11,000 feet in early summer.

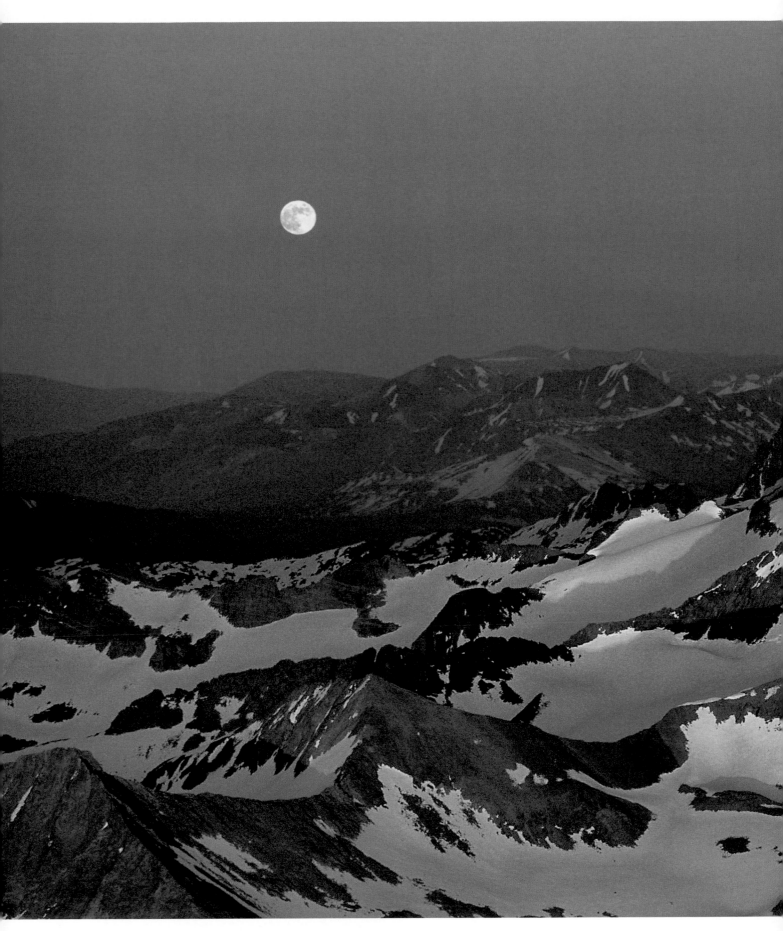

86–87 A full moon rises over the source of the Tuolumne River— Yosemite's largest glacier on 13,110-foot Mount Lyell.

87 top Twilight suffuses the Yosemite High Country with a warm glow as seen from the summit of Cathedral Peak.

87 center The High Sierra takes on a Himalayan appearance in mid-winter as seen from 13,500 feet on Mount Whitney.

87 bottom Evening comes to an unnamed lake at timberline in the Ansel Adams Wilderness south of Yosemite National Park.

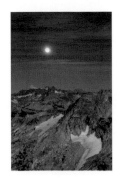

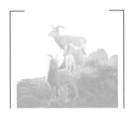

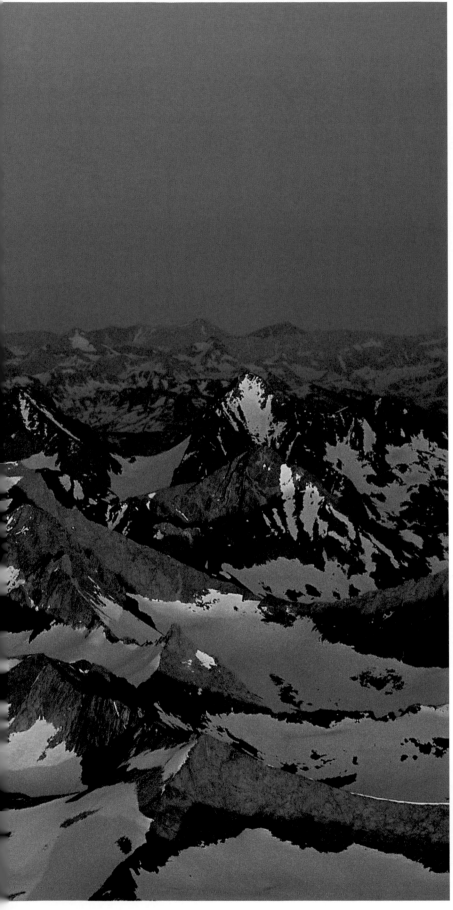

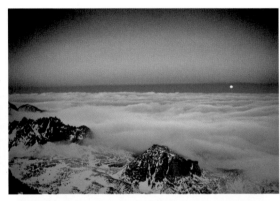

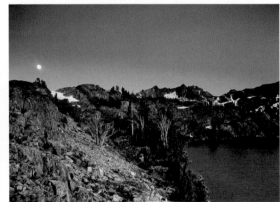

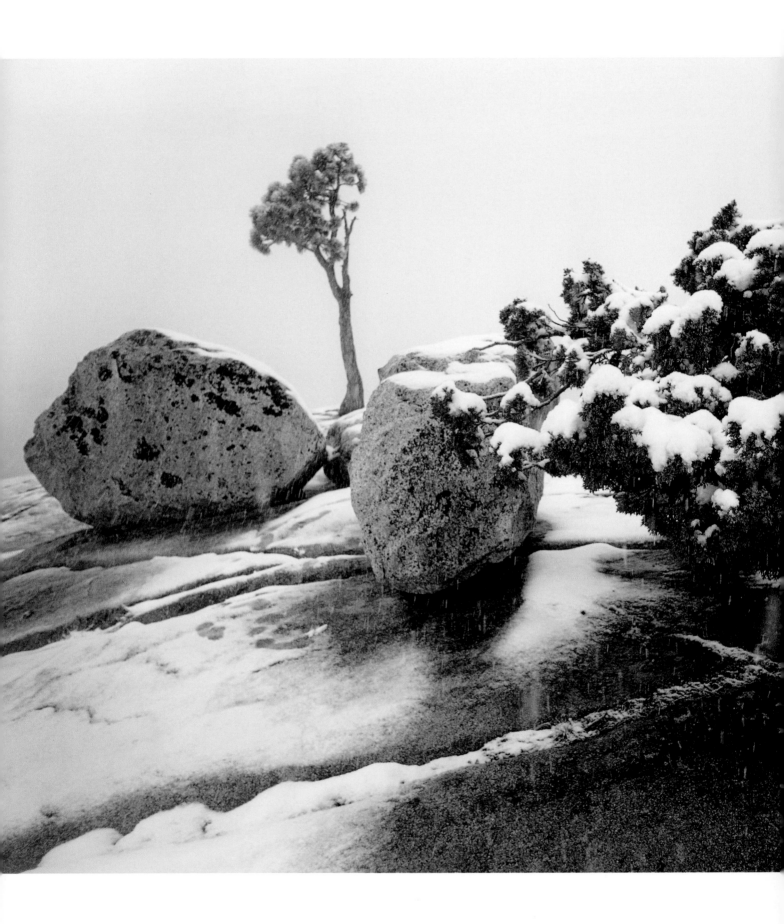

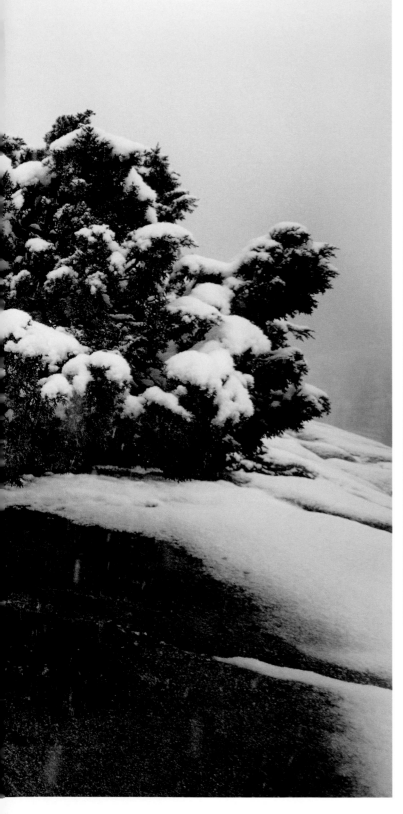

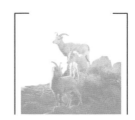

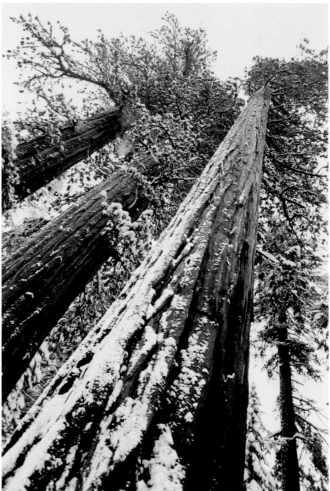

88–89 Snow falls on a natural bonzai garden atop a glacier-polished dome at Yosemite's Olmsted Point. Boulders left by the last recession of the ice share a lonely perch with dwarfed juniper and Jeffrey pine trees sprouting from nearby cracks.

89 Giant sequoias soar skyward out of Yosemite's Merced Grove.

90–91 A crimson sunset at the end of a storm fringes the Evolution Peaks along the John Muir Trail in Kings Canyon National Park.

92–93 In an otherworldly telephoto view on a rare −22°F winter morning, the full moon sinks behind Wheeler Crest at the moment of sunrise.

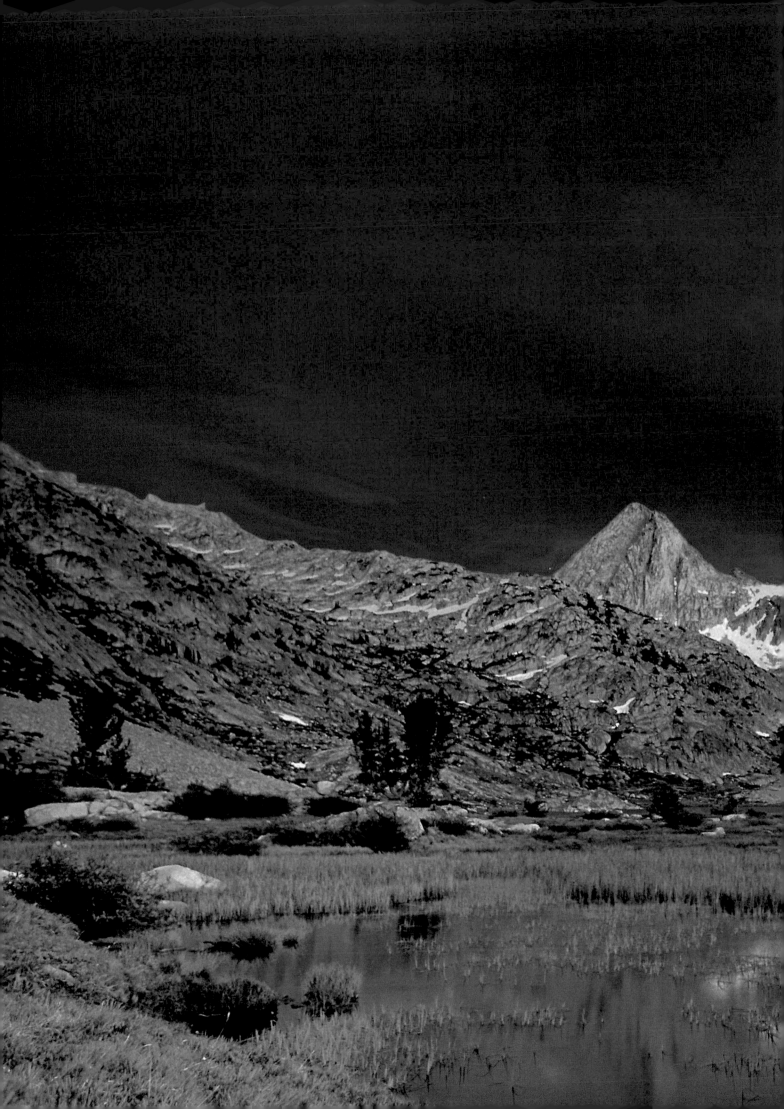

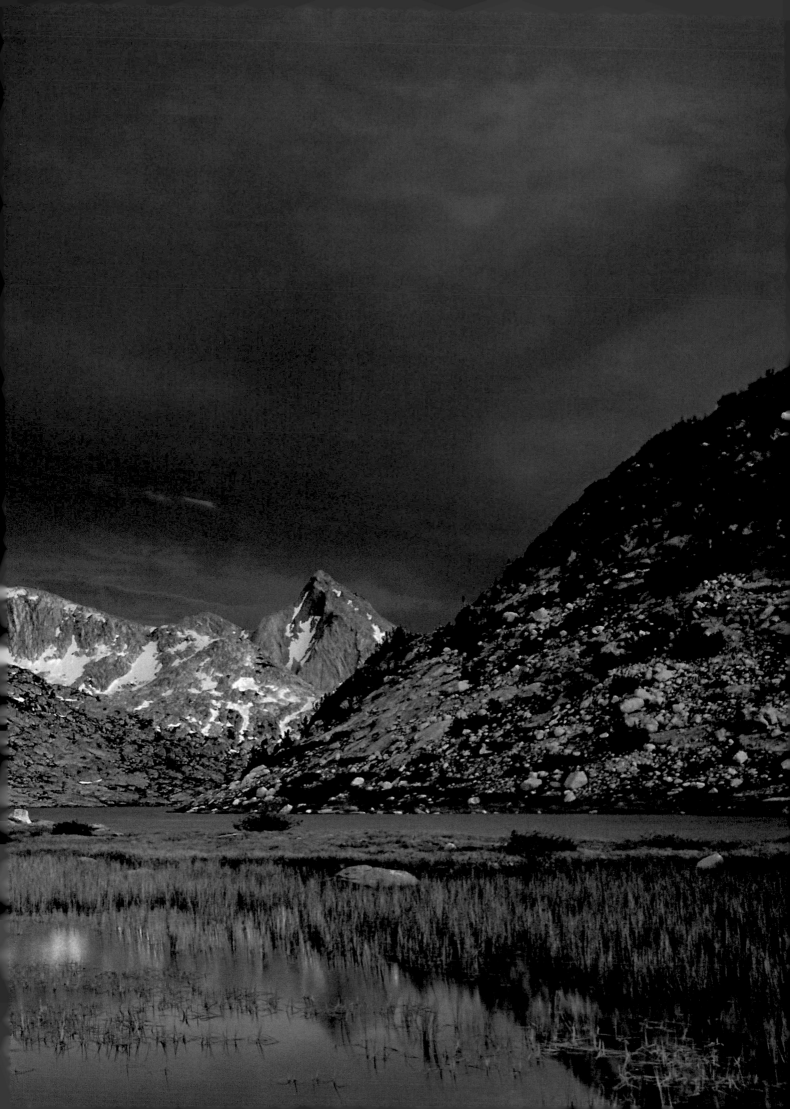

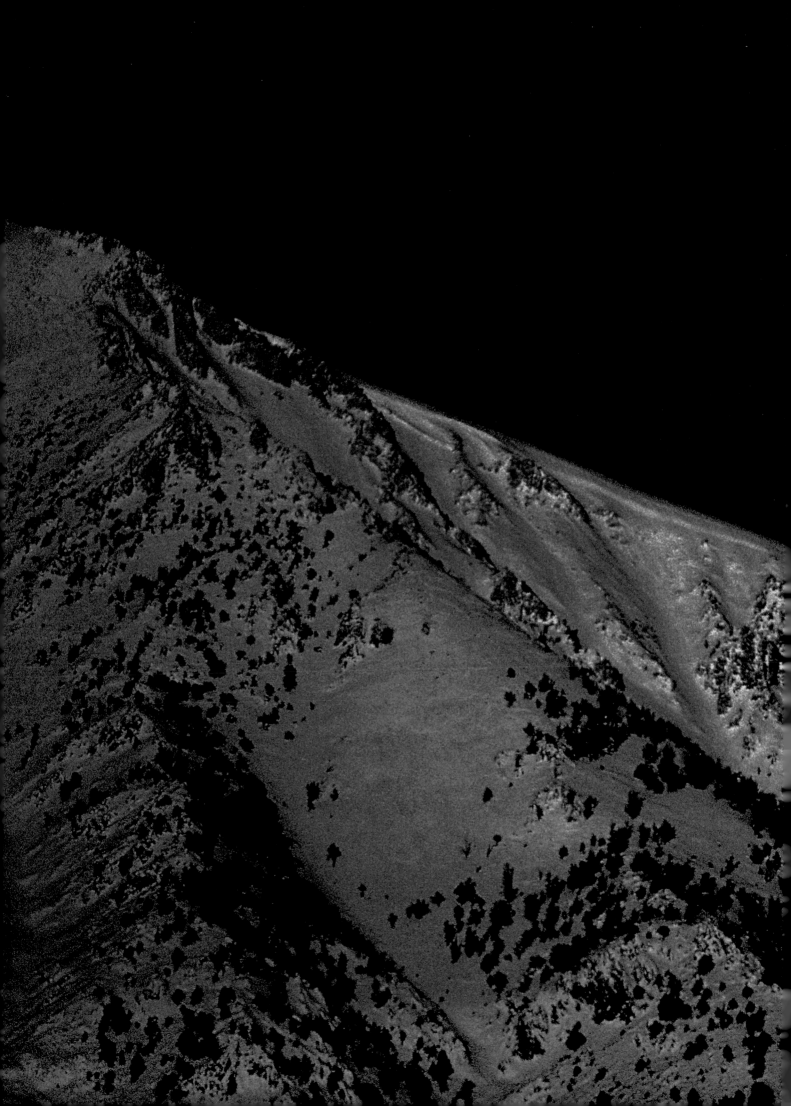

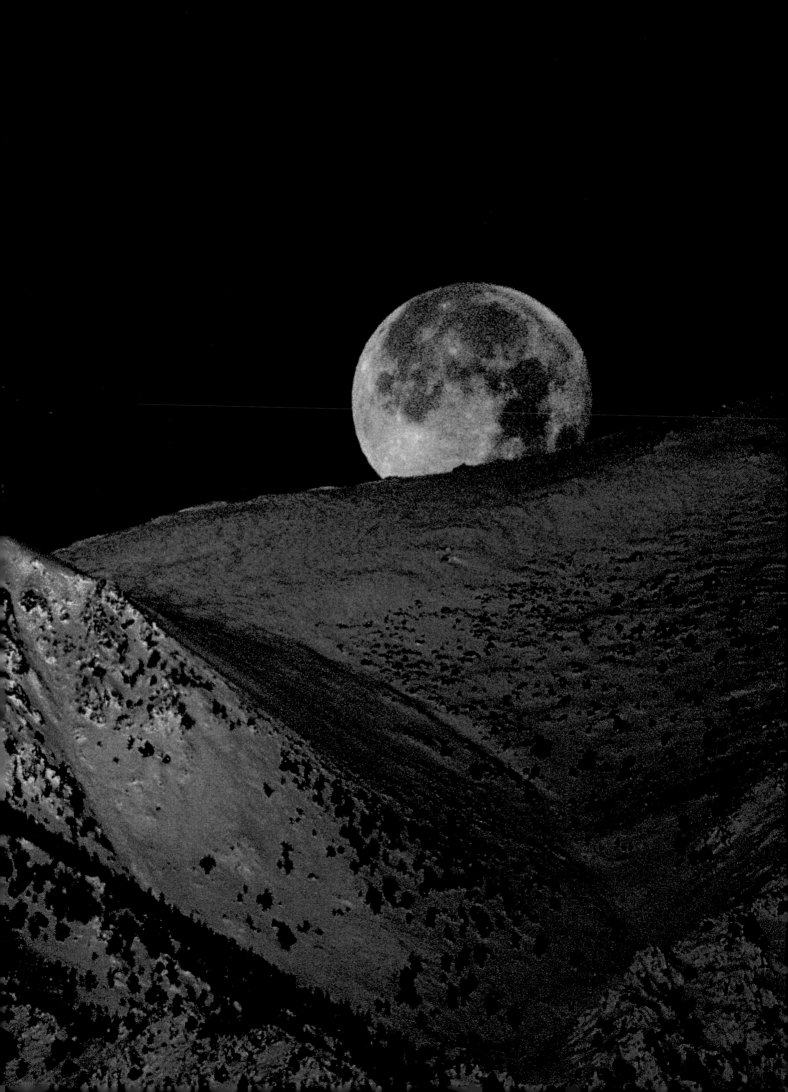

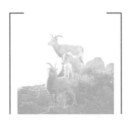

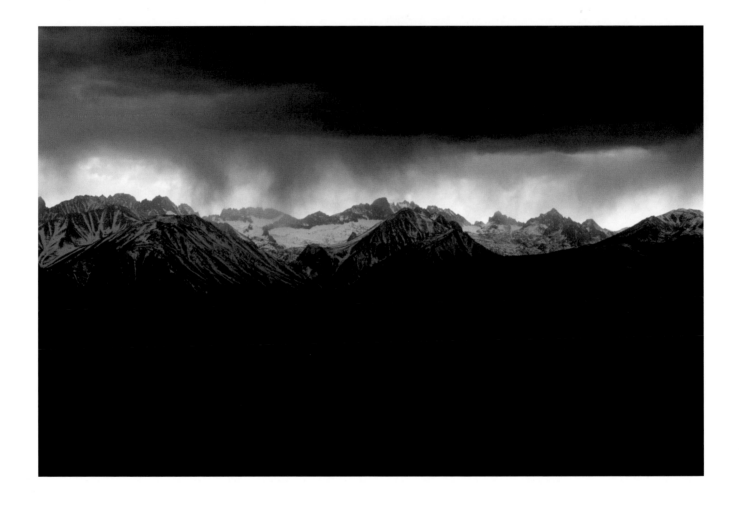

94 A summer thunderstorm closes in on the 14,000-foot peaks of the Palisade Range above the Sierra Nevada's largest glaciers.

95 Melt water from late summer snow reflects last light on 14,384-foot Mount Williamson, the second highest peak in the Sierra Nevada Range.

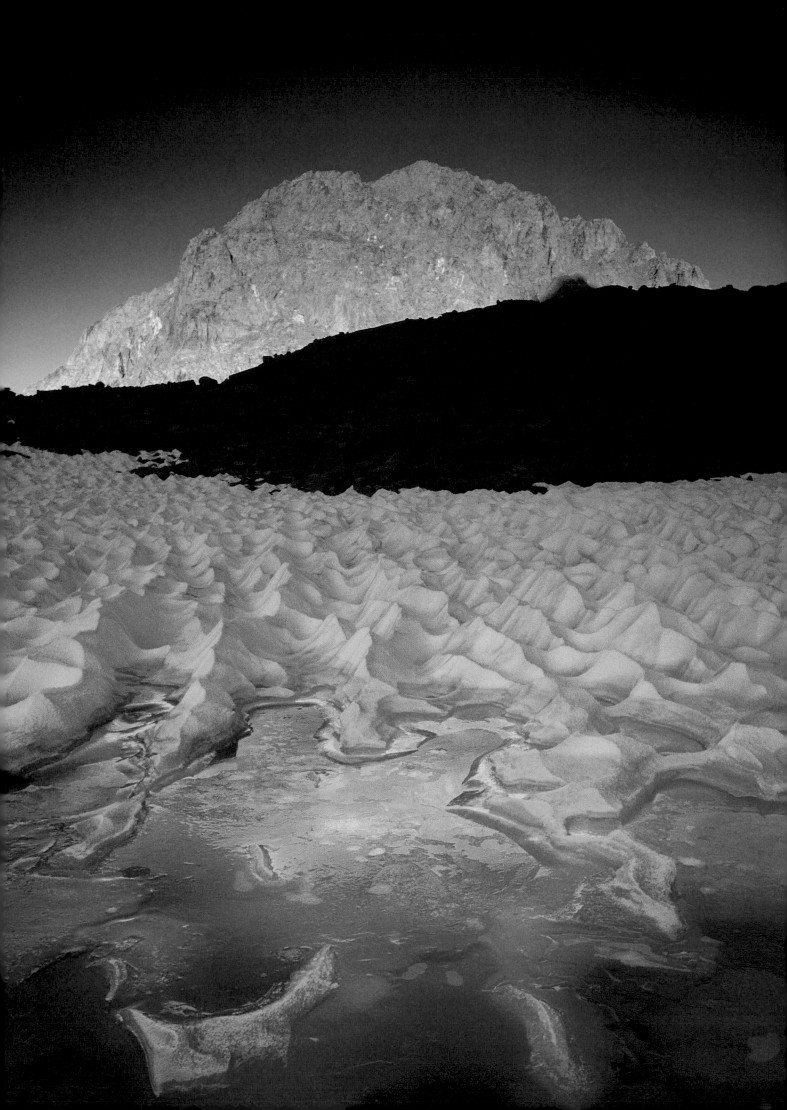

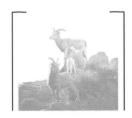

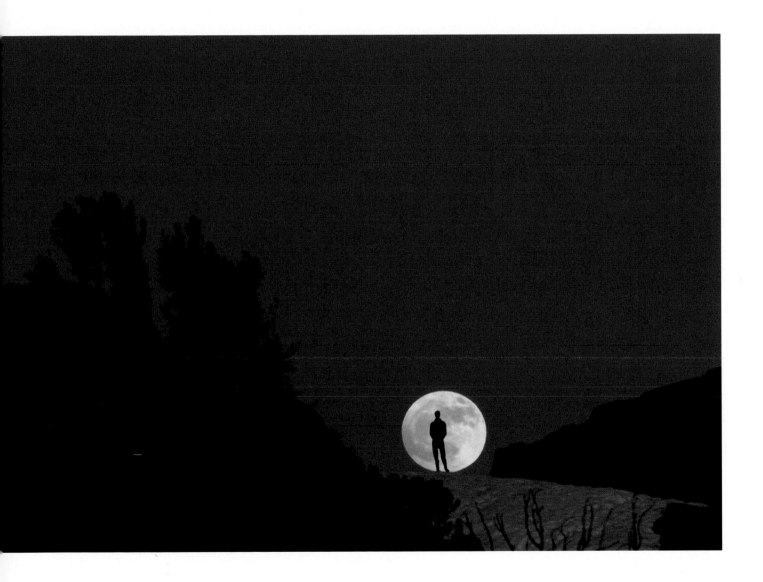

96 A hiker watches the full moon rise at sunset from a snowy gap below Mount Ritter in the Ansel Adams Wilderness.

97 The full moon sets behind a forested ridge above Lake Tenaya as seen from Olmsted Point in the Yosemite High Country.

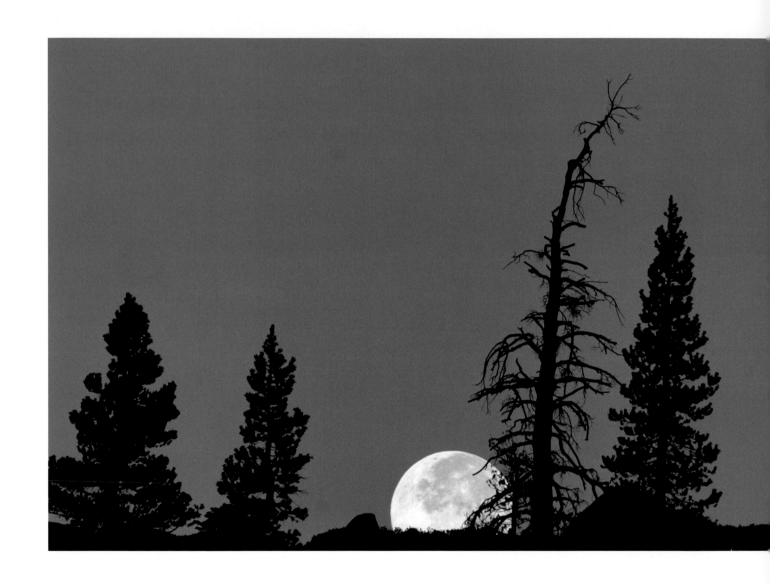

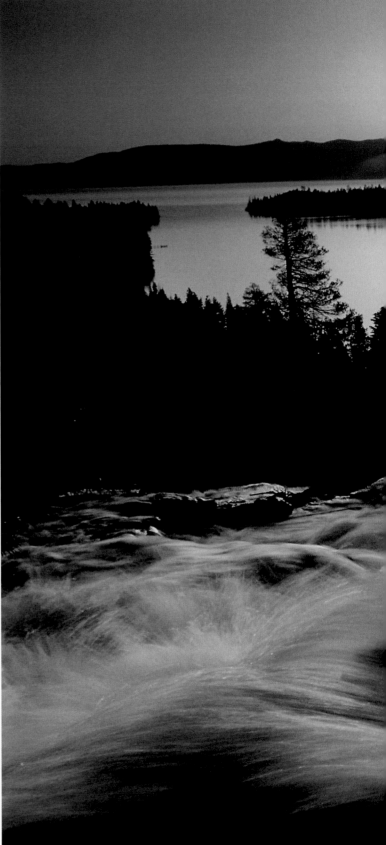

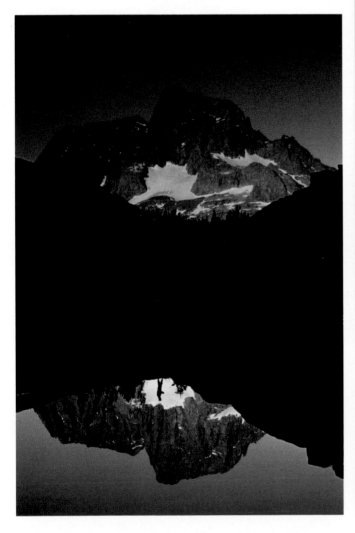

98 bottom Hidden by shadow and perspective, a hiker's presence is belied only by his reflection beneath Banner Peak in the Ansel Adams Wilderness.

98–99 Silky waters at the brink of Eagle Falls plunge toward Emerald Bay on the California side of Lake Tahoe.

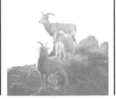

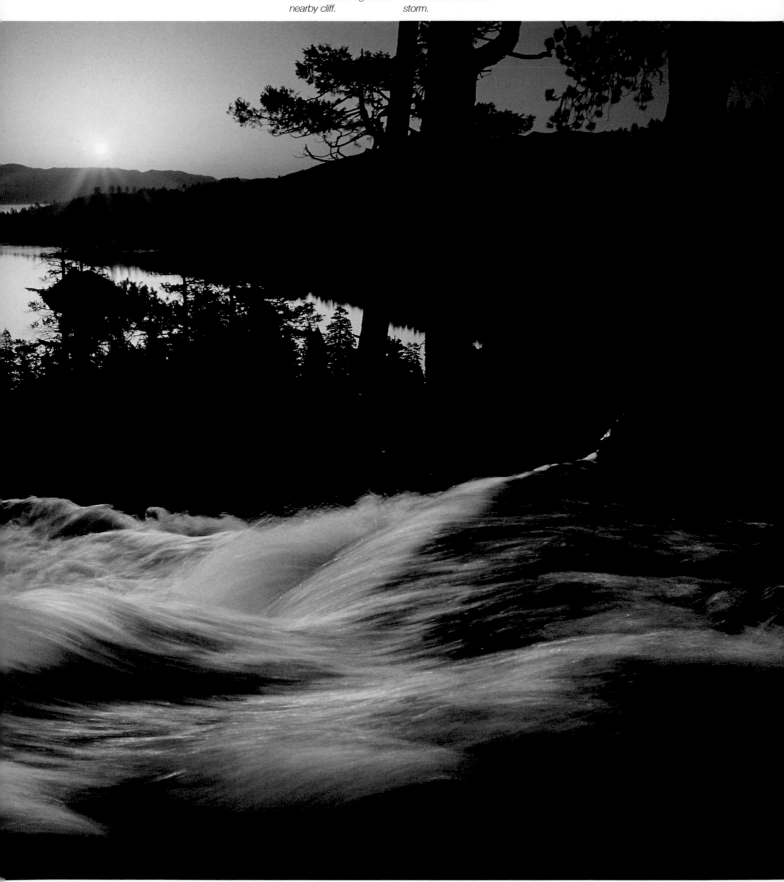

100 Alpenglow on Keeler Needle and Mount Whitney cast a hiker's shadow against a nearby cliff.

100–101 Lenticular clouds at dawn over Tioga Pass forebode Yosemite's first winter storm.

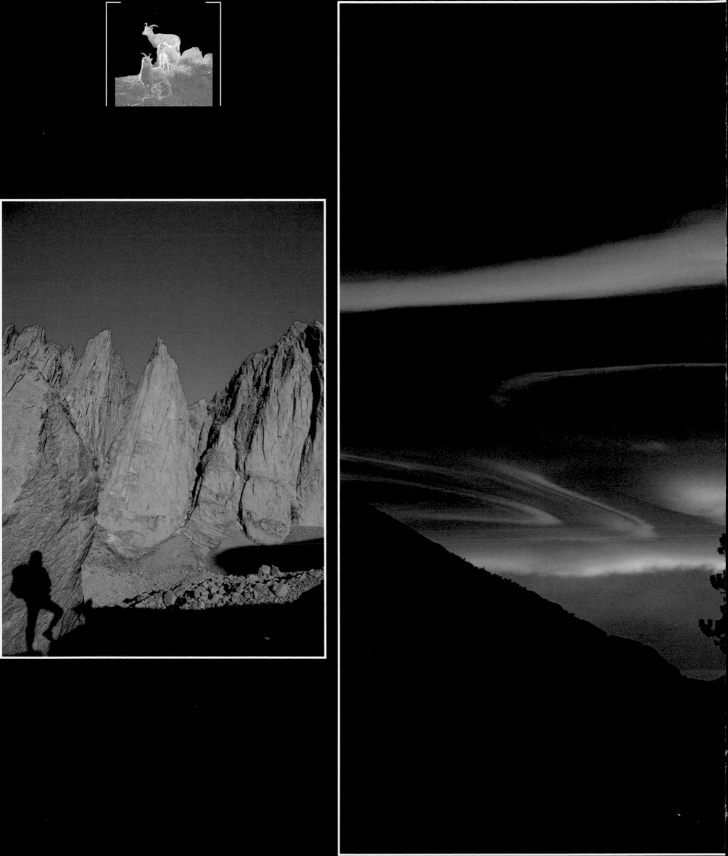

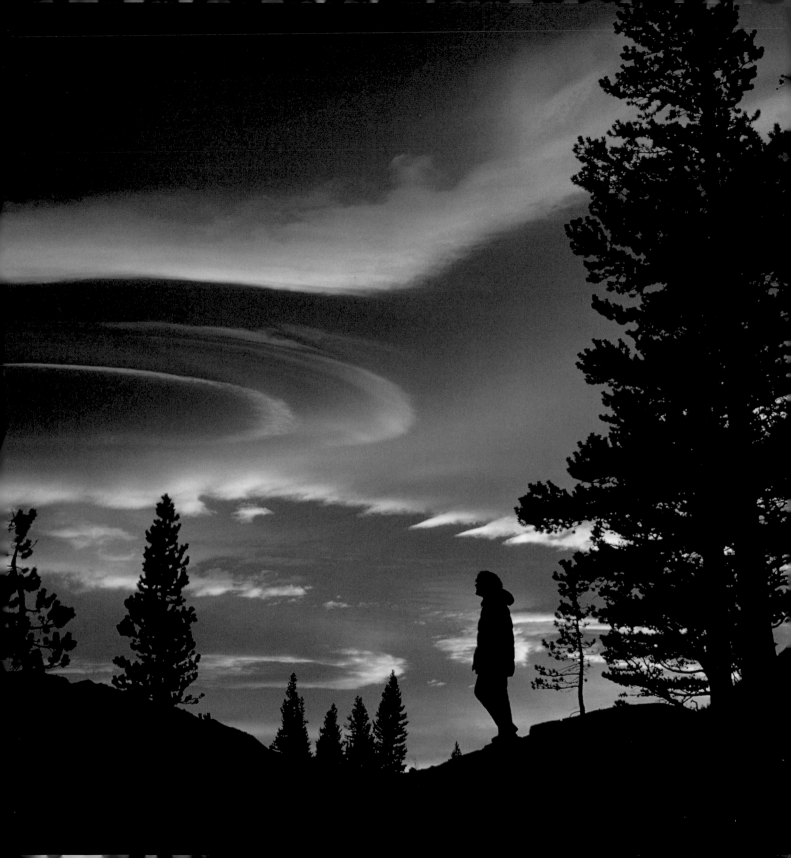

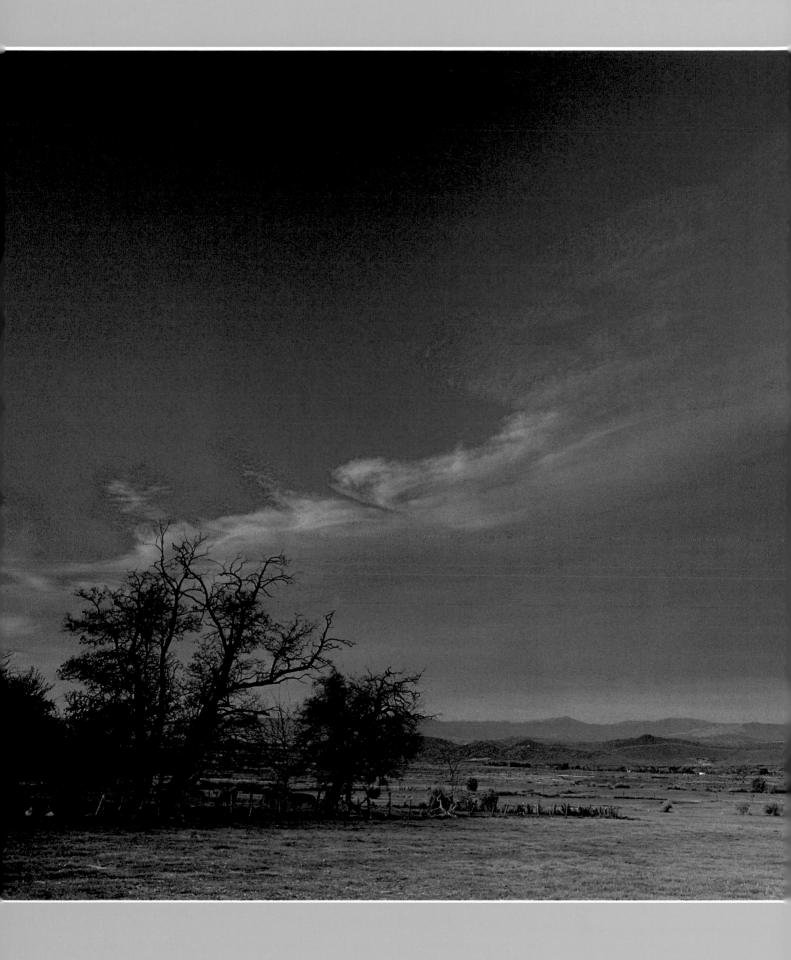

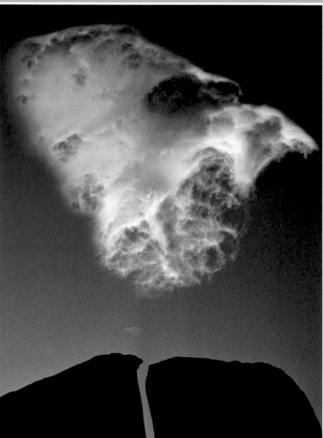

The Great Basin

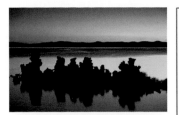

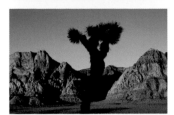

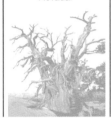

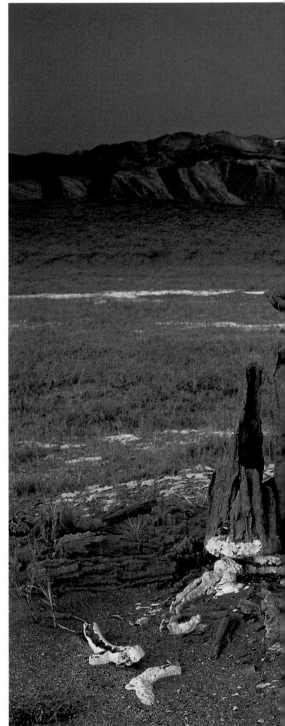

Modern travelers, conditioned to the bustle of metropolitan life, are pleasantly mesmerized by the endless empty expanses of the Great Basin. They know they can travel in air-conditioned comfort on the highways, visit special destinations, and return to civilization at will. Nineteenth-century pioneers in covered wagons on their way to the gold fields of California described these same dry valleys and desert ranges as useless, ugly, and life-threatening badlands to be passed through to reach the fabled paradise of California—the land of plenty. The day when any of these arid landscapes would be preserved for their scenic beauty, to spiritually enrich souls overwhelmed by too much of everything in the cities, was not remotely imaginable.

That day arrived only during my own lifetime. As a child, I crossed Nevada and Utah on summer vacations with my parents in the middle of the night. My father tied burlap "desert water bags" that cooled by transpiration to the sides of our 1940 Chevrolet, rarely stopping on our way to the cooler heights of Colorado, Wyoming, or Montana.

Crossing the desert in a modern, air-conditioned, sport-utility vehicle makes for a very different experience. With climate control in broad daylight, the beauty and symmetry of the exposed bones of the Earth can now be appreciated with stereo music playing and a cold drink in one hand. Even so, most people obliviously cross the Great Basin on Interstate 80 over the same dry valley bottoms traversed by the pioneers, unaware of the islands of montane meadow and forest on the heights of nearby desert peaks, or the stark beauty of the shores of shallow alkaline lakes where there were once vast inland seas.

The famous explorer and raconteur, Captain John Fremont, searched in vain during the 1840s for the "Buenaventura River," the region's supposed drainage to the sea, drawn on previous maps as ending up in San Francisco Bay. He finally immortalized this empty quarter of the American West as The Great Basin, a land without a natural outlet to the sea.

Had Fremont come 200,000 years earlier, he could have sailed vast inland seas through the same broad valleys he found filled with sagebrush. The Great Salt Lake in Utah, Pyramid Lake in Nevada, and Mono Lake in California are three of the best-known relics of these Ice Age seas. With no outlet, minerals in the water have no way to escape, and through evaporation, the salinity of these lakes now far exceeds that of the ocean. Islands in all three lakes house nesting colonies of California gulls, which migrate from the Pacific each spring to breed beside the last remnants of their ancestral home. The lakes are also staging areas along the Great Basin Flyway for millions of other birds.

When Mark Twain first saw Mono Lake in 1870, he described it as "a solemn, silent, sailless sea." Its shores were barren and its waters salty. No lush forests or sandy beaches lapped its edge. Because the Great Basin didn't match the American notion of scenic beauty, the city of Los Angeles was able to gain legal entitlement to surrounding streams. An eleven-mile tunnel was dug to connect clear streams coming down from the mountains into the Owens River before they, too, merged with the briny lake. Farther south, the entire river was diverted into the Los Angeles Aqueduct for a 300-mile journey out of the Great Basin to a growing city on another shore without enough natural clear water.

Since the city of Los Angeles began taking water from the Mono Basin in 1940, the level of the lake has drastically lowered. In the 1970s, I wrote the first national magazine story about the plight of Mono Lake. At that time, a top executive for the city of Los Angeles told me, "We have legal rights to that Mono Basin water and we won't reduce our export one bit unless someone sues us and we lose. The odds of that happening are mighty small."

After the big winter of 1983 flooded Rush Creek with more water than Los Angeles could export, a vacationing lawyer caught trout in the usually dry stream bed. He found an obscure law against lowering the level of a stream with game fish beyond where they could survive. A court heard evidence

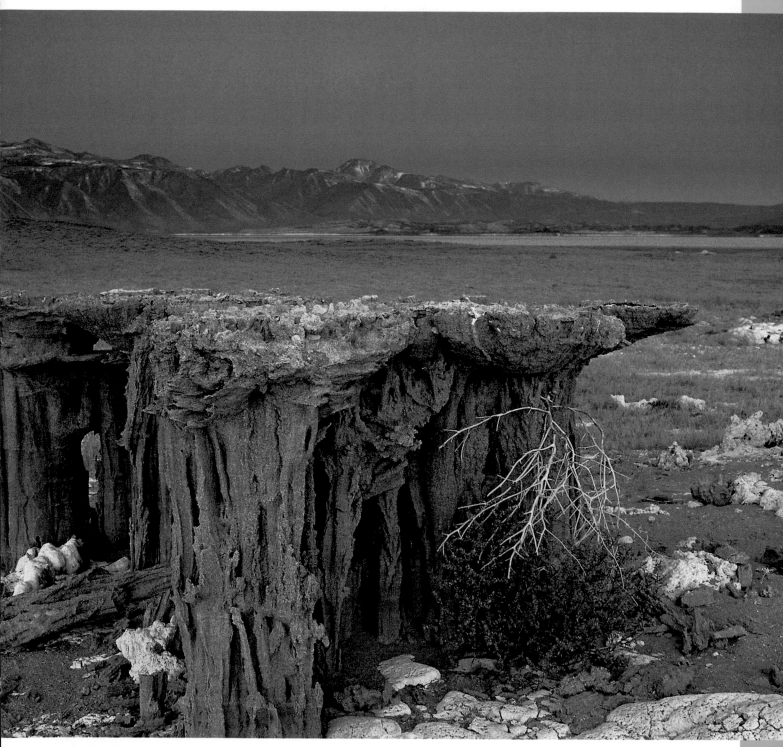

104–105 Alkaline sand columns that formed in the receding waters of Mono Lake stand high and dry on the arid plain of the Mono Basin, which forms the Great Basin's western edge against the High Sierra of eastern California.

Near the end of the last ice age about 20,000 years ago, Mono Lake was many times its present size, fed by a glacier descending from Yosemite's Tioga Pass that calved icebergs into the lake.

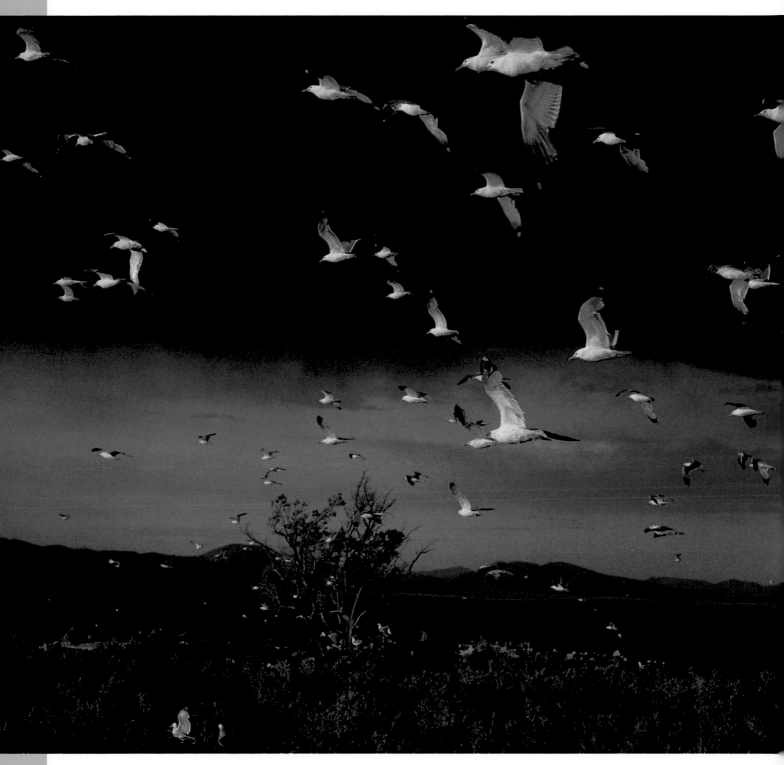

106–107 Gilded by the rays of the setting sun beneath dark clouds, California gulls soar above their largest nesting colony on Mono Lake's Negit Island in eastern California. Since 1940, export of water to Los Angeles has greatly reduced the water level of the lake, causing Negit Island to become connected to the mainland by an isthmus in the 1970s. Predators almost destroyed the colony before dredging and legal action to maintain the lake's level finally saved the island's sanctity.

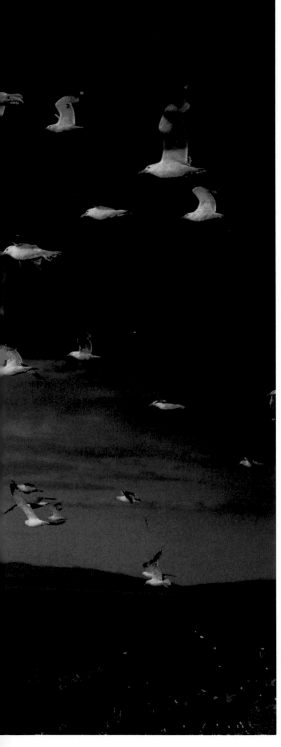

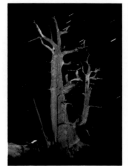

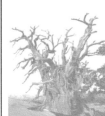

107 An ancient bristlecone pine bares its limbs against a starry sky in California's White Mountains.

that increased alkalinity threatened the entire natural food chain of Mono Lake, beginning with billions of brine shrimp that nourish the lake's plankton, brine flies, gulls, grebes, and shoreline predators. After a long battle, Los Angeles agreed to maintain Rush Creek and Mono Lake itself at viable levels.

While Mono Lake's flora and fauna were threatened by the export of water, its scenic appeal increased. Other-worldly towers of white tufa created by the lake's alkalinity rose ever higher above the receding waters. In a scene that has become one of America's most photographed landscapes, the hushed waters of the lake turn scarlet at dawn from light filtered through desert haze with the strange white towers profiled against the snowy High Sierra in the distance.

East of Mono Lake, an undulating carpet of sagebrush appears to roll toward the Nevada horizon all the way across the basin to Utah, but such is not the case. Seen from space, the topography of the Great Basin looks like a bunch of caterpillars crawling south. Nevada has 236 mountain ranges, with more than fifty rising over 9,000 feet in an alternating basin-and-range pattern similar to that of the ocean floor. Each of the higher ranges has its own special places. Some are accessible by paved roads or jeep roads. Others can be reached only by foot or by ski in the winter. To get to know the Great Basin, it is essential to leave the broad valleys of old explorers and modern highways to see firsthand these alpine islands that seemingly float above a sagebrush sea. Even Las Vegas has one nearby. Mount Charleston, complete with a ski area and extensive forest, rises to nearly 12,000 feet just thirty miles from town.

Nevada was conspicuous among Western states in not having a single national park until 1986, when Great Basin National Park was created around 13,063-foot Wheeler Peak, the highest peak wholly in the state. On the shady side of the peak's 2,000-foot northeast face is a remnant of the largest Pleistocene Great Basin glacier, now the nation's most southerly permanent icefield. About 5,000 years ago, an event called "The Little Ice Age"

pushed a fresh lateral moraine eastward at an altitude of 10,750 feet. Bristlecone pine seedlings took root on the fresh, open ground. One of them survived until 1964, when a geographer enlisted the help of the U.S. Forest Service to cut it down with a chain-saw to count its rings: 4,844 plus a rotten core for a total estimated age of 4,900 years—the Earth's oldest known living thing.

In 1974, before the creation of the park, I found the stump and published photographs for the first time ever in the popular press. Today, neither its location nor its existence are acknowledged in park literature. Each time I visit the park, I make a personal pilgrimage to where it once stood. Nearby, other fine specimens still stand, dated by corings at least a thousand years younger. Each tree has been sculpted over the ages into a unique form by the relentless west wind, yet this common force also makes each tree appear to be caught in the same motion, as if a troupe of dancers were all pirouetting with arms pointed skyward.

More than 400 miles away on the opposite side of the Great Basin is the world's oldest-known-living-thing by default—Methuselah, a 4,600-year-old tree in the White Mountains along the California—Nevada border. I also frequently visit this range by road, by trail, and by ski, once spending sixteen days skiing its entire length through bristlecone forests and over a 14,000-foot summit with bird's-eye views of the parallel High Sierra the entire way.

In between these two 14,000-foot ranges, the Owens Valley is the deepest in America, dropping to 4,000 feet. Thanks to Los Angeles owning most of the water rights along 150 miles of the eastern Sierra, the large land area of the Owens Valley is sparsely populated. Though locals deride Los Angeles for having stolen the area's water, had the city not done so the fertile soil would surely have been irrigated into vast farms punctuated by faceless cities, as along the western slope of the Sierra in the Central Valley, where sprawling Fresno and Bakersfield are more than twenty times larger than the biggest towns in the Owens Valley.

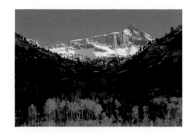

108 top June snows grace the peaks of the Ruby Mountains above Lamoille Canyon in eastern Nevada. The once-remote desert peaks are now the site of exceptional powder skiing by helicopter.

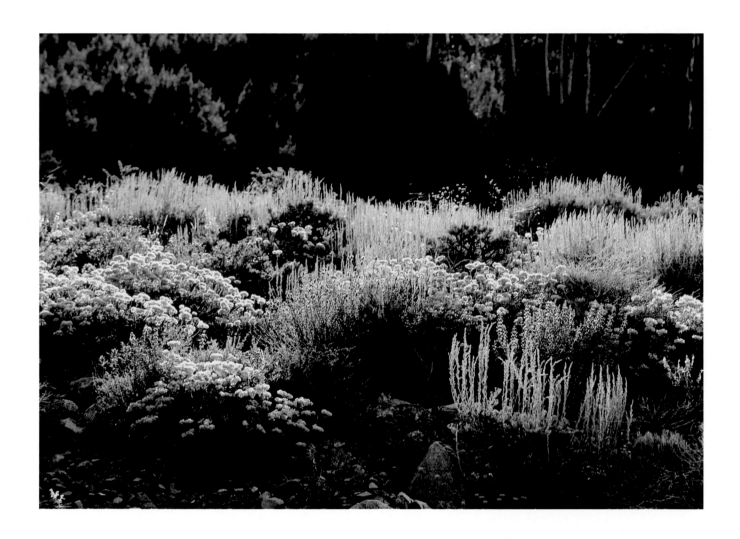

108 bottom East of the Sierra Nevada along the June Lakes Loop above Grant Lake, summer wildflowers tint a field of Great Basin sagebrush in a well-watered side canyon.

109 At the height of fall, a few of the aspens of the Great Basin go beyond the normal shift of green to yellow leaves to rival the richest reds of the forests of New England.

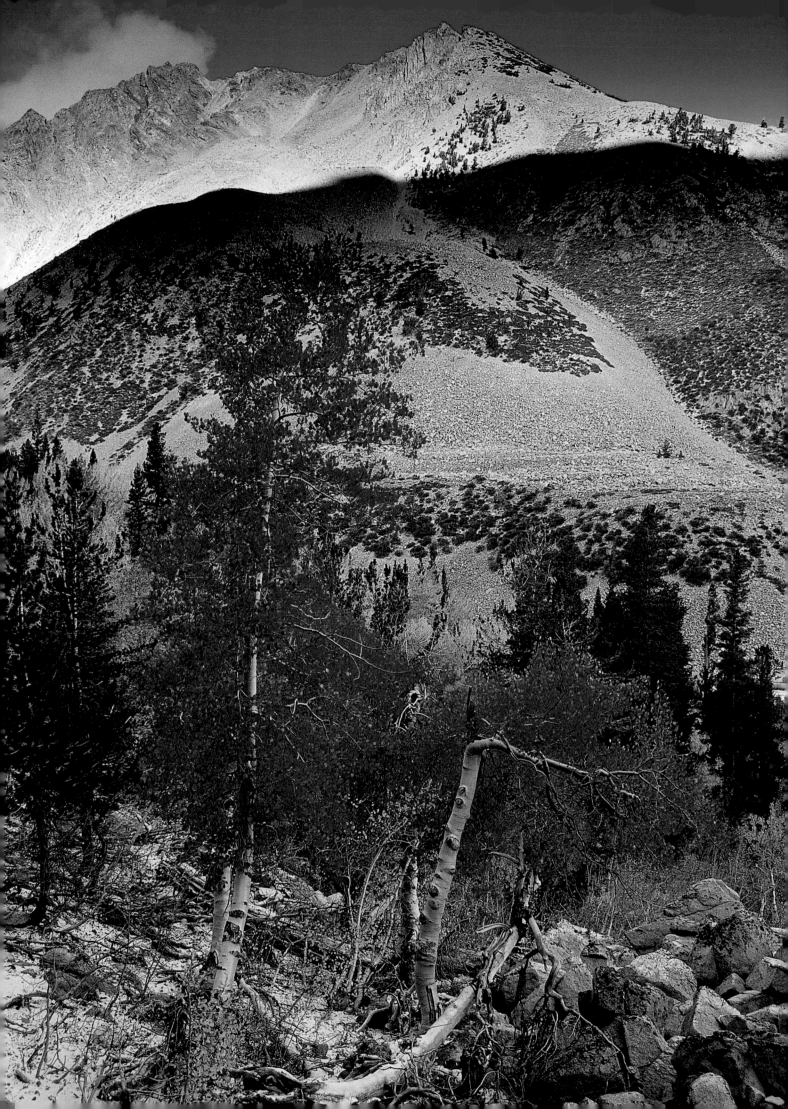

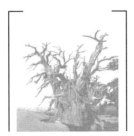

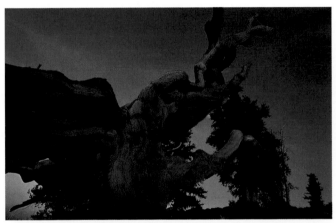

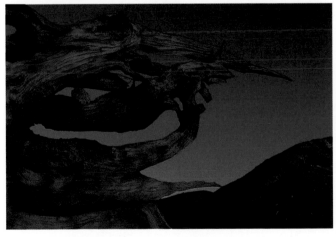

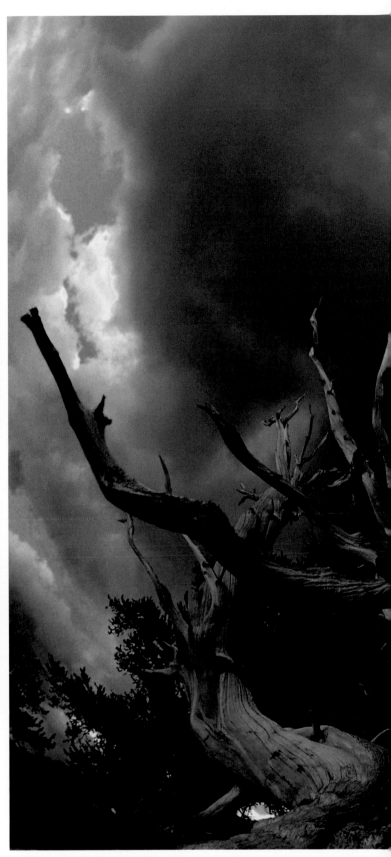

110 Eroded by eons of blowing wind and snow, the twisted shapes of bristlecone pines in California's White Mountains suggest their great age. World's oldest living thing — a 4,600-year-old bristlecone named Methuselah — continues to survive here in an undisclosed location in Schulman Grove.

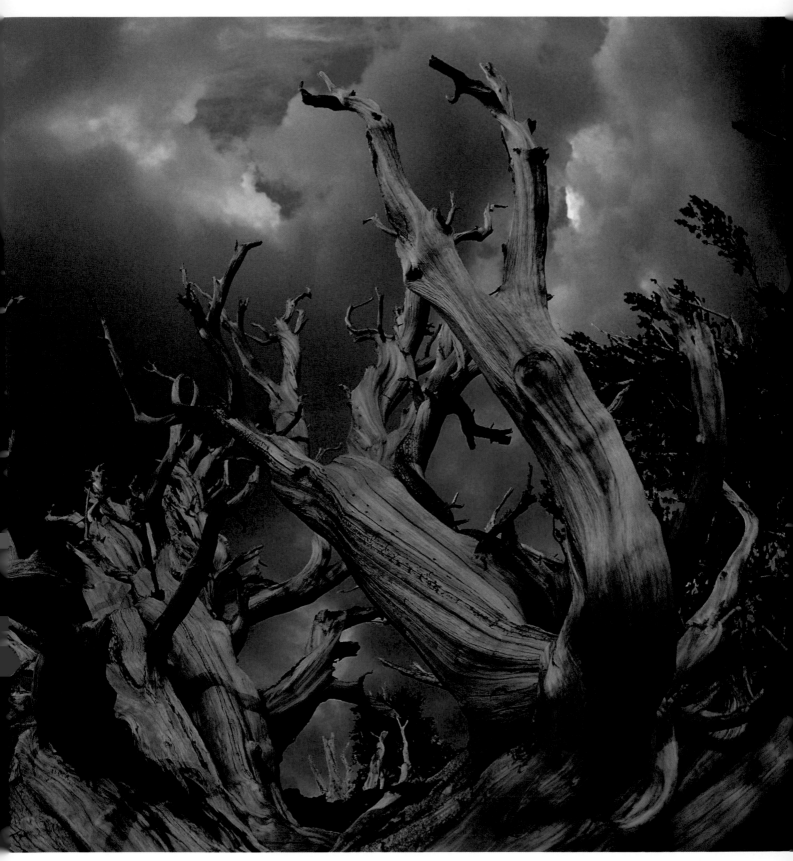

110–111 The barren limbs of a bristlecone pine glow in the setting sun at 11,000 feet beneath a stormy sky over the White Mountains. Though this tree appears dead, it is very much alive, shunting its life force to a few green limbs.

112–113 In midwinter on the crest of the White Mountains at over 11,000 feet, Patriarch Grove is framed through the dead limbs of a living tree. Ring widths of bristlecones record the pattern of ancient climates, while ring counts of these oldest continuously living organisms also led to a major recalibration of radiocarbon dating.

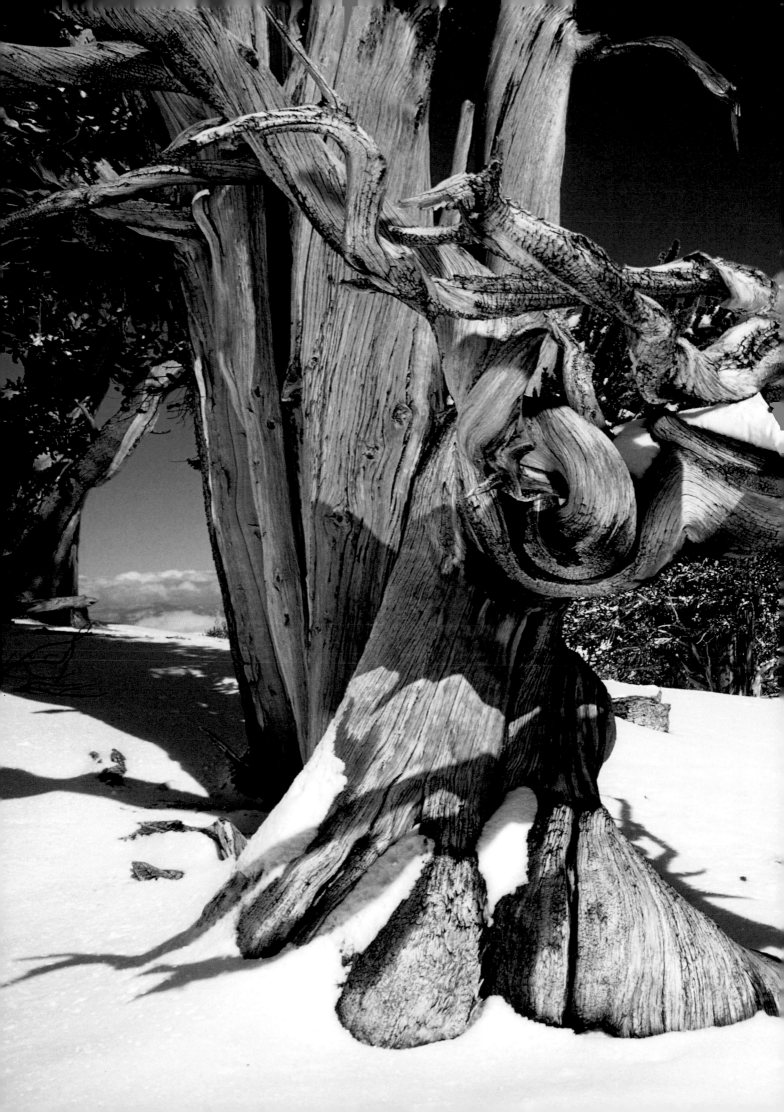

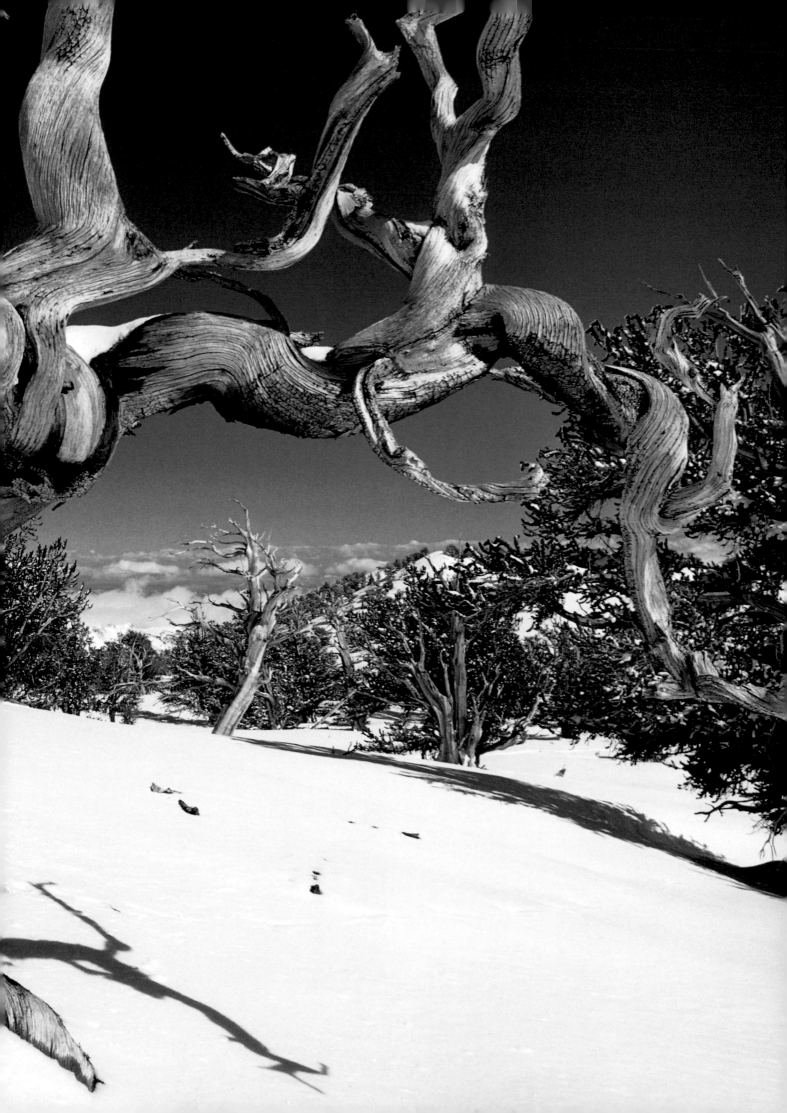

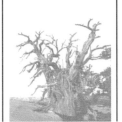

114 *A rainbow arcs over the sage flats of the Owens Valley, America's deepest, on the western edge of the Great Basin.*

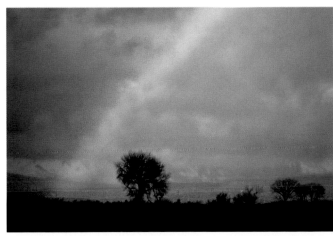

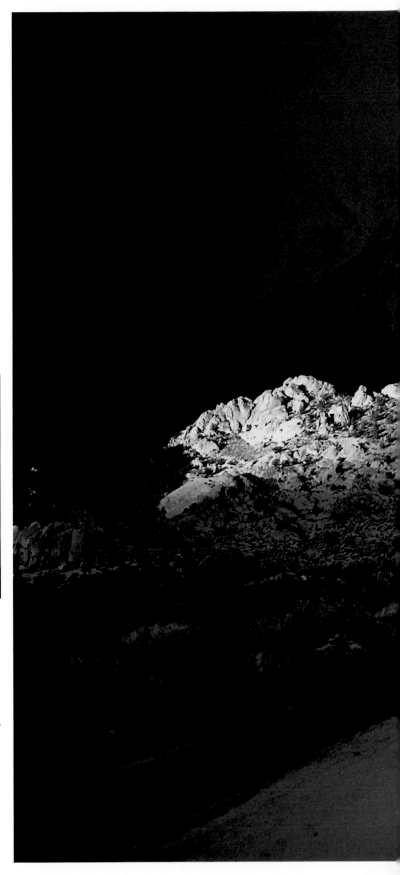

114–115 On a stormy Great Basin morning high over Buttermilk Road near Bishop, California, peaks of the snowy High Sierra remain in blue shadow while beams of warm light touch the desert floor.

116–117 The Sierra Wave, a stationary cloud front formed by high winds and moisture from the Pacific, sits far above the 14,000-foot crest of the White Mountains, as seen over the Owens Valley at sunset.

118–119 A bristlecone forest thrives high on Mount Charleston above Las Vegas.

119 Bristlecones are found near the tops of over fifty ranges of the Great Basin, including Nevada's Ruby Mountains.

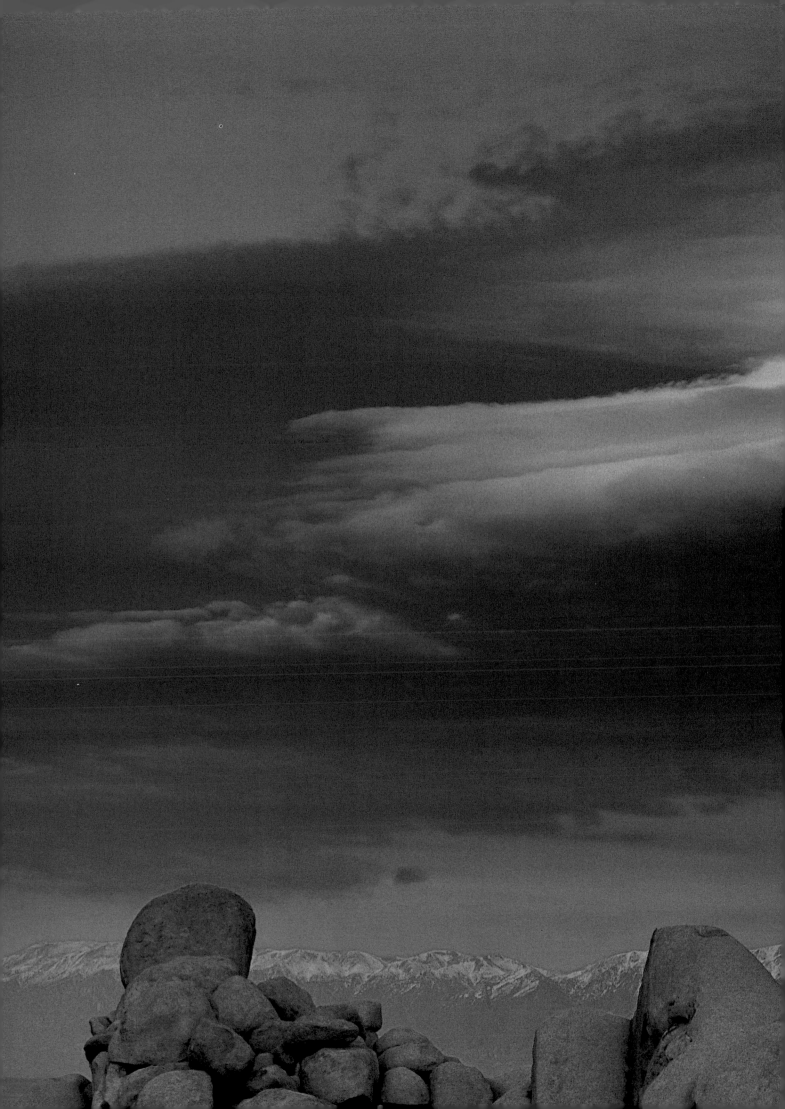

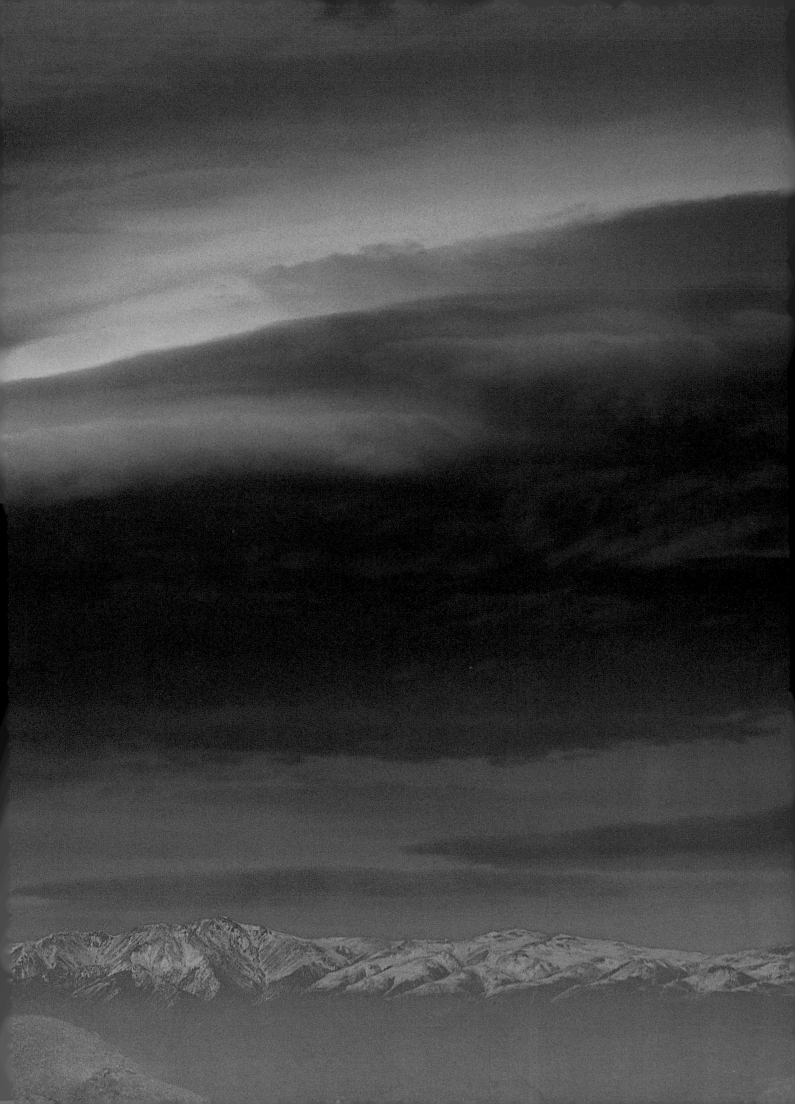

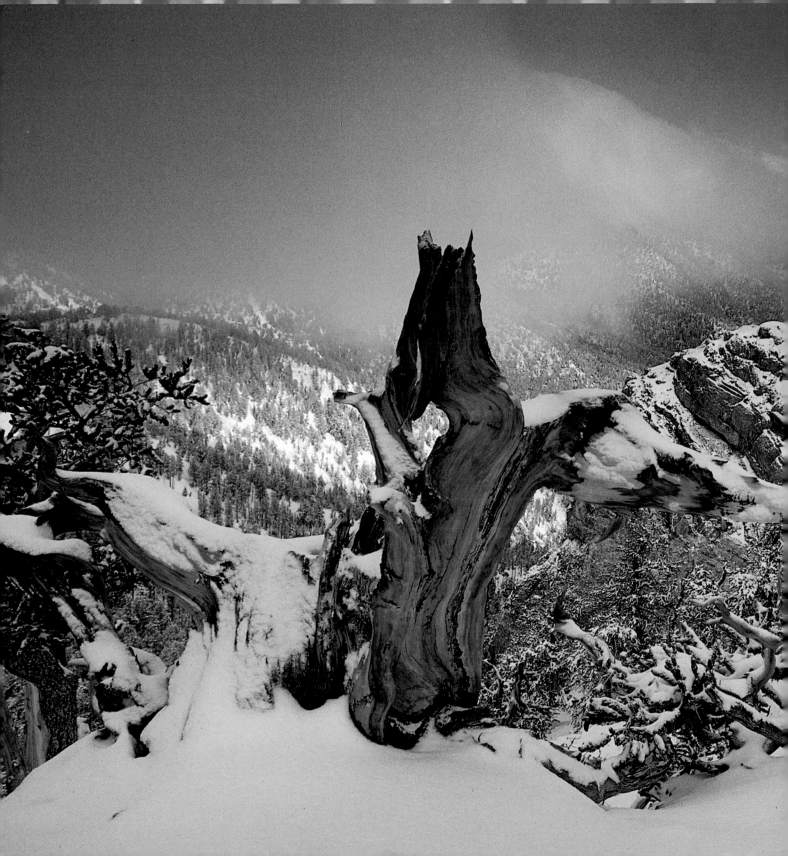

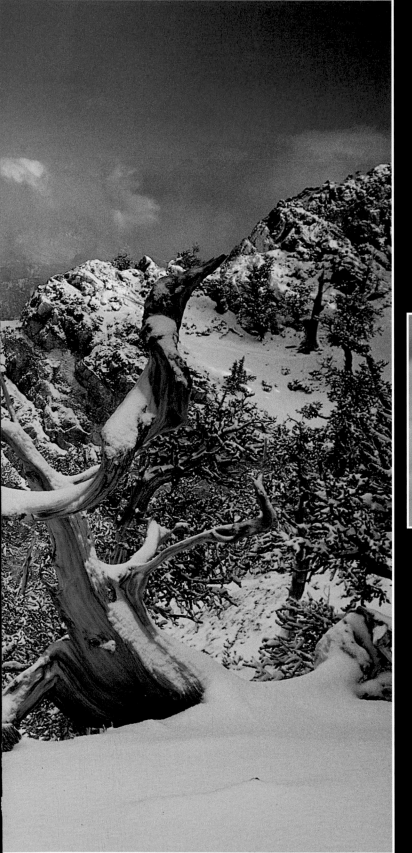
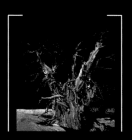
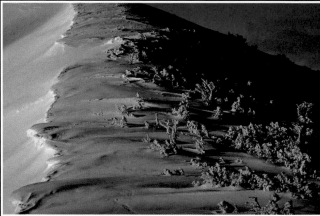

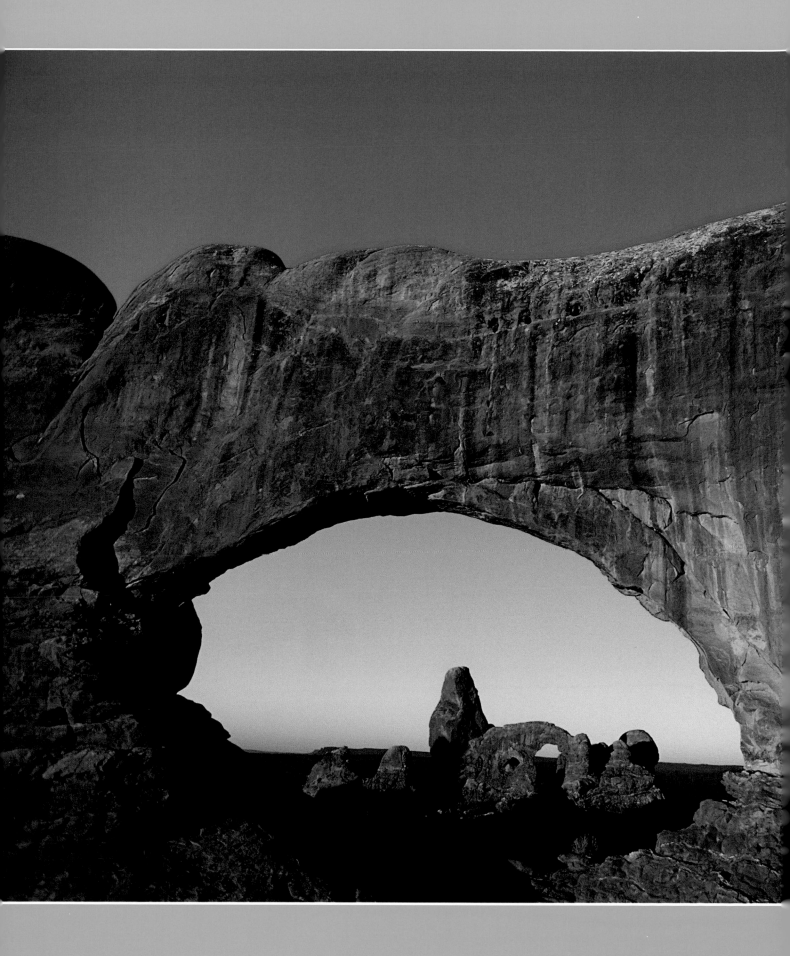

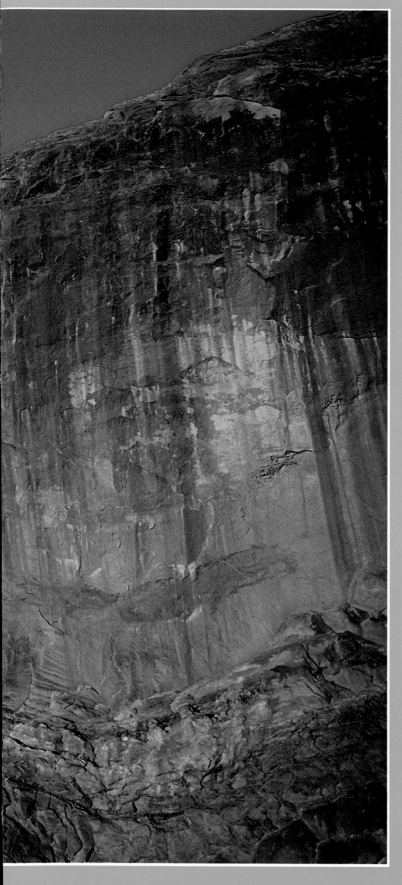

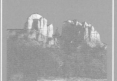

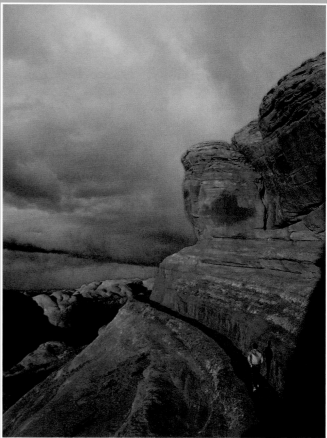

The Southwest

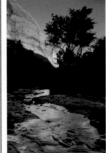

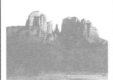

122 A tributary of Utah's Escalante River reflects sunset on the red sandstone cliffs of Coyote Gulch on the Kaiparowits Plateau where the recently created Grand Staircase-Escalante National Monument borders Glen Canyon National Recreation Area.

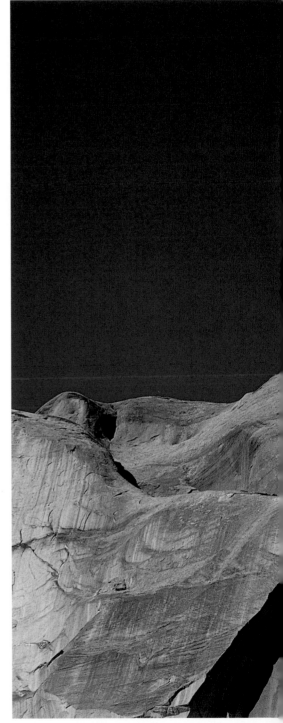

Today, the American Southwest is internationally recognized as one of the greatest concentrations of outstanding natural and cultural features on the planet, but this awareness is recent. Until most of today's myriad national parks, monuments, recreation areas, and Native American tribal parks became officially protected in recent decades, surprisingly few international visitors came to see these unique open spaces of "Slickrock Country."

The Southwest's scenic areas are clustered in two distinct regions. The first is around Zion and Grand Canyon, two older national parks created in an era when only the grandest superlatives were considered worthy of park status. The deepest of all Grand Canyon, normally seen from its south rim, was an obvious choice for a park, as was Zion Canyon, with its drive-through "Yosemite-in-Technicolor" giant rock walls. (In 1967, my party spent months seeking special permission to make the first-ever Zion wall climb up the face of the Great White Throne).

This first region in western Utah and Arizona is often called "The Grand Circle," where visitors can drive a rough circuit of Grand Canyon, Glen Canyon, Pipe Spring, Zion, Bryce, Cedar Breaks, and Lake Mead. The second region is called Four Corners, where eastern Utah and Arizona meet western Colorado and New Mexico. The only older national park in this region is Mesa Verde, created to preserve ancient cliff dwellings. Beyond Four Corners near Sante Fe, New Mexico, Bandelier National Monument also preserves cliff dwellings and extensive rock art.

The gateway to Four Corners from the north is Arches National Park, near Moab, Utah. This remarkable assortment of natural arches of all shapes and sizes was so little visited in the sixties that a resident park ranger, Edward Abbey, often found himself to be the only person in what was then a national monument. He recounted those days, as well as solo explorations of nearby labyrinth canyons now within Canyonlands National Park, in *Desert Solitaire*, a book that awakened the

American counterculture to both the wild appeal of the Colorado Plateau, as well as threats to its sanctity from floods of water by dams and floods of people by commercial tourism.

Moab, once described by Abbey as a sleepy little cow town, has been transformed into a major mountain biking, rock climbing, and river rafting center. While every sort of guided tour is available, it is still possible to drive out of town, walk a few minutes across the redrock desert, and feel totally alone in a landscape that appears to be primeval.

Four Corners sits on the mile-high, 15,000-square-mile Colorado Plateau, which has a major outlet to the sea, unlike the adjoining Great Basin. As soft sedimentary rocks began to uplift about 10 million years ago, the Colorado River cut like a hot knife through butter because its course draining the Rocky Mountains to the sea already existed. Most of Grand Canyon's depth was cut during the last 3 million years, but the United States Bureau of Reclamation attempted to stop the process virtually overnight by building a series of dams planned to divert 90 percent of the Colorado River waters that now flow through the Grand Canyon. Defeating this process during the fifties and sixties gave birth to the American environmental movement as a national poltical force.

A major turning point in public support came in 1966 when the executive director of the Sierra Club, David Brower, took out a full-page ad in the *New York Times* about a dam slated to flood into the Grand Canyon with the bold heading: "Should we also flood the Sistine Chapel so tourists can get closer to the ceiling?"

I doubt that I would have become an environmental writer and photographer, were it not for my involvement with a proposed dam within Dinosaur National Monument on a tributary of the Colorado River more than a decade earlier at the tender age of thirteen. A term paper I wrote began my lifelong fascination with the relationship between preserved areas and the individuals who have gone out of their way to save them.

During that summer of 1953, I'd walked the

banks of the wild river at Echo Park with my father as he told me that it might be no more. When I decided to write about it, he suggested that I interview our neighbor, David Brower, who had testified before Congress against the dam, making the Sierra Club's first environmental stand outside California, where the small mountain outing club my family belonged to was based. Brower later became known as the "archdruid of conservation,"

twice nominated for the Nobel Peace Prize.

After Echo Park Dam was defeated, a larger dam was built on the Colorado River at Glen Canyon. Some of the nation's finest red sandstone wilderness outside national parklands was inundated with no major opposition from the Sierra Club. Brower, now in his late eighties, wrote me in 1999 to say "the loss of beautiful Glen Canyon due in part to my own inaction is one of my biggest

regrets." He urged me to support restoration of Glen Canyon by decommissioning the dam and draining massive Lake Powell, which could become a political reality in the near future.

Another battle concerns the new Grand Staircase–Escalante National Monument, created by presidential mandate in 1996 in the canyonlands of southern Utah after state and local opposition defeated a bill to make it a national park. Hostile

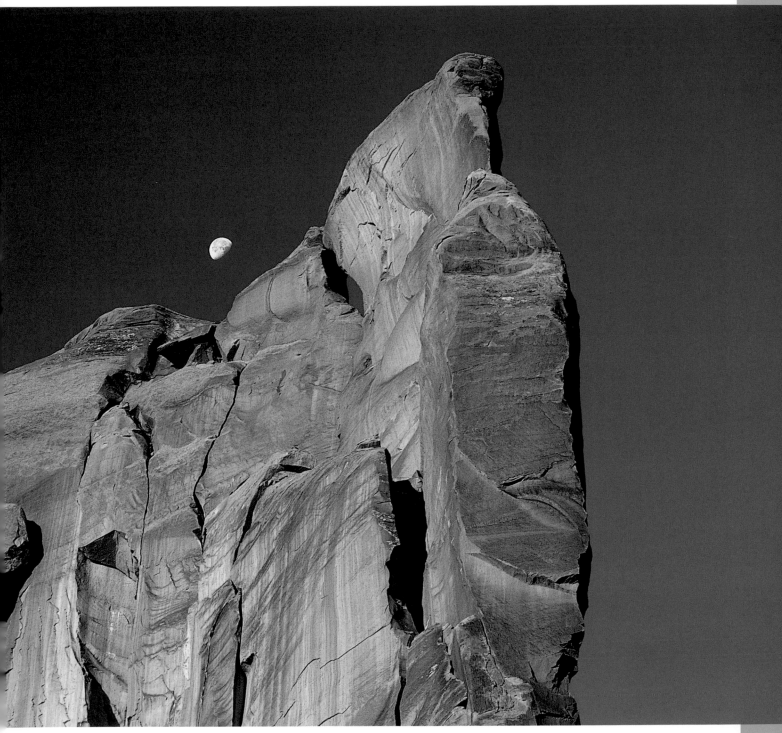

122–123 The moon peeks over the top of a wild sandstone spire near Gouldings Trading Post on the edge of Monument Valley, a Navajo Indian tribal park on the Utah-Arizona border.

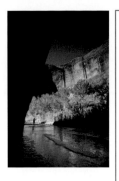

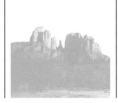

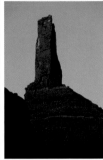

local governments have gone so far as to bulldoze foot trails into broad roads both within the monument and Capitol Reef National Park, citing an obscure access law in a reactionary move against so much land being taken out of their control for future development.

Luckily, this is not the case in most of the Southwest, where after more than a century of exploitation, the grand sandstone monoliths have taken on an enduring sacred significance, much like the castles and cathedrals of Europe. Few of today's visitors who come to see the landforms realize that these arid lands were once populated by the major Southwestern component of a biomass of wild mammals exceeding that of any other area on earth, including the Serengeti Plain of Africa. In the Southwest after 1850, over a million buffalo a year were wantonly shot until the last one fell in Texas in 1879. Large-antlered Merriam's elk that ranged throughout the Southwest became totally extinct. As late as 1924, government mismanagement of predators to protect cattle and

sheep precipitated the annihilation of the Kaibab Game Reserve on the north rim of the Grand Canyon. After 6,000 coyotes, wolves, bears, and cougars were destroyed, deer herds expanded into the hundreds of thousands, decimated the natural vegetation cover, and promptly starved to death.

When settlers from the East first came to the Southwest, the most arid lands were considered intrinsically worthless. Towns and farms lined rivers on the flatlands, while many of the wildest and most unique landforms were given to the Indians as reservations. One example is Monument Valley, now an icon of the American West depicted in bank and cigarette advertisements, travel brochures, and almost every picture book of America. As these wildest, steepest, and most beautiful sandstone towers of the Southwest drew ever more tourists, the Navajos created their own tribal park, charging admission to travelers, who often complain to no avail that their annual pass to all national parks should gain them entrance.

Antelope Canyon and other slot canyons near Page, Arizona, are also controlled by Native Americans. The sites, which can only be visited with a native guide, are as impressive in their arm's-width narrowness as the Grand Canyon is for its enormity. Within the Grand Canyon but outside the national park, the Havasupai Indians now charge substantial fees to visit the most beautiful side valley of all, where Havasu Fall pours over red sandstone into a turquoise pool bounded by white travertine and lush greenery in a scene straight out of Tahiti.

Mexamericans in the Southwest also have a right to feel disenfranchised. In the early nineteenth century white settlers from the East arrived to exploit resources and claim lands for the United States, culminating in Mexico ceding possession during the 1840s, despite a Spanish-speaking majority. Though these Latin peoples became United States citizens, their cultural ties remain with the south and their environment—arid, rugged, and sparsely vegetated—merges imperceptively with that of northern Mexico.

Meanwhile, many former pueblos of the Southwest burgeoned into veritable moonbases, dependent on life support from elsewhere. Sprawling megacities such as Tucson, Phoenix, Dallas, and Albuquerque could not have reached their current size without the three A's of modern Southwest living: air conditioning, automobiles, and aqueducts. Their growth anticipated the influx of tourists as large airports with flights from both coasts began to bring visitors from all over the world.

The same recent comfort and economic success has also drawn many immigrants from south of the border. Communities where Spanish is spoken more often than English are increasing, giving the ancient legend of Aztlan, the first land of the Aztecs, a modern interpretation. The geography of the American Southwest matches some descriptions of Aztlan in a legend that says the sons of the Aztec will once again occupy their ancestral homelands and cause a new civilization to flourish. Some Latin Americans have begun to refer to the five major states of the Southwest as Aztlan.

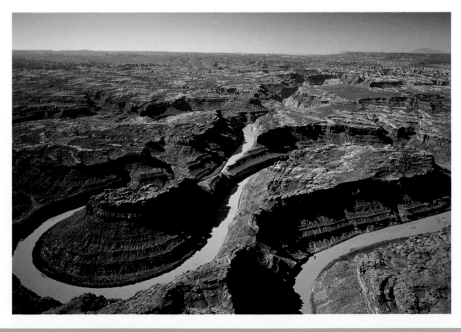

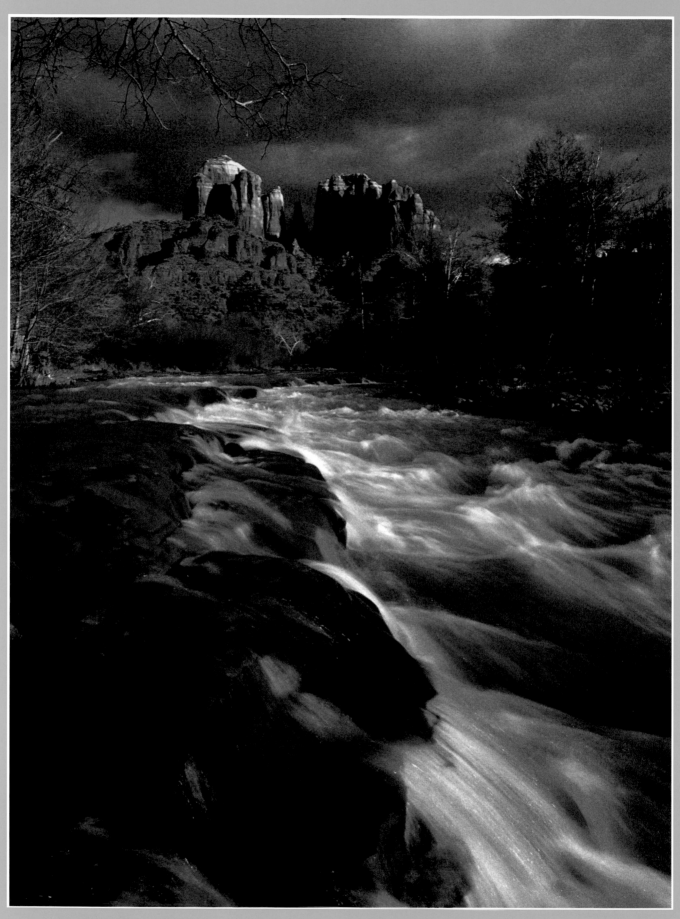

124 bottom Oxbow bends of the great Colorado River meander through Utah's Canyonlands National Park.

125 Cathedral Rocks catch evening light high over Oak Creek Canyon near Sedona, Arizona.

126–127 The countless spires of Utah's Bryce Canyon are singled out in the crystalline air of a winter dawn.

The natural amphitheater suddenly erupts from the forested Paunsaugunt Plateau at over 8,000 feet.

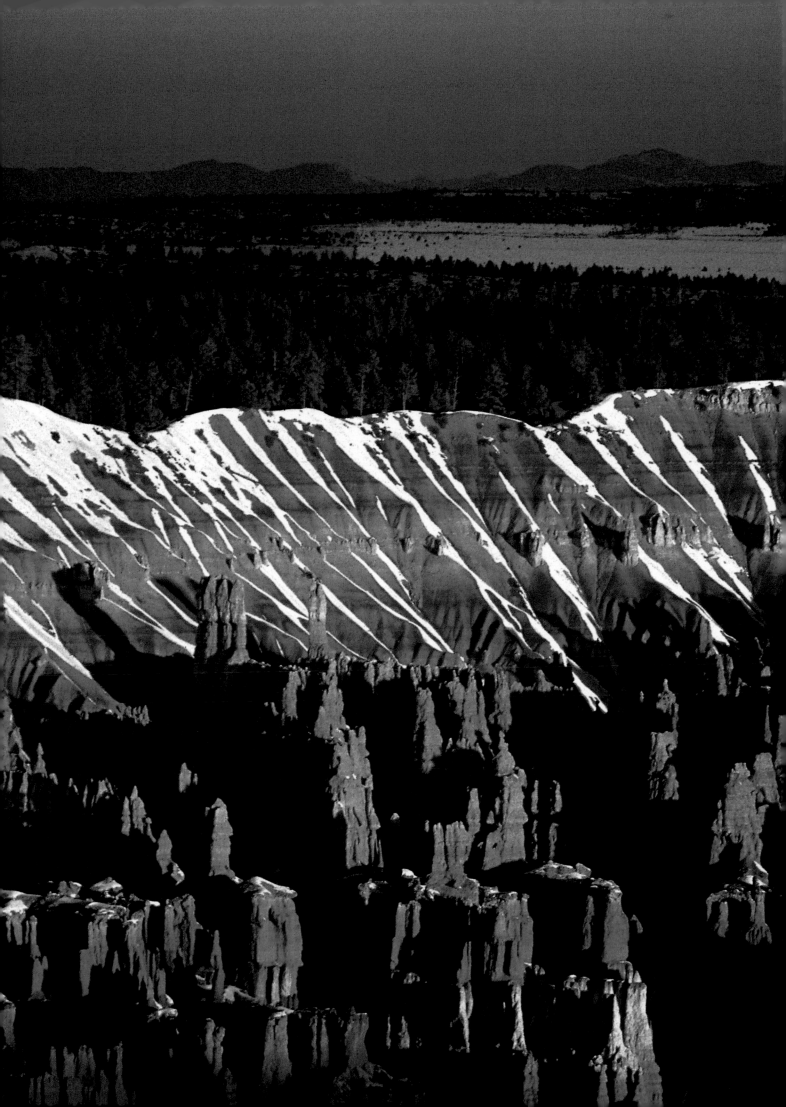

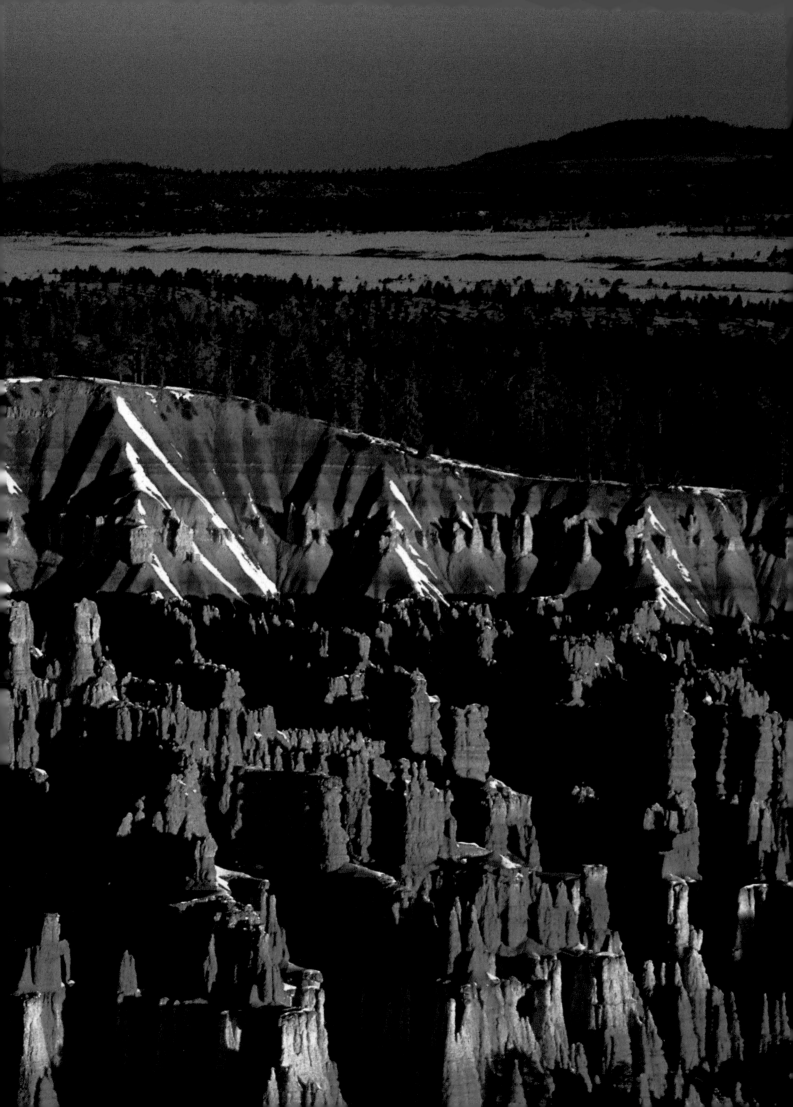

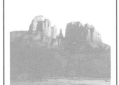

128 A crescent moon stands out in predawn twilight over the buttes of Monument Valley on the Utah-Arizona border.

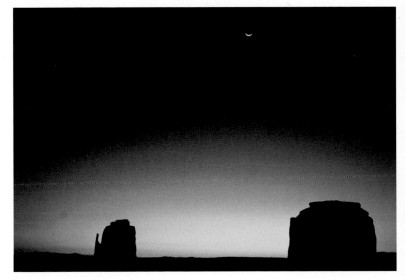

128–129 The Mitten Buttes of Monument Valley appear to stand alone in evening twilight after a dusting of winter snow on the Colorado Plateau. Seen in countless movies, picture books, and advertisements, they are among the most familiar icons of the Southwest. A 14-mile dirt road loops through the 29,817-acre Navajo tribal park.

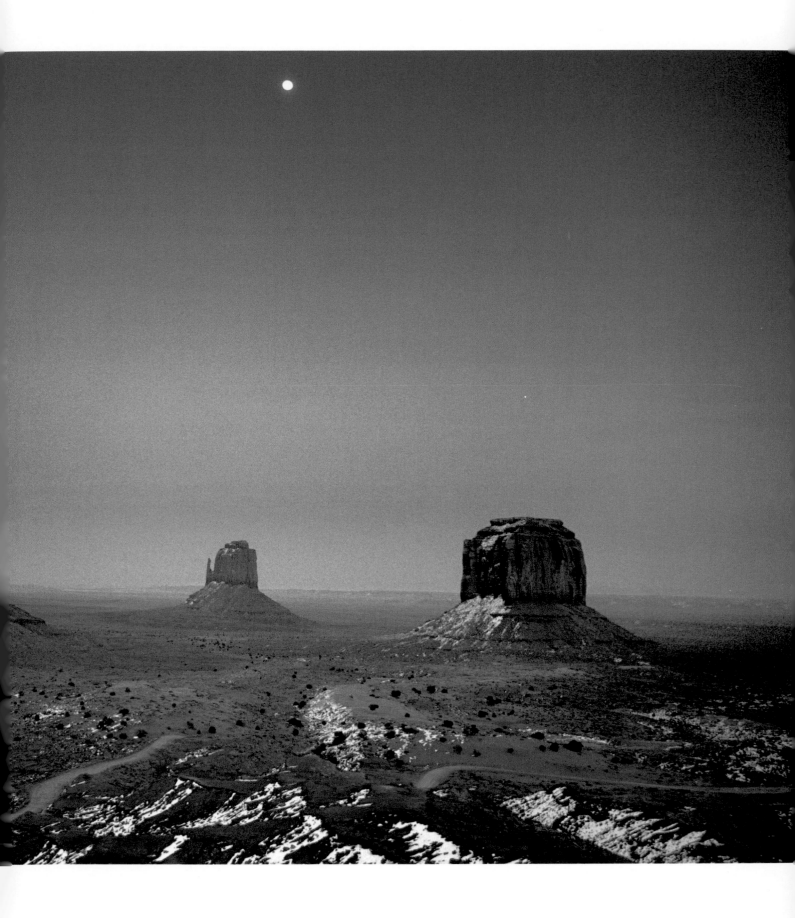

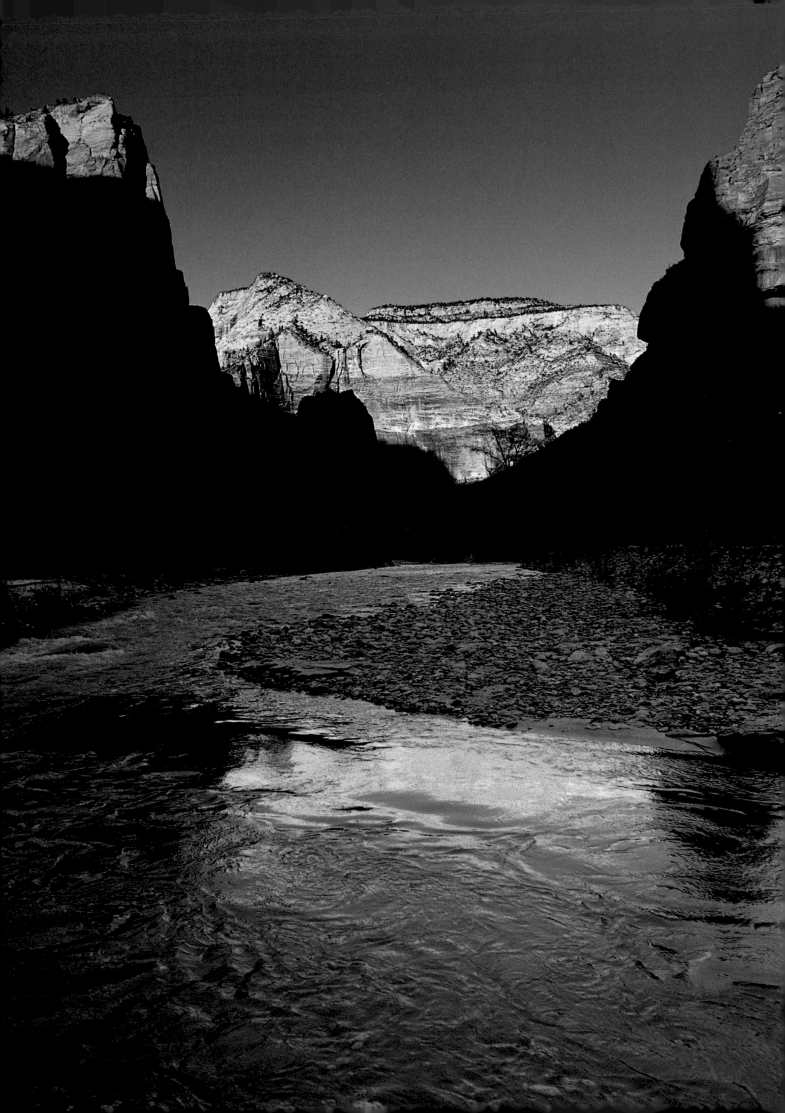

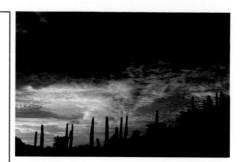

131 top In the heart of the Sonoran Desert of Arizona, tall sagauaro cacti stand profiled against a classic Southwest sunset in Tucson Mountain Park.

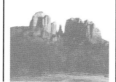

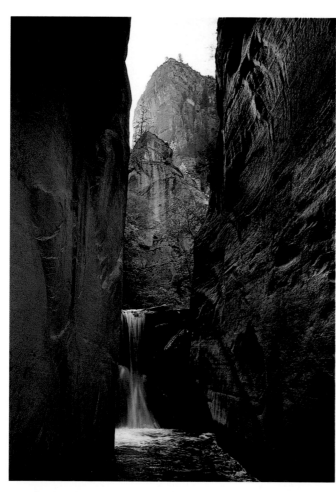

131 bottom left The Narrows of the Virgin River force the waters of the stream that carved massive Zion Canyon into a narrow defile 4,000 feet below the rim of the valley.

131 bottom right Spring wildflowers carpet the floor of the fertile Verde Valley near Sedona, Arizona. Well-preserved Anasazi Indian ruins surround the valley.

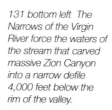

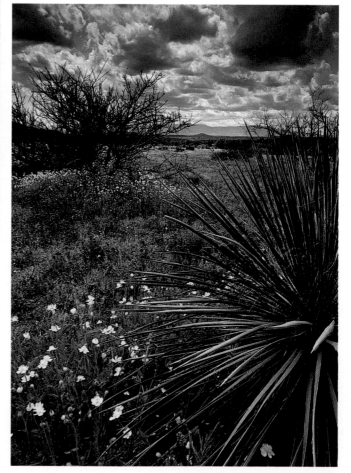

130 The Virgin River flows through Zion Canyon beneath Angels Landing on a fall evening in Utah's Zion National Park. Cliffs of red and white sandstone rising vertically up to 4000 feet above the river have earned Zion the nickname of "Yosemite Valley in Technicolor."

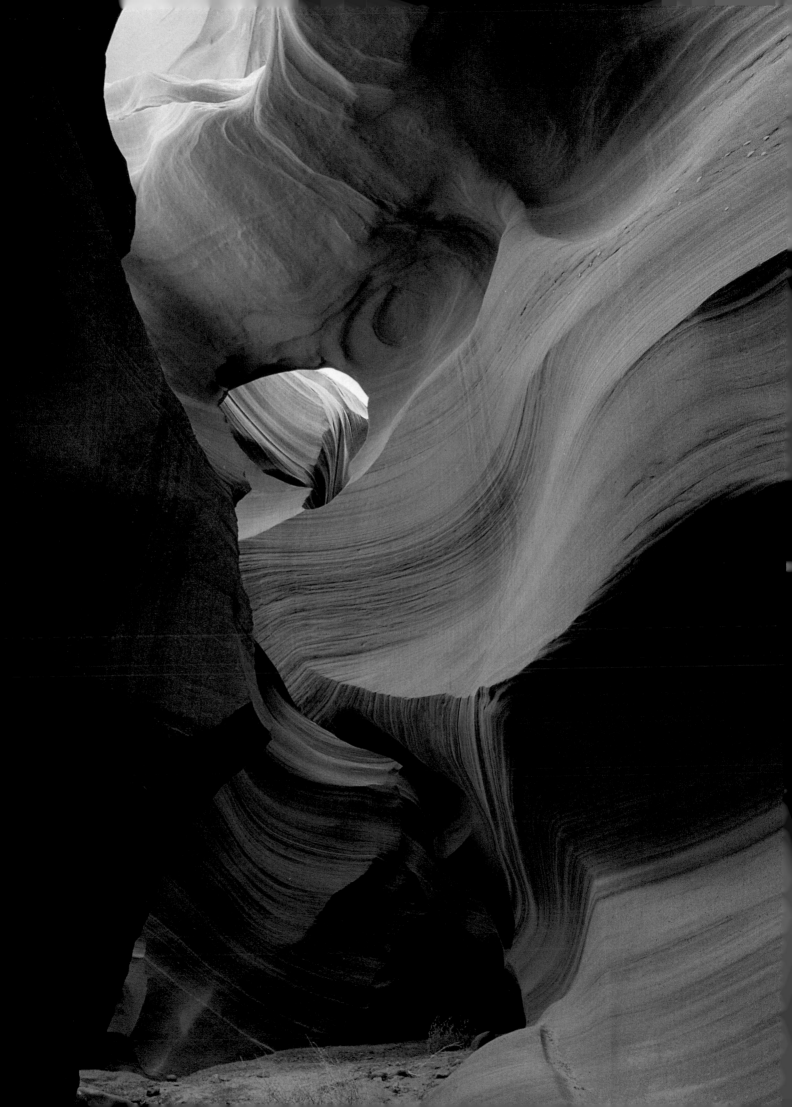

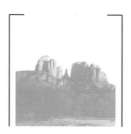

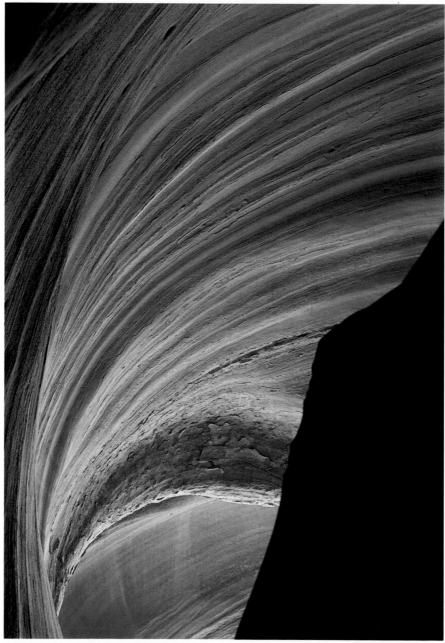

132 Lower Antelope
Canyon near Page,
Arizona is one of the the
Southwest's most
amazing slot canyons,
dropping out of nowhere
from a dry wash.

133 The fluted walls
of nearby Upper
Antelope Canyon catch
sunlight that turns ever
more red as it bounces
back and forth between
the cliffs.

134–135 Hidden
clouds to the east
cast a sunset afterglow
into the Grand
Canyon below
Lookout Studio
on the South Rim.

135 Winter snows
blanket Humphreys Peak,
12,655 feet, highest of
the San Francisco Peaks
near Flagstaff, Arizona,
and sacred to both the
Hopi and Navajo.

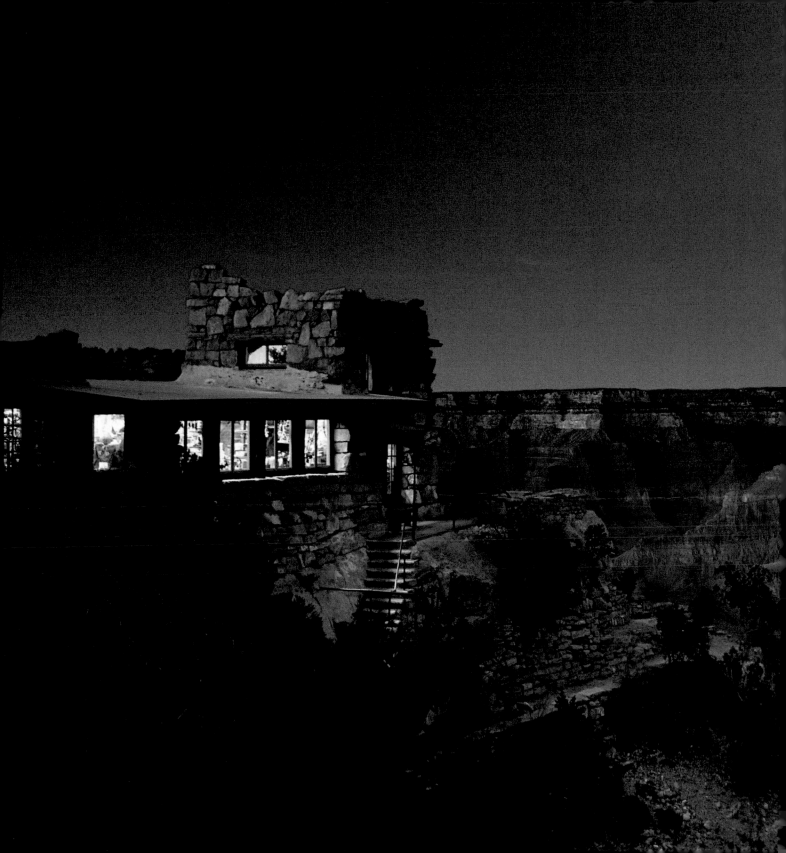

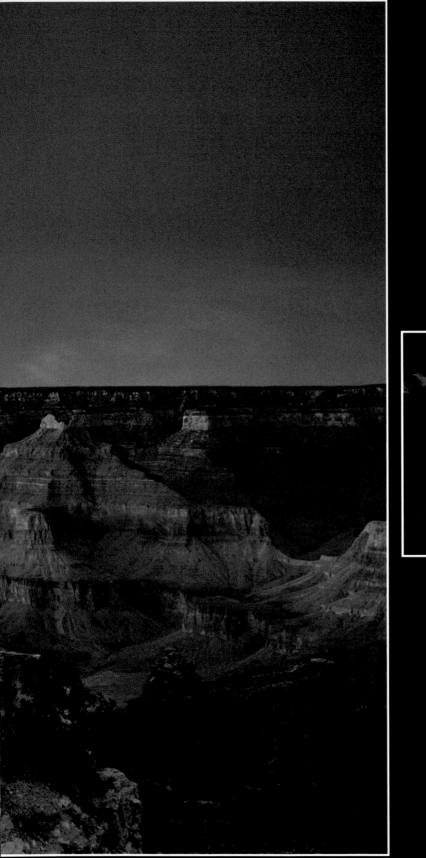
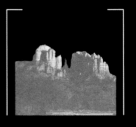
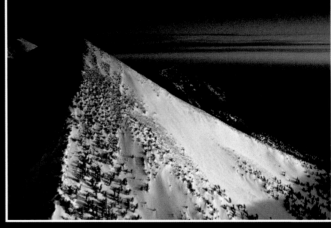

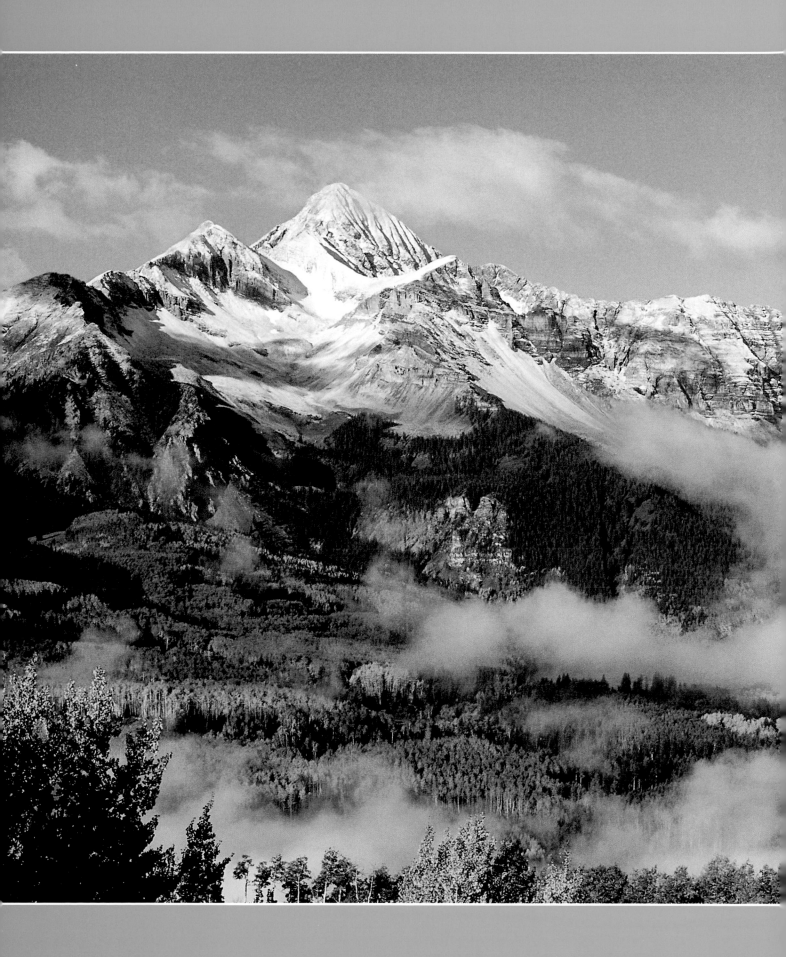

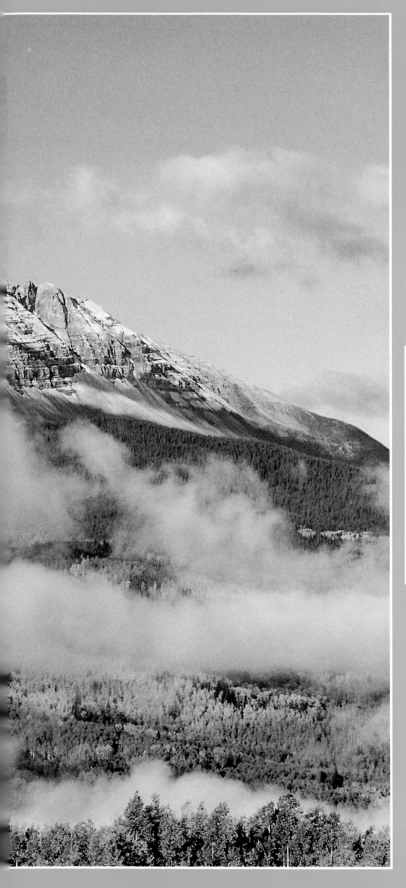

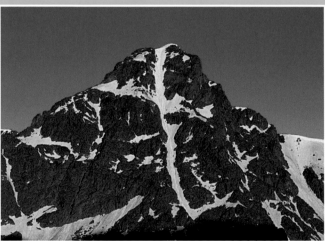

The American Rockies

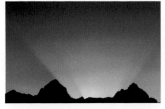

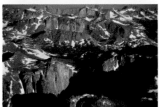

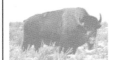

I f I were asked to sum up the Rocky Mountains in a sentence or two, I'd be at a loss for words. Unlike the singular Sierra Nevada Range of my home state, over a hundred separate mountain ranges make up the 3000-mile swath of the Rockies that extends from Mexico to the Canadian Arctic. The succession of ranges, up to 350 miles wide, defies all attempts to generalize.

The American Rockies are so much more than the Wyoming geysers, waterfalls, lakes, and bison herds that led to Yellowstone becoming the world's first national park. They are also more than the icy Montana mountains lapped by densely flowered meadows with mountain goats and grizzlies of Glacier National Park. Yet for others they are no more than the urban sprawl of Denver, Boulder, and Fort Collins connecting into yet another American megacity flanked by Colorado's Front Range.

Other examples in the same states are equally disparate. Compare Wyoming's Grand Tetons seen through the window of a plush Jackson Hole resort to "The Bob," as the heavily forested, utterly remote Bob Marshall Wilderness of Montana is known to the rugged few who visit it on foot. Compare the empty feeling of the Great Sand Dunes of the southern San Juan Range in Colorado with that of the usually empty second homes lining the ski slopes of Vail in the same state.

Perhaps because they are so much like the Sierra Nevada, The Wind Rivers are my favorite range in the American Rockies. Warm, relatively dry summers make "The Winds" a paradise for backpackers, fishermen, and climbers. The range has hundreds peaks over 12,000 feet with sheer rock walls, glaciers, and snows that last well into summer. Melt waters cascade into alpine basins filled with meadows, open pine forest, and countless lakes before joining into larger rivers that flow toward the Atlantic or the Pacific, depending on whether their source was east or west of the Continental Divide, which follows the crest of the range.

The Winds have the tallest peak in Wyoming, Gannett Peak, which rises slightly higher than the Grand Teton, a hundred miles to the west. In 1842 John C. Fremont claimed to have climbed the highest peak in the Rockies, but climbed either what is now called 13,745-foot Fremont Peak, 59 feet shy of Gannett Peak, or 13,502-foot Mount Woodrow Wilson, just a mile from Gannett.

Many modern climbers come to the Winds to attempt some of the finest spires and wall climbs in North America. The most popular area is the Cirque of the Towers, usually accessed from a southern trailhead called Big Sandy. The Cirque can also be reached by a 20-mile hike from the north on the Lander side of the range. In 1990 I ran 19 miles over a high pass from Big Sandy to join three of America's top rock climbers beneath seldom-visited Mount Hooker, which has the longest continuously vertical cliff in the Rockies, a 2000-foot north wall that had never been free-climbed. Awaiting me there were Todd Skinner, Paul Piana, and Tim Toula, who had hiked in from the Lander side with a horse packer with enough food and gear for us to complete the first free-climb of the face (using ropes and anchors for safety only, not for upward progress). We spent our final three days living on the side of the cliff, only to emerge onto a large summit plateau of meadows and wildflowers, suspended above the rest of the world.

Most of Colorado's 54 summits above 14,000 feet are extremely conducive to day hikes or mountain runs. High trailheads exceeding 11,000 feet translate into a few hours—or less—of uphill exertion for a reasonably fit person. After teaching all-day photo workshops at Vail every summer, I used to drive an hour or so and take my pick of well-maintained trails to reach the top of a new fourteener before sunset. One evening I summitted a cluster of four, but the most memorable was having the fell fields of alpine flowers that lead to the top of 14,431-foot Mount Elbert—the highest peak in all the Rockies—all to myself.

During years of photographing every summer in the backcountry of the Gore and Sawatch Ranges near Vail, the best wildflower display I saw was on lower Meadow Mountain, less than a mile off Interstate 70. Around Aspen area, the vista of the Maroon Bells from Maroon Lake is especially compelling when blue columbine, the Colorado state flower, are in bloom. Near Telluride, Yankee Boy Basin has one of the greatest summer profusions of wildflowers in wet years.

Though roads go all the way to the top of 14,264-foot Mount Evans and 14,109-foot Pikes Peak, the peaks hold great endurance challenges. Bicycling the paved Mount Evans road is a fabulous way to reach the top and see herds of mountain goats and bighorn sheep. I've also run the course of the Pikes Peak Marathon up the Barr Trail that begins at 6,700 feet at Manitou Springs.

Where Pikes Peak merges with the Great Plains on the outskirts of Colorado Springs, the red sandstone cliffs of the Garden of the Gods encircle a level park that stays green throughout the spring and summer. Rocky Mountain National Park near Estes Park, Colorado, also has road access high into the Rockies. Because Colorado is so blessed with steep rock formations close to towns, it has attracted an unusual number of top climbers, and even famous high-wire performers, over the last century. However, mountain sport was not the goal of the first people of European descent to visit the Rockies. Gold, furs, and well-watered farmland were high on their priorities. When Lewis and Clark crossed the Rockies through Montana and Wyoming in 1804, they were surveying resources for exploitation, rather than public enjoyment.

How America's first national park came into being has long been a national legend, but a recently published history, *Searching for Yellowstone*, by Paul Schullery, puts the myth into political perspective. As the legend goes,

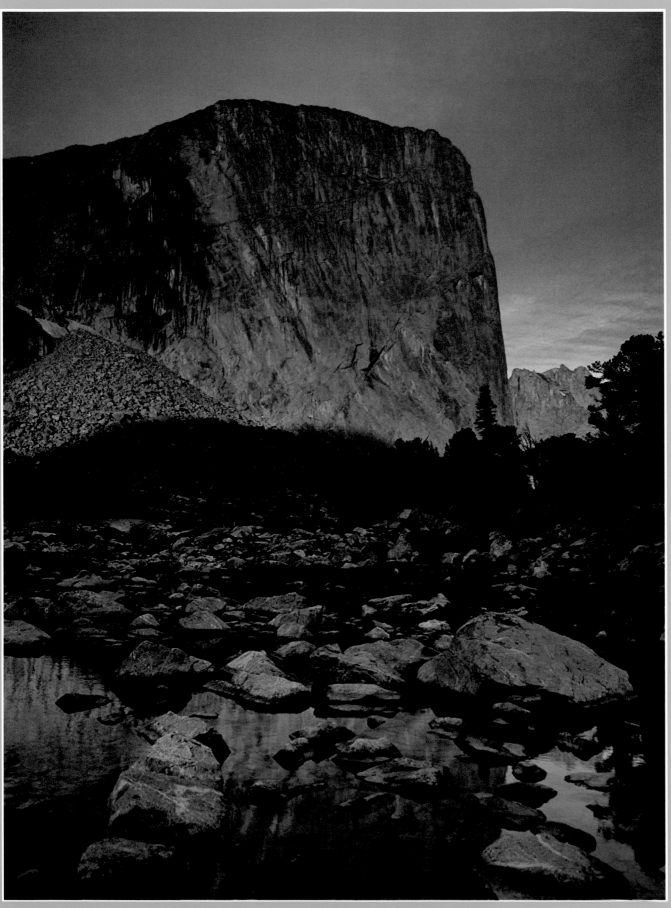

139 Alpenglow at dawn paints gray gneiss crimson on 12,504-foot Mount Hooker in a remote part of Wyoming's Wind River Range. The 2000-foot north face is the highest continuously vertical cliff in the Rockies. While rivaling the face of Yosemite's Half Dome in height, this face is in a far wilder, higher, colder, and remote area, a long 19 miles by trail from dirt roads on either side of the massive range.

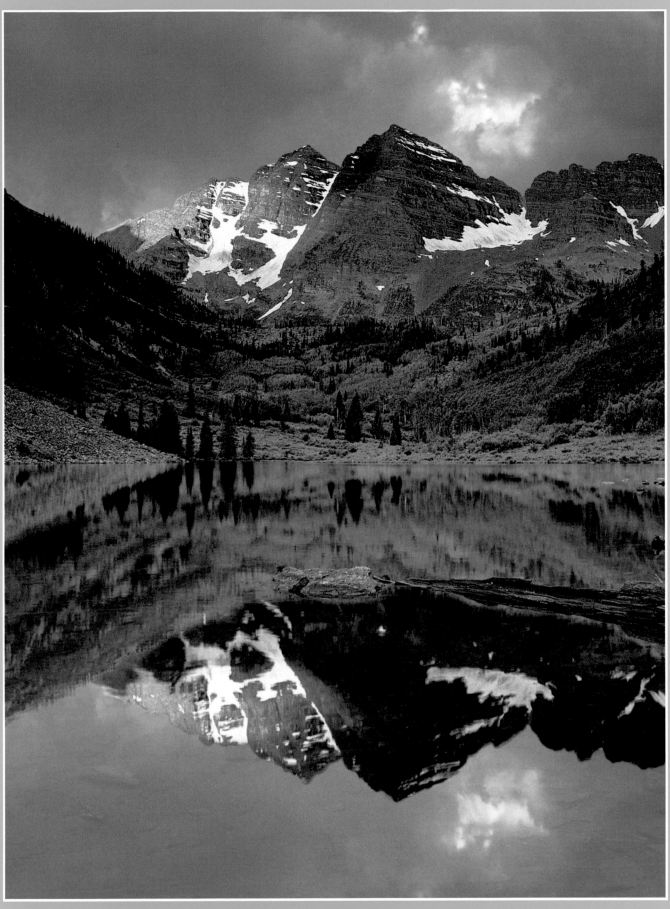

140 The 14,000 foot summits of Colorado's aptly named Maroon Bells catch a spot of sun at the end of a summer thunderstorm. *Reflected in the waters of Maroon Lake at 9,600 feet, the peaks are part of the Aspen–Snowmass Wilderness, a large* roadless area set aside from all future development above the rapidly growing ski towns of Aspen and Snowmass.

141 top Blue columbine, the Colorado state flower, blooms throughout the Rockies at higher elevations.

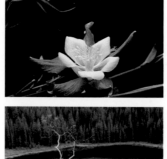

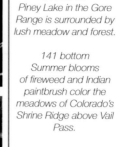

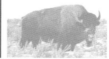

141 center
Piney Lake in the Gore Range is surrounded by lush meadow and forest.

141 bottom
Summer blooms of fireweed and Indian paintbrush color the meadows of Colorado's Shrine Ridge above Vail Pass.

Yellowstone became the first park as the result of a conversation around a campfire in Wyoming Territory on a September night in 1870. The Washburn expedition had been marveling at the grandeur and majesty of geothermal displays set amidst the splendor of the Rocky Mountains. As several of the party discussed ways to profit from what they had seen, one member insisted the land should become a park for all Americans to see. His convincing arguments changed their minds and the rest is history. Well, not quite . . .

Congress did not establish Yellowstone National Park in 1872 because some scruffy expeditioners said to preserve it in its natural condition. The railroads, state and federal officials, as well as private transport and tourism enterprises all lobbied for the park in their own self-interest for commercial exploitation. That conflict between preservation and providing for public enjoyment has greatly escalated in modern times.

Despite the most abundant display of large mammals of any of the 375 units of the U.S. National Park System—antelope, bear, bighorn sheep, bison, cougar, coyote, deer, elk, and the recently reintroduced wolf—Yellowstone officials readily admit that the park has a decreased quality of visitor experience due to overcrowding and increased pressure on the Greater Yellowstone Ecosytem beyond park borders. Development is virtually uncontrolled and park animals that temporarily wander outside are often hunted. The State of Montana recently shot 1,100 of the remaining 4,000 bison of the Yellowstone herd, ostensibly to protect a similar number of cattle grazing a nearby national forest for a few dollars a year from brucellosis, a disease that has never been documented to cross between wild bison and cattle.

At the turn of the twentieth century, bison almost went extinct in the United States. A herd of the last twenty Yellowstone bison began to slowly increase only after Wyoming declared a closed season on the animals, wherever they roamed. In 1908 a National Bison Range was set aside near Missoula on the other side of Montana, the first National Wildlife Refuge created by Congress. Today, the large expanse of open hillsides with forested canyons supports hundreds of bison as well as bighorn, elk, mule deer, and a full complement of predators.

In Wyoming, a National Elk Refuge in Jackson Hole protects winter range for the largest elk herd in America. More than a thousand animals can often be seen from the main highway during the winter months. Montana's Glacier National Park is also a splendid place to observe wildlife from the road in a spectacular setting. Mountain goats are almost always seen grazing by the road near the crest of Logan Pass on the Going-to-the-Sun Highway. The surprisingly level Highline Trail that traverses the sides of the peaks for miles from Logan Pass is a great place to see goats, bighorn, mule deer, coyote, and sometimes grizzly bears.

Wildlife is not as abundant in the Wasatch Range of Utah, but powder snow is. Resorts such as Alta, Deer Valley, Park City, Snowbird, and Sundance have some of the world's lightest and deepest powder. The moist air from the Pacific Ocean dries in a special way as it travels over the deserts of the Great Basin and rises up over the mountains to drop its gentle snow crystals on the peaks.

My favorite Wasatch Peak is Mount Timpanogas, which rises to 11,750 feet above Sundance, the ski resort built by Robert Redford in the 1970s after he starred in the movie, Downhill Racer. In winter and spring, Timpanogas rivals the most spectacular peaks of the Canadian Rockies when the giant panoramic glacial cirque that rents its upper face is coated with ice and snow. Summer trails wander through alpine meadows past lakes and forest to a rocky summit above timberline.

The highest peaks in the Rockies of New Mexico are over 13,000 feet in the Sangre de Cristo Range that crosses the state's northern border from Colorado. Visible from Sante Fe and Taos, this range is by far the best known, but the more obscure Mogollon Range that rises to 10,778 less than a hundred miles from the Mexican border holds a special place in conservation history.

Here in 1924 the first designated Wilderness Area in North America was created forty years before the Wilderness Act of 1964 through the visionary efforts of the conservationist and national forest land manager, Aldo Leopold, who conceptualized the now familiar phrases, "ecological conscience" and "land ethic." In 1916 he foresaw tourists in automobiles as degrading future wildlands as much as hunting and logging, so he studied six areas to be declared roadless Wilderness. By 1921, only the headwaters of the Gila River were still roadless. His original 574,000-acre Gila Wilderness Area was later reduced to 438,000 acres after less enlightened land managers allowed a road to be built through part of the preserve.

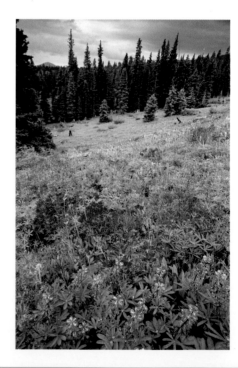

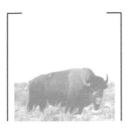

142 top Vivid fall colors line the edge of a lake on the floor of Jackson Hole in Wyoming's Grand Teton National Park.

142 bottom Aspens take on an orange glow against late afternoon shadows at the foot of Garnet Canyon below the Grand Teton.

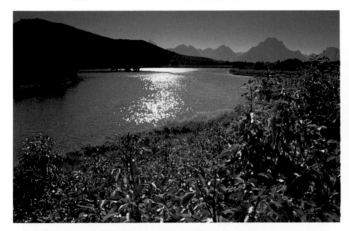

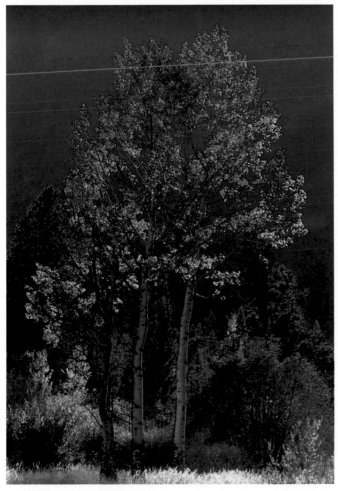

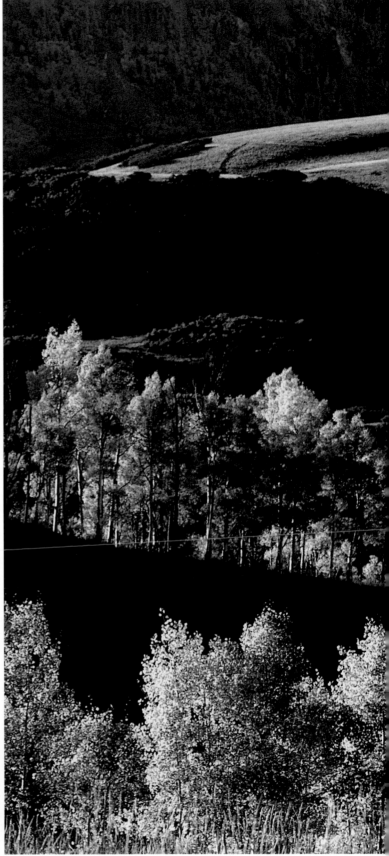

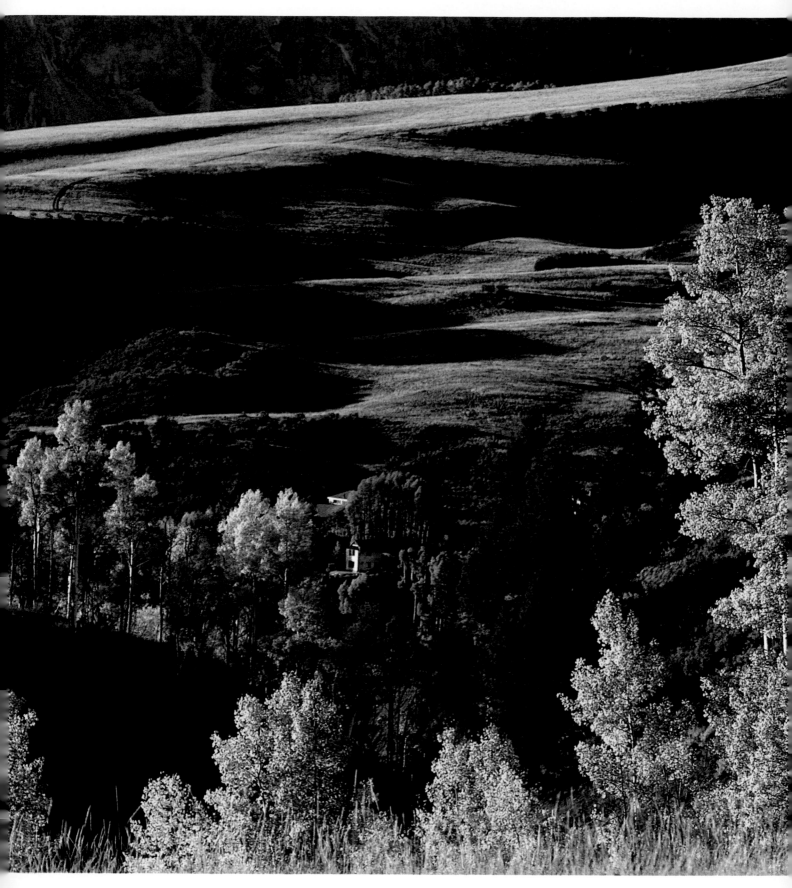

142-143 Aspens flow like rivers down open hillsides of the San Juan Range almost everywhere around Telluride, Colorado. Their common root systems following well-watered courses link them together into flowing patterns across the landscape. The elite ski resort of Telluride, formerly a frontier mining town, is surrounded by 14,000-foot peaks in a high basin.

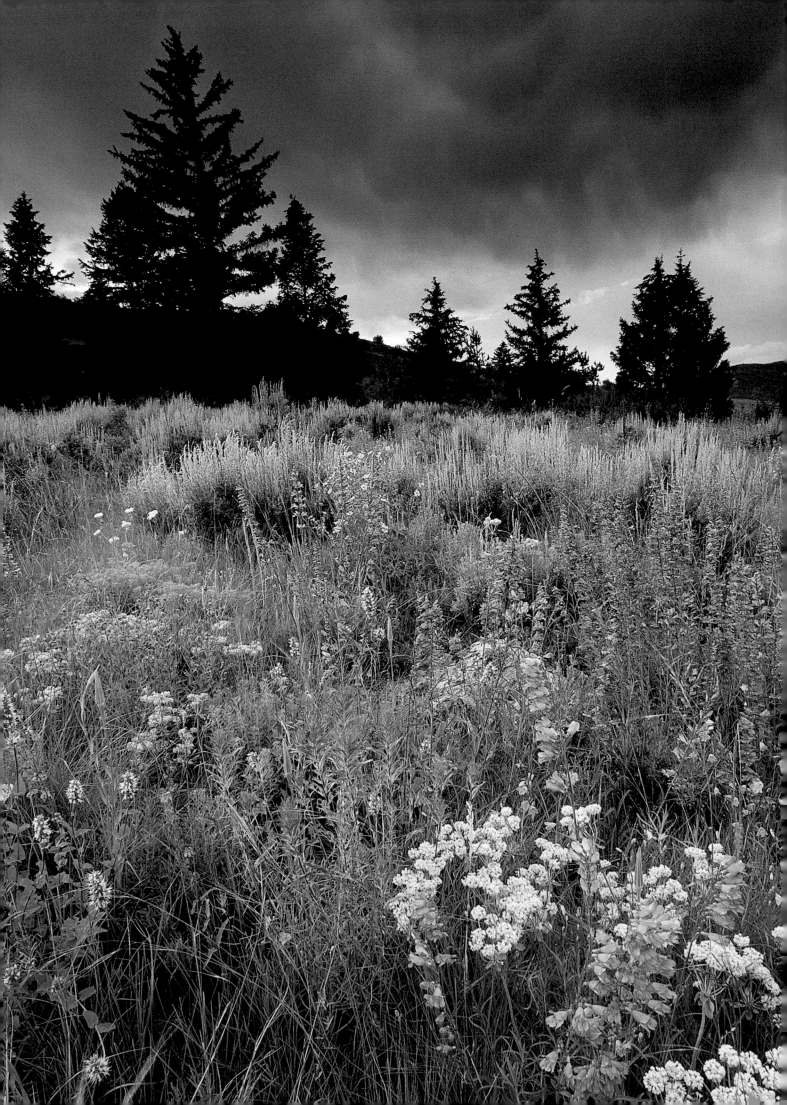

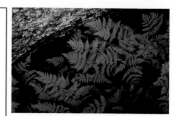

144 A field of sagebrush comes alive with summer wildflowers on the lower slopes of Meadow Mountain a few miles west of Vail, Colorado.

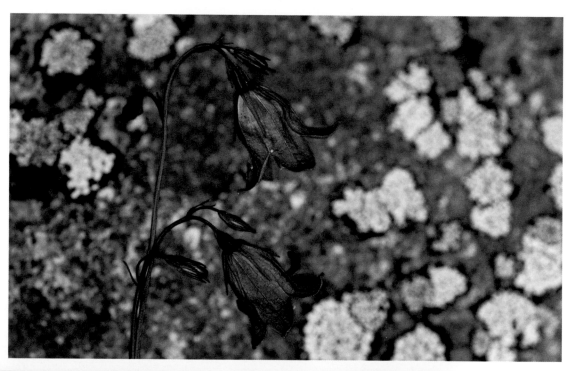

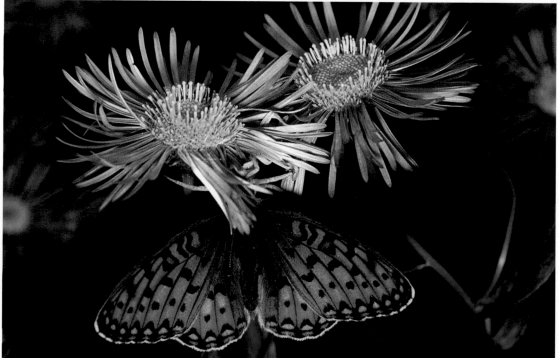

145 top Far below the icy peaks of Glacier National Park in Montana, lush ferns grow along the shadowed watercourse of Avalanche Creek.

145 center Mountain harebell is set off by the abstract patterns of lichens growing on the quartzite of the Gore Range in Colorado.

145 bottom A butterfly landing to gather nectar from asters blooming on Meadow Mountain near Vail is seized by a spider hidden beneath the petals.

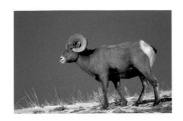

146 top A Rocky Mountain bighorn ram grazes a windblown ridge in the mountains of northern Yellowstone National Park in midwinter.

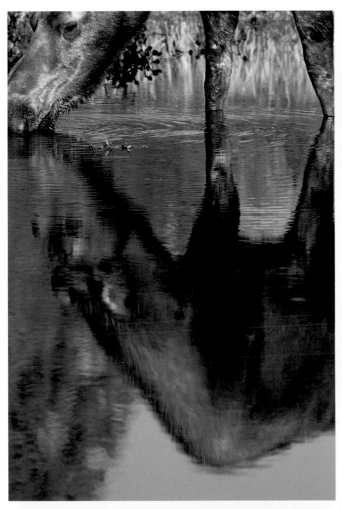

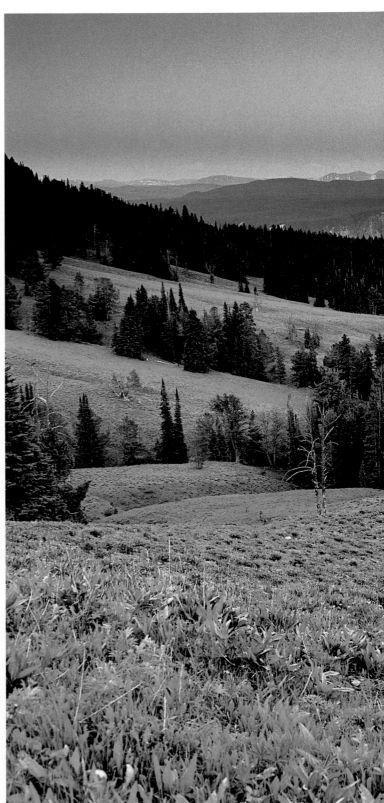

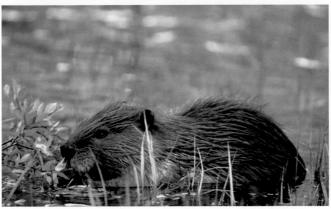

146

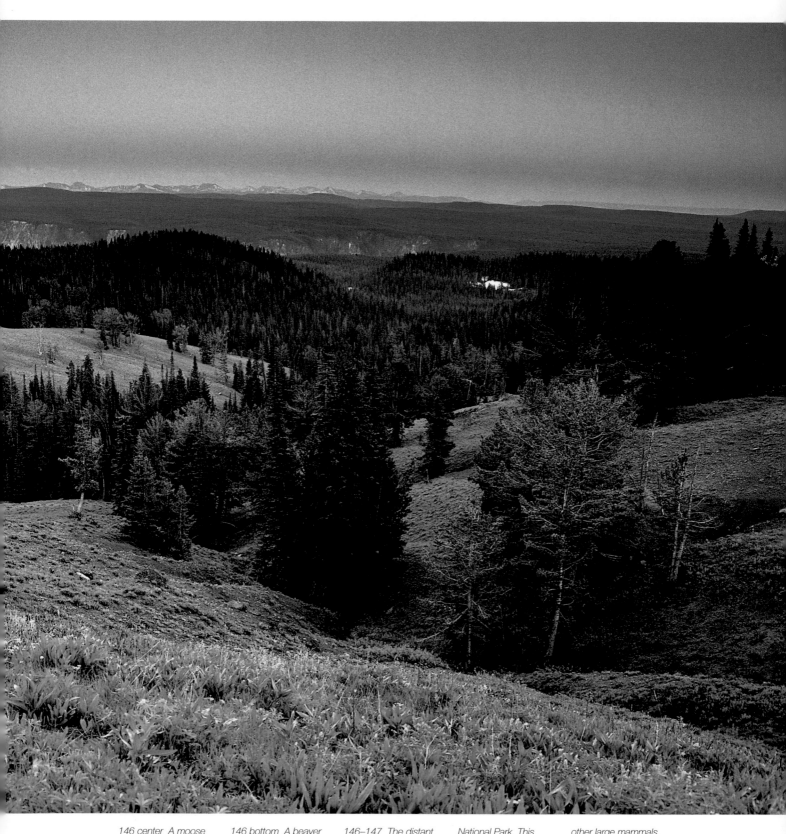

146 center A moose drinks from an eddy in the Snake River in Wyoming's Grand Teton National Park.

146 bottom A beaver tows a willow branch to build a dam across a stream in the Gore Range of Colorado.

146–147 The distant Absaroka Range glows on the horizon in twilight over the green hills of northern Yellowstone National Park. This roadless wilderness is home to some of the Lower 48's last grizzly bears, as well as many other large mammals, including antelope, bighorn, cougar, coyote, deer, elk, lynx, moose, mountain goat, and wolf.

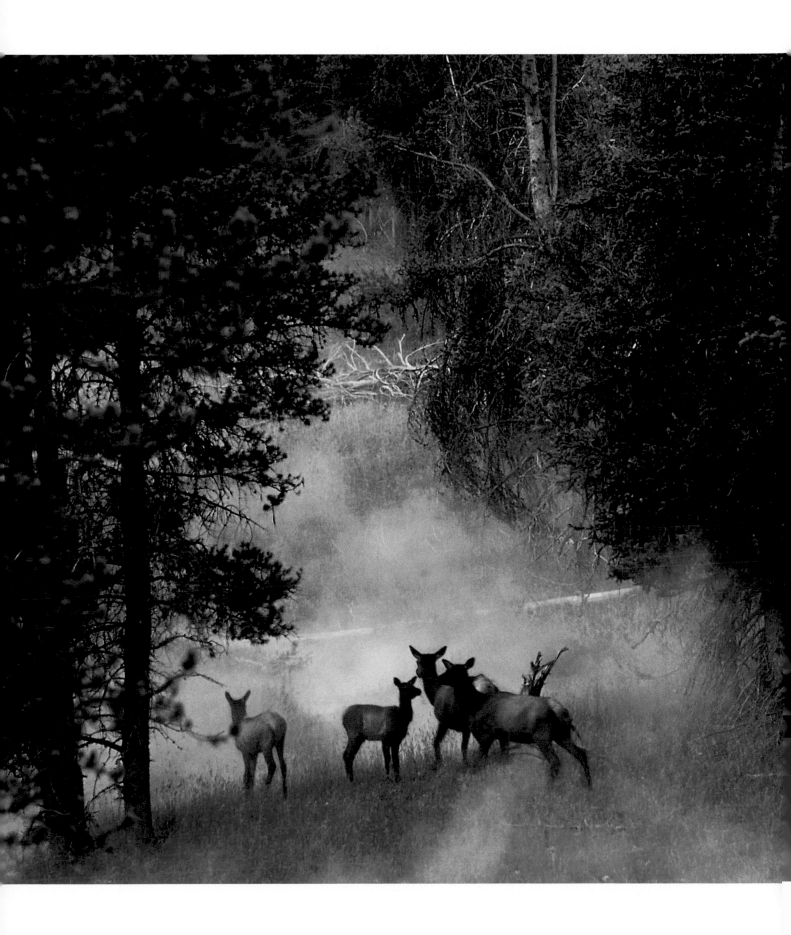

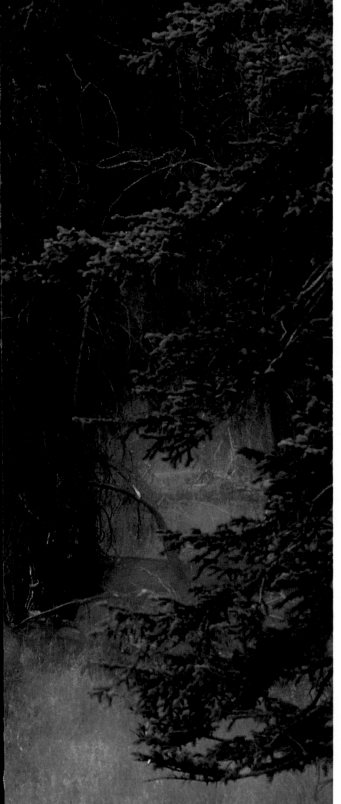

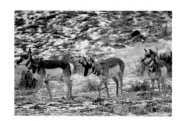

*148–149 A herd of elk
graze a forest clearing
veiled in the mist of
nearby hot springs in
Yellowstone National
Park.*

*149 top Pronghorn
antelope browse the
windblown plains of
northern Yellowstone,
near Gardiner,
Montana.*

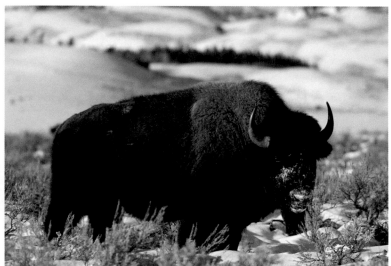

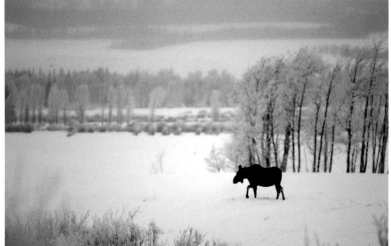

*149 center On a
−30°F winter morning,
a lone moose wanders
into the open plains of
Jackson Hole below
the Grand Tetons.*

*149 bottom
An American bison,
commonly known as a
buffalo, grazes one of its
last strongholds in
Yellowtone National Park.*

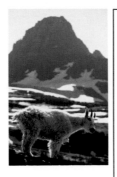

150 top *A mountain goat stands profiled against a peak above Logan Pass in Montana's Glacier National Park.*

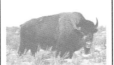

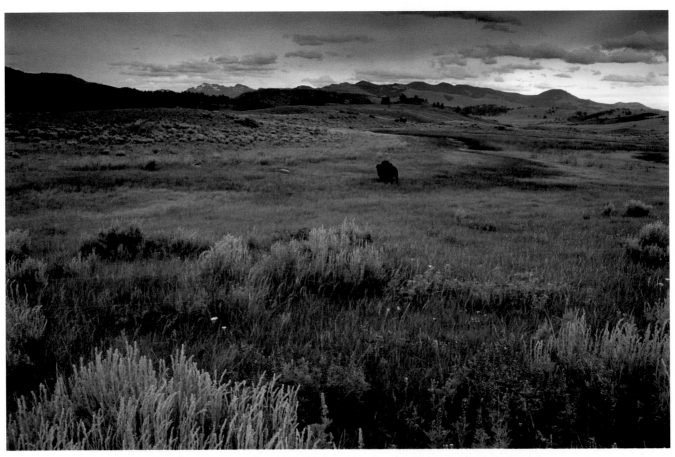

150 bottom *A lone bison grazes a lush meadow fringed with sagebrush and purple lupine in the Lamar Valley of northern Yellowstone National Park. In this expansive valley, wolves were recently reintroduced back into the Greater Yellowstone Ecosystem, to the delight of ecotourists, but not ranchers.*

151 *Unique double falls occur where two creeks from opposite sides of a high valley join each other above Logan Pass in Glacier National Park. On the horizon, an August sunrise paints the sky above peaks of the Continental Divide that overlook the route of the Going-to-the-Sun Highway.*

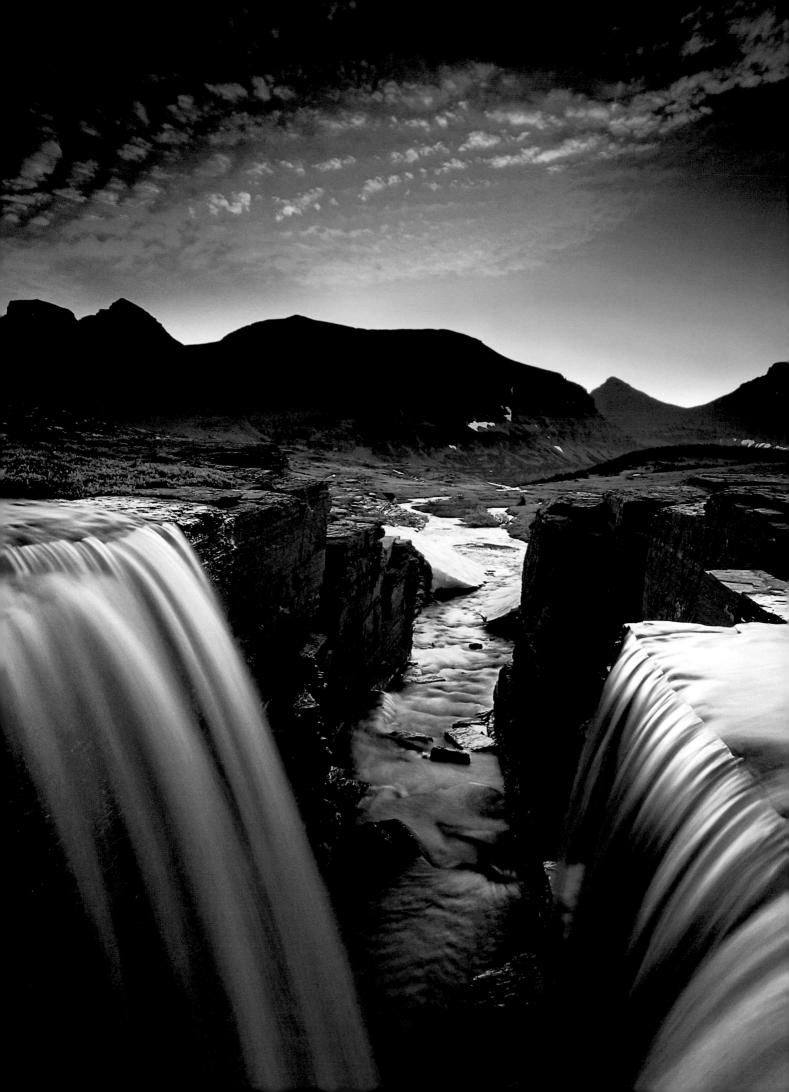

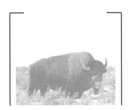

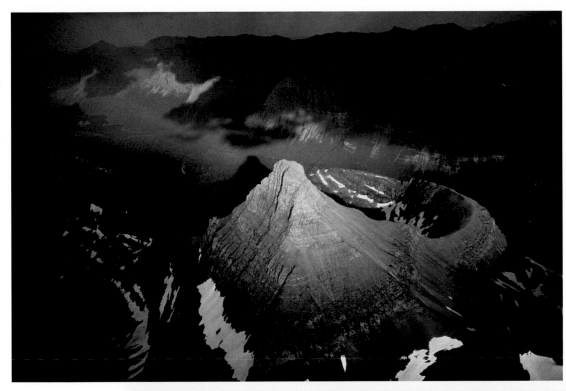

153 A reflection in a
pool filled by spray from
Avalanche Gorge
mirrors a hemlock forest
in Montana's Glacier
National Park.

154–155 Also in
Glacier, fresh grasses
beside Lake Sherburne
are set off by the
crimson glow of a
stormy summer sunrise.

152 top Seen from the
air, Mount Reynolds
crowns Logan Pass in
Glacier National Park.

152 bottom From the
ground on Logan Pass,
mule deer gambol
beneath the peaks of
Glacier's famous
Garden Wall.

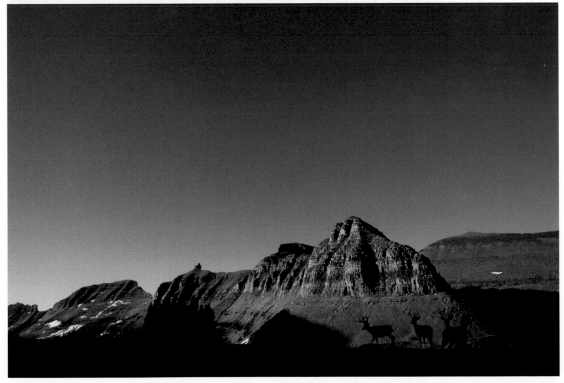

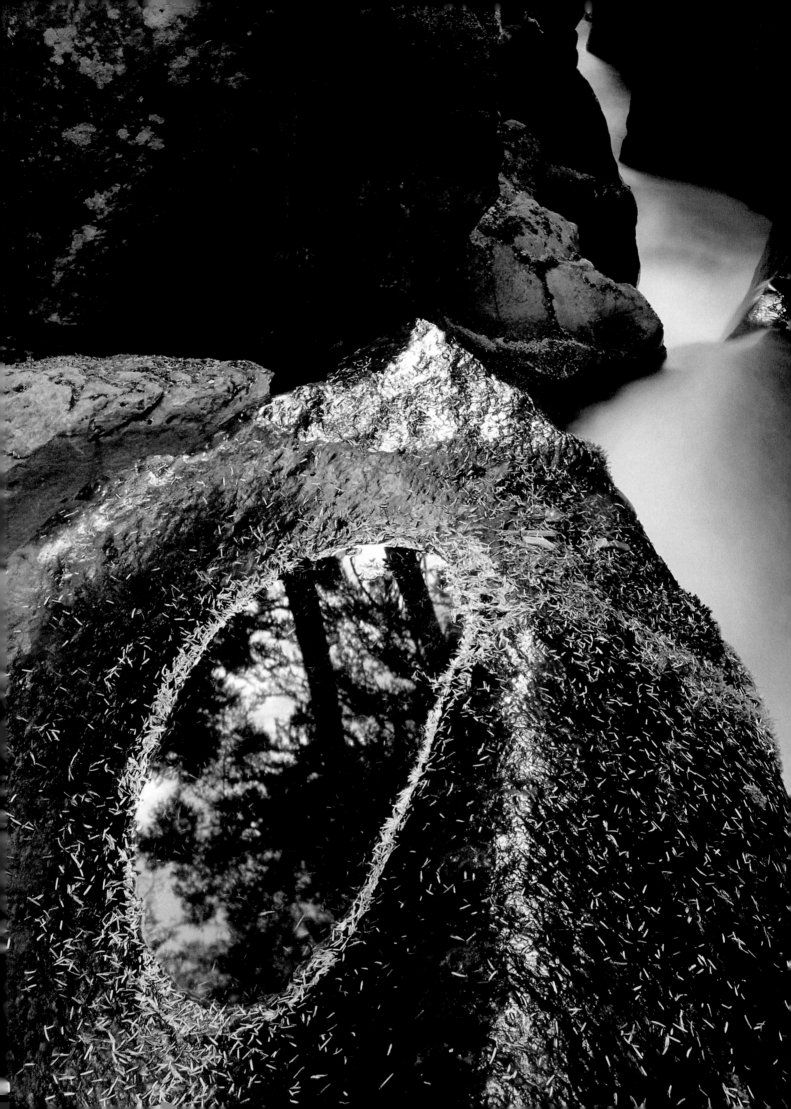

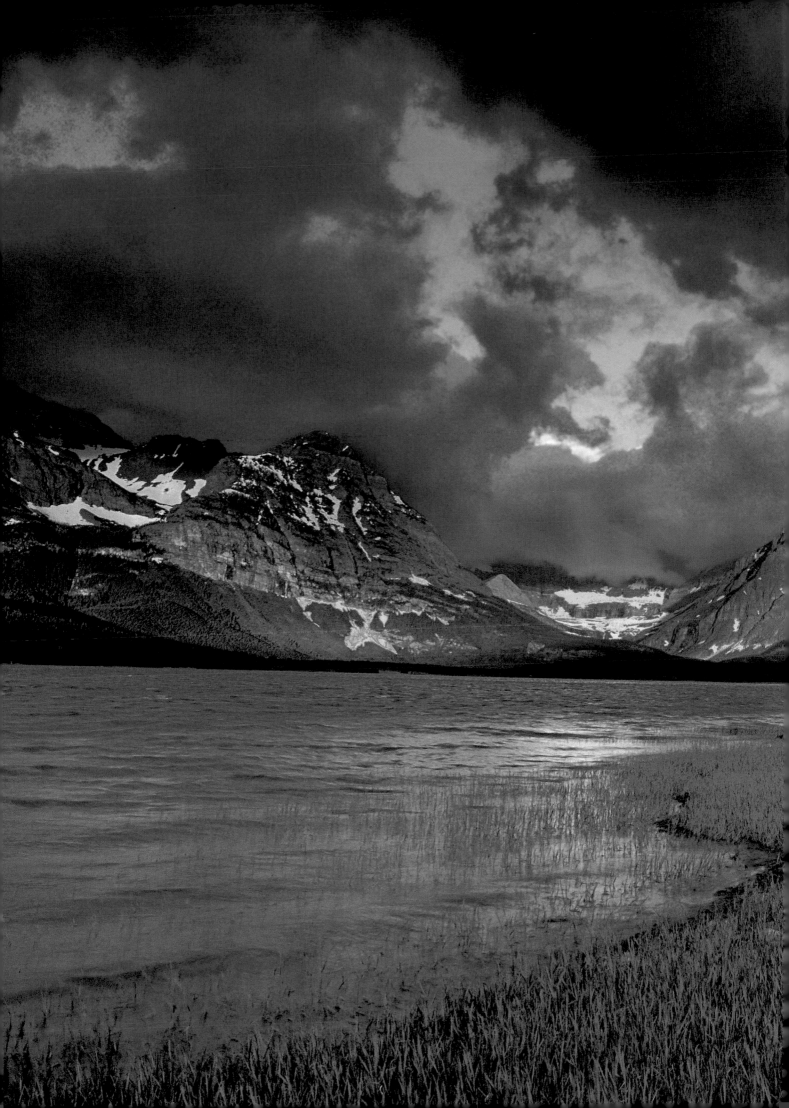

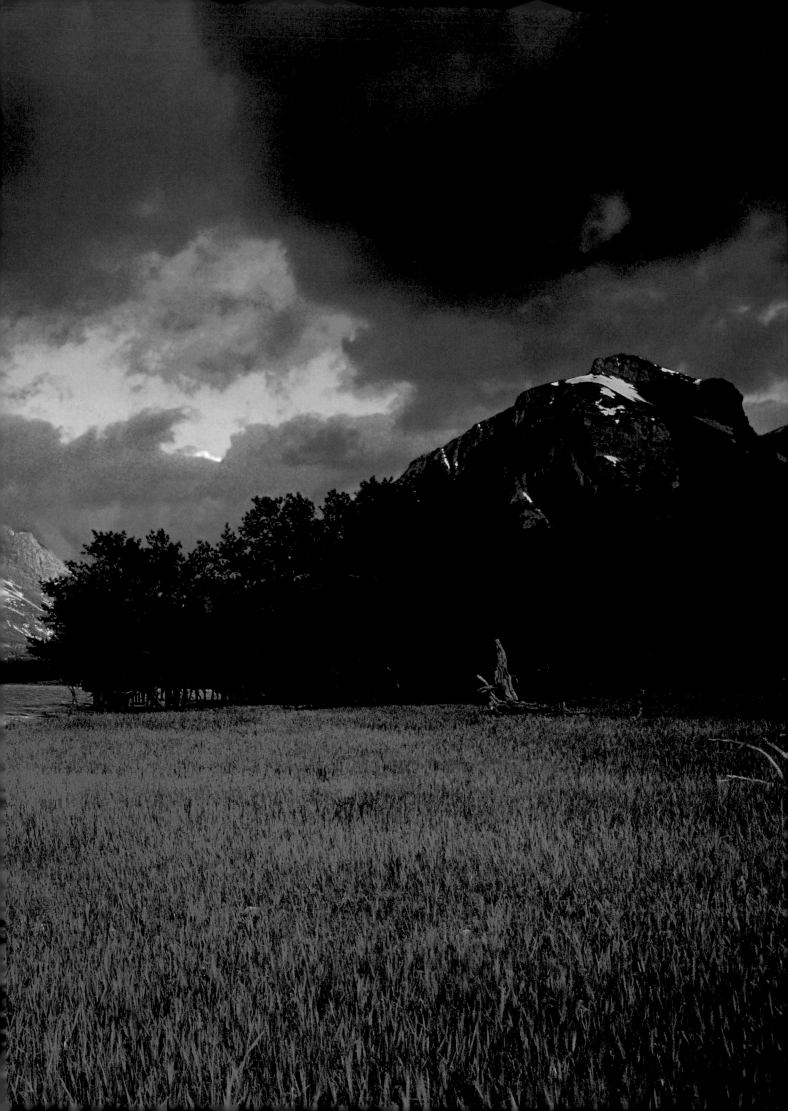

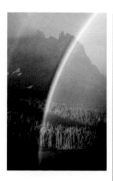

156 top A rainbow over St. Mary's Lake in Glacier National Park accents a classic Rocky Mountain vista of dawn light on lake, forest, and mountain.

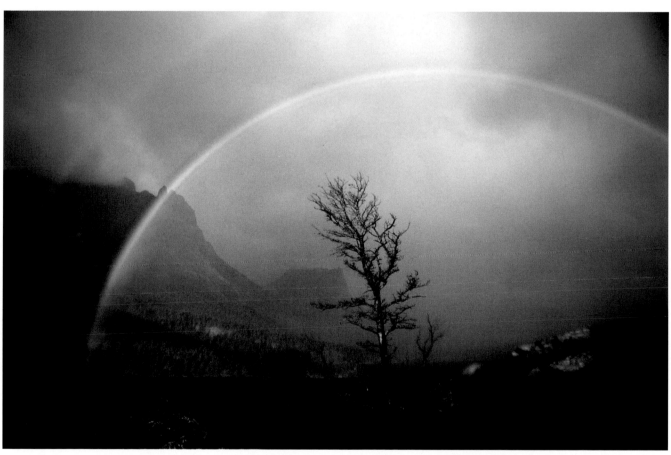

156 bottom On a summer morning when rainbows lasted for over an hour, an extreme wide-angle lens captures a broader vista of the same scene depicted at the top of the page and to the right, including the fierce rainstorm lit from beneath that created the appearance of the rainbow from aptly named Sunrise Point.

157 In a telephoto view to the right of the other two incomplete rainbows, a double rainbow casts a mysterious warm glow through a heavy downpour over Going-to-the-Sun Mountain. The predominant reds and yellows of this rainbow's prism, with blues and greens almost absent, are due to the warm color of light near the moment of sunrise.

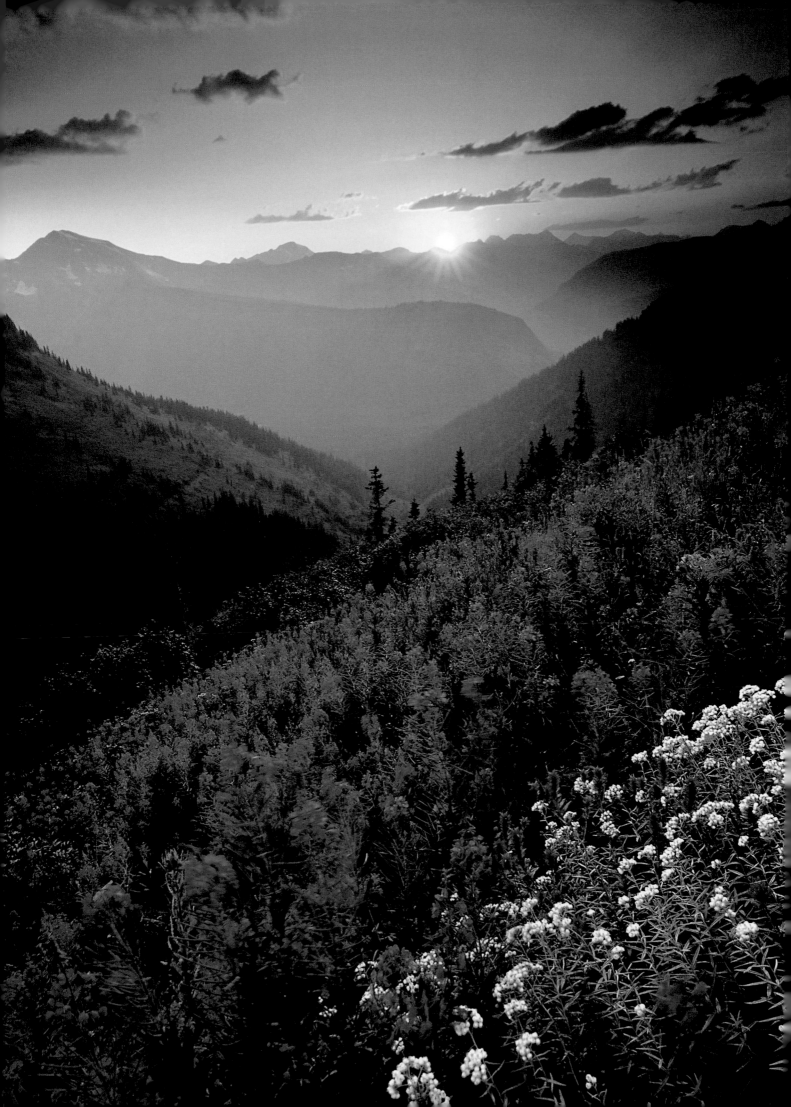

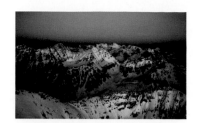

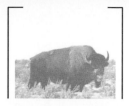

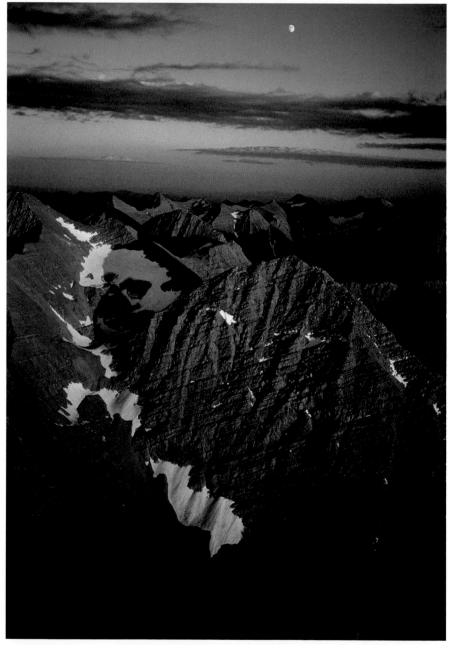

158 A field of fireweed atop Logan Pass in Glacier National Park brushes the landscape purple in this slow exposure made in the last warm rays of light on a windy evening in August.

159 top A spring view of Colorado's Maroon Bells shows why they hold world-class ski resorts.

159 bottom South of Glacier, last light touches the wild Mission Mountains.

160 A hiker watches an evening rainbow arcing across a hidden valley beneath Cathedral Peak on the east side of the Wind River Range of Wyoming.

160–161 Beneath a full moon in predawn twilight, the Grand Tetons rise majestically above the verdant sagebrush plains of Jackson Hole near Jenny Lake.

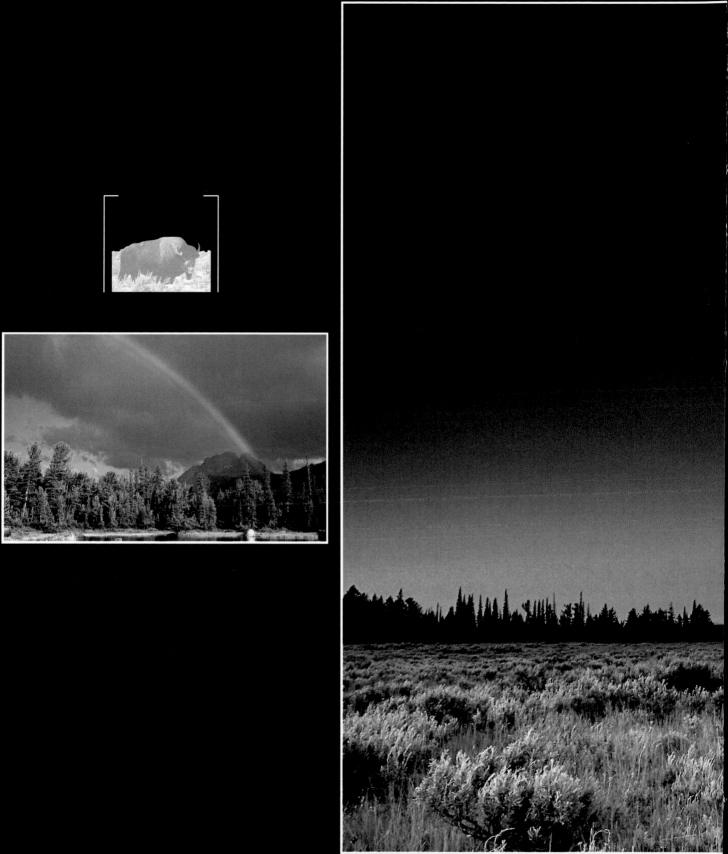

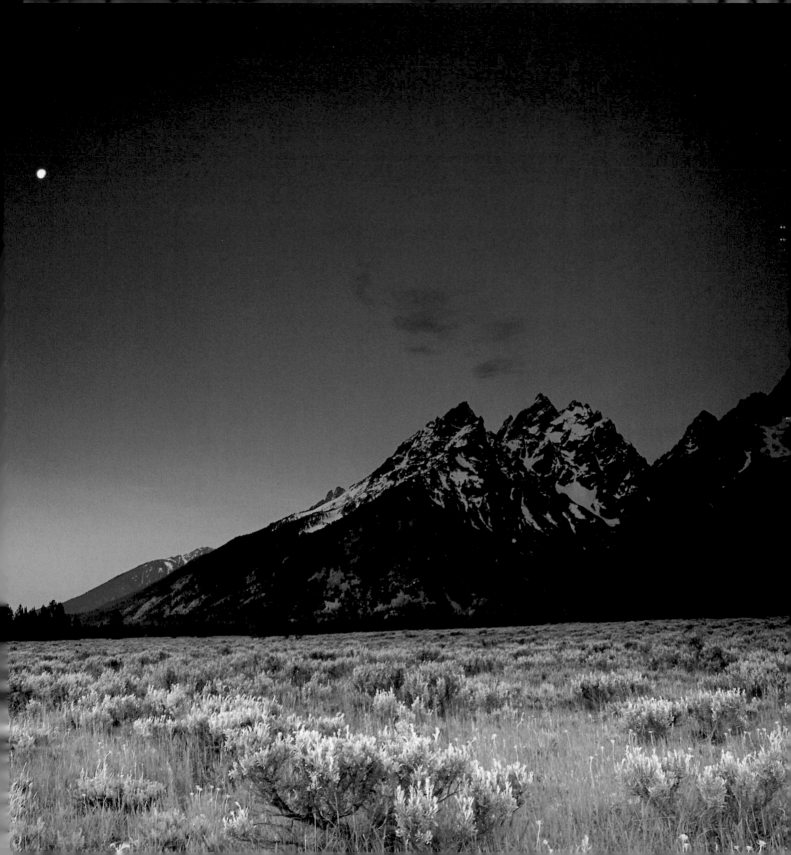

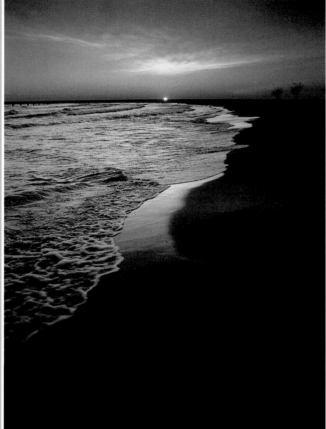

162–163
Spring flowers
carpet the Great
Plains in the
"Big Sky" country
of eastern Montana.

The Great Plains and Heartlands

163 Dawn comes
to the shores
of Lake Michigan
in Lincoln Park
within the city
of Chicago.

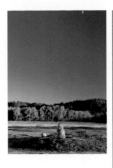

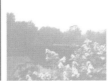

164 top A prairie dog stands at alert beside its hole in Devils Tower National Monument on the plains of eastern Wyoming.

The Great Plains of the American Midwest have not become photographic icons, like the waterfalls of Yosemite or the gorge of the Grand Canyon. Their essence—a continuous level horizon—cannot be touched by hand or made accessible in the two dimensions of a photograph. To truly experience the plains is to be immersed hip deep in a tall-grass prairie.

The "Big Sky Country" that stretches from the front ranges of the Rockies to the hardwood forests of the East used to hold a greater biomass of wildlife per square mile than the Serengeti plain of Africa. A thousand years ago, the sun rose and set between the legs of the greatest herds on Earth—buffalo, elk, deer, bighorn sheep, and antelope. Twelve thousand years ago, mammoths, camels, yaks, llamas, great sloths, lions, cheetahs and saber-toothed tigers walked the same prairie.

In 1803, the United States doubled in size by way of the Louisiana Purchase from Napoleon. President Jefferson commissioned Meriwether Lewis and William Clark to explore these vast lands stretching from the Mississippi River to the Rocky Mountains and forge a route to the Pacific. Throughout their journey, Lewis and Clark encountered many grizzly bears, now gone entirely

from the plains. They reported a herd of 300,000 buffalo and far larger flocks of passenger pigeons, the most common bird in America. John James Audubon estimated one flock at over 2 billion, yet wanton shooting exterminated the species by 1900, when the last wild pigeon was shot in Ohio.

During one year in the 1870s, "Buffalo Bill" Cody shot 4,280 buffalo for the Union Pacific Railroad. As Francis Parkman predicted in 1872, "A time would come, when those plains would be a grazing country, the buffalo give place to tame cattle, farmhouses be scattered along the water courses, and wolves, bears, and Indians be numbered among the things that were." The Great Plains were soon homesteaded as farmland, while the Rockies and the Great Basin remain mostly public land, with national forests, parks, and wildlife refuges.

With the great majority of the plains under cultivation or used for grazing cattle or sheep, very little of the original tall grass prairie remains in this "breadbasket" of North America. Without natural grasses and large mammals, most federal preserves are restored areas, rather than wilderness.

Toward the east where the land begins rolling toward the Alleghenies and the Appalachians, the plains merge into the "Heartlands" of the Midwest.

Cuyahoga National Recreation Area within metropolitan Cleveland has become a premier example of restored wildlands. During the 1960s, the Cuyahoga River became so polluted by heavy industry that it burst into flames. Today, the area is once again a paradise of open meadow and hardwood forest beside clear waters.

The Cuyahoga River pours into Lake Erie, the most polluted of the five Great Lakes where fish and birds of prey almost died out during the 1970s but have since begun to recover. To the North, larger Lake Superior has fared far better. Along American shores in Minnesota and Michigan, as well as on the Canadian side, wild areas abound.

My father was born in a log cabin in Minnesota in 1884. As I was growing up, my family drove across the plains of eastern Wyoming, Montana, South Dakota, and Iowa several times to visit the old family farm. We often stopped to watch prairie dog "towns" all across the Great Plains, but by the time I became a photographer, prairie dogs were gone except in such protected areas as the Badlands of South Dakota and Devils Tower in Wyoming, where these large rodents pop in and out of closely spaced holes like living pinballs, always with an eye for the shadow of a hawk or the stalk of a coyote.

Devils Tower, rising 900 feet out of the plains in vertical volcanic columns, is so improbable that it was chosen as the site where aliens land in the movie, *Close Encounters of the Third Kind*. Because it was falsely depicted as barren and lifeless, *Audubon* magazine assigned me to document its wildlife. I climbed it with a partner, spent a night on top, and photographed falcons diving through pigeons, as well as woodrats stealing our food. We descended into golden October grasses, glimpsing herds of deer and a coyote by moonlight in a memorable vision of what all the Great Plains must have once been like. John Muir, who grew up in Wisconsin in the 1850s, described seeing passenger pigeon "flocks streaming south in the fall so large that they were flowing over from horizon to horizon in an almost continuous stream all day... like a mighty river in the sky."

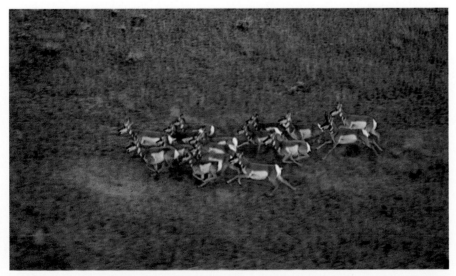

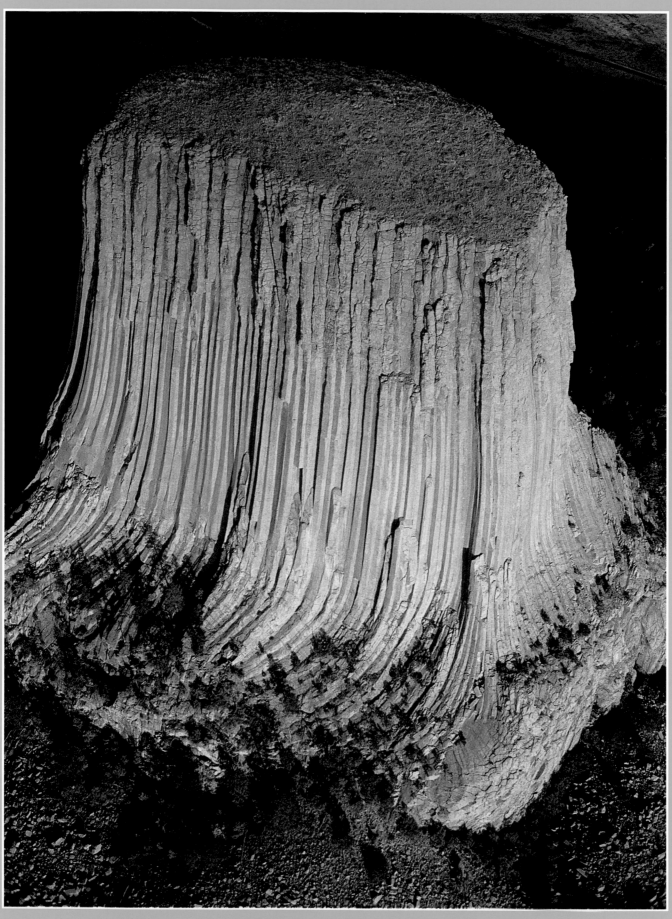

164 bottom A herd of pronghorn antelope race across the plains near the Wyoming–South Dakota border. North America's fastest land animals, they can sprint up to 61 mph and cruise longer distances at 30 mph.

165 The volcanic columns of Devils Tower appear to erupt from the Wyoming plains. The 900-foot tower was slowly exposed by erosion after lava welled up beneath the surface about 50 million years ago.

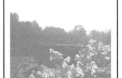

166 top   Migrating Canada geese glide across a pond on a misty morning near Columbus, Ohio.

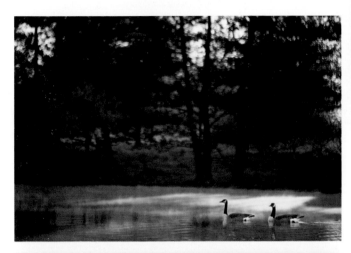

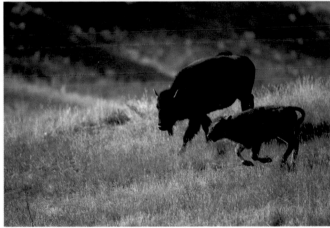

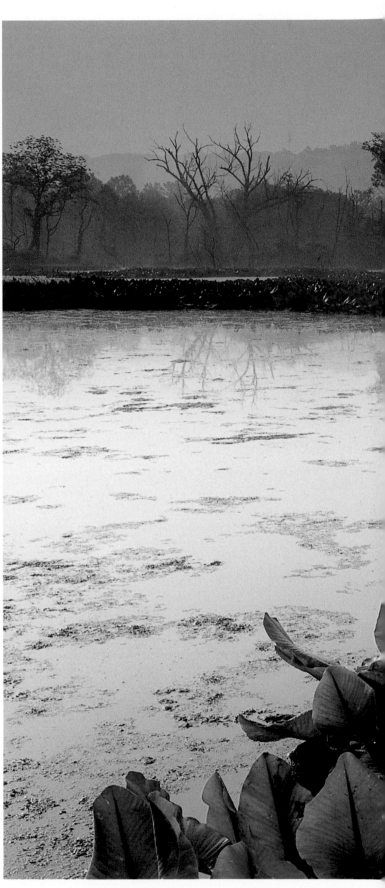

166 bottom   A bison with her young calf traverses prairie grasslands in Montana's 18,542-acre National Bison Range, created in 1908 by President Roosevelt to protect the last 300 wild bison. Herds were estimated at over 70 million a century before.

166–167   The restored watershed of the Cuyahoga River, once so incredibly polluted by industry that it caught fire, is now protected by Ohio's Cuyahoga National Recreation Area in metropolitan Cleveland.

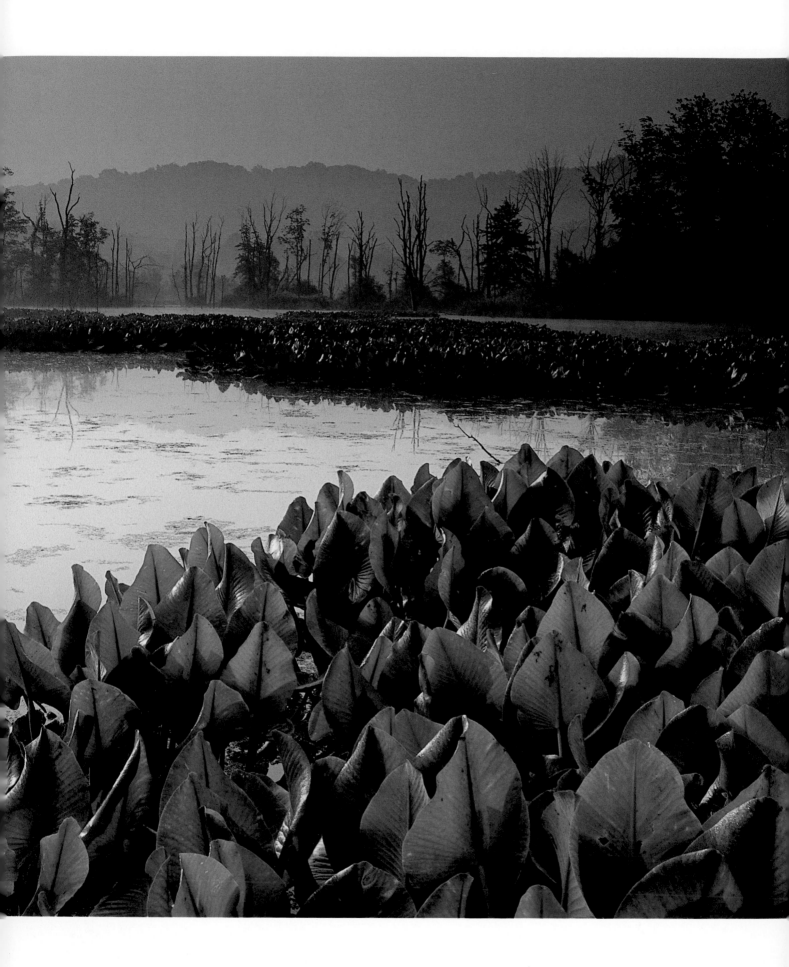

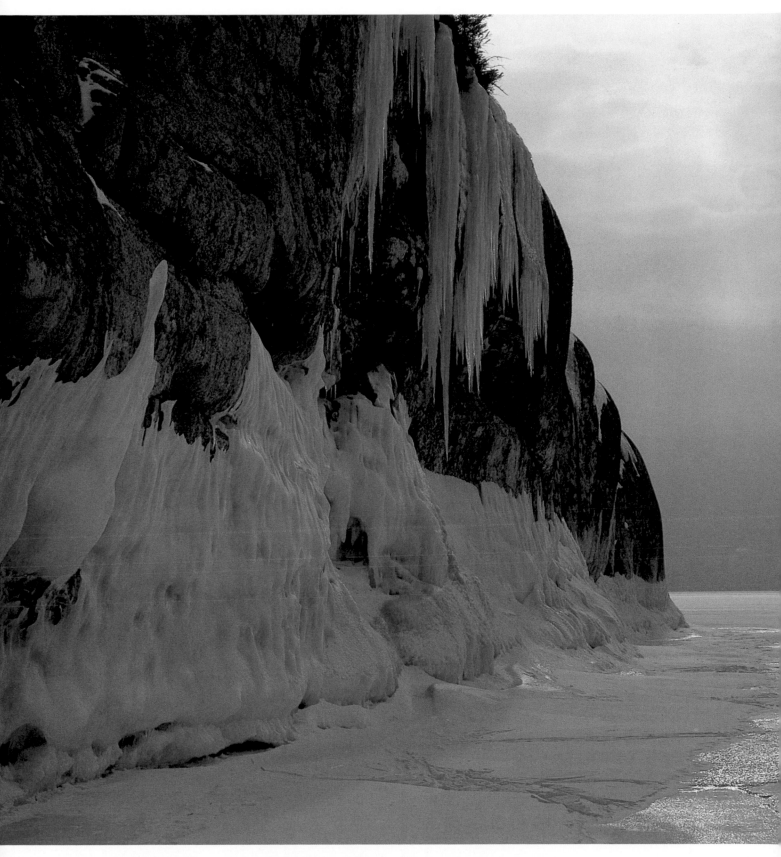

168–169 Lake Superior, the world's largest freshwater lake, lies frozen in midwinter beneath cliffs of granite and ice on the Canadian side. One of the five Great Lakes, its area exceeds that of Connecticut, New Hampshire, Massachusetts, and Vermont combined.

169 top Waves bred by winds on the oceanic expanse of Lake Superior in summer crash against the Michigan shore.

169 bottom Sandstone cliffs drop into the lake's deep green waters at Pictured Rocks National Lakeshore in Michigan.

170–171 Sunrise lights up mists rising over the Cuyahoga River in Ohio's Cuyahoga National Recreation Area.

171 A pond fringed by flowers and surrounded by hardwood forest holds a primeval vision of America's heartlands.

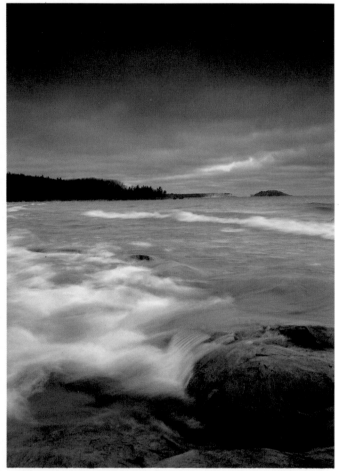

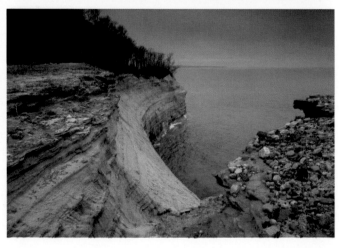

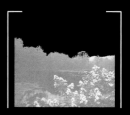

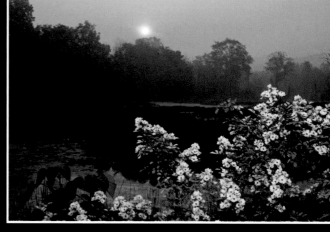

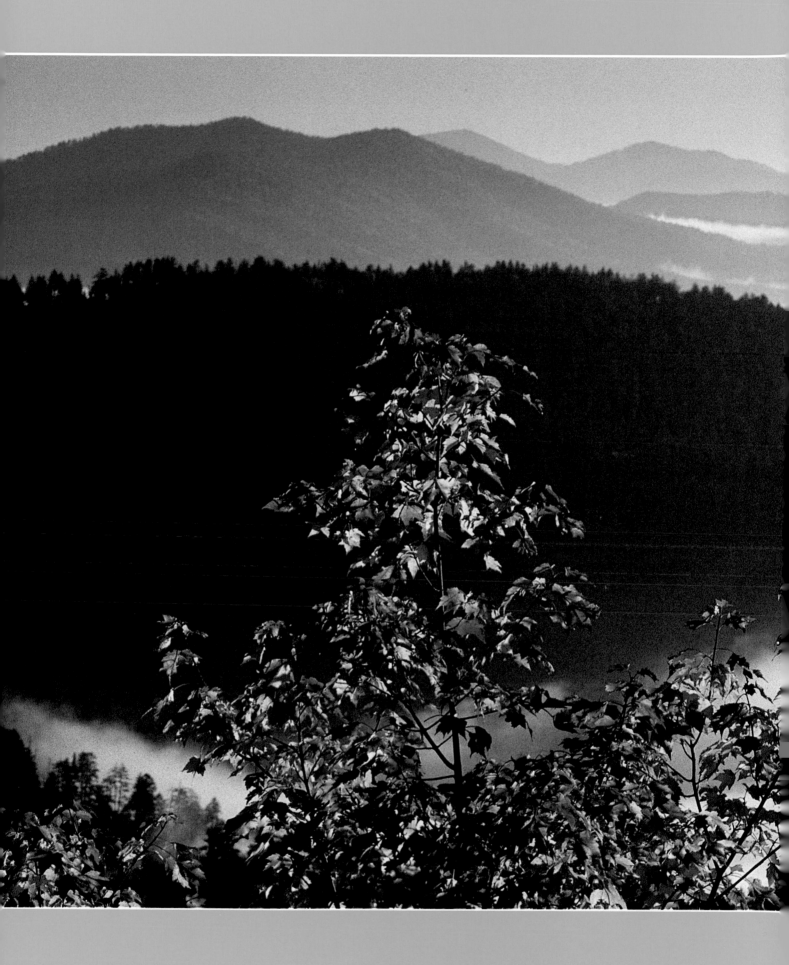

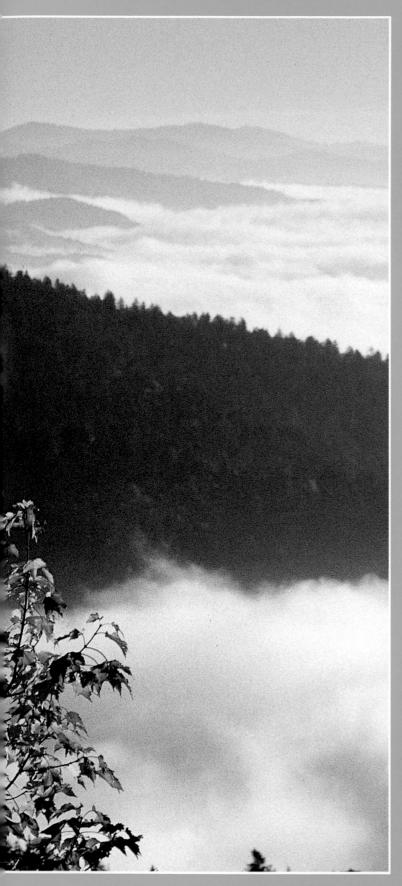

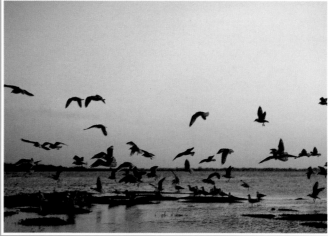

The Appalachians and the Atlantic Coast

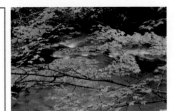

174 top left A birch tree gleams in the morning sun in New York State's Hudson River Valley.

174 top right Fall foliage overhangs a stream in the highlands of North Carolina.

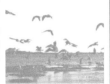

As a wide-angle photograph overemphasizes near subjects, the most famous cover of *The New Yorker* magazine exaggerates the way residents of the island of Manhattan perceive America. The avenues are clearly numbered, the equally wide Hudson River fades off into a New Jersey of similar breadth, and somewhere out in the distance a strip of like width holds all of Texas, Utah and California.

Though my perception of wild North America may be based from the West, I've visited enough wildness in the East to know not only what is there, but also what has been lost in this area of early settlement by Europeans. Despite long wilderness hikes, climbs, and mountain runs from Maine to Georgia, my most mind-altering Atlantic experience happened on a simple morning jog in Manhattan's Central Park.

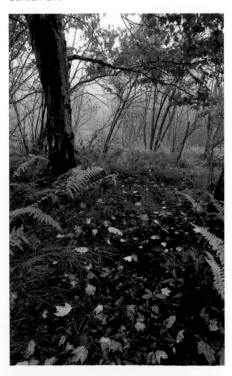

In my hotel room, I strapped on my camera chest pouch, hoping at best for a nice sunrise silhouetted through trees. When the clouds closed in before dawn, I forgot about my camera and continued running into the deepest forest of this giant public garden, marveling how natural it looked even though I knew the history of its creation by America's greatest landscape architect, Frederick Law Olmsted (who also ventured 3000 miles overland to California in the 1860s to design parks, college campuses, and write the charter for North America's first federal nature preserve in Yosemite).

Just as I was thinking about not being in a truly natural park with wild animals, I spotted one of Central Park's resident ground hogs in the bushes. After I managed a photograph of the slightly wary creature, we stood facing each other for long minutes with a piece of wild New York forest to ourselves.

When the first pilgrims arrived in the 1620s, wildlife was splendidly abundant all across the Adirondacks, the Appalachians, and the Atlantic Coastal Plain. In Olmsted's day, most of New York State was still wild. As late as 1890, the state paid 107 bounties on cougars and several more on wolves. Both animals vanished after the turn of the twentieth century.

Though buffalo, caribou, and elk were exterminated, white-tailed deer are more abundant today than in primeval times, when predators other than humans culled their numbers. I saw more deer during a week of hikes and trail runs in the Blue Ridge Mountains, than in decades of trail activities in Yosemite.

The seedy casinos of Atlantic City, New Jersey, seem an unlikely place to spot non-human wildness, and yet across Delaware Bay the salt marshes of Brigantine National Wildlife Refuge teem with bird life. I spent days that passed like hours photographing egrets and herons against the sunrise as well as geese and mergansers in the sloughs, plus a host of small shorebirds on the sandy banks, all with high-rise buildings in the distance.

In the fall, the hardwood forests of New England take on some of the richest natural colors on Earth. Broad-leafed maples and oaks turn every warm hue imaginable as greens give way to yellows, oranges, crimsons, maroons, and violets set against green pines, blue skies, and white clouds. I've chased these colors in many national and state parks, as well as little local wild spots of at least equal beauty, such as Punkatasset Woods amidst homes on the outskirts of Concord, Massachusetts. The colors I photographed there were as rich and wild as anything I searched out in the heart of Vermont or Maine.

Henry David Thoreau found the much smaller Concord of the 1850s too populous for his tastes. He moved out of town into a cabin on Walden Pond, where he wrote his seminal book, *Walden*, considered the original manifesto of American environmental philosophy. His description of 26 months alone in the forests of New England reflects on nature, rather than humanity, as being at the core of the meaning of life. His phrase, "In wildness is the preservation of the world," has literally reverberated around the world, influencing poets, photographers, and policy makers.

Many of Thoreau's equally strong opinions have been less quoted. He realized that "true art is but the expression of our love of nature. It is monstrous when one cares but little about trees and much about Corinthian columns, and yet this is exceedingly common." His special reverence for the way natural light affects appreciation of nature is strikingly similar to that of today's top nature photographers, who have learned to re-experience Thoreau's rapt attention to Nature's tiny details, rather than only more obvious natural wonders. Like Thoreau, the best photographers come to know that a single tree, or even a single leaf of that tree, shimmering in the October backlight of a New England afternoon, can hold its own with a giant Sequoia, geyser, or Grand Teton. Thoreau understood just when "the oaks, hickories, maples, and other trees imparted a brightness like

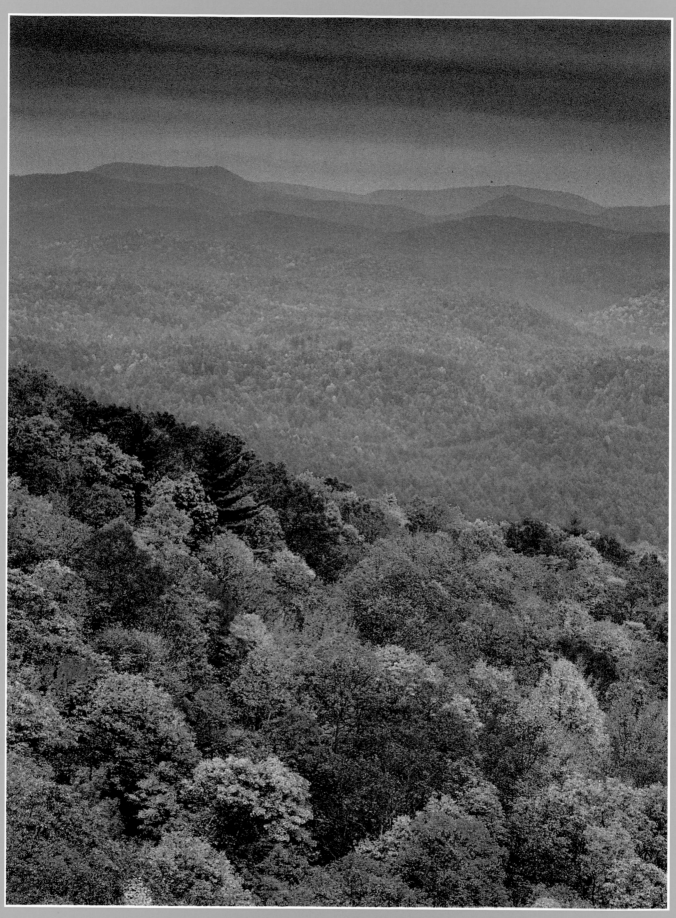

174 bottom Fall leaves color the lush forest floor of North Carolina's Pisgah Wilderness Area near Asheville.

175 More than beautiful to the eye, the many fall colors of the highlands of North Carolina indicate the presence of America's most diverse temperate broadleaf forest. Southeastern forests hold 190 native species, 27 of them endemic to a region reported by World Wildlife Fund to hold "the richest temperate herbaceous flora in the world."

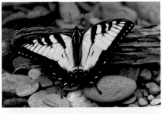

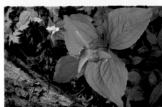

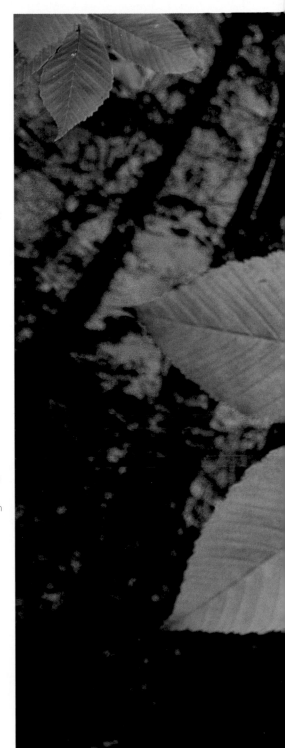

sunshine to the landscape" and recognized that "every day a new picture is painted and framed, held up for half an hour, in such lights as the Great Artist chooses, and then withdrawn, the curtain falls."

Because fall colors don't require great wild surroundings to be appreciated, New England has gained popularity as a place to experience nature in rustic comfort that speaks of an era, more than a century past along most of the East Coast, when farms and stores were locally owned and a person could step out their door into enough wildness to feel renewed.

While New England's lack of development guarantees its charm well into the twenty-first century, the Great Smokies have already been sold short by Gatlinburg, Tennessee—America's most dreadful national park village. The crowded coagulation of tacky amusements, motels, fast

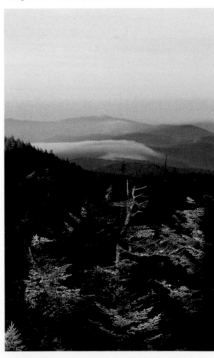

food, and Dolly Parton's Dollywood theme park is at odds with the burbling cascades and giant trilliums that line the nearby floor of this heavily forested and visited park in the heart of the southern Appalachians.

The highest point in the Smokies hasn't fared much better. A space-age concrete ramp leads to an artificial viewpoint atop 6,642-foot Clingman's Dome. Great sunrise photos across multiple hazy ranges—partly from industrial pollutants—can be made before the crowds arrive, but I no longer focus closely on the dying trees, suffering from an exotic pest invasion.

On the plus side, the park is honeycombed by over a hundred wilderness trails, which only a tiny percentage of the park's 10 million annual visitors use. Thirty-seven of the two thousand miles of the Appalachian Trail run through the heart of the park. The rustic Mount LeConte Lodge near the tip of the park's third highest peak is an ideal place to stay and venture out for sunrises and sunsets, if you can get reservations.

I've hiked or run many sections of the Appalachian Trail from its northern terminus atop Mount Katahdin in Maine to its southern one in Georgia. Each area has its special appeal, such as the Blue Ridge Mountains of Virginia's Shenandoah National Park or the Highlands of North Carolina, but for me, the granite and ice of the White Mountains of New Hampshire have the most wilderness character. Thoreau described "the most rugged scenery in New England" above North Conway, where the extreme steeps of Tuckerman Ravine have attracted generations of world-class skiers and the 6,288-foot summit of Mount Washington long held the world's ground-recorded wind speed record at 234 miles per hour.

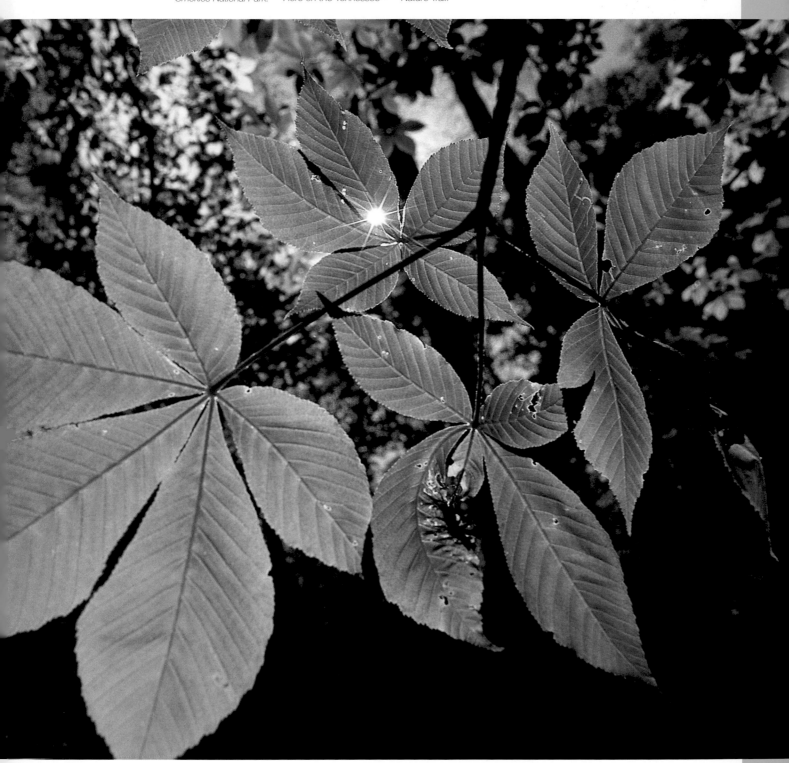

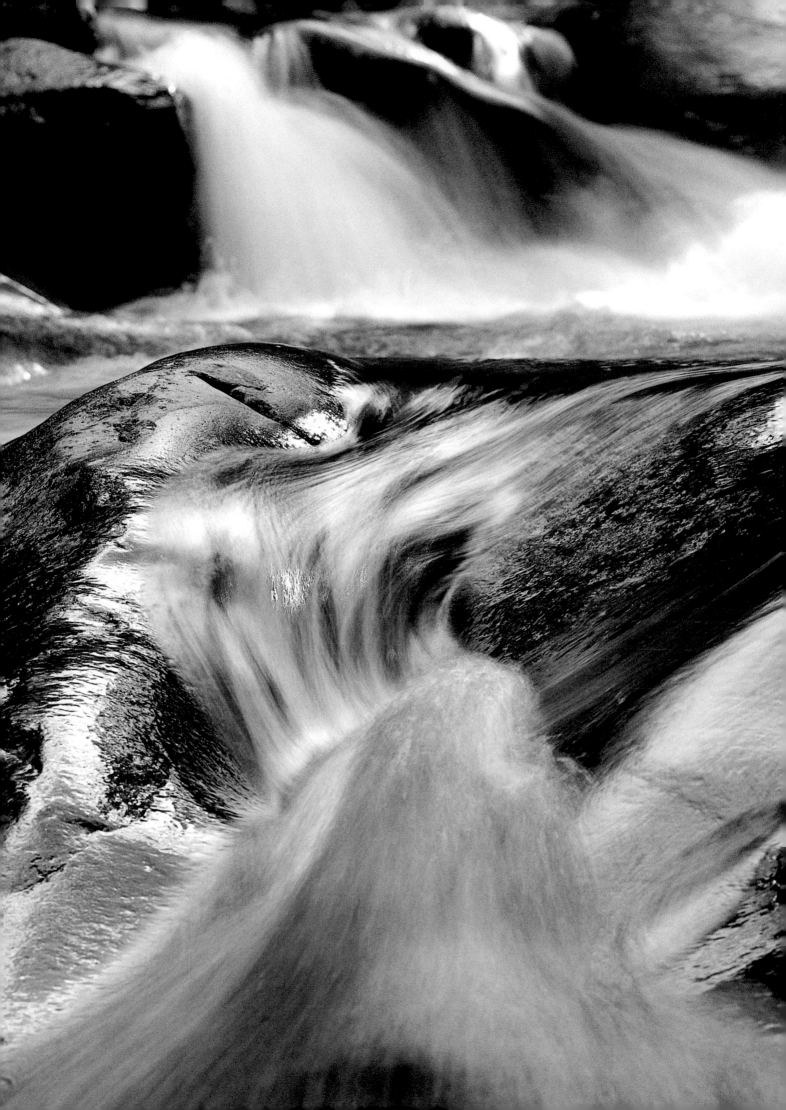

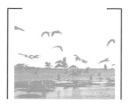

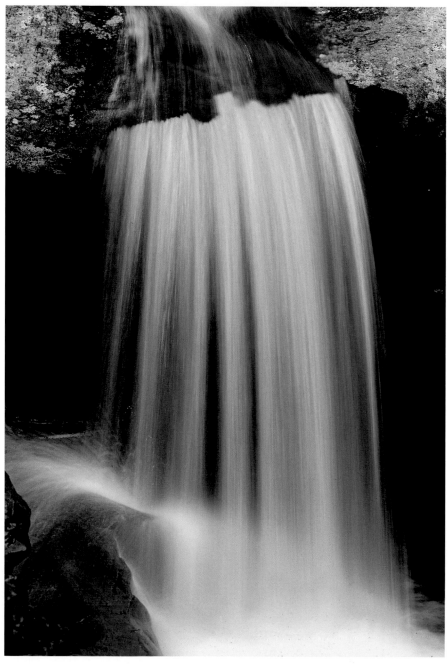

178 and 179 Great Smokies National Park is one of those unique places where it is impossible not to hear the sound of falling water almost anywhere within its half-million acres of forest and mountain. Storm systems moving across the Southeast rise and drop their moisture over the high crests of the Southern Appalachians, resulting in countless cascades that surge over polished rock and waterfalls that drop over frequent cliffs on the rugged slopes.

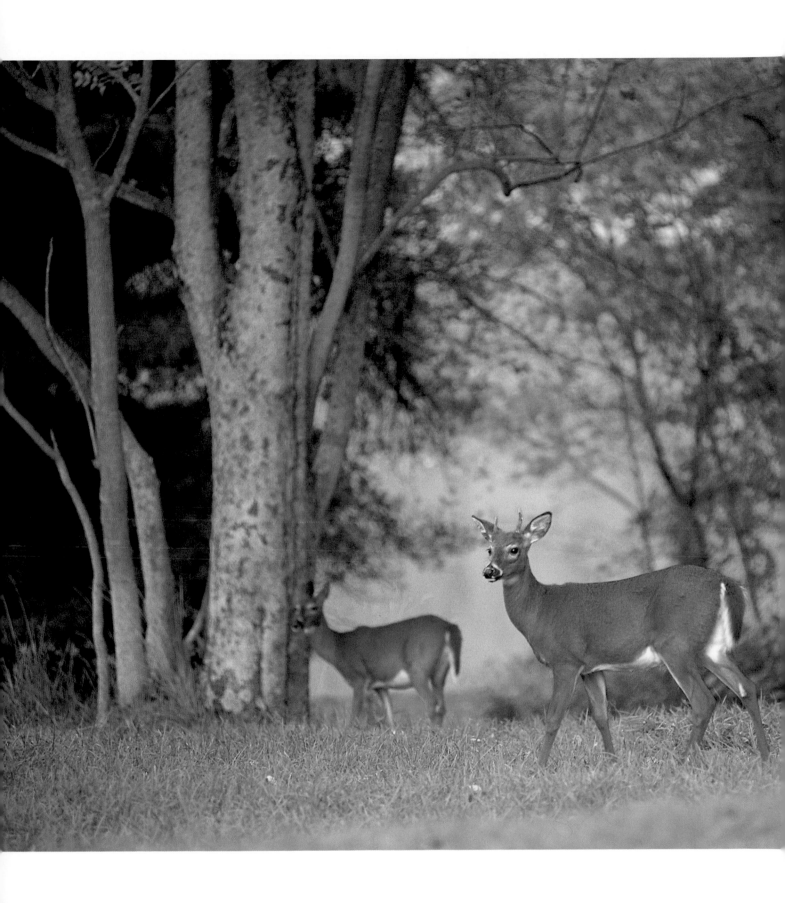

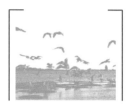

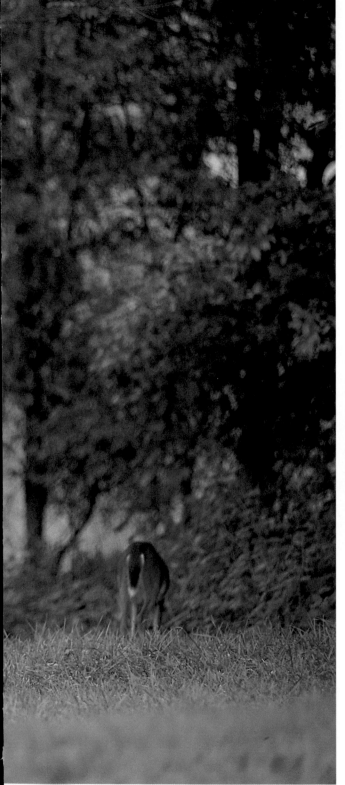

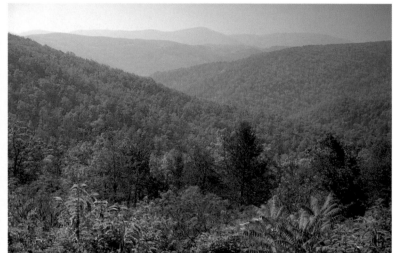

180–181 White-
tailed deer browse
an open meadow
in the Blue Ridge
Mountains in Virginia's
Shenandoah National
Park, where Skyline
Drive parallels the
course of the
Appalachian Trail
for 105 miles.

181 Maples, oaks, and
birches display early fall
colors on the crest of
the Blue Ridge
Mountains, which hold
one of the few extensive
remnants of hardwood
forests that once
blanketed the East from
the Atlantic to the
Mississippi.

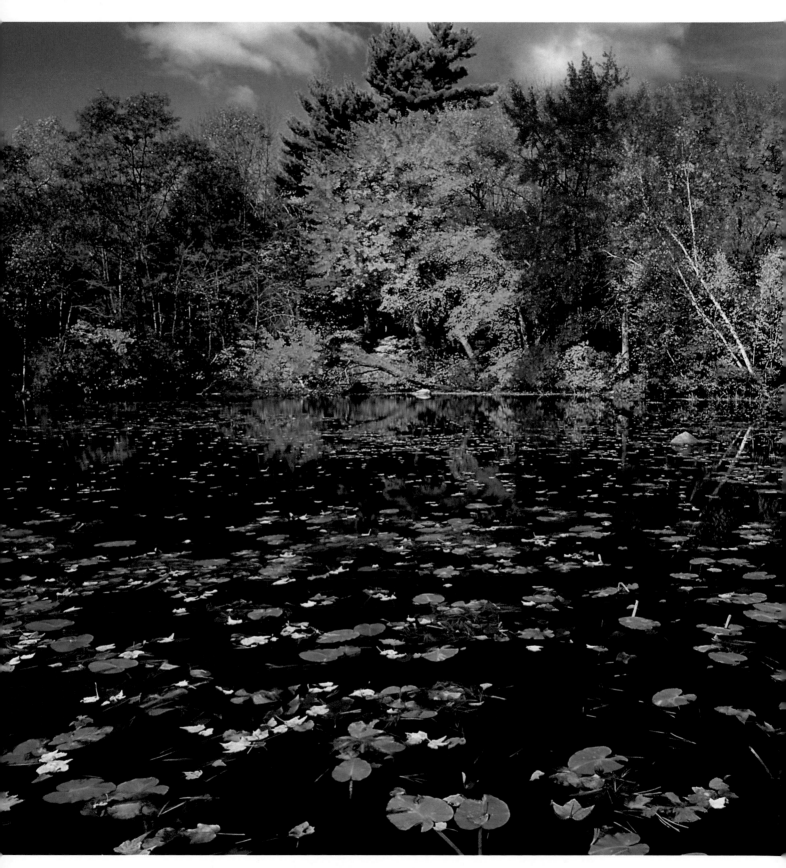

182–183 Punkatasset
Woods show the full
range of New England
fall colors over a pond
near Concord,
Massachusetts.

183 top A groundhog
appears after a winter
of hibernation in a
secluded forest area
of New York City's
Central Park.

183 center Late
afternoon backlight
intensifies fall colors
above Smalls Falls in
the deeply forested
interior of Maine.

183 bottom Maples
begin to turn their
famous fall colors in late
September in the dense
Maine Woods of Deer
Isle.

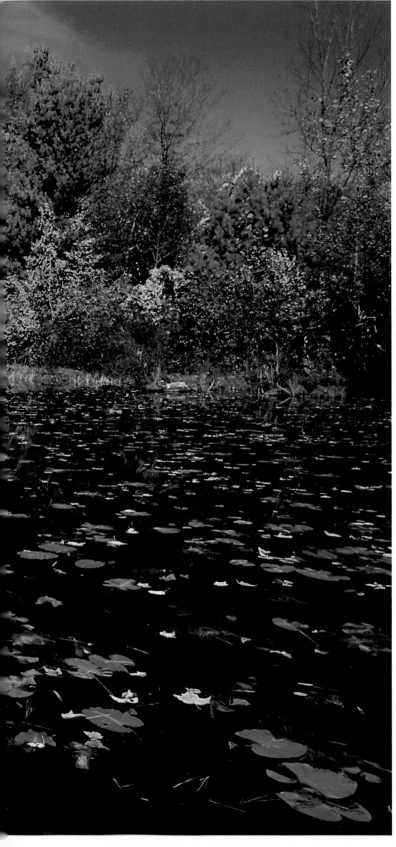

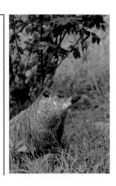

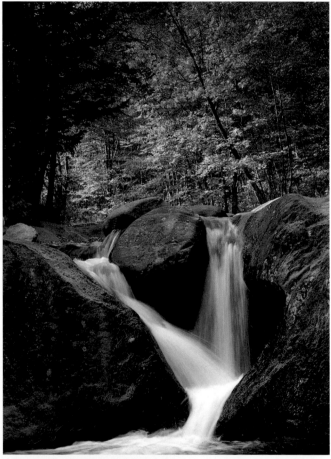

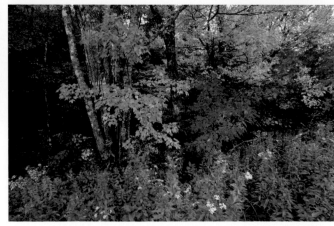

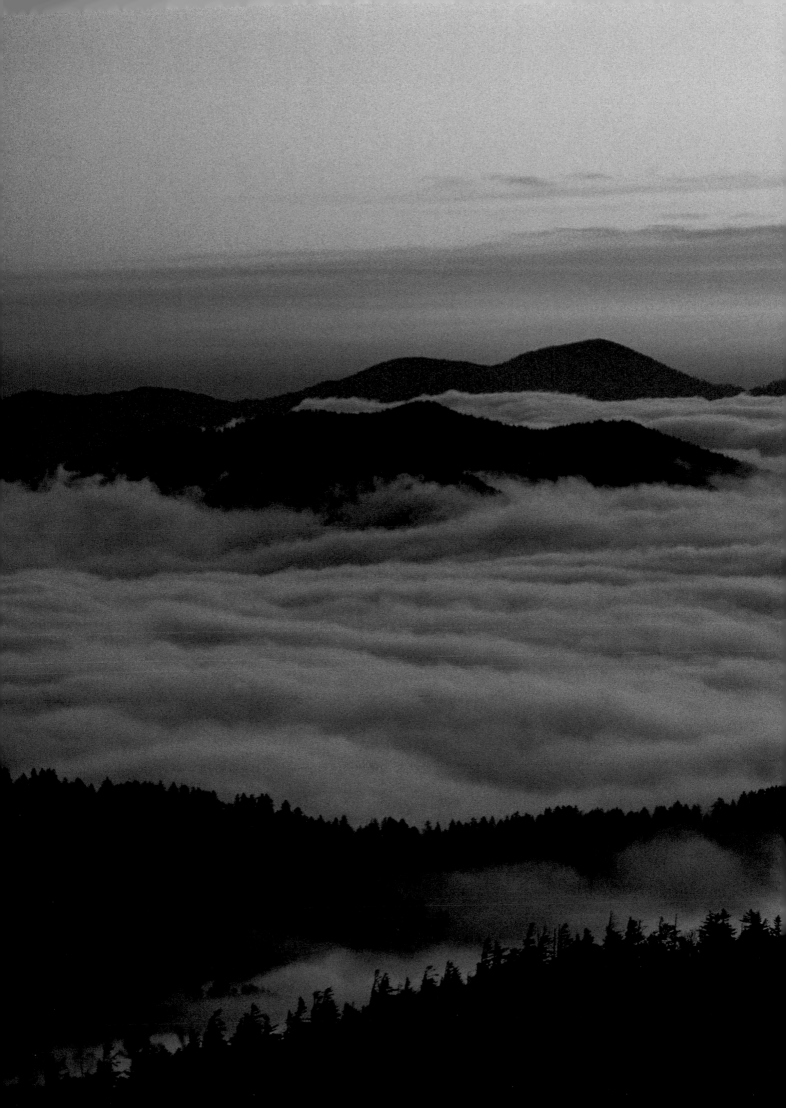

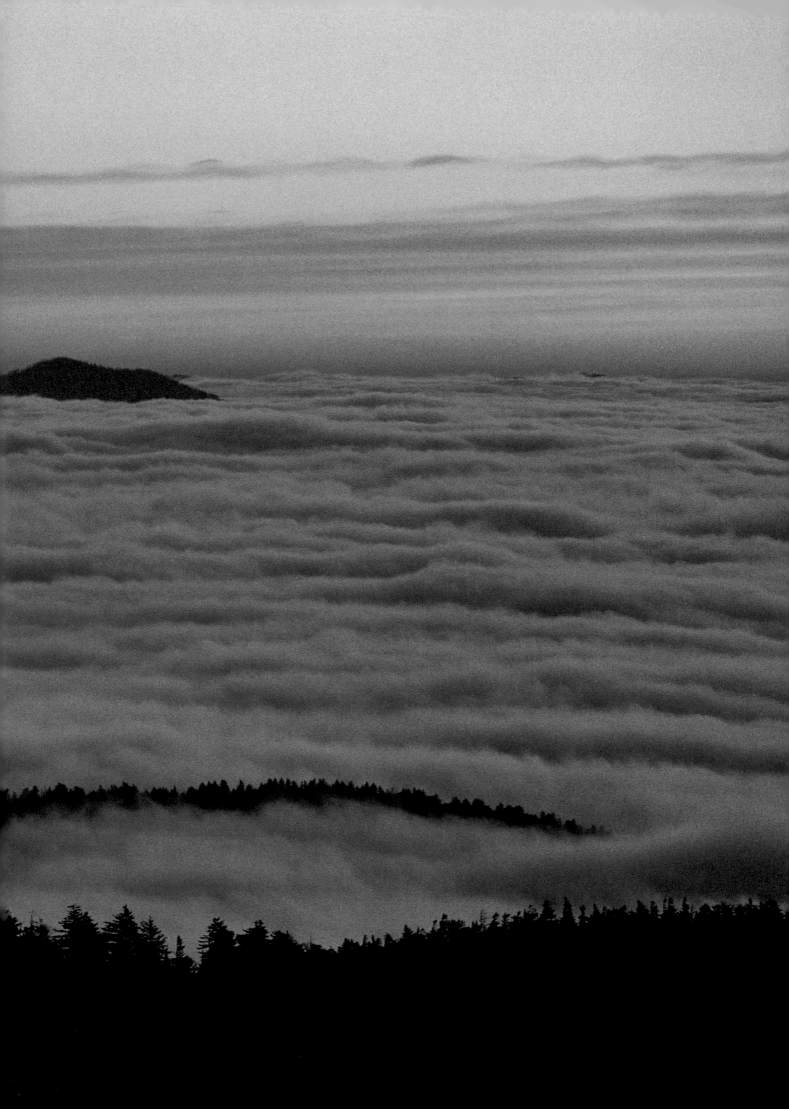

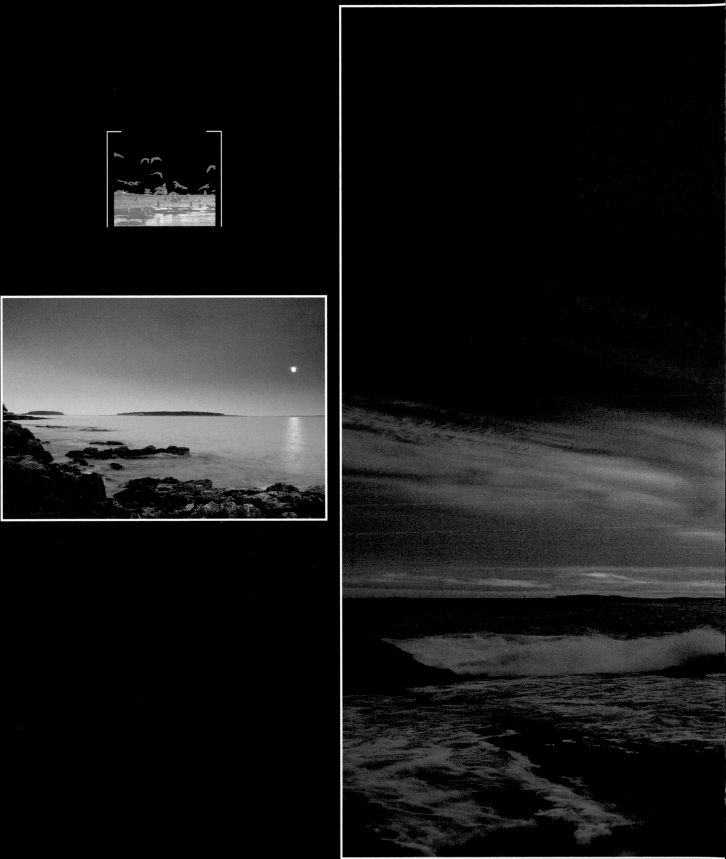

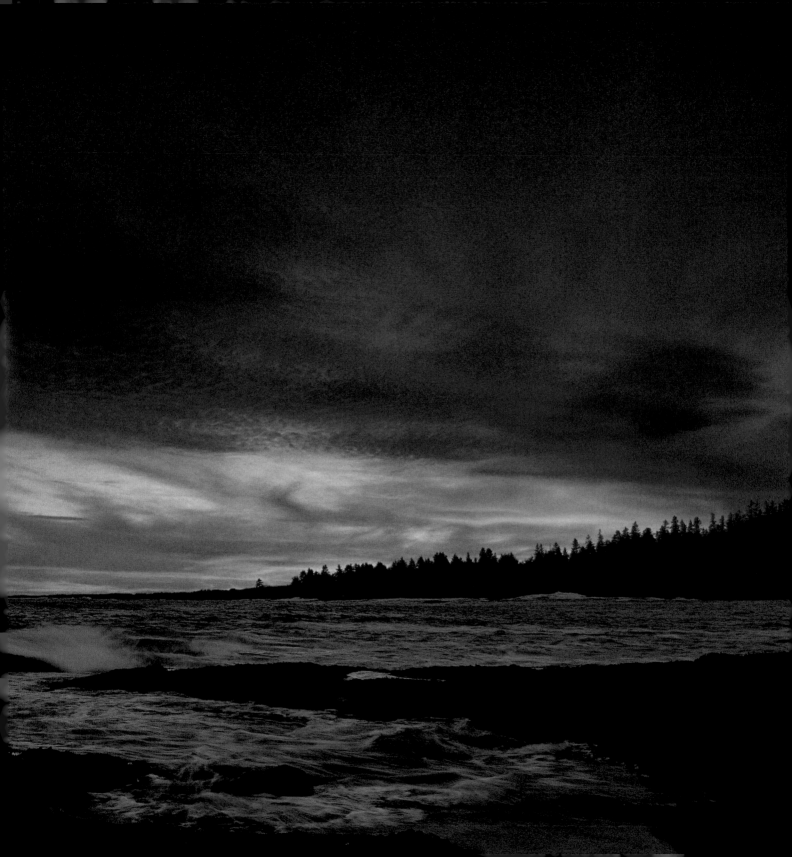

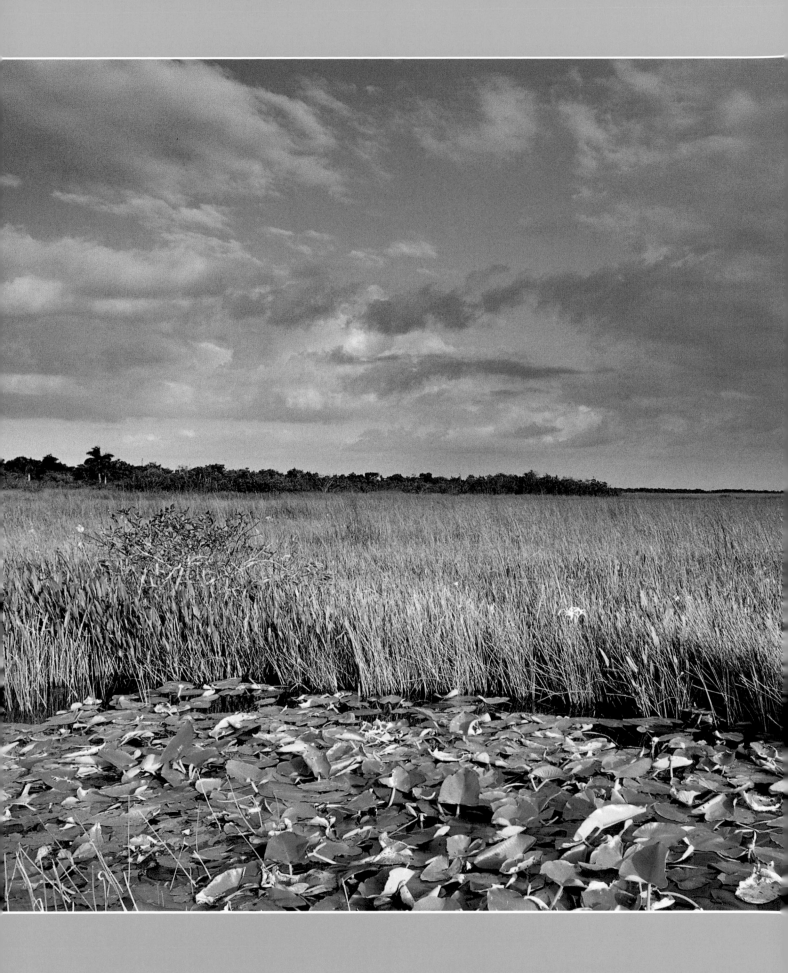

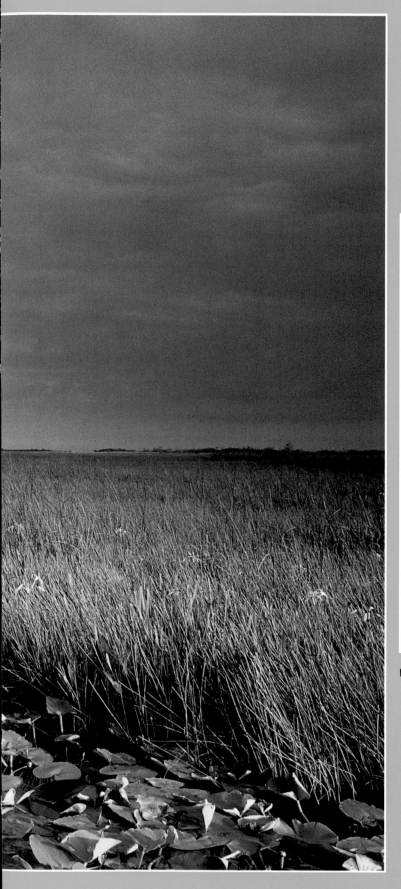

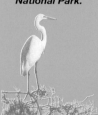

188–189 A river
of grass stretches
to the horizon from
the Anhinga Trail
in Everglades
National Park.

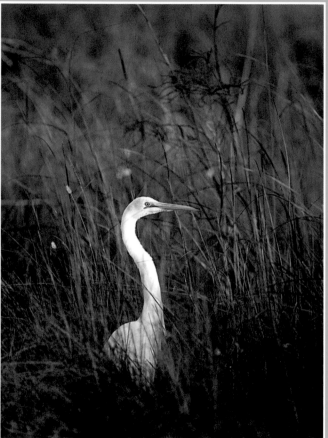

The Everglades

189 A great
egret stalks
the sawgrass prairie
of the Florida
Everglades
at dawn.

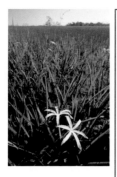

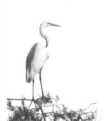

190 top Swamp lilies bloom in the flooded sawgrass prairie of Pah-hay-okee in Everglades National Park.

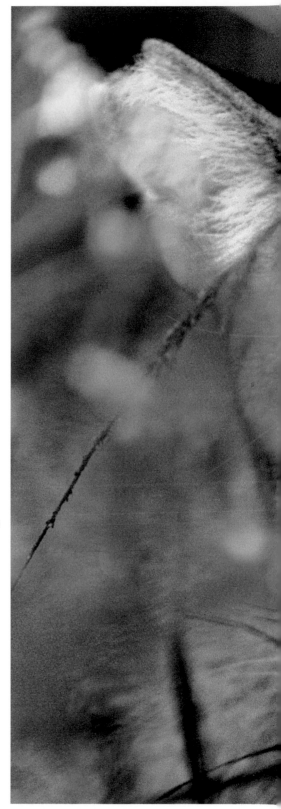

hen the Spaniard, Ponce de Leon, became the first European to tread on what is now the United States in 1513, he was seeking the fountain of youth. He landed on a massive peninsula bordering the Gulf of Mexico and called it Florida. Its southern half was indeed a fountain where the fresh waters of 730-square-mile Lake Okeechobee flowed southward in a broad sheet over a hundred miles long that averaged less than six inches deep. The dominant wetlands were submerged sawgrass prairie, with mangrove swamp, pineland, and hardwood hammock complicating potential settlement.

Indian arrows routed Ponce de Leon before he penetrated this watery expanse now known as the Everglades. In a geological sense, they really are a fountain of youth, existing for just the last 5,000 to 7,000 years as a semi-tropical freshwater marsh within a vast limestone basin only a few feet high, created while Near Eastern civilizations and global sea levels were simultaneously rising after the last ice age. By comparison, the rocks of the Canadian Shield are 3,000 to 4,500 *million* years old.

The fragile flowing lake and rain water that takes up to two years to reach the ocean created an ecological Eden—a subtropical garden filled with millions of birds, mammals, and wildflowers that bloom all year. Here where tropical and temperate species merge, giant orchids are found near pine forests. The American alligator is the top water predator, with the Florida panther at the top of land predators. Both have been listed as Endangered or Threatened. With humans now atop this fragile, unique food chain, the National Park Service has called Everglades "the most threatened of U.S. national parks."

The Everglades ecosystem has four national park areas—Everglades, Big Cypress, Biscayne, and Dry Tortugas—plus designations as an International Biosphere Reserve, a World Heritage Site, and a Wetland of International Significance. The tale of its decline goes back to what Ponce de Leon was seeking and what American retirees believed they were finding as they began flocking to Florida's warm climate at the beginning of the twentieth century: a place to extend their lives in comfort. They soon wanted not only to drink from the natural fountain but also to divert it from flooding their towns and farmlands during the wet season. Local boosters fostered the 1969 selection of the Everglades as the site for world's largest airport. The plan to bulldoze 39 square miles to service 65 million passengers a year was defeated only when Big Cypress National Preserve adjoining the Everglades park was created in 1974.

The fragile Everglades National Park ecosystem has a maximum elevation difference, from the highest pine ridge to the bottom of huge Florida Bay (bigger than many states) of just 14 feet. After World War II, more than 1,000 miles of levees, dikes, and canals were constructed, routinely shunting billions of gallons of potential Everglades water into the ocean. Wading bird populations have dropped more than 90 percent, yet at the right time, particular ponds and sloughs still appear to teem with some of North America's largest and most colorful birds. In

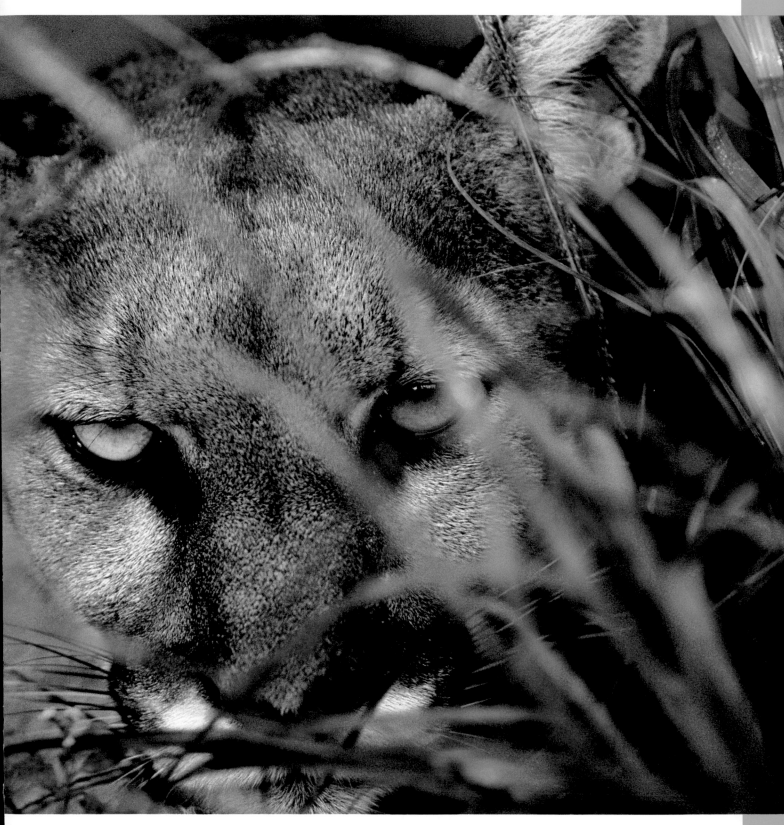

190 bottom
A swallowtail butterfly gathers nectar from a flower beside Shark Slough in Everglades National Park.

190–191 An extremely endangered Florida panther peers out of Everglades grasses in the large enclosure of an animal rehabilitation facility beside Everglades National Park. Before major efforts to save the species were made in the 1980s, this southern race of mountain lion was reduced to less than thirty in south Florida by hunting and massive habitat destruction.

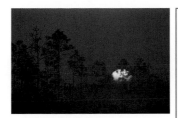

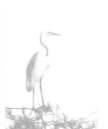

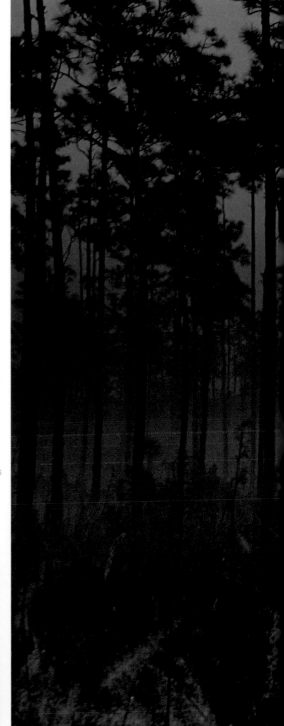

the old days, herons and ibises were counted by acres, not individuals.

After my first trip to the Everglades in the late 1970s, I took it for granted that the Anhinga Trail, just four miles from the park entrance, would always have herons, egrets, ibis, and anhinga within camera shot of the boardwalk during the prime winter season. After all, the trail runs beside Taylor Slough, one of the park's major waterways from Lake Okeechobee. On a later trip I found only parched earth in the slough and no birds.

Though I created a good collection of photographs over the course of several Everglades trips, I decided to go back for five days at the end of October 1998 on assignment for my 1999 World Wildlife Fund book, *Living Planet*.

To my present surprise, every one of the Everglades photographs selected for that book as well as this one were from that recent outing where mists rose at dawn in the pinelands, alligators basked beside the Turner River of Big Cypress for hours, and sunsets turned every shade, reflected in the waters of a wet year.

Despite massive environmental problems and a human population expected to double in fifty years, southern Florida still has a tremendous wealth of wildness. Many of the best known older sites continue to be the best places to photograph, with boardwalk access and creatures habituated to harmless human approach. In the large parking lot at Shark River Slough (where about half the Everglades waters pass) I photographed a red-shouldered hawk with a snake in its talons perched in a tree just above arm's reach. On the Anhinga Trail, I used a normal lens with flash fill in the shadows from just four feet to make the anhiga portrait in this book. As I continued down the trail, the bird never moved.

Whether the Everglades survive the next century depends not only upon billions of dollars of Congressional appropriations for major acquisitions and restorations, but whether people will care enough to consider the Everglades as sacred ground as the Parthenon or Westminster Abbey. If not, these wild wetlands are doomed. As Everglades Park Superintendent Richard Ring puts it, "Unless we figure out a way that changes how we grow and build, the built system is going to continue to move into the natural system."

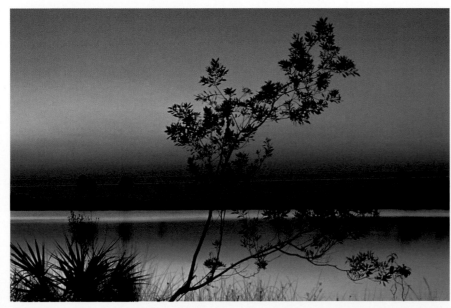

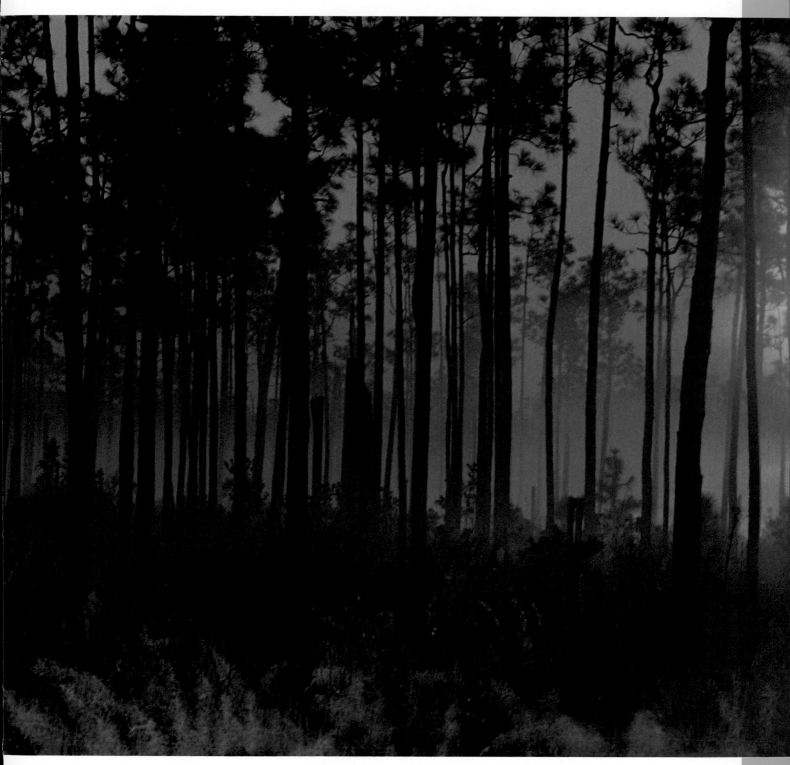

192 bottom A sunset over Pineglades Lake in Everglades National Park merges the separate worlds of mangrove, pine, palmetto, and water.

192–193 Sunrise colors rising mists on Long Pine Key, an area of pine forest that grows atop limestone bedrock elevated about two feet above the seasonal flooding of the Everglades. Nearby Rock Reef Pass, the highest point in the national park, is all of three feet above sea level. These tree islands are home for many large animals of the Everglades, as well as 30 species of endemic plants.

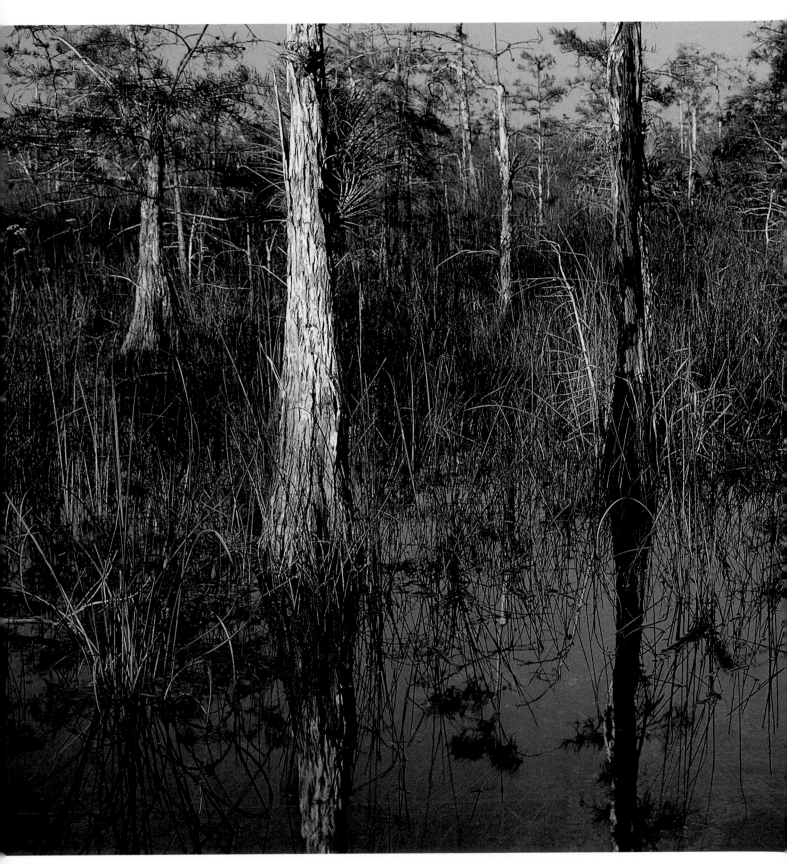

194–195 A cypress swamp at Pah-hay-okee is typical habitat for water birds as well as rare key deer and river otters.

195 top A red-shouldered hawk perches out of the noonday sun on the limb of a Shark Valley tree, shortly before pouncing on a snake.

195 center An anhinga dries its feathers in the morning sun after a dive in Taylor Slough beside the Anhinga Trail.

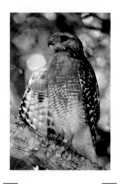

198 The stately great egret, frozen in position in search of fish, is the symbol of the National Audubon Society.

198–199 A tricolored heron stalks through sawgrass prairie in Shark Valley near the Tamiami Trail.

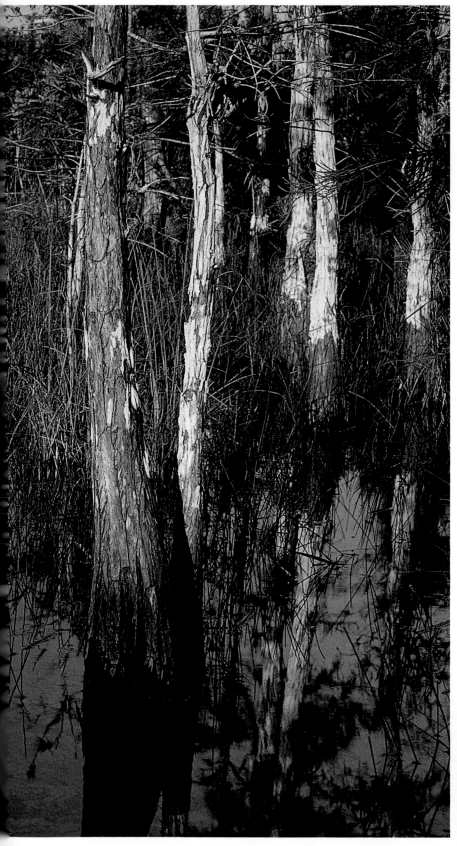

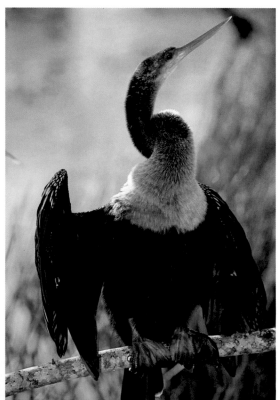

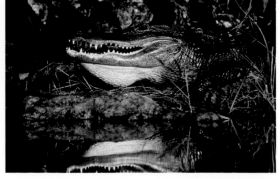

195 bottom An alligator basks beside the Turner River in Big Cypress National Preserve, north of Everglades National Park.

196–197 The sun breaks under evening clouds over Pine Glades Lake in Everglades National Park.

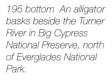

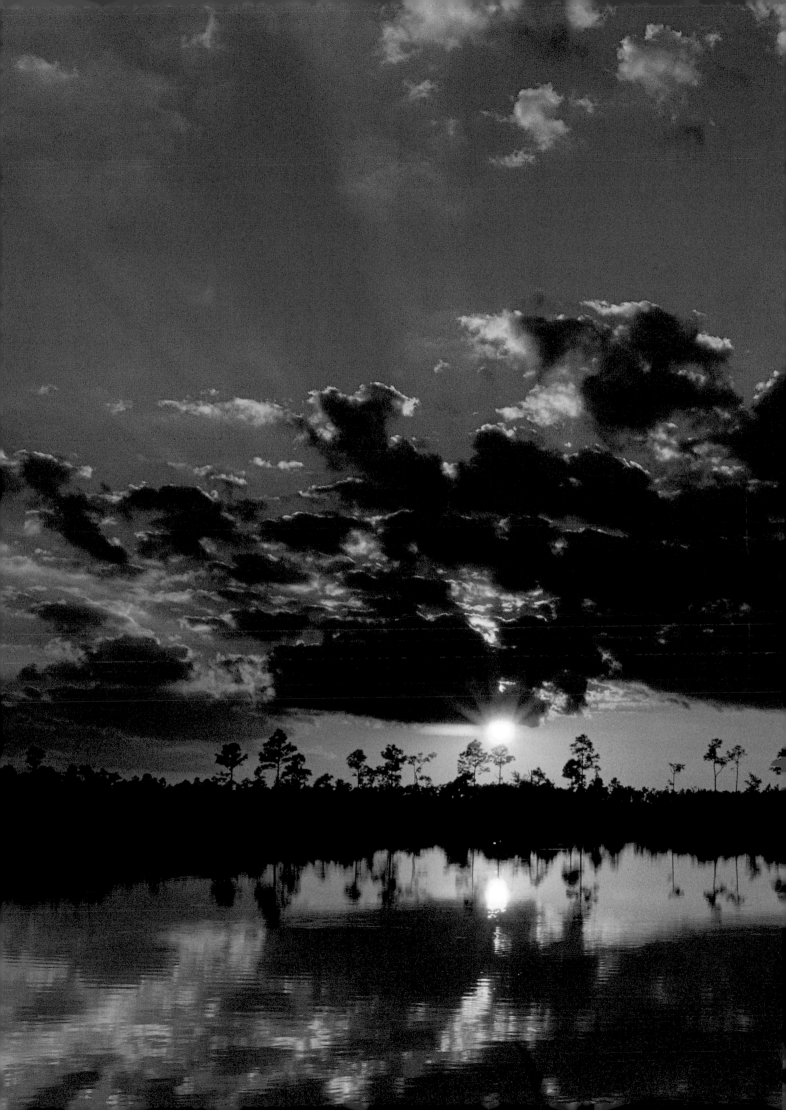

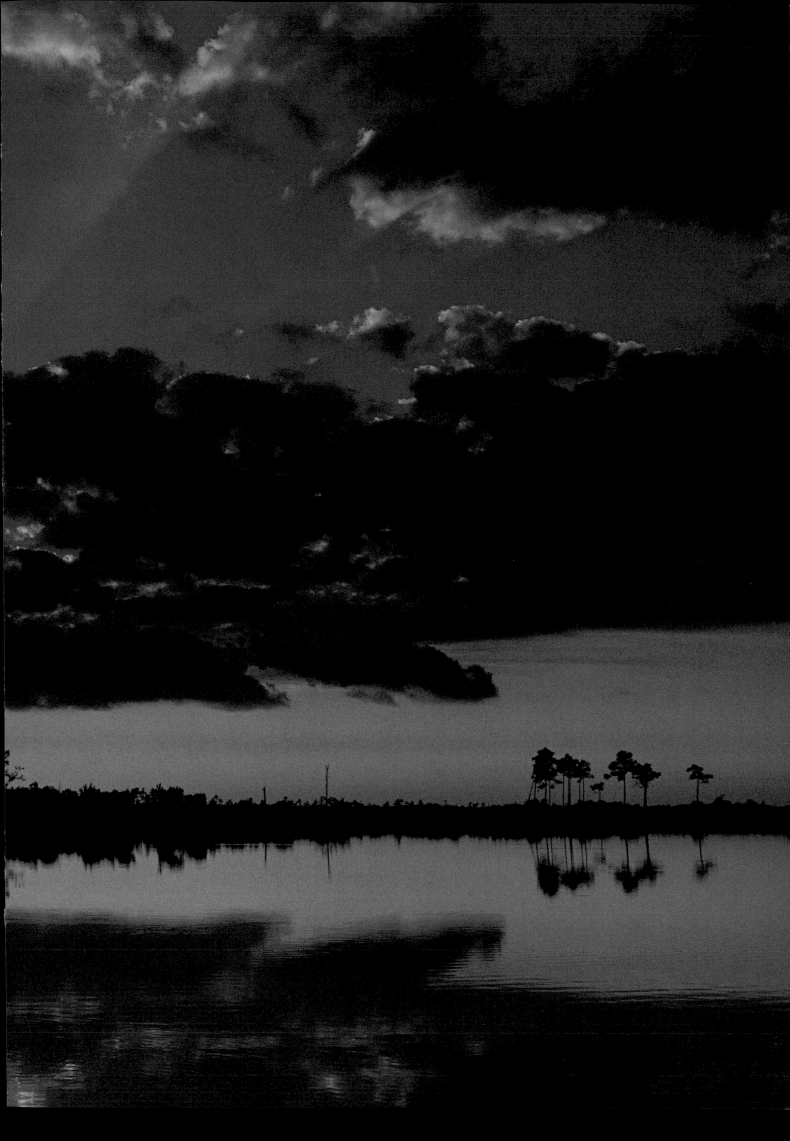

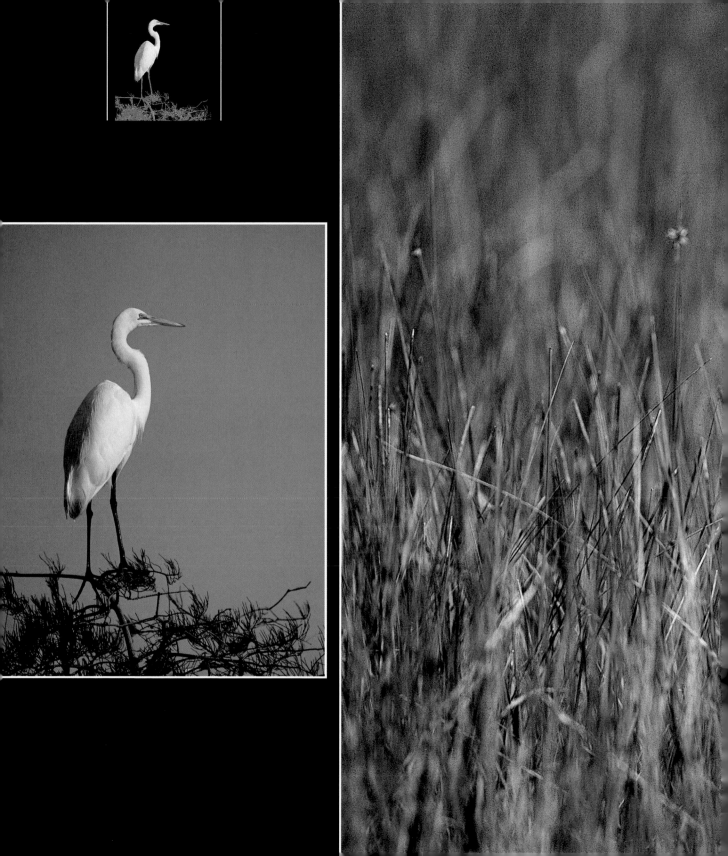

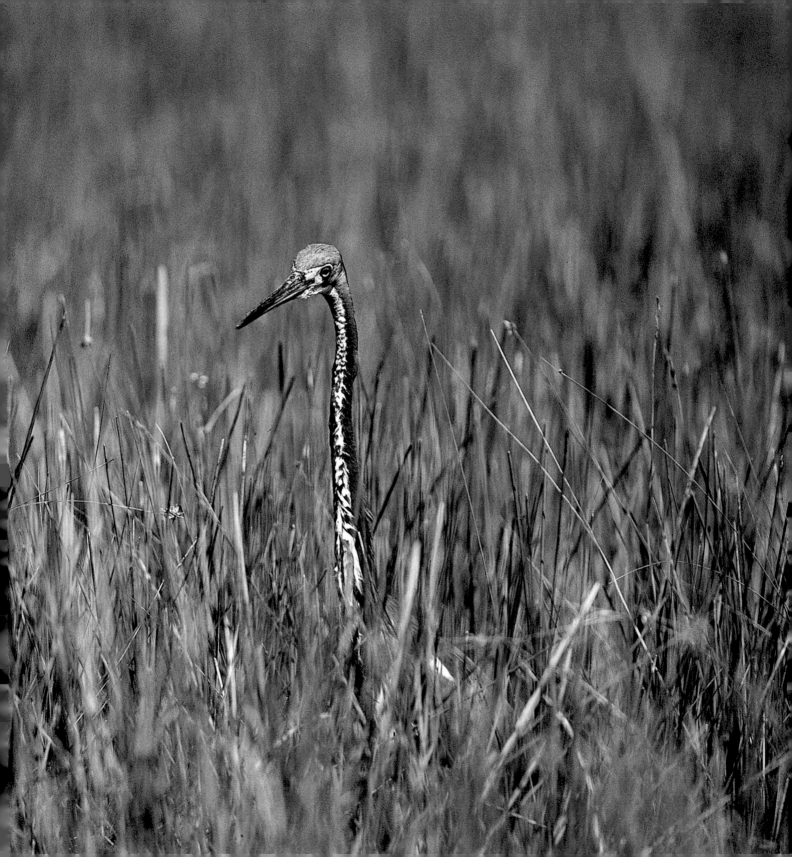

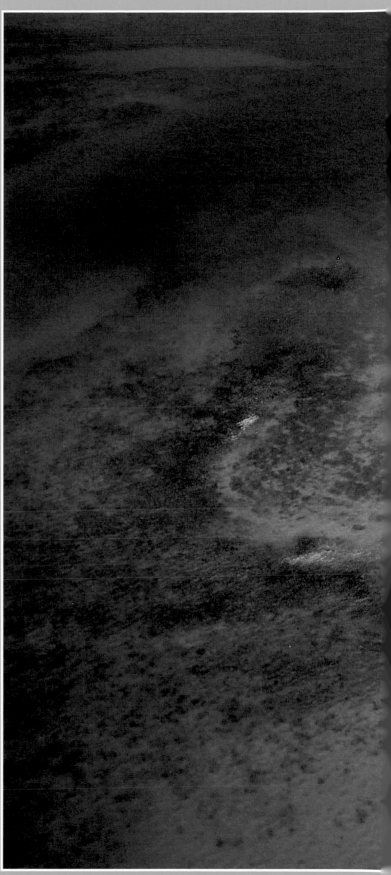

200 Dominica became known as "The Nature Island" because it holds the best preserved natural habitat of the Caribbean Islands.

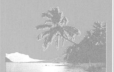

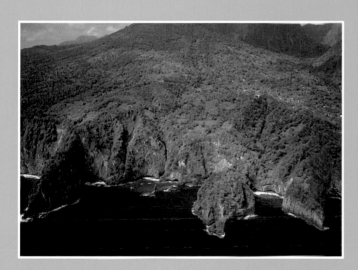

The Caribbean

200–201 A tiny island of coral sands and palms off the coast of Anguilla symbolizes the universal appeal of the Caribbean.

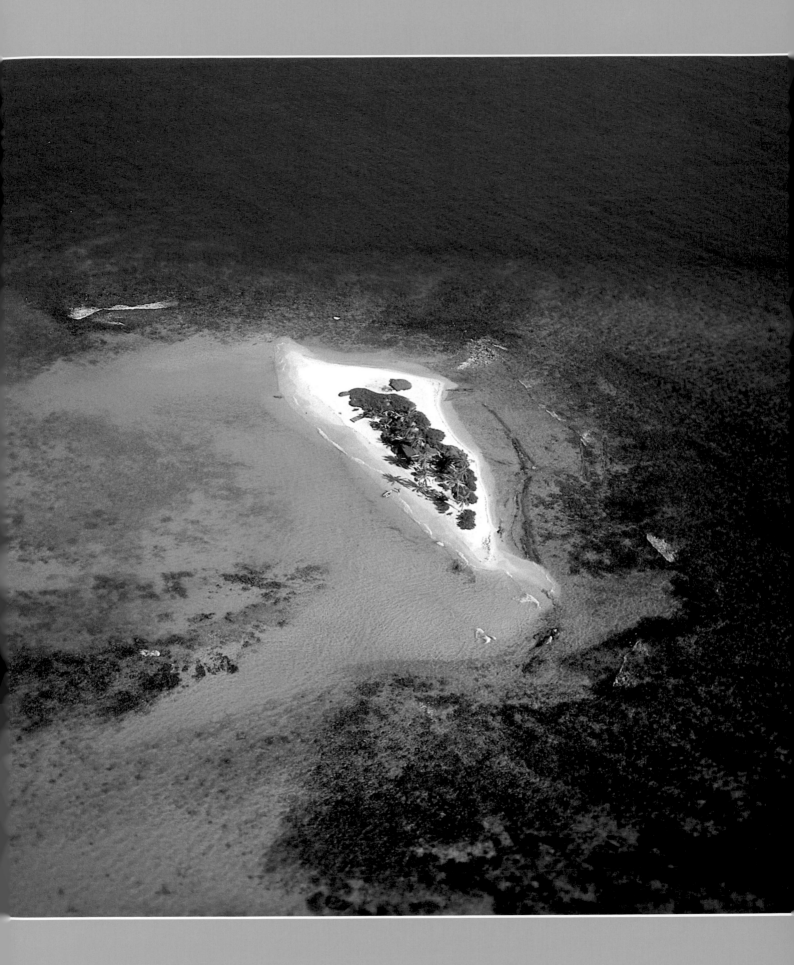

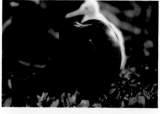

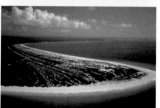

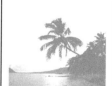

202 top A male frigatebird inflates its throat to attract a mate in a mangrove swamp on Barbuda Island.

202 center Empty white beaches arc around the rest of the little island.

Many Americans speak of vacationing "in the Caribbean" like going to Hawaii, but this most politically and geographically complex part of North America is hardly a singular place. Here in 1492 about 400 miles out to sea in a string of islands that stretch a thousand miles from near Florida almost to Venezuela, a terribly confused Italian sailor named Christopher Columbus proclaimed for Spain the discovery of what he called "The West Indies." He believed he had found a passage to Asia. After he fell out of favor with Spanish royalty, the New World became known as America, named for his provision contractor, Amerigo Vespucci, who made later voyages of his own.

Days before touching shore, Columbus anticipated a vast land mass by the large numbers of birds passing over his ship. Modern ornithologists suspect he saw only pelagic shearwaters and petrels that live far out at sea. He made landfall in the long irregular chain of the Bahamas, now an independent nation. A second voyage reached the major island of the Greater Antilles now known as Cuba. Columbus thought it was the Asian mainland. On his fourth and final voyage, Columbus cruised the Central American coast, looking for the Ganges.

He never landed anywhere in what became the continental United States.

Few of the islands ended up under Spanish control as the British, Danish, Dutch, French, Irish and Swedes fought bitterly with each other, the natives, and pirates such as Blackbeard and Captain Kidd. The United States gained Puerto Rico in 1898 after the Spanish-American War and three of the Virgin Islands from the Danish in 1917. A federal study in the thirties recommended against a Virgin Islands national park because of altered flora and fauna. Expansive sugar cane fields had been overrun by mongoose introduced to control rats escaped from ships. Forests were second or third growth. Only after the Rockefeller family bought most of St. John Island to donate much of it as a park did Congress establish one in 1956. The coast is deservedly the main attraction. The coral sands of Trunk Bay have been rated as one of the world's top ten beaches. The world's first signed "underwater trail" is beneath the surface and not a single high-rise hotel rises over the lush surrounding forests.

Other major islands have not been so lucky. Cane plantations, population expansion, poverty, and mass tourism have taken their toll, leaving surprisingly little land in its natural condition. Politics, crime, and overpopulation have run amok over their

wildness as effectively as affluence has paved Nassau in the Bahamas.

When my wife and I island-hopped through the Caribbean in her small airplane, we decided each day where to spend the night. Though we landed in the Dominican Republic, where Pico Duarte crowns the Caribbean at 10,400 feet, we sought out the smaller islands of the Lesser Antilles, such as Anguilla, known for its incredible turquoise water and white sands. On nearby Barbuda a local fisherman poled us through a mangrove swamp in his small dory to photograph a large nesting colony of frigatebirds.

The four Greater Antilles – Cuba, Puerto Rico, Jamaica, and Hispaniola (split into Haiti and the Dominican Republic) – also have areas in natural condition. Half an hour's drive from San Juan, Puerto Rico is the El Yunque rain forest. Farther afield are some of America's most extensive limestone caves. Fifty miles offshore, the island of Mona is a nature refuge that has been called the "Galapágos of the Caribbean," uninhabited except for research scientists and visitors on special permits.

Our most spectacular aerial view was looking down at jade and turquoise waters surrounding the green hills of the Grenadines as white surf broke over coral reefs just below the surface. Our favorite ground visit was on Dominica, rightly called "The Nature Island." Volcanic peaks rising to nearly 5,000 feet draw 300 inches of annual rainfall out of passing clouds, far more than elsewhere in the Caribbean. In the midst of lush vegetation, reached by a wild jungle trail past cascading streams and waterfalls, is the "Boiling Lake," once billed as the only such body of water in the world (the only other one is in New Zealand). Abundant water flowing into an active volcanic steam vent continuously bubbles at the boiling point, despite temperatures that would evaporate all the water away in more arid conditions.

We spent other days on Tobago's coral beaches, beside St. Lucia's 2,000-foot forested Pitons, and around North Cacos's flamingo ponds, before a final night beneath cruise ships in the Bahamas en route to Miami, the northern gateway to the Caribbean.

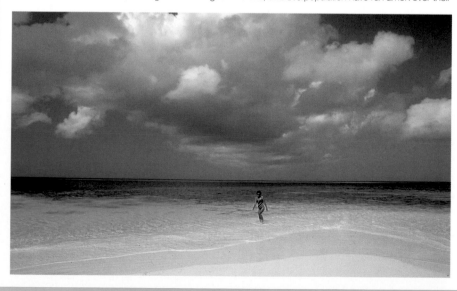

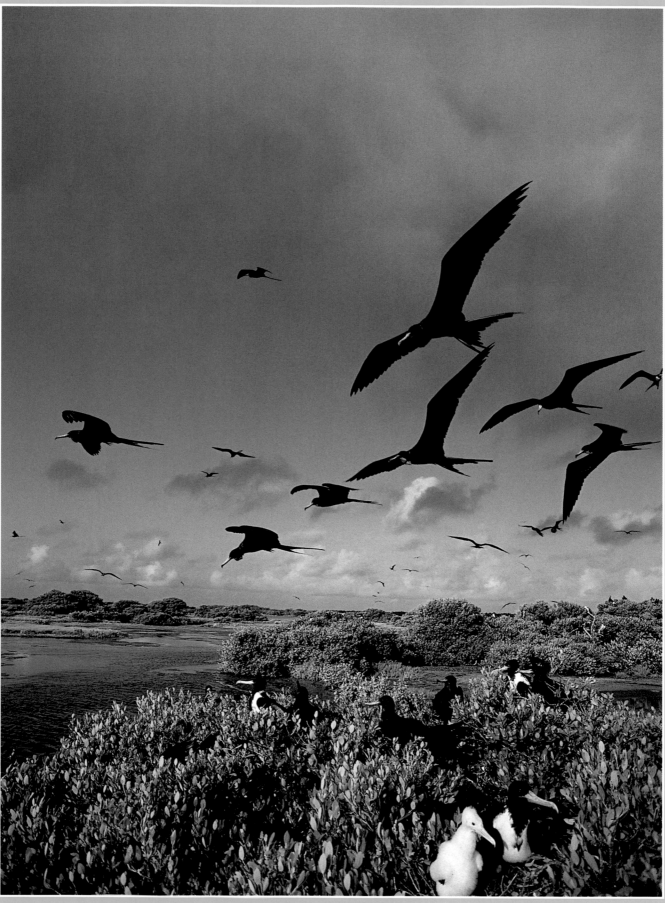

202 bottom
Emblematic of the
Caribbean, the white
coral sands and
turquoise waters of
Barbuda Island
remain pristine
because of limited
access and few
accomodations other
than a $1500-per-
night resort.

203 Far off the
beaten track of
normal tourists, a
breeding colony of
magnificent
frigatebirds thrive in
a mangrove swamp
on the inner shores
of an uninhabited
Barbuda bay.

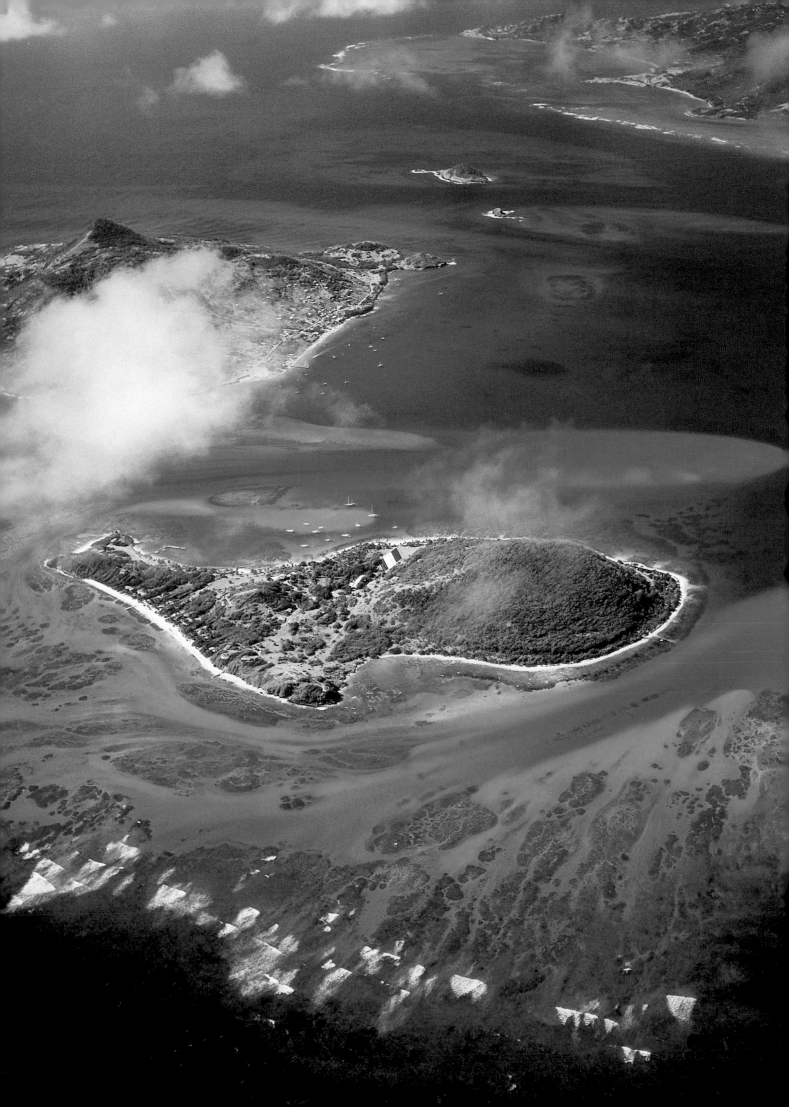

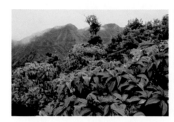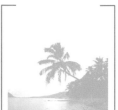

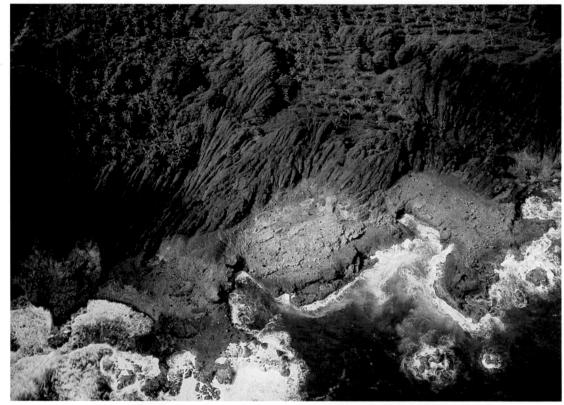

205 bottom The double spouts of Trafalgar Falls pour through tropical rainforest from the 5,000-foot heights of the wild island of Dominica.

206 A tiny sailboat glides through shallow turquoise waters colored by a coral reef not far below the surface in the northern Bahamas, close enough to Florida for weekend sailors to enjoy.

206–207 A long exposure of the rugged coral shores of Anguilla's Road Bay turns breaking waves to silky mist. Once the Caribbean's best-kept secret with little rain and white coral sands, Anguilla now touts world-class resorts.

204 White surf breaks over a barely submerged coral reef surrounding the Grenadine Islands, as seen from a small airplane. Stretching from St. Vincent to Grenada, the islands have been called the most beautiful sailing waters in the world.

205 top Lush jungle carpets the heights of Dominica beside the trail to the island's famous boiling lake, heated by a volcanic steam vent.

205 center Seen from the air, the hurricane-blown pattern of natural forests on the shore of Dominica stands out from the ordered arrangement of one of the island's few palm plantations.

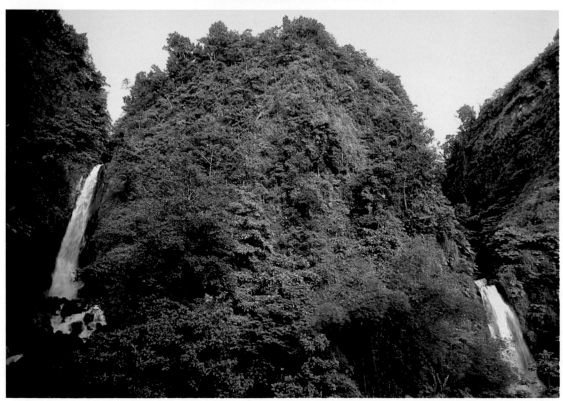

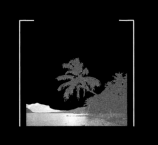

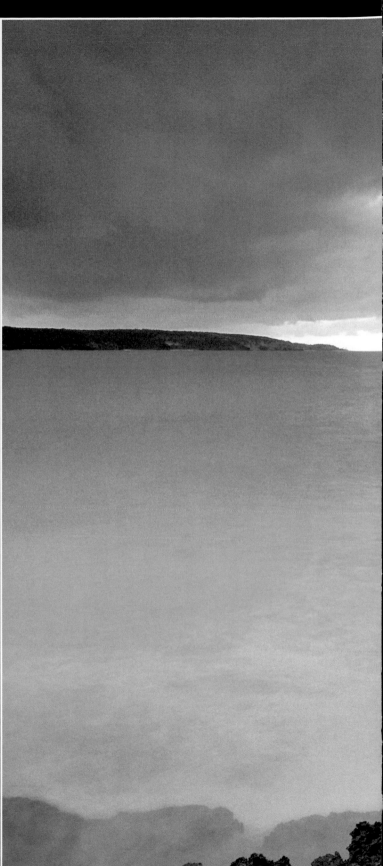

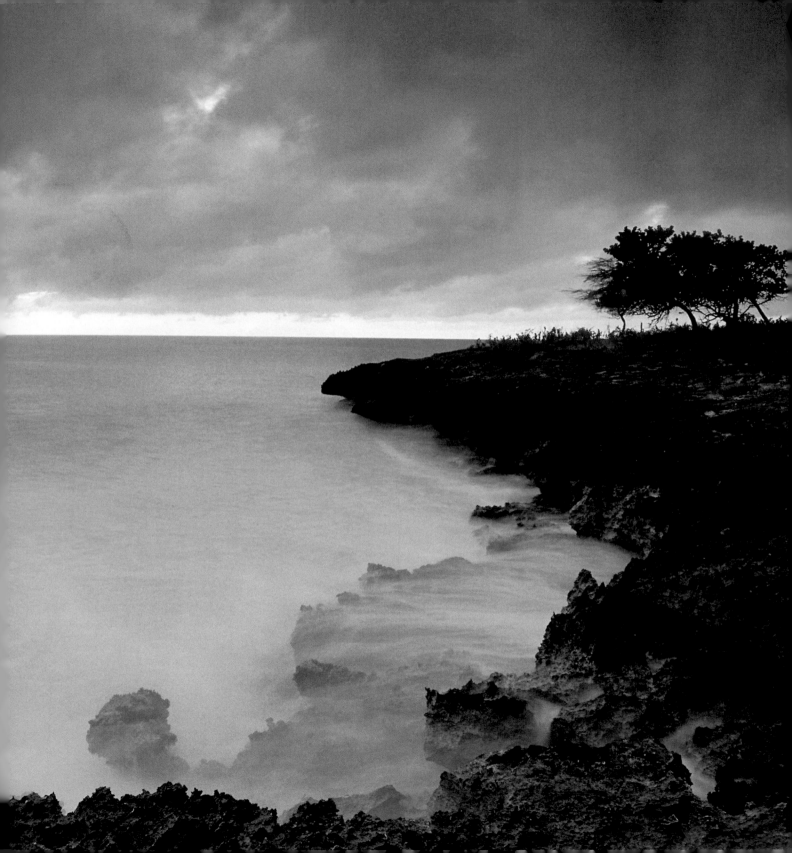

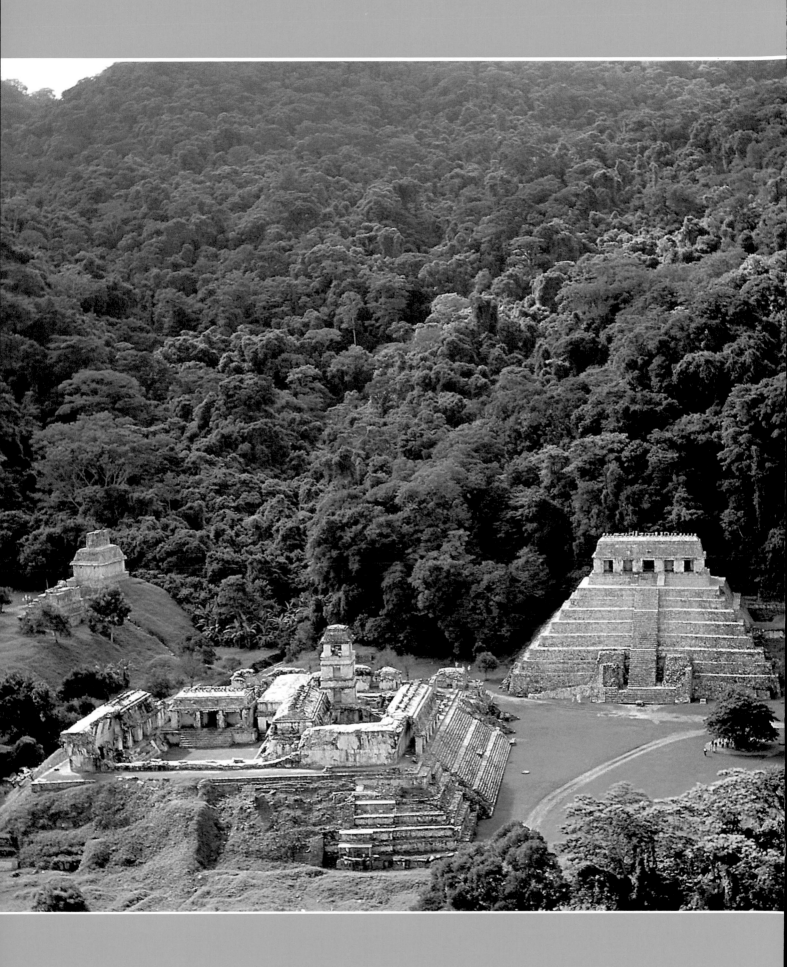

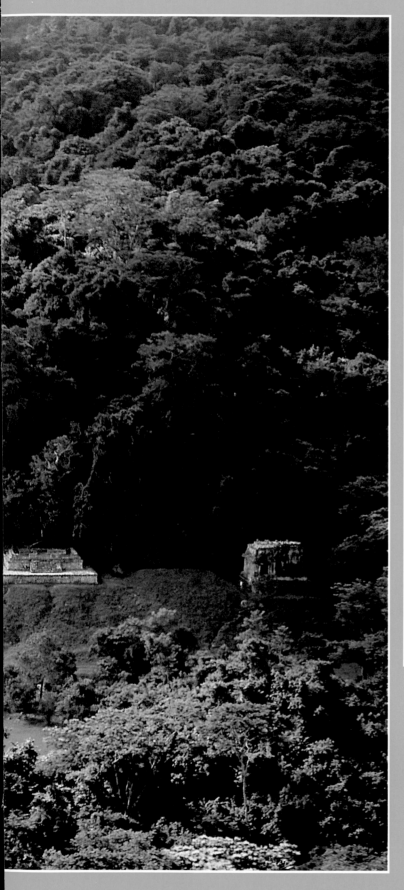

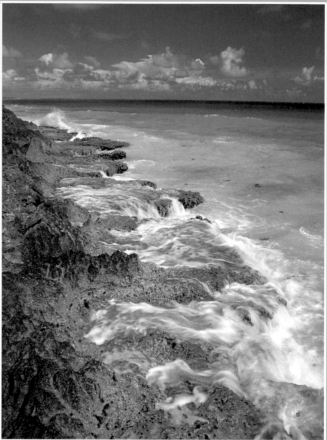

The Mexican Mainland

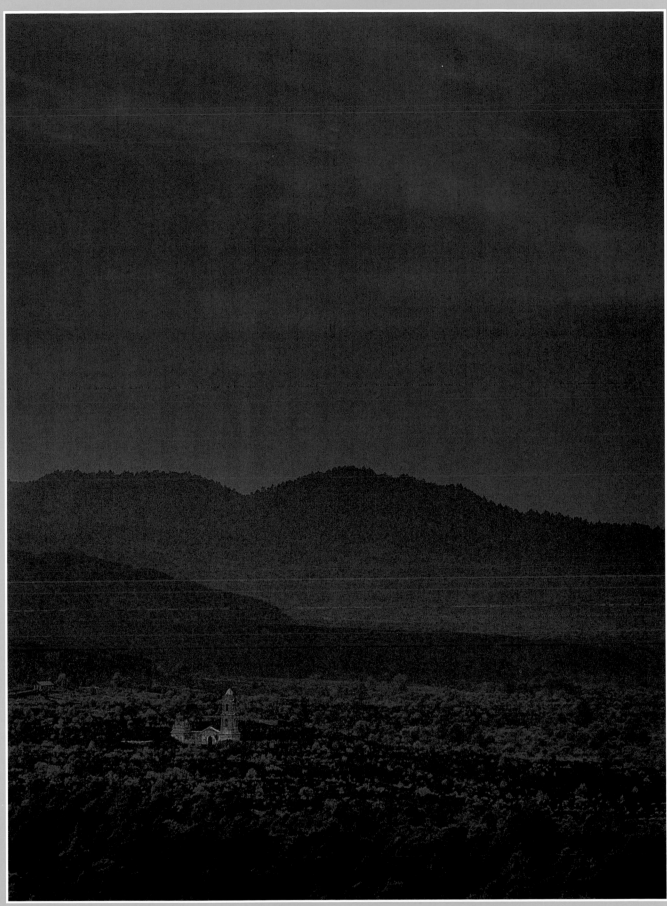

210 A church steeple rising out of bare lava is all that can be seen of the Indian village of San Juan de Parangaricutiro in Michoacán. In 1943, a volcano erupted out of nowhere in a farmer's corn field. The village, several miles away, was buried by the flow of molten lava. The brand new conical volcano, rising 1,500 feet above the former fields, became known as Volcán Paracutín.

211 top A lake in the highlands of the Sierra Madre reflects the wonderful colors of sunrise in the state of Guanajuato.

211 center In the Michoacán mountains near El Rosario, up to 100 million monarch butterflies winter in a fir forest, comprising the entire population from the Atlantic to the Rocky Mountains from both the United States and Canada. The now-protected area was only found in 1974 by a Canadian biologist who spent 40 years searching for these 100 acres of monarch wintering grounds.

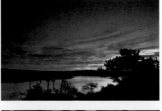

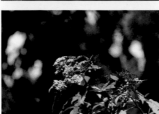

211 bottom
Cacti rise into a predawn sky like organ pipes atop a 9,000-foot ridge near Tapalpa in Jalisco.

"To see Mexico from the air," attests Mexican writer Carlos Fuentes, "is to look upon the face of creation... a portrait of water and fire, of wind and earthquake, of the moon and the sun." When my wife and I flew the entire length of Mexico in her small plane, we sensed the same elemental glory from afar, along with a powerful desire to get down on the ground and experience its multicolored culture and landscape in person.

Mexico is indeed water, 6,000 miles of coastline lined with rugged cliffs, deep harbors, white beaches, and warm turquoise waters on both its Pacific and Caribbean sides. It is also fire erupting from 17,888-foot Popocatépetl and 11,500-foot Volcán de Fuego as I write these words. These peaks of the Cordillera Neovolcánica are among the most consistently active volcanoes in North America, culminating in the dormant cone of 18,503-foot Orizaba.

Hurricane winds sometimes rip the teeming inland jungles and palm-beached east coast of the Yucatán, while 8-point tremblors periodically shake the western highlands around the juncture of three tectonic plates. Yet spending a week soon after a massive hurricane in a traditional beach bungalow at Akumal was to hardly be aware that a storm had passed, except for newly naked palms and disturbed coral reefs below the surface. To visit Miamified Cancún, an hour to the north, was to experience far greater devastation of the Mexican landscape.

We found Fuentes' moonscapes in the heart of ancient craters near León, filled with cracked alkali from eons of evaporation with no outlet. Worship of the sun, so central to Mayan cosmology, came across to us not only in the ancient ruins of Chichén Itzá, Palenque, and Tulum, but also in this day and age along the Mexican Riviera. Here beside the Pacific, some of the earth's most consistent coastal sunshine lures millions into a realm where no two places are alike. We saw the flamboyance of Mazatlán, the high-rise indulgence

of Puerto Vallarta, the unpretentiousness of Barra de Navidad, the gated seclusion of a Club Med, and the decline of the ancient port of Manzanillo. Farther south, the old pueblo of Zihuatenejo, with its narrow streets and beachfront cafes, outwardly resembles the Italian Riviera, while romantic Acapulco Bay, where sport divers leap high cliffs and bikinis outnumber skirts, is like nowhere else.

This incredible variety of experience continues across the central plateau of the Sierra Madre Occidental, averaging 6,500 feet and stretching 950 miles in a maze of crooked valleys, locked between countless mountain ranges, and split by deep ravines. The largest of these ravines, Barranca del Cobre or "Copper Canyon," exceeds the Grand Canyon in depth. Though some of it can be seen from the wild Chihuahua al Pacifico railroad that runs from Las Mochis to Creel, at its heart is the roadless home of the Tarahumara, an indigenous tribe which escaped Spanish enslavement in the silver mines 400 years ago and became legendary for endurance running.

Barbara and I have often visited historic towns of the Sierra Madre, such as the old silver (and briefly national) capital of Guanajuato, which has been called the most beautiful city in the Americas. Its European-styled cathedrals, opera house, and university stand apart from ribbons of rainbow-hued traditional homes flowing on either side of a deep and narrow canyon. An hour away, San Miguel de Allende combines an historical town preserved by decree with an expatriate community of writers, artists, and retirees. Also in the area, elegant Querétaro, with its ancient Roman-styled aqueduct and Plaza de la Independencia, was the seat of the 1810 revolution against Spain.

One of my earliest childhood memories is of my father showing me a news photograph of a volcano in Michoacán State that had just erupted in a farmer's corn field. Volcán Paricutín rose thousands of feet out of nowhere in 1943, engulfing a village several miles away so deeply

that only the steeple of the unfinished church remained above the molten ocean.

I visited first the church and then the volcano by traversing about fifteen miles of lava fields with a Parapuecha Indian guide. As we scrambled toward the summit, a side cone steamed with vapors, yet the main crater, hundreds of feet deep, was absolutely dormant. It had ceased to be active after just nine years.

My vote for Mexico's most unusual natural phenomena goes to another remote site in Michoacán. In 1974, after 40 years of searching, a Canadian scientist discovered the wintering grounds for virtually the entire population of monarch butterflies east of the Rocky Mountains in Canada, the United States, and Mexico in a fir forest near El Rosario at over 10,000 feet. From November to April, up to 100 million monarchs blanket the trees and ground of just 100 acres of what has become an official sanctuary. Their life span is so short that the arriving butterflies are the third to fifth generations of those who left the previous spring. Navigation over a period of months to a site they have never seen thousands of miles away has defied complete explanation. However, when I visited the sanctuary in 1999, the butterflies were reduced to just 13 acres without fully blanketing trees. Scientists blamed a savage El Niño year combined with other factors. Only time and preservation of habitat will tell whether the eastern monarch population fully recovers.

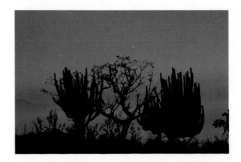

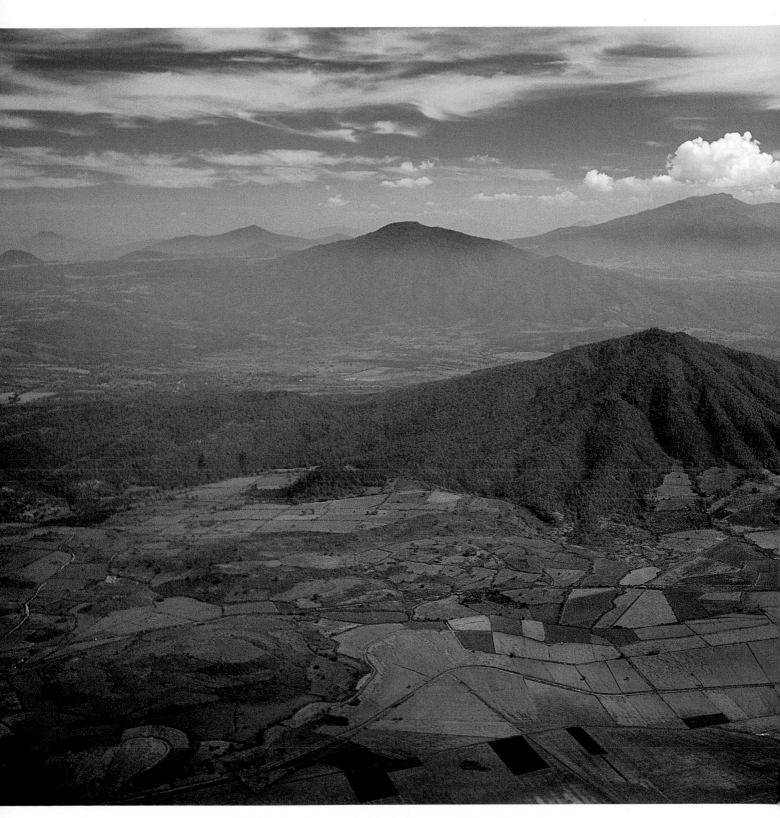

212-213 Seen from the air, forested old volcanoes rise above cultivated plains south of Guadalajara. This part of the Sierra Madre is called the Cordillera Neovolcánica, a region that holds several of America's most consistently active volcanoes.

213 top Steam vents sit below the now dormant cone of Paracutín, Mexico's newest volcano, which erupted out of a corn field in 1943.

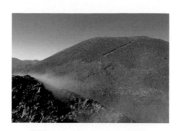

213 center A brine lake, totally hidden from view from the surrounding plains of the Sierra Madre, fills one of many extinct volcanic craters in the state of Guanajuato.

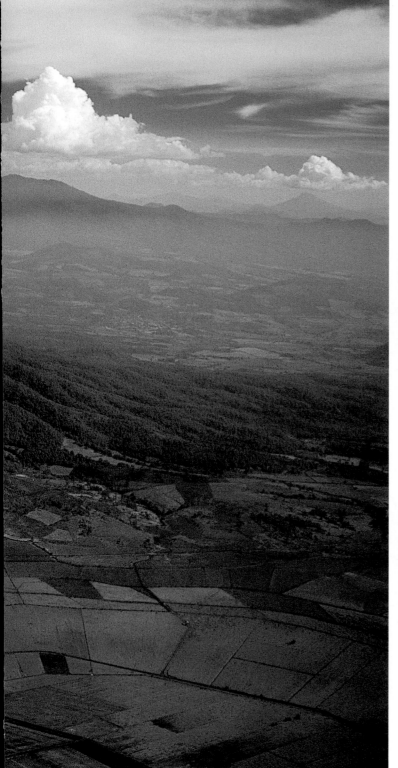

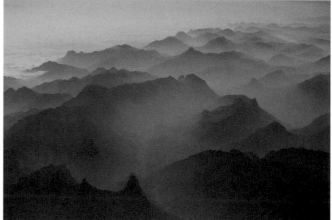

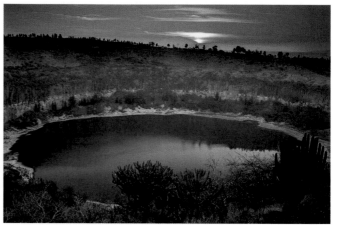

213 bottom The seemingly endless desert ranges of the Sierra Madre Oriental rise to over 12,000 feet in central Mexico south of Monterrey.

214–215 A tropical storm brews over ancient Mayan ruins at Tulum, where the Yucatán Peninsula meets the Caribbean Sea.

215 An extinct crater near León is filled with thick alkaline deposits evaporated over eons from a lake without an outlet.

213

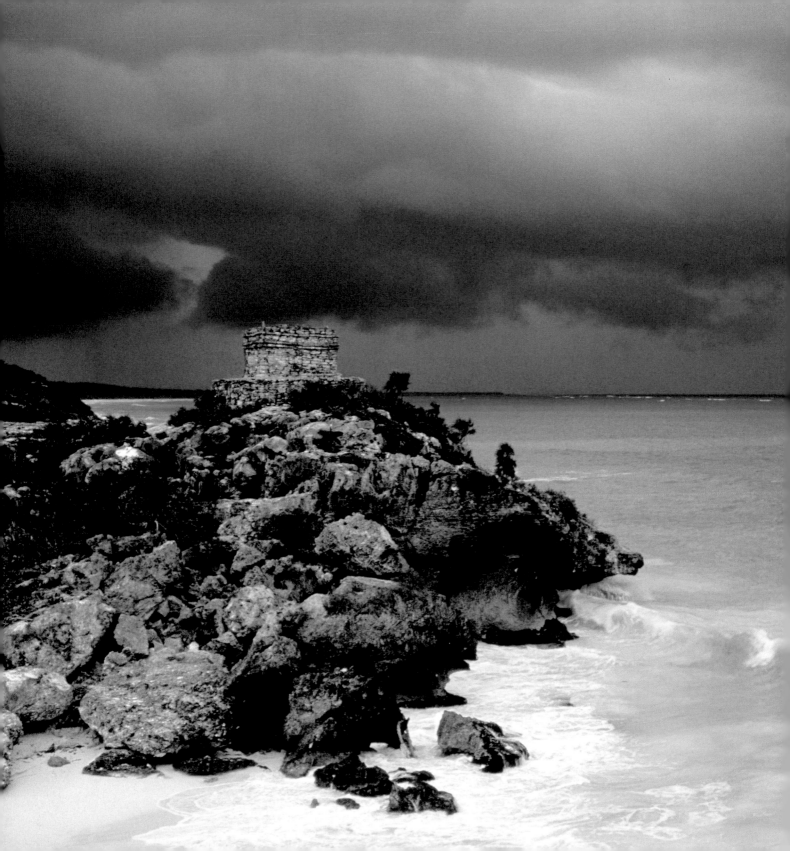

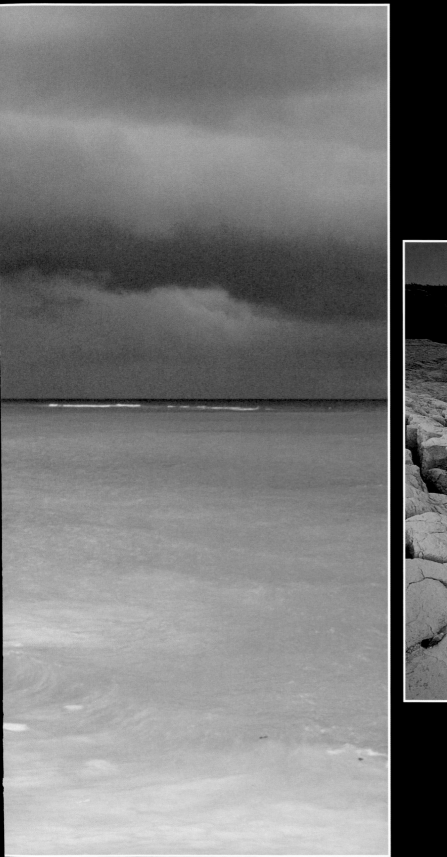
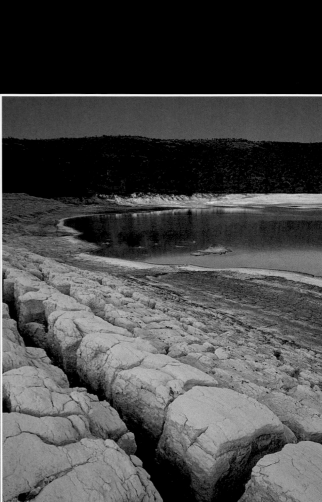

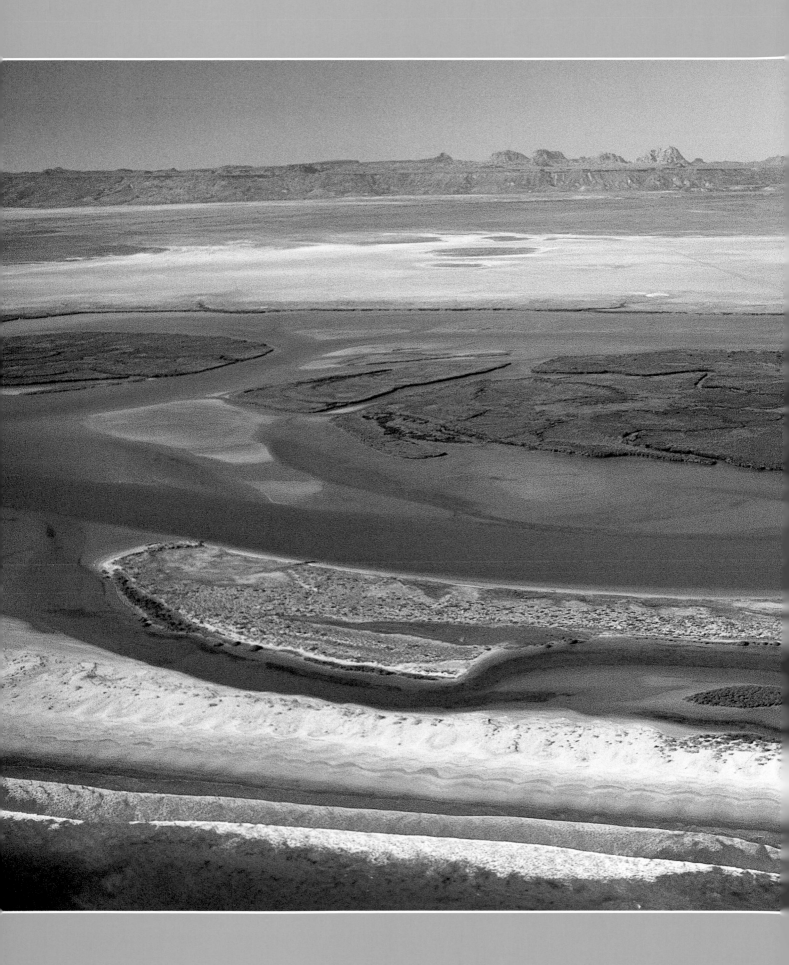

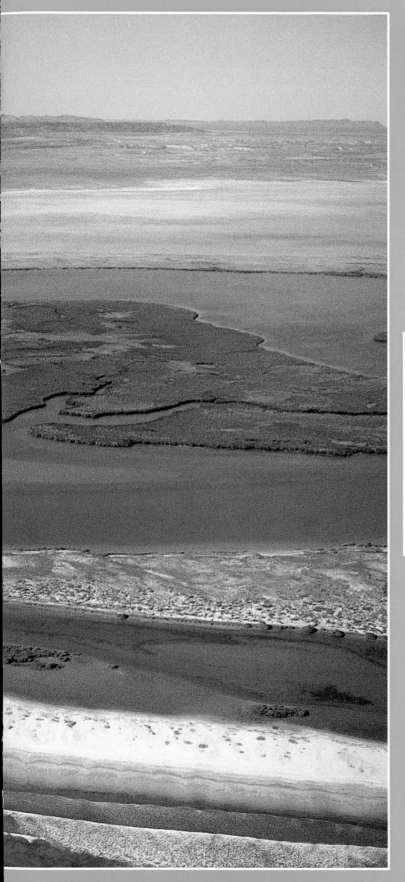

216–217
The protected waters of San Ignacio Lagoon are one of the Baja Peninsula's three major breeding grounds for gray whales.

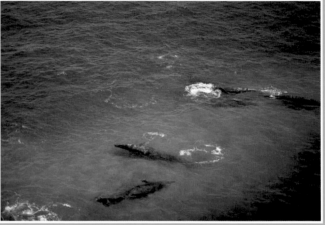

The Baja Peninsula

217 California gray whales breed in San Ignacio Lagoon on the Pacific Coast of Baja.

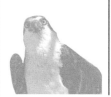

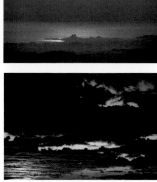

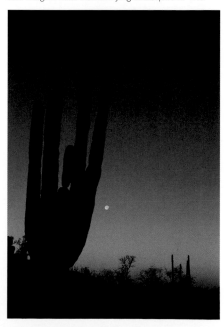

When the Spanish conquistadors first set foot on the Baja Peninsula in the early 1530s, lured by tales of golden cities and a kingdom of warrior women, they believed they had discovered an island. In 1839, one of Hernán Cortés' lieutenants sailed up what is now known as the Sea of Cortés and arrived at the delta of the Colorado River. Only then did the Spanish realize that Baja was actually one of the world's largest peninsulas, 800 miles in length. In places, the slender ribbon of land is only thirty miles wide.

Baja was connected to mainland Mexico until sometime during the Pliocene epoch, probably about four million years ago. The same giant San Andreas Fault that periodically shakes San Francisco has gradually split off the peninsula. When sea levels were much higher, the Sea of Cortés reached up the Imperial Valley north of the present location of Palm Springs.

The peninsula has been under Mexican rule since shortly after the country gained independence in 1821, though the United States later fought naval battles trying to acquire it. The northern half did not officially become the state of Baja California until 1952. The half south of the 27th parallel remained a frontier until the state of Baja California del Sur was created just after the completion of the controversial 1058-mile Transpeninsular Highway in 1973. Also until that year, American settlement of Mexican land in Baja was held back by regulations forbidding foreign ownership within 50 kilometers (31 miles) of the sea or 100 kilometers (62 miles) of the border. The government decided to lure foreign currency into the new state by creating a way for foreigners to essentially own coastal property by establishing land trusts, with themselves as beneficiaries. More than 50,000 Americans now "own" homes in Baja.

Long before the highway opened, American nature writer Joseph Wood Krutch called Baja "a wonderful example of how much bad roads can do for a country. Bad roads act as filters. They separate those who are sufficiently appreciative of what lies beyond the blacktop." Despite the paved Transpeninsular Highway, which I've found as friendly to drive as any country road in the United States, more than 85 percent of the peninsula's population remains concentrated in the northern border towns of Tijuana and Mexicali. Outside major cities, the arid peninsula has less than one person per ten square miles, an extremely low population density.

More because of isolation than preservation, most of Baja remains wild and undeveloped. Baja's two national parks lie along the spine of the inland mountains. Sierra San Pedro Martir National Park in the north has the peninsula's highest mountain. The sometimes snow-fringed summit of 10,126-foot Picacho del Diablo rises its steep granite walls high over ponderosa pine forests and canyons in a scene much like California's Southern Sierra Nevada. The National Park of the Constitution of 1857 in the Sierra de Juarez mountains features a lake named after an American settler who was eaten by a cannibal. Things are safer now, though Baja still has its share of bandits off the main roads.

Just before World War II, the American author John Steinbeck sailed around the Sea of Cortés on a scientific research voyage and ventured ashore to describe the essence of what sets the lower elevations of the Baja Sierra apart from ranges to the north. He visited a "deep cleft in the granite mountains" where "a tiny stream of water fell hundreds of feet from pool to pool. There were palm trees and wild grapevines and large ferns, and the water was cool and sweet." He also described the miraculous air in which "outlines of reality change with the moment."

On seemingly waterless slopes of the Sierra grow the world's tallest cacti, the cardón, which can stand sixty feet and weigh twelve tons. The peninsula contains the greatest variety of cacti in the world, plus a botanical bonanza of over 4,000 plant species, many found nowhere else.

The subtropical Baja coast remains temperate all year. California gray whales, long on the endangered species list, make the longest migration of any mammal, 12,000 miles from the Bering Sea in the Arctic, to breed in shallow lagoons on the Pacific Coast of Baja. In 1857 whaling captain Charles Scammon followed a pod into the lagoon near Guerrero Negro that now bears his name. Within twenty years, half of all the gray whales had been slaughtered. By 1910 they neared extinction. Not until 1972 did Mexico finally establish a reserve around Scammon's Lagoon. The other two major breeding areas, Magdalena Bay and San Ignacio Lagoon, received lesser protection some years later.

Shortly before the turn of the millennium, international conservationists such as Jean-Michel Cousteau and Kathryn Fuller (president of World Wildlife Fund) met separately with President Zedillo of Mexico in response to a Mitsubishi/Mexican Government joint venture to build the world's largest salt works within the Vizcaino Biosphere Reserve in San Ignacio Lagoon. Under tremendous pressure from without, the government aborted its plans.

Years ago, my wife flew me in her Cessna 206 over all three lagoons enroute to camp on an island in Magdalena Bay with Doug Peacock, seasonal desert rat and author of *Baja!*, a narrative of the peninsula's history and wild appeal. To awake each morning to Sonoran Desert sands rising out of turquoise waters filled with breaching whales was one of my life's most memorable experiences.

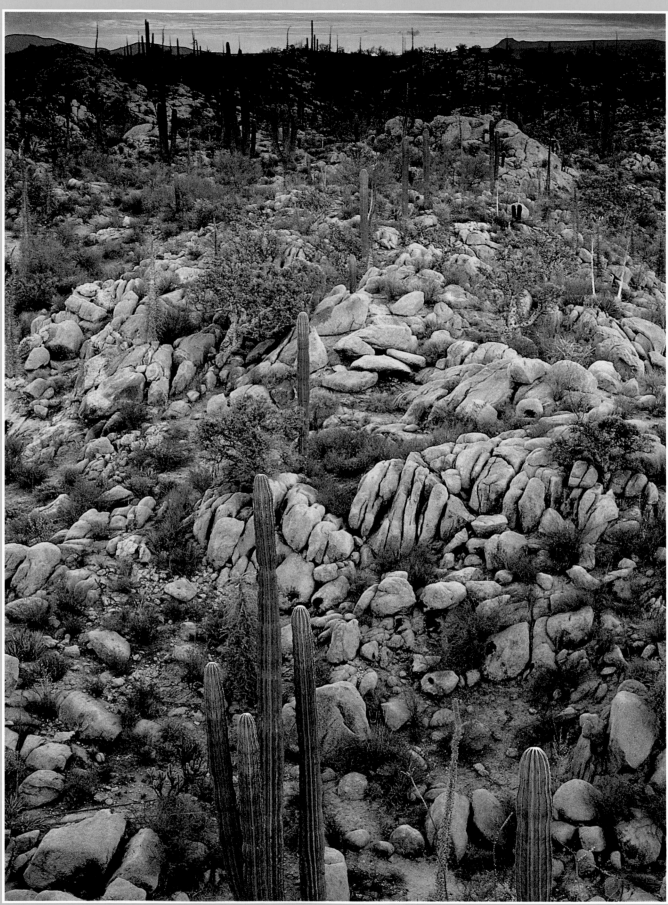

218 bottom Cleaving the evening sky like a devil's trident, a giant cardón cactus stands 40 feet above the desert near Cataviña.

219 In Desierto Central de Baja California Natural Park, cardón cacti and elephant trees grow out of fields of house-sized boulders. Once a hindrance to travel and settlement, this rugged land in which all level passages are guarded by cacti has become a park attracting photographers, climbers, and desert botanists since the completion of the Transpeninsular Highway in 1973.

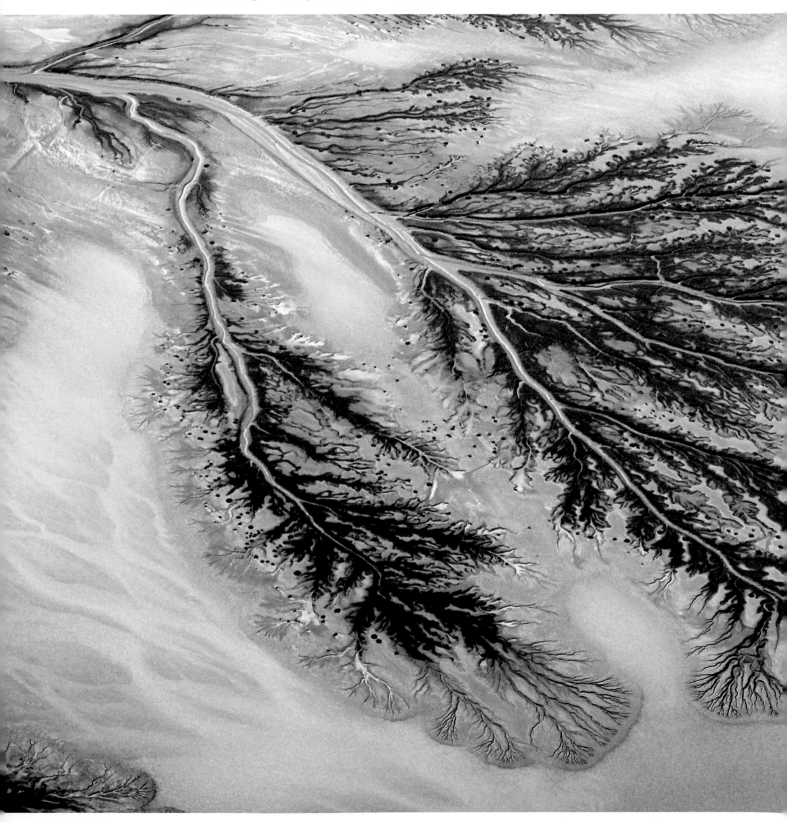

220–221 Like a giant leaf upon the desert, the mighty Colorado River disappears into the sands of Baja before reaching the Sea of Cortés during years of low rainfall. Evaporation from huge reservoirs along the river in the United States, as well as massive diversions for irrigation and city water have reduced the river to, at best, a trickle into the delta of the Sea of Cortés, which used to hold a fantastic concentration of wildlife.

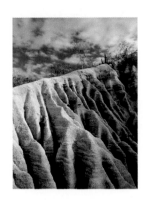

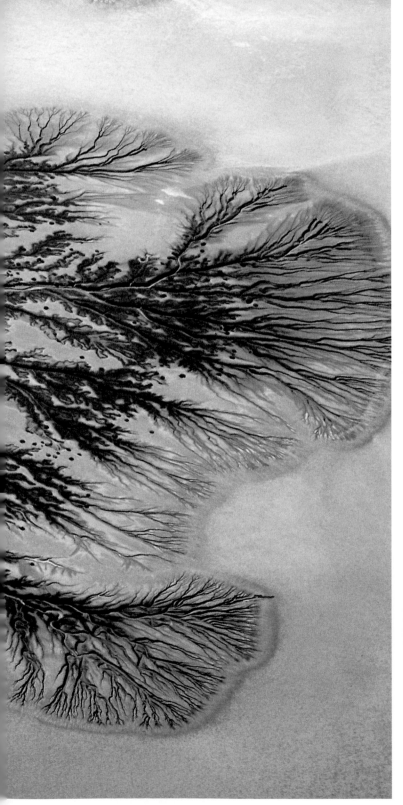

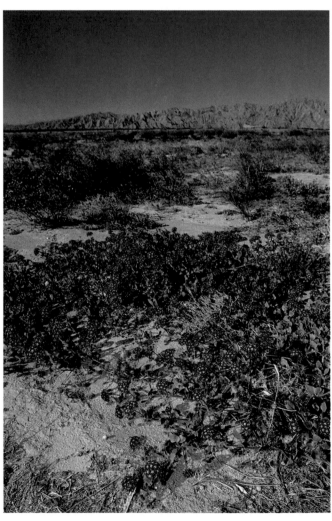

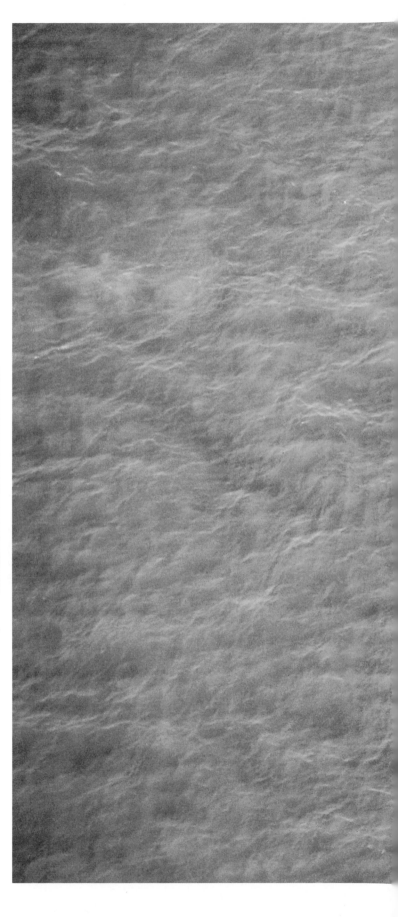

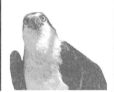

222 Seen from an island, a gray whale breaches in Magdalena Bay.

222–223 Seen from the air, a gray whale and its calf cruise the shallow waters of the same bay.

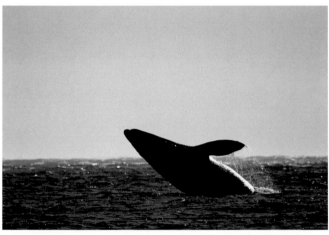

224 Gulls ride breaking waves on the Pacific Coast of the island of Santo Domingo at Boca de Soledad near protected Magdalena Bay in Baja California Sur.

224–225 A wild Baja sunset drops behind giant cordon cacti atop eroded granite hills in Desierto Central de Baja California

Natural Park near Cataviña.
Also present are smaller cacti: cholla, cirio, candelabra and prickly pears.

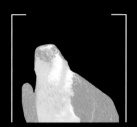

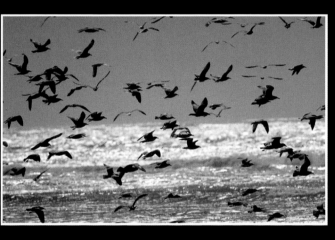

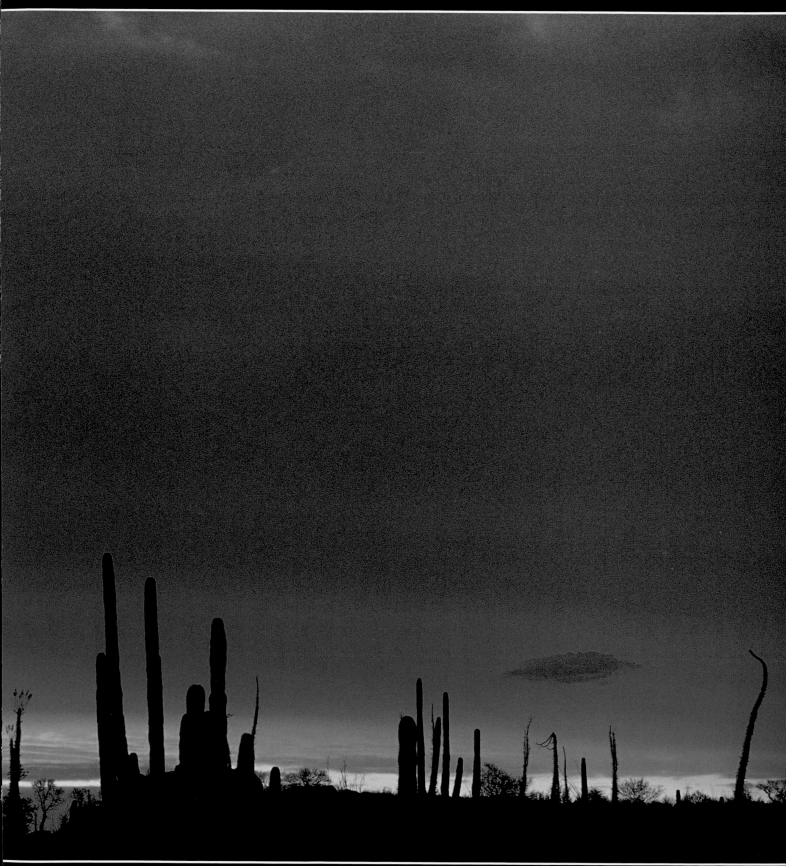

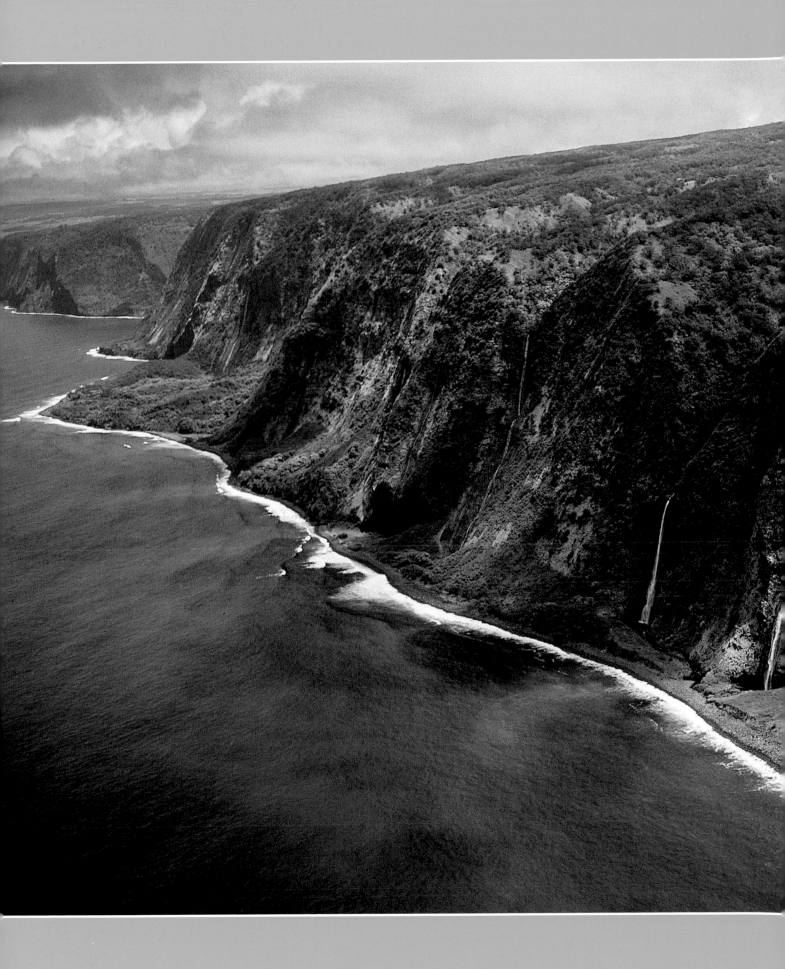

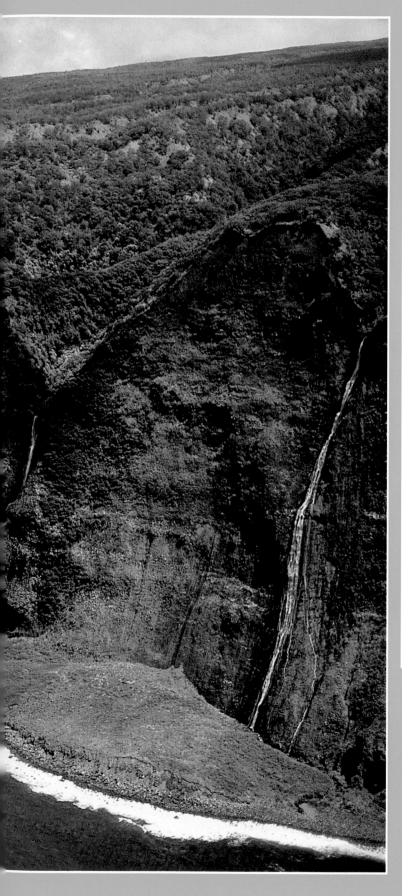

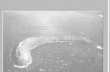

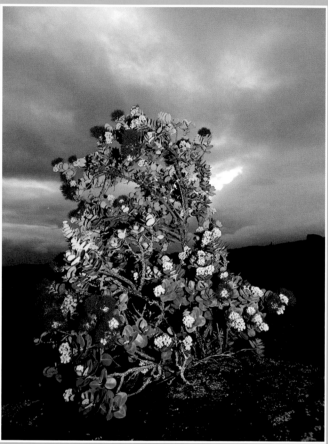

Hawaii

228–229 *The turquoise and violet lagoon of Hanauma Bay fills a sunken crater just ten miles from Honolulu on the island of Oahu. The unusually shaped bay was formed about 6,000 years ago when the side of the crater of Koko Head collapsed and ocean water rushed in. A large coral reef at the entrance to the bay insulates its relatively quiet waters from much of the wave action on the exposed point of land jutting into the Kaiwi Channel. Officially a state nature preserve, the bay was set aside to be an underwater wildlife park.*

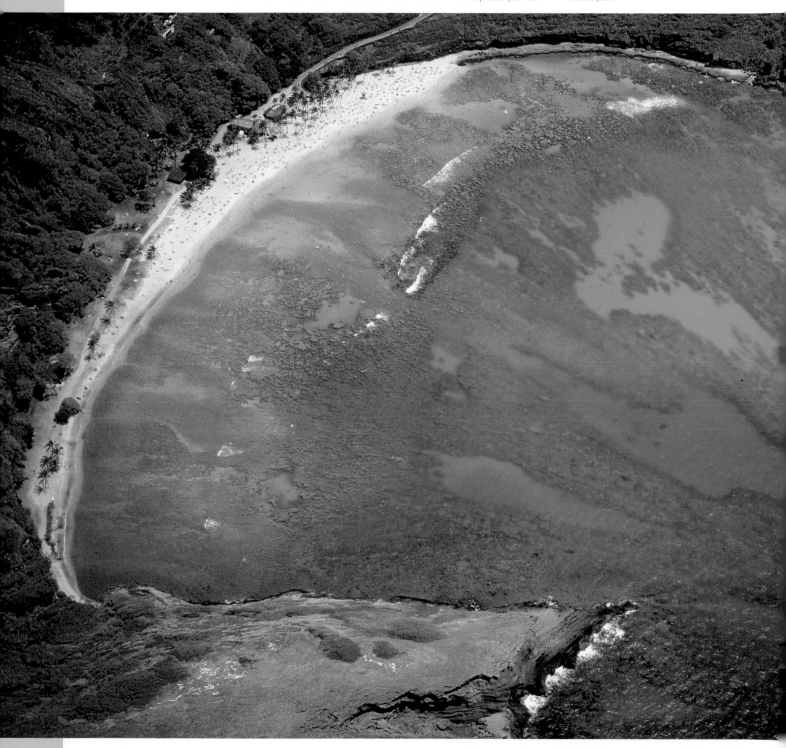

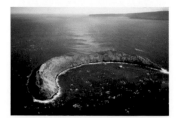

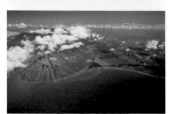

229 top Tiny Molokini Island off the coast of Maui is the top of a submerged crater.

229 bottom Seen from high above, the West Maui Mountains appear as a single volcano rising out of the ocean.

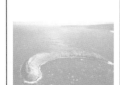

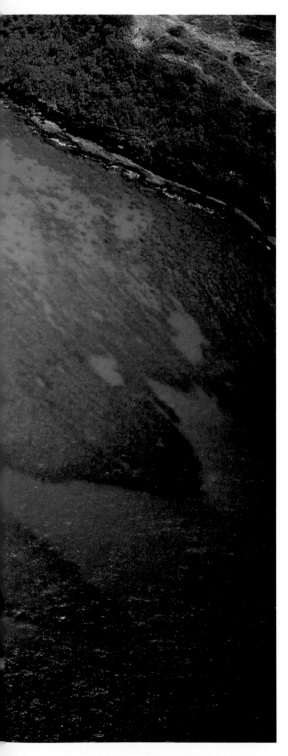

Two of my friends who live at different ends of the island of Maui use the same effective speech mannerism whenever they mention their place of residence during brief visits to us less fortunate souls confined to the main North American continent. No matter how casual or fast-paced their banter, they utter the name "Maui" with a master orator's pause.

Most Americans can't help themselves from breaking into a smile of sheer pleasure at the first mention of this Pacific garden of Eden, where the vegetation is always lush, the beaches are always white, the air is always warm (but never too hot), and the sun always shines. "You really *live* there?" is a typical response.

So well does this romantic image fit the coastal resorts and surfing beaches of most of Hawaii that tourism has evolved into the major industry, netting over $10 billion per year and far exceeding the old mainstays of sugar cane and pineapple plantations, military installations, and commercial fishing. Nowhere else in America does tourism bring in anything close to Hawaii's annual average of $10,000 per resident, but it has exacted a heavy price on the "Main Island" of Oahu, where Waikiki has outlived its reputation as Hawaii's beach of dreams. Girded by 40-story buildings, 30,000 hotel rooms, 70,000 visitors a day, and 400,000 people in the encroaching city of Honolulu, this once-exquisite two-mile stretch of beach may well be the world's most overdeveloped natural resort area. It's little wonder that Maui has taken over as modern Hawaii's dream destination.

Though beach after beach and the wild Hana Coast hold the lion's share of public attractions and accommodations, it is the wild character of the inner island that gives Maui so much more of a unique ambiance than Oahu.

Three-quarters of Maui's interior consists of protected wildlands. The "Highway to Heaven" climbs over 10,000 feet through the open landscape of Haleakala National Park to the rim of a massive crater, 27 miles in circumference and 3,000 feet deep. Concessions are often booked for rapid mountain bike descents from the summit to the sea, but to spend quiet time trekking through the crater itself is to experience a totally different Hawaii. Here above timberline, where morning temperatures hover around freezing, is a misty moonscape of arid, undulating desert. Dark pastels of rounded cinder cones and rugged lava flows, punctuated here and there with clusters of endangered silversword, replace the white beaches and surf of the coast.

When Mark Twain traveled to wild places throughout the American West in the 1860s, he witnessed a dawn over Haleakala and called it "the sublimest spectacle I ever witnessed." Really two islands in one, Maui consists of two dormant volcanoes linked by an isthmus that allows commercial jets to land directly from the continent. The West Maui Mountains could hardly be more different than Haleakala. Clothed in dense rain forest all the way to their 5,788-foot highest summit, these peaks receive 400 inches of rain a year, making them the *second* wettest spot on the islands.

The most northerly major island of Kauai garners the earth's highest average rainfall—over 460 inches—on the upper reaches of 5,148-foot Mount Waialeale. During some years over fifty feet—600 inches—of water has fallen from the sky. Because the islands are the most isolated on the planet, furthest away from the influence of a continent, unique species and unusual evolutionary patterns have evolved in these well-watered highlands. An extraordinary 95 percent of the native species of the rain forests of Hawaii are found nowhere else.

230–231 and 231 top The southern shores of Molokai are the most colorful of all the Hawaiian Islands. Centuries ago, native Polynesians fished these shallow waters and configured ponds to aid their catch and breed marine life — the forerunner of modern aquaculture. The colors are the result of differing flora in the old ponds, many of which have been restored to be once again used as fish farms by modern Hawaiians.

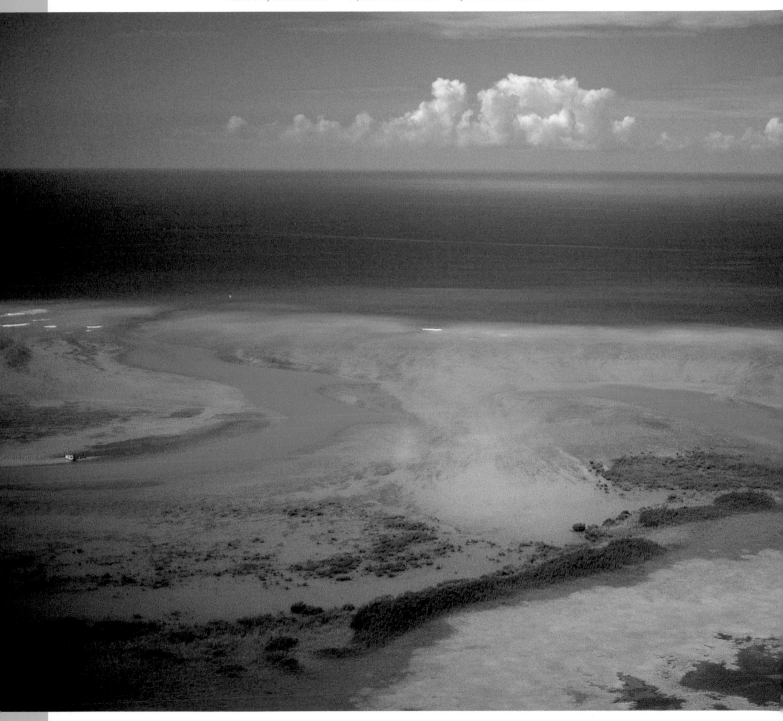

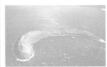

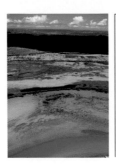

Unfortunately, the over 1,700 unique Hawaiian plants have become outnumbered by over 2,000 introduced species that have completely taken over most of the lowlands. Many native species are now extinct. When the Sierra Club ran a photo of a Hawaiian jungle on the cover of their magazine to celebrate protected wildlands on the islands, a botanist wrote to say that not one plant in the apparently wild scene was native. What tourists think of as Hawaiian—coconut palms, pineapple, guava, and bamboo—have all been introduced.

My wife, Barbara, was born on Oahu. She left the islands with her military family at five and rarely returned. Neither of us had seen the islands closely from the air until *Islands* magazine assigned us to rent a small plane for her to fly while I photographed a feature. To see the islands erupting from the sea in both a visual and a literal sense was to deeply appreciate their primeval character.

In an underpowered Cessna 172 filled with our luggage and cameras, we had seemed to circle endlessly to be able to climb to 11,000 feet over Haleakala on a perfect morning. When we flew on to the "Big Island" named Hawaii, the weather was marginal and we caught only glimpses of the snow-dusted, 13,788-foot hulk of Mauna Kea through the clouds. Days later, as we departed without flying into turbulent katabatic winds rolling off the upper reaches of the broad dome, I looked back across the waters and perceived the peak as geologists see it: not as a summit slightly lower than the 14,000-foot continental high points of the Sierra Nevada, Cascades, and Rockies, but as the world's tallest mountain, rising directly 32,000 feet from the ocean floor.

During a break in the weather, Barbara had flown over the much lower expanse of Kilauea, the world's largest active crater. As we skimmed over the top of Pu'u O'o vent while strong winds held a column of steam to the side, I glimpsed a surge of bright-red lava just as I snapped the shutter. The giant crater in Hawaii Volcanoos National Park has spewed an estimated two billion tons of lava since 1983, building the Big Island ever bigger. Luckily for park visitors, the consistency of Hawaiian lava is such that it flows rather than blows, like the top of a Mount

Vesuvius or St. Helens.

As Barbara later wrote in *Plane and Pilot* magazine, "On good days you can see from one island to the next, with the exception of Kauai. . . . On bad days, pilots have been known to fly out to sea and disappear forever." We were not permitted to fly the rental aircraft across 75 miles of open ocean to Kauai, so after photographing five of the six major islands— Oahu, Maui, Hawaii, Molokai, and Lanai—we hopped a commercial flight.

We first explored the deep gorges of Waimea Canyon by car and foot at the height of an unusually fine wildflower bloom. Then we chartered a helicopter and timed our departure to fly with the door off just as the sun was breaking at the end of an afternoon rain storm. Having studied the physics of rainbows, I directed the pilot to fly a course where they repeatedly appeared in front of us over the lush green rain forests of Mount Waialeale and the crimson sea cliffs of the wild and roadless Na Pali Coast. Then I asked him to hover just above a sunlit wet cloud where he was excited to see his first-ever, 360-degree true rainbow. It took up so much of the sky that I needed to use my widest fish-eye lens to record it all in one image.

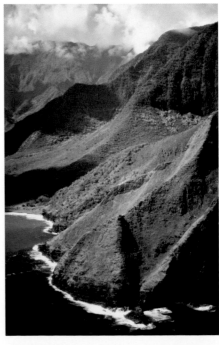

232 *The rugged green slopes of 5,788-foot Pu'u Kukui, "Hill of Light," drop toward the sea in the highlands of the West Maui Forest Reserve. Just out of sight behind the peaks is the resort town of Lahaina.*

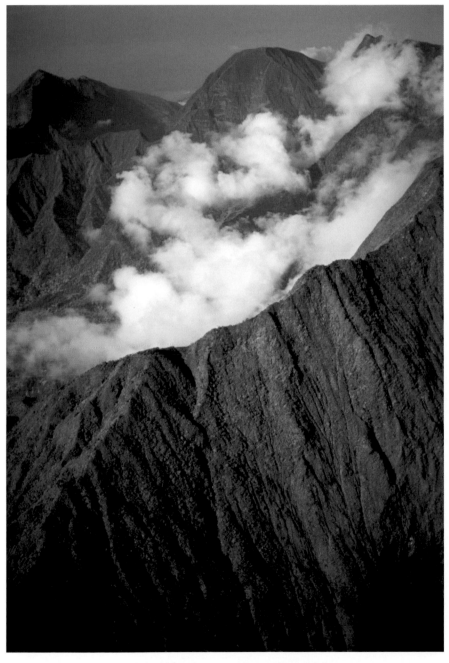

233 *A rainbow arcs over the wild Na Pali Coast of Kauai Island. The wholly roadless area of canyons, jungle valleys, and waterfalls is only accessible by the 11-mile Kalalau Trail or by kayak or small boat in good weather.*

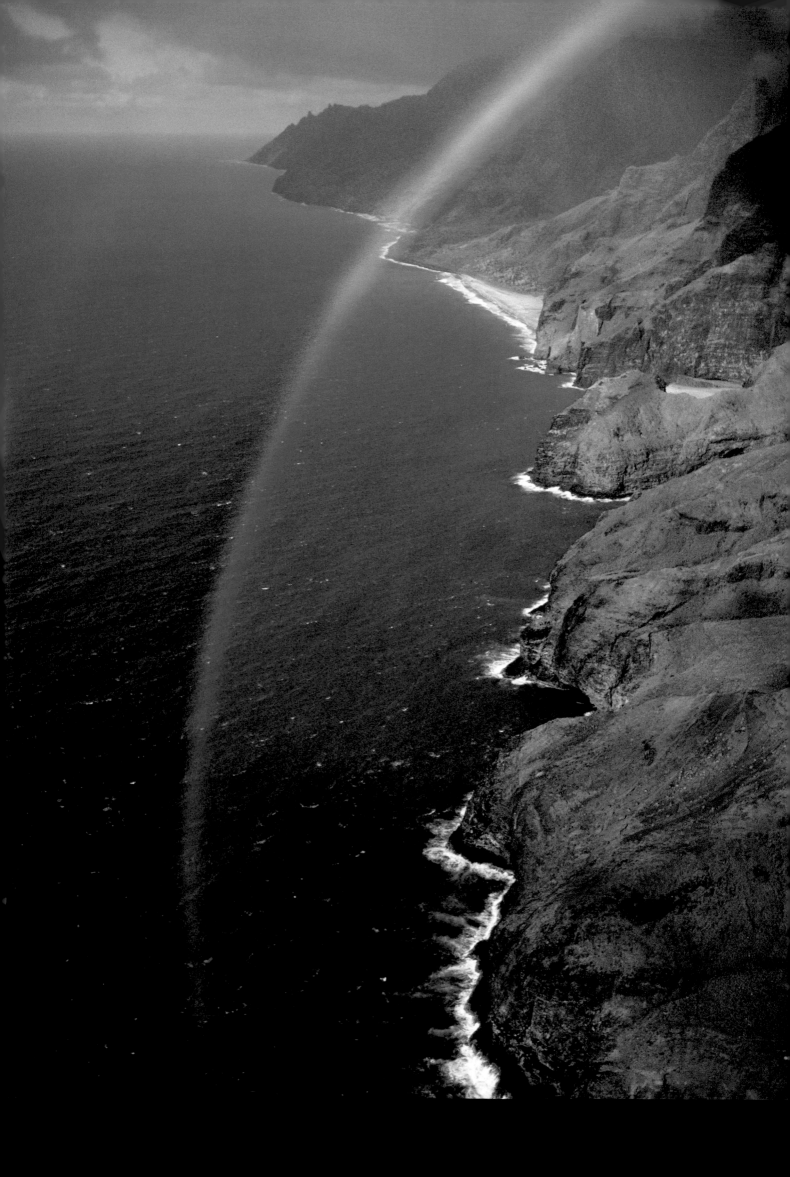

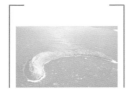

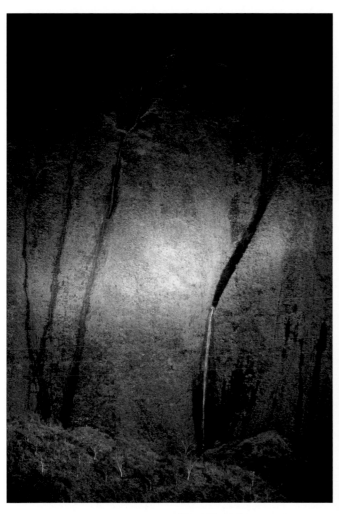

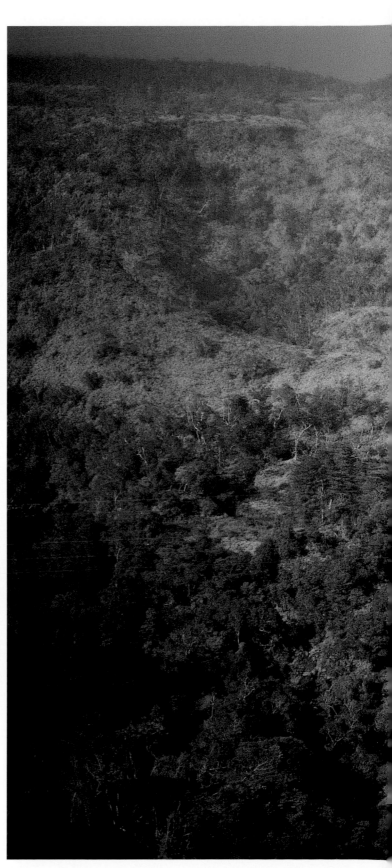

234 A waterfall drops out of the Hawaiian rainforest into Kilohana Crater in the roadless interior of Kauai, where the only way to see the features of the jungled landscape is from the air.

234–235 A rainbow arcs over rainforest high on the slopes of Mount Wai'ale'ale, usually hidden in cloud with the world's highest average annual rainfall of 460 inches—over fifty feet per year.

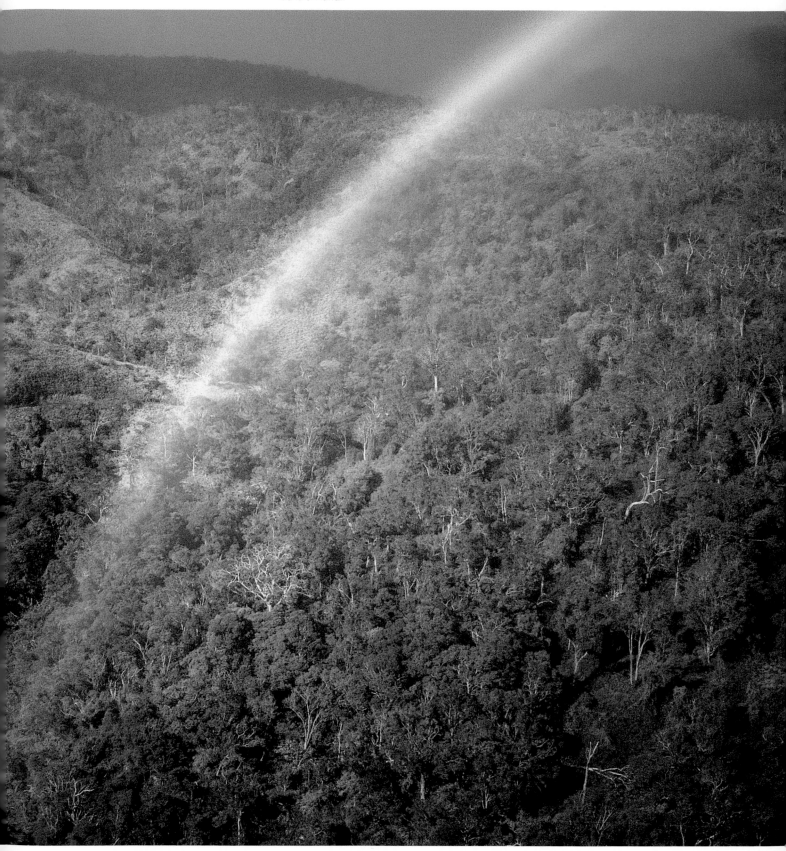

236 Molten lava erupts in the continuously active crater of Pu'u O'o Vent in Hawaii Volcanoes National Park on the big island of Hawaii.

236–237 Flowers burst into bloom at the top of Waimea Canyon on Kauai shortly after a severe hurricane. When Mark Twain visited the 3,600-foot deep gorge in the 1870s, he called it "The Grand Canyon of the Pacific."

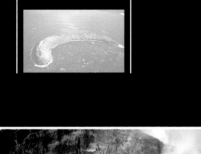

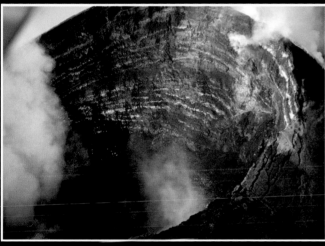

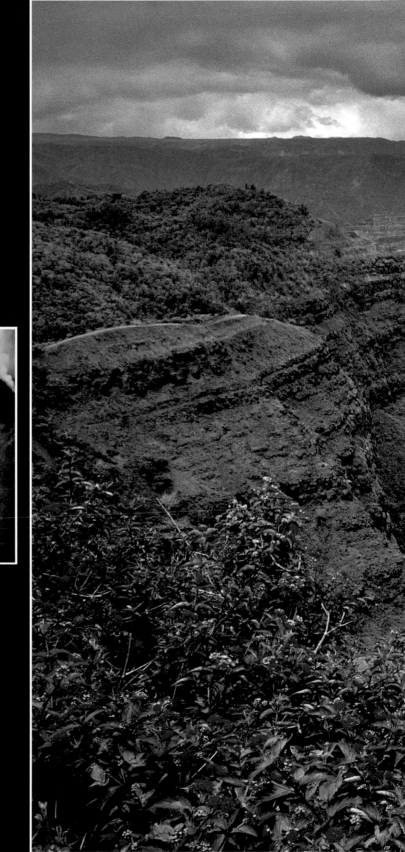

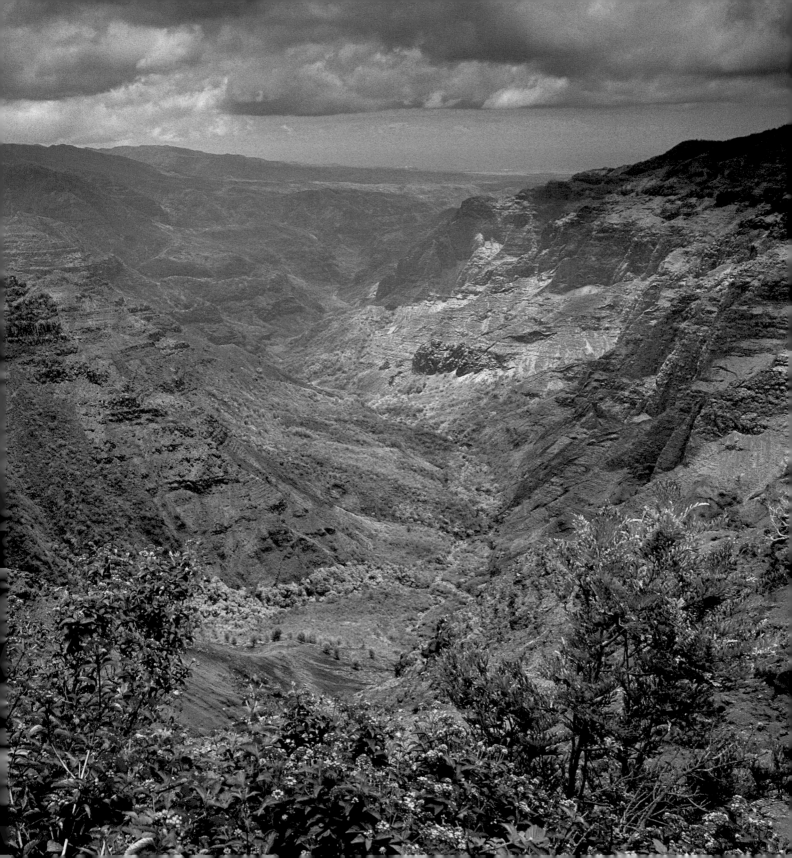

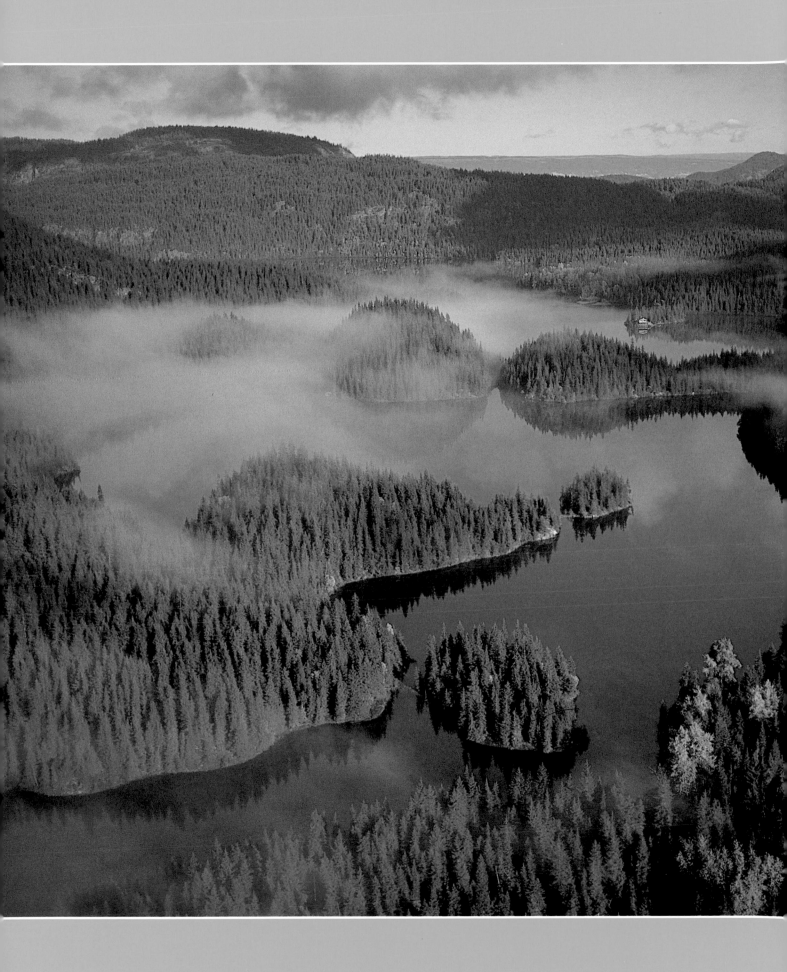

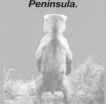

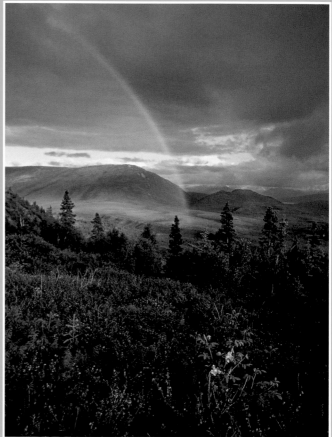

Alaska

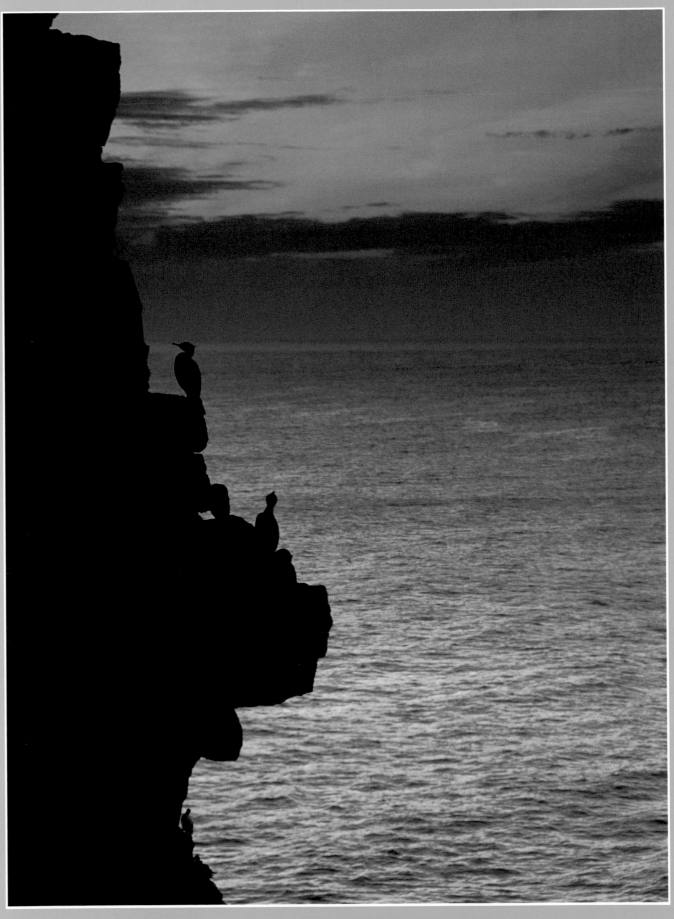

242 and 243 bottom
The Pribilof Islands
in the Bering Sea
between Alaska and
Siberia hold the
world's greatest

concentration of
mammals and
seabirds. Uninhabited
until 1786, the very
remote islands were
controlled by Russia

until 1867, when the
United States
bought Alaska. Aleut
natives brought by
the Russians to
harvest seals now

manage tourism to
seacliffs that teem
with murres,
kittiwakes, puffins,
and a host of
unusual species.

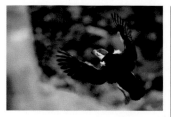

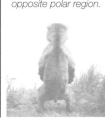

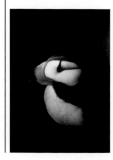

243 top Horned puffins breed on seacliffs and catch fish in the breaking surf. Their coloration and comical appearance parallel the evolution of penguins in the opposite polar region.

amidst enormous populations of sea mammals: otters, seals, walruses, and whales.

The explorers often described by historians as the "first Westerners" to visit Alaska were actually Easterners. Russians pushing eastward to the mouth of the Lena River claimed the Siberian Coast in 1620, the same year that pilgrims sailing west on the *Mayflower* settled in New England. In 1724, Peter the Great hired the Danish explorer Vitus Bering to confirm if Asia and America were one, as Columbus had suspected. When Bering returned from a land journey without clear proof, the czar sent him back by sea. In 1741, Bering finally touched Alaskan soil and claimed it for the czar.

Fur resources were rapidly exploited after trading posts were set up all along the "Panhandle" of Southeast Alaska as far south as Northern California. In little more than a century, large sea mammals were in serious decline and the Alaskan race of musk oxen had been exterminated. In 1867, Russia sold Alaska to the United States for $7.2 million— about 2 cents an acre.

I got a taste of remaining Russian heritage when I first visited the Pribilof Islands in the Bering Sea in 1979. They were uninhabited in 1786, when Russian fur trader Gerassim Pribilof happened upon the world's largest concentration of mammals and seabirds. Natives from the Aleutian Islands were enslaved to slaughter fur seals by the millions. Their Aleut descendants with Russian surnames live on these remote islands along with the 800,000 seals, still the world's largest colony, thanks to the end of commercial sealing and the richness of the seas.

Despite grizzly bears being the most common icon of Alaskan wildlife, they also have a strong Eurasian connection. Subspecies of the same bear once inhabited temperate and sub-polar wilds all across Asia, the Middle East, and Europe. Gone from most populated areas by the time of Columbus, they survive in large numbers only in Siberia and Alaska.

Solitary grizzlies can often be seen from the 90-mile dirt road through Denali National Park, but the finest places to see these largest of all land predators are at their annual gatherings to catch salmon. Where waterfalls are common, the bears are solitary, but where waterfalls are rare, many bears congregate. At McNeil Falls on the Alaska

Peninsula I saw 31 bears at once vying for salmon. Prime locations where fish leaped high out of the rapids, like real estate atop the hills of a great city, were possessed by those who wielded the most power. These venerable bears, weighing up to 1,200 pounds, bore scarred faces and bodies in mute witness to the value of their hard-won turf.

Unfortunately, the turf for bear watching at McNeil has become equally contentious. An annual state lottery selects fifteen people per day out of thousands of applicants to visit the falls during the salmon run with an armed naturalist-guide. Brooks Falls in Katmai National Park has fewer bears in a more photogenic location. Viewing is limited chiefly by the few campsites and accommodations.

Seeing polar bears in Alaska is nowhere near as predictable as going to Churchill in Canada, where the bears gather every fall. I've been lucky enough to have one look down the barrel of my 600mm lens near Barrow and jump back into the sea. I also had a rare simultaneous sighting of a polar bear coming from the sea as a grizzly family walked across the tundra on the grounds of the Prudhoe Bay oil complex. To my pleasant surprise, I saw more wildlife within the protected area of the complex than outside along the 414-mile dirt Dalton Highway that parallels the Alaska Pipeline. Beyond the other end of the pipeline in Prince William Sound, I was equally surprised to visit beaches hit by the 1989 *Exxon Valdez* oil spill exactly a year to the day later and see no evidence of a problem, unless I turned over rocks to look for oil scum or paid attention to the unnatural silence. I had heard many birds on previous visits, both to the same coastline on Prince William Sound and exquisite Kachemak Bay to the north.

If Alaska has a dark side, it's cold winter nights that seem longer than summer days. Tourists don't experience the length of these winters, where what used to be known as cabin fever runs rampant under the newer epithet, "seasonal affective disorder." An increasingly popular way to escape cabin fever and see wild landscapes veiled in snow is to take up Alaska's official sport since 1972, dogsledding. However, as white Alaskans were re-discovering this classic means of Arctic transportation and re-inventing it as competitive sport, native Eskimos were figuring out that

snowmobiles could be parked in the spring without having to be fed for the rest of the year.

One winter I tried my hand at mushing my own team through 100 miles of Gates of the Arctic National Park as part of a group led by a musher who had raced the 1,100-mile Iditarod Trail. I'll never forget the glow of the wood fire that warmed us as northern lights danced across the sky, knowing that I'd be home in California within two weeks. I sensed a tremendous difference between dogsledding as adventure tourism and as a way of life in a vanished, pre-mechanized world.

My mother, who visited Alaska in 1933, recounted the following impressions of how air travel was changing things to an oral historian more than half a century later: "Flying was absolutely nothing, or I should say everything! There were no roads in Alaska... nothing open between any towns. It was the healthiest place to live. Nobody ever heard of locking doors because who could escape? You don't run a dog sled with stuff you've just taken from someone's house! Every little town had it's own little, tiny airplane, those little one-seater things. That was communication in 1933 . . . it wasn't in the United States at all."

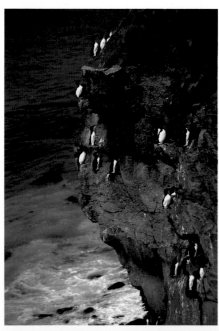

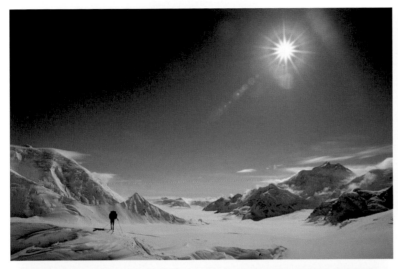

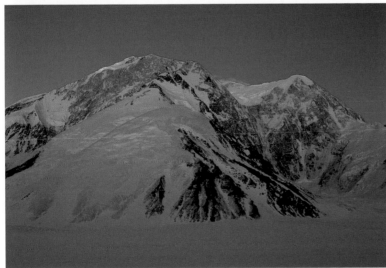

244 top In a part of Denali National Park that has yet to emerge from the last ice age, a mountaineer skis the Kahiltna Glacier below Mount McKinley.

244 bottom Midnight sun shines on the upper Northwest Buttress of 20,320-foot Mount McKinley, North America's highest mountain.

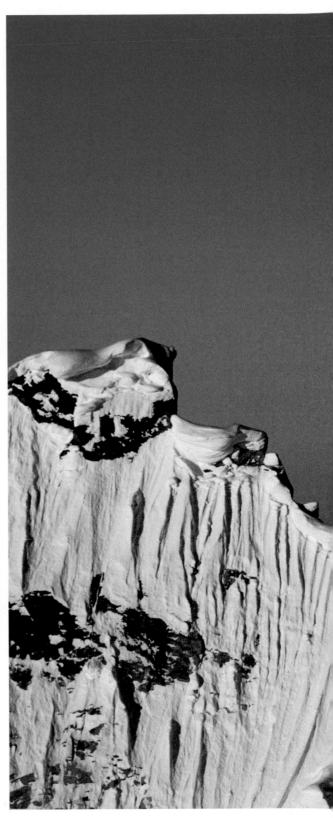

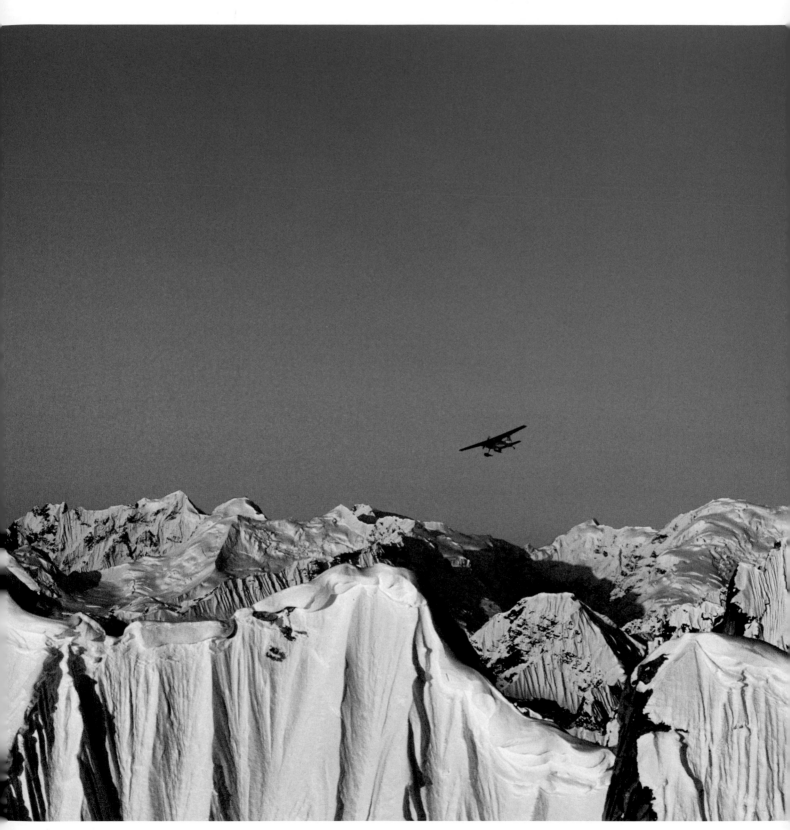

244–245 A bush pilot flies a single-engine plane over the icy ramparts of the Alaska Range south of Mount McKinley in Denali National Park. Until the 1970s and 1980s, when mountain adventurers began regularly hiring bush pilots to land their ski-equipped planes on glaciers beneath sheer walls of rocks and ice in ever more remote valleys, the summits were mostly unclimbed and the entire region was little explored by ground. On this spring morning, pilot Doug Geeting has hired out his plane for "flightseeing" without landing on the ice—a rapidly growing part of his business.

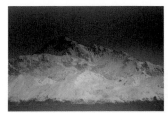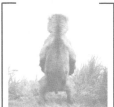

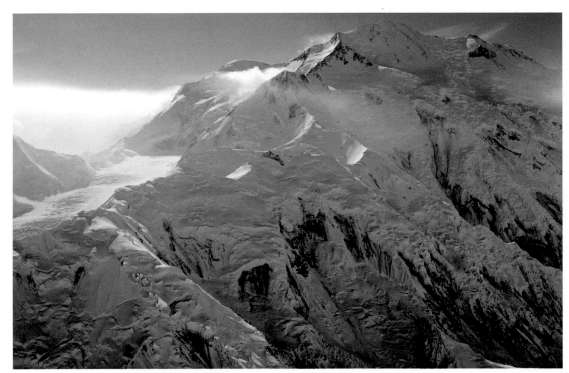

246 bottom Wildly sculpted Mount Huntington in the shadow of Mount McKinley is considered by many to be North America's most beautiful mountain.

247 A corniced ridge at 16,500 feet on Mount McKinley separates midnight sun from blue shadow on a −22°F June night.

246 top Alpenglow lights up the south face of Mount McKinley at dawn as seen in a distant telephoto from the Anchorage-Fairbanks Highway.

246 center On the north side of the mountain, the wild Wickersham Wall drops 12,000 feet from the 20,320-foot summit to the Peters Glacier.

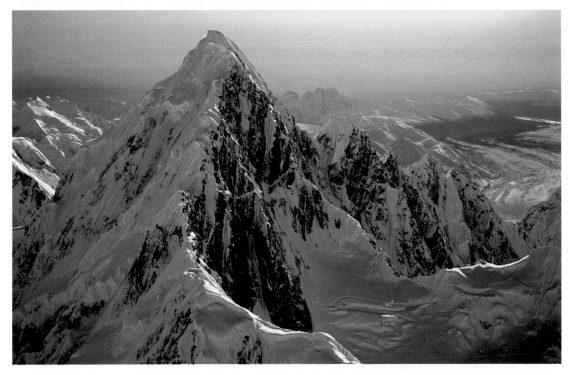

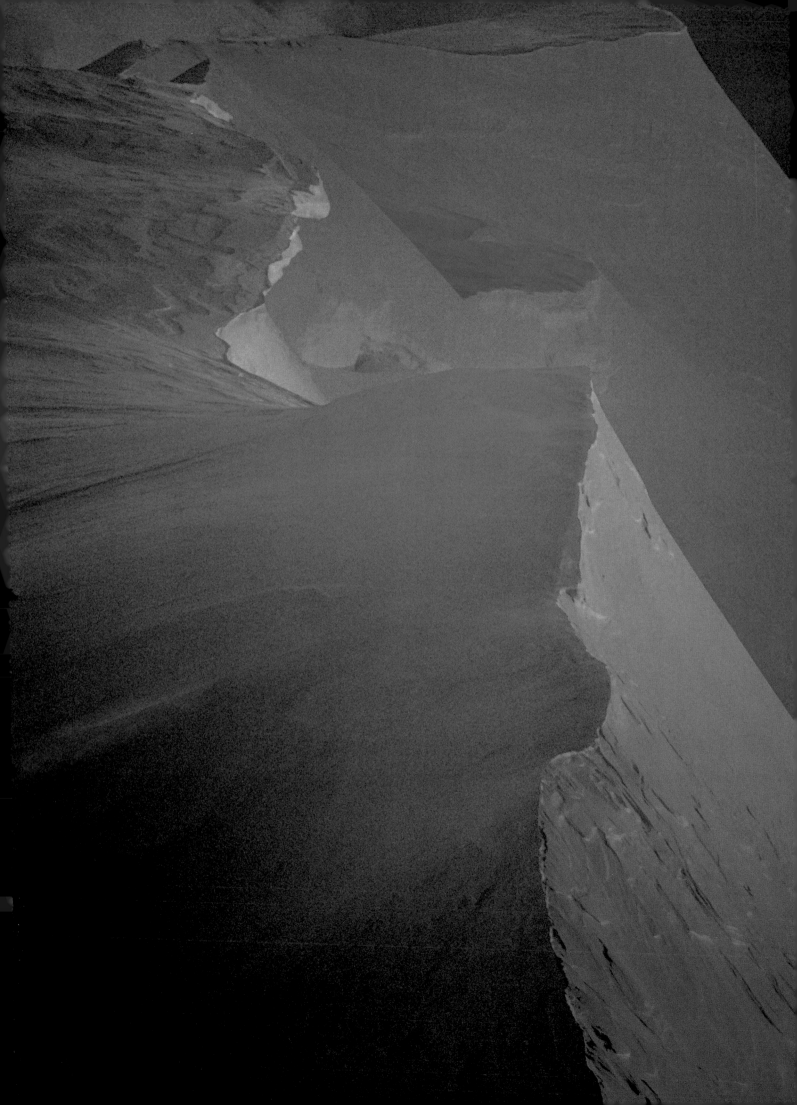

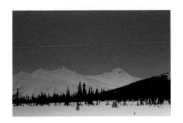

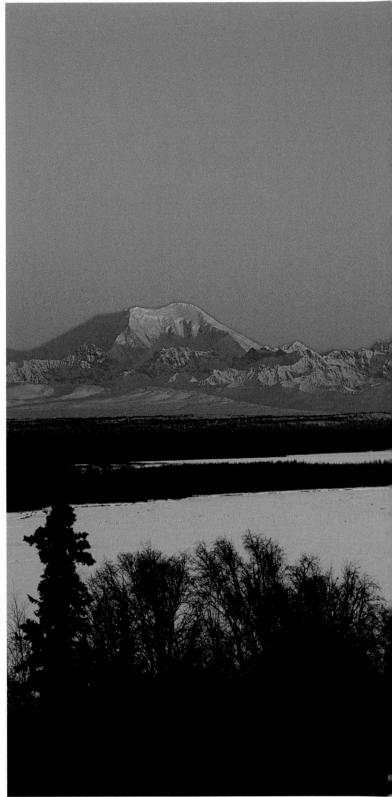

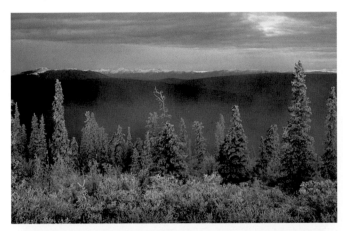

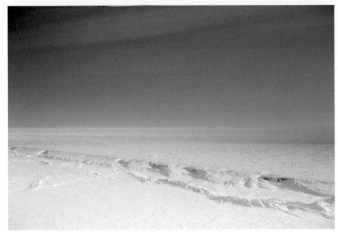

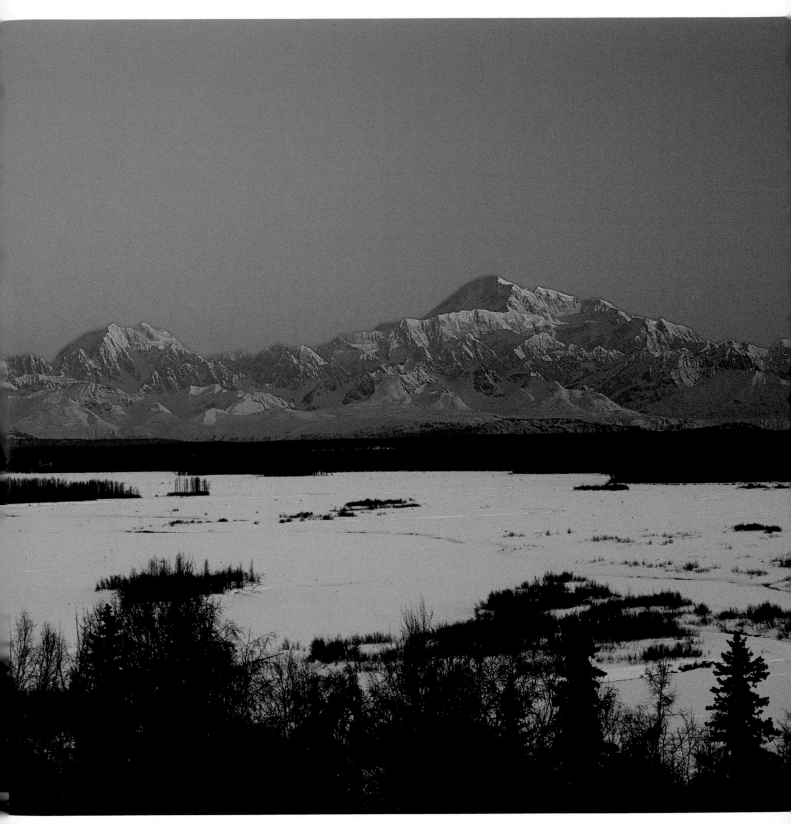

248 and 249
The Alaskan interior and Arctic shores are locked in winter for more than half the months of the year. Temperatures below −70°F have been recorded in the Brooks Range (left, top) as well as the valleys surrounding the Yukon River near the Yukon border (left, center). On the Arctic Coast near Point Barrow (left, bottom) snow over treeless tundra and sea ice blurs the clear distinction between ocean and land that we take for granted along warmer coastlines. Seen from a hilltop near Talkeetna (above), a winter sunrise over the frozen Susitna River and its floodplain lights up the highest summits of the Alaska Range. From left to right are 17,400-foot Mount Foraker, 14,573-foot Mount Hunter, and 20,320-foot Mount McKinley.

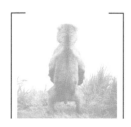

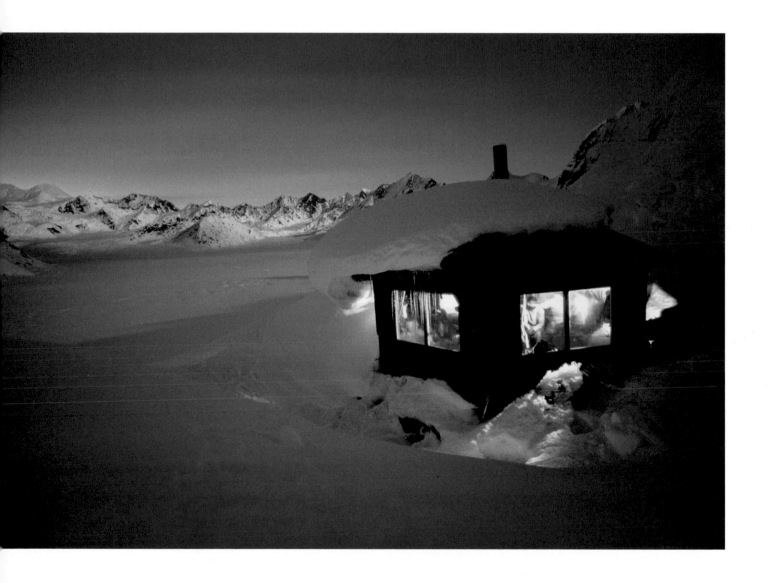

250 A fire in a wood stove sets a cabin aglow in a winter time exposure made during the first ski circumnavigation of Mount McKinley. Don Sheldon's Mountain House, the only structure in over 1,000 square miles of Denali National Park south of McKinley, was built by the legendary bush pilot on a rock spur above a favored landing site before the area was included in the park.

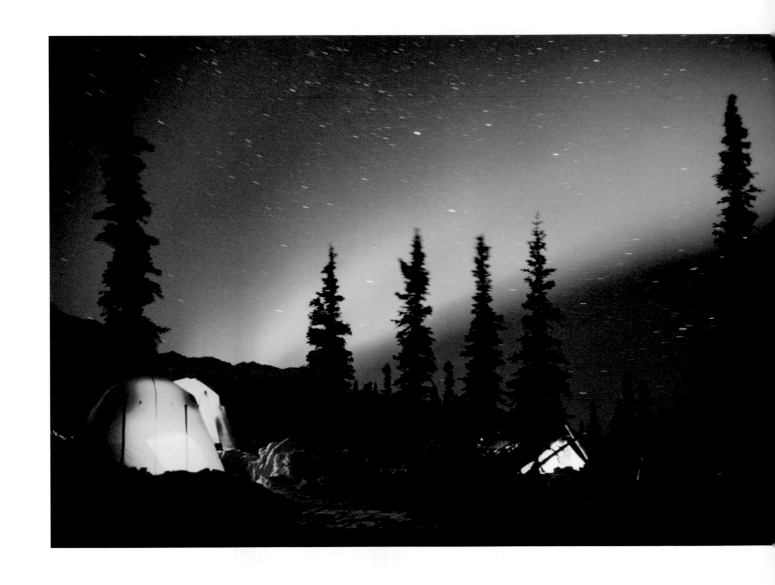

251 The aurora borealis, commonly known as the northern lights, glows above the tented camp of a winter dogsledding expedition through the Brooks Range in Gates of the Arctic National Park.

The stars appear streaked by the earth's rotation during a three-minute exposure, while the aurora has been rendered as a glowing blur, rather than the dancing beams of light seen with the eye.

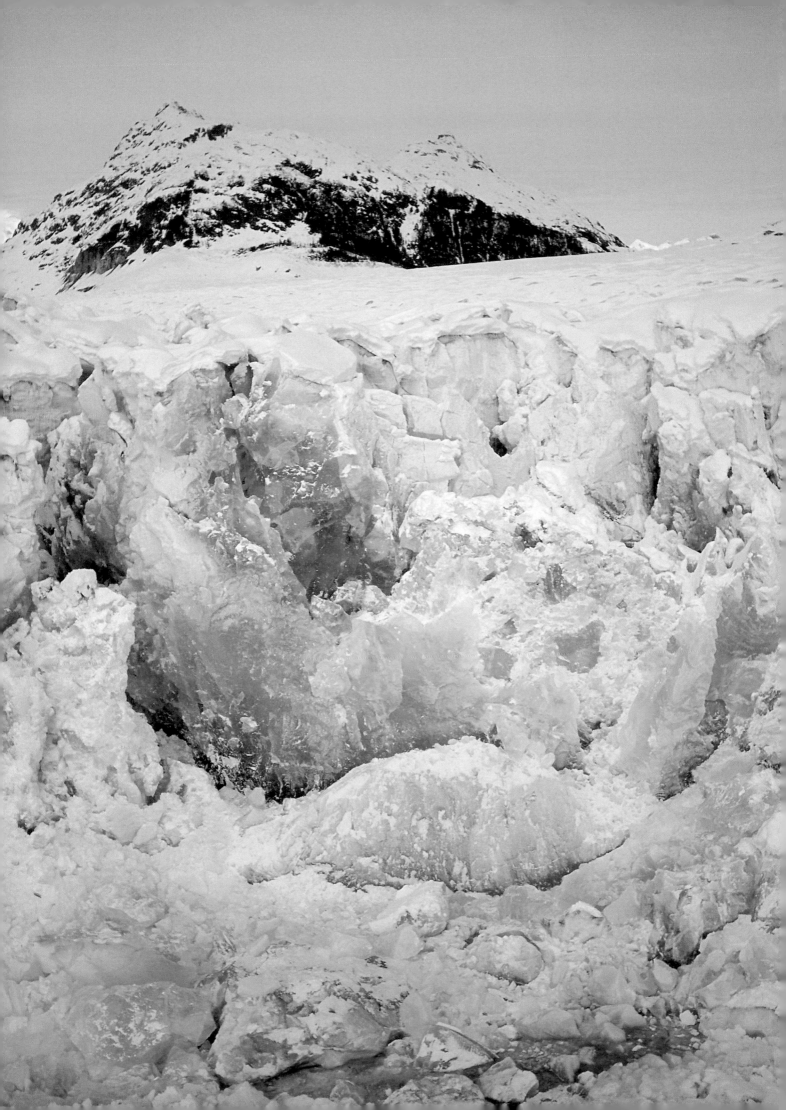

252 The tidewater ice cliff of the massive Columbia Glacier calves icebergs into Prince William Sound near Valdez.

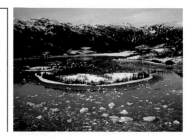

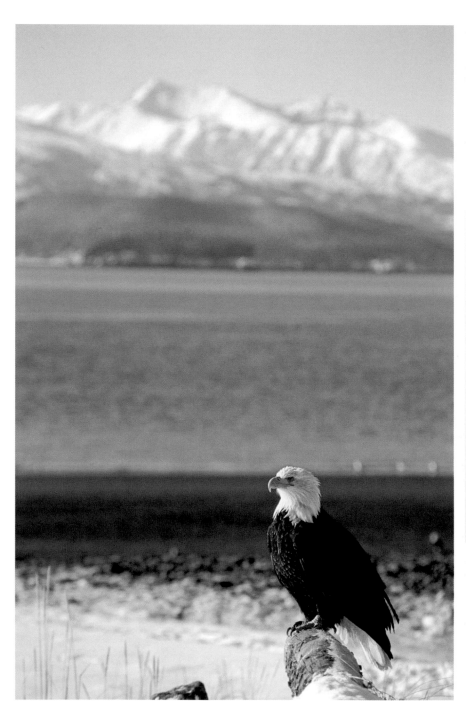

253 top Icebergs dot Prince William Sound off the Gulf of Alaska during spring break-up near the site of the infamous Exxon Valdez oil spill of 1990. Though wildlife declined, the area quickly regained its pristine appearance.

253 bottom left A bald eagle surveys Kachemak Bay between the Kenai and Alaska Peninsulas.

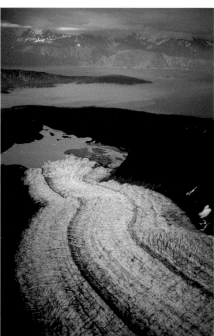

253 bottom right A tidewater glacier drops from the heights of Chilkat Range into the sea in Southeast Alaska's Glacier Bay National Park and Preserve.

254–255 In Portage Lake beneath the Chugach Mountains south of Anchorage, icebergs melt into abstract forms after breaking off from the Portage Glacier.

253

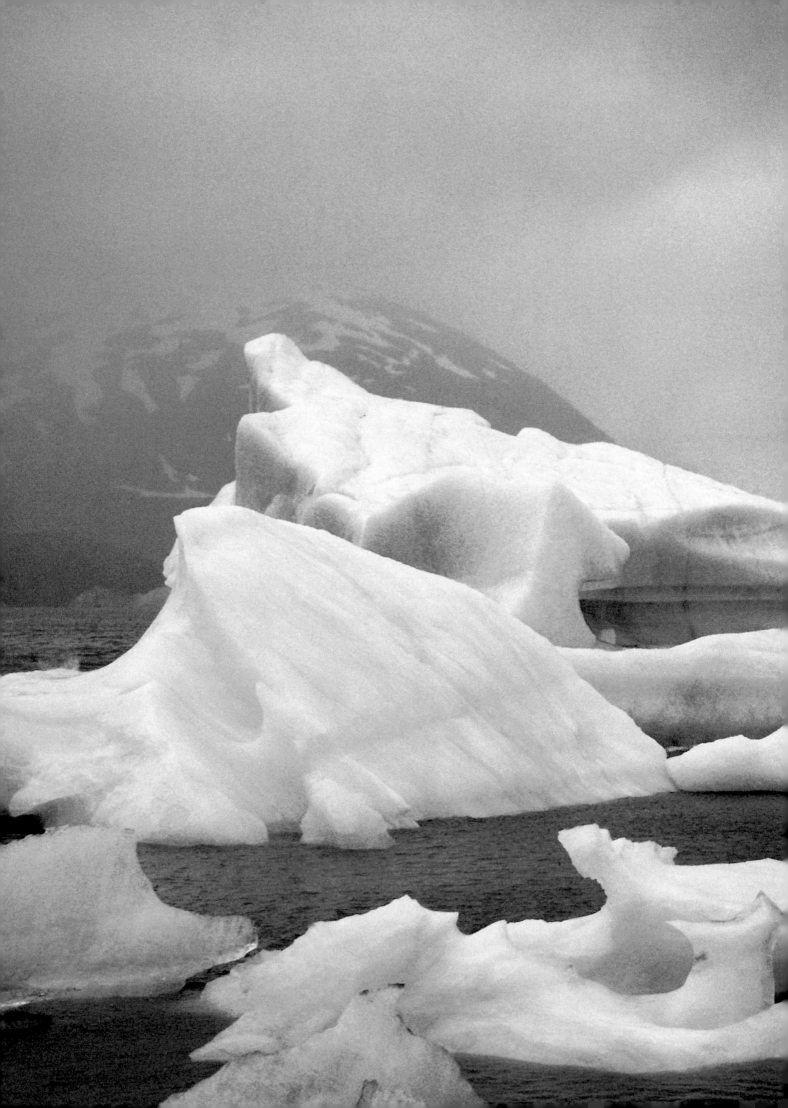

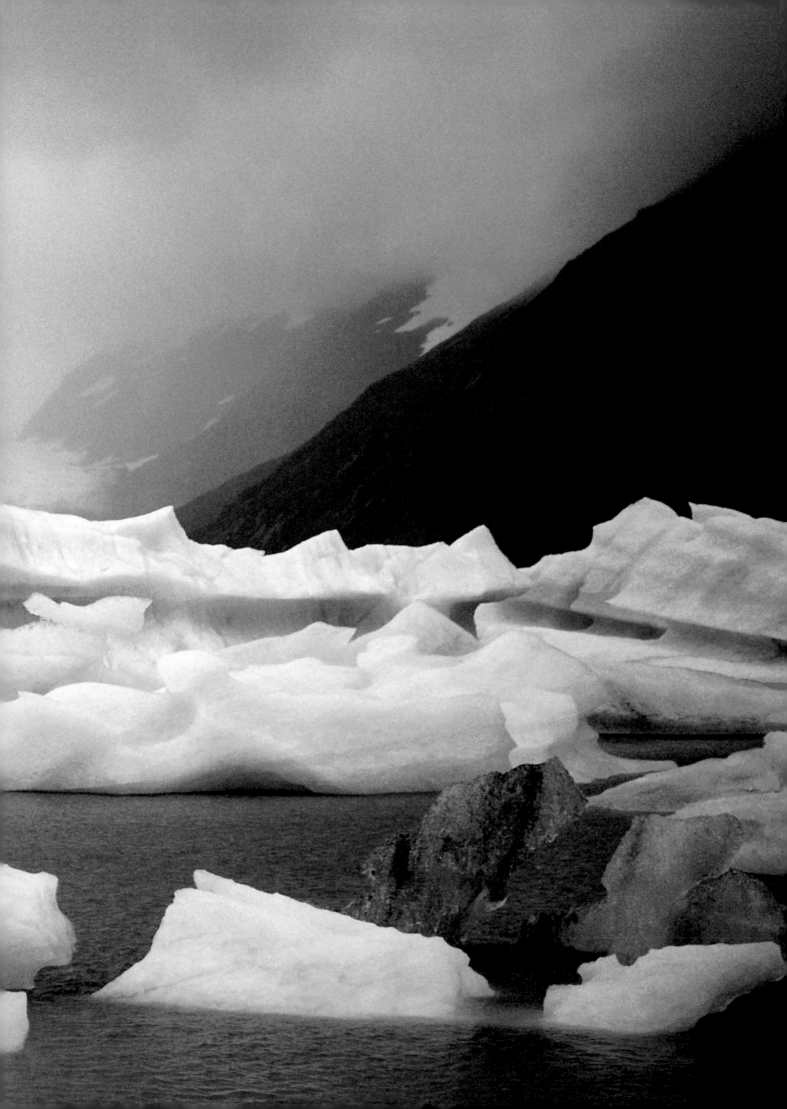

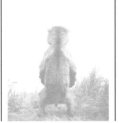

256 The sun sets over the Harding Icefield, a true ice-cap burying all but the tips of countless peaks, on the heights of Kenai Fjords National Park.

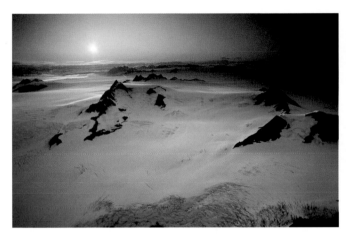

256–257 Blocks of sea ice, raised by a pressure ridge on the frozen Chukchi Sea, transmit an eerie glow in the setting sun a few miles out from Alaska's most northerly town of Barrow.

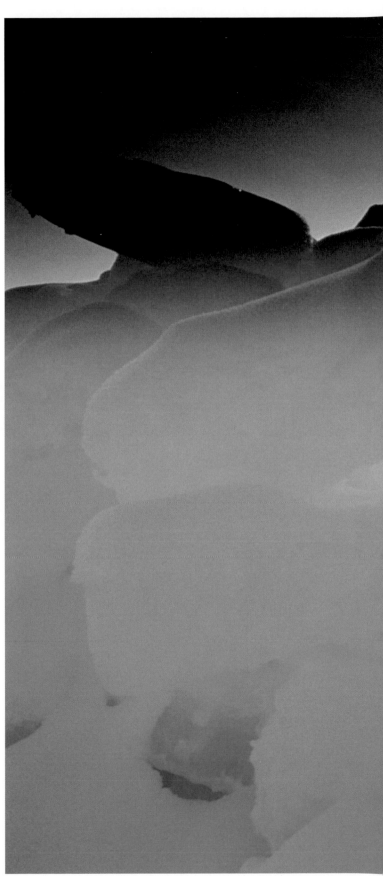

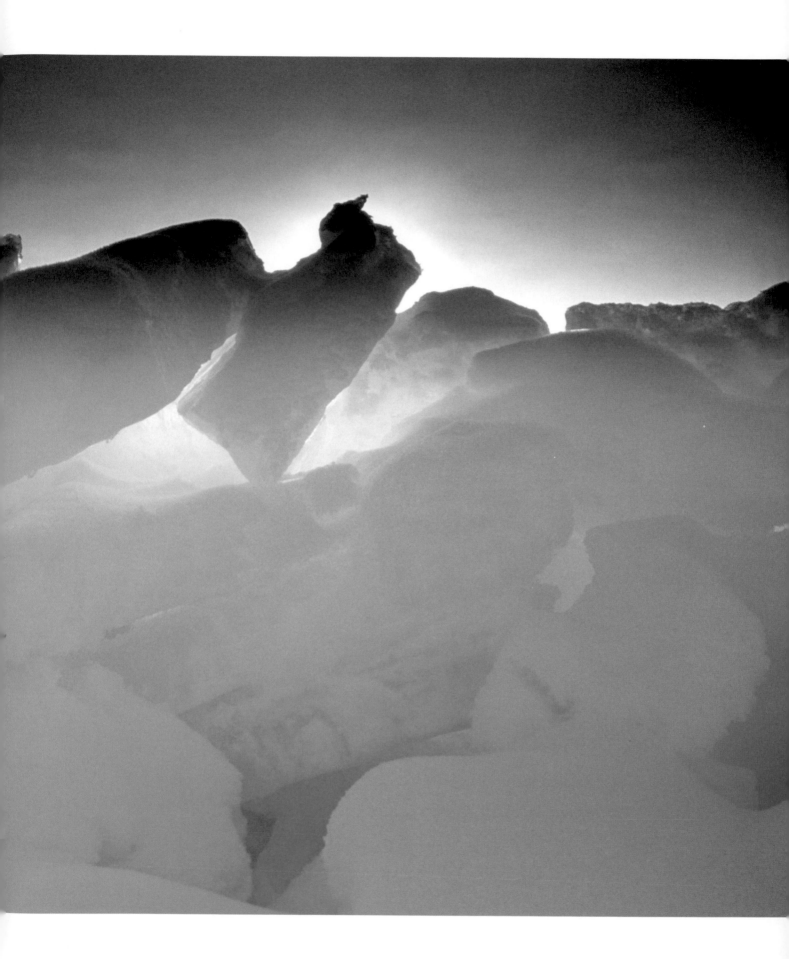

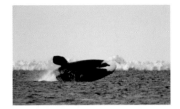

258 top A bowhead whale performs an unusual (for this species) full breach in an open lead of the frozen Chukchi Sea near Barrow.

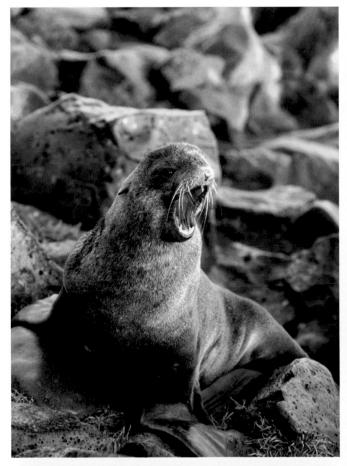

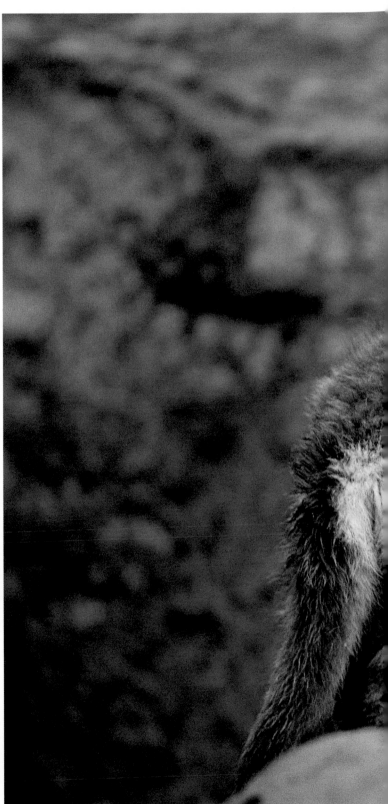

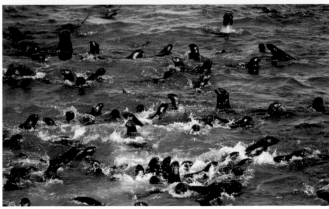

258 center A young male northern fur seal wards off an intruder with a dominance display, as seen from a blind at a breeding colony on the Pribilof Islands.

258 bottom Northern fur seals cavort in the Bering Sea beside the Pribilof Islands, where 800,000 breed in the world's largest concentration of mammals.

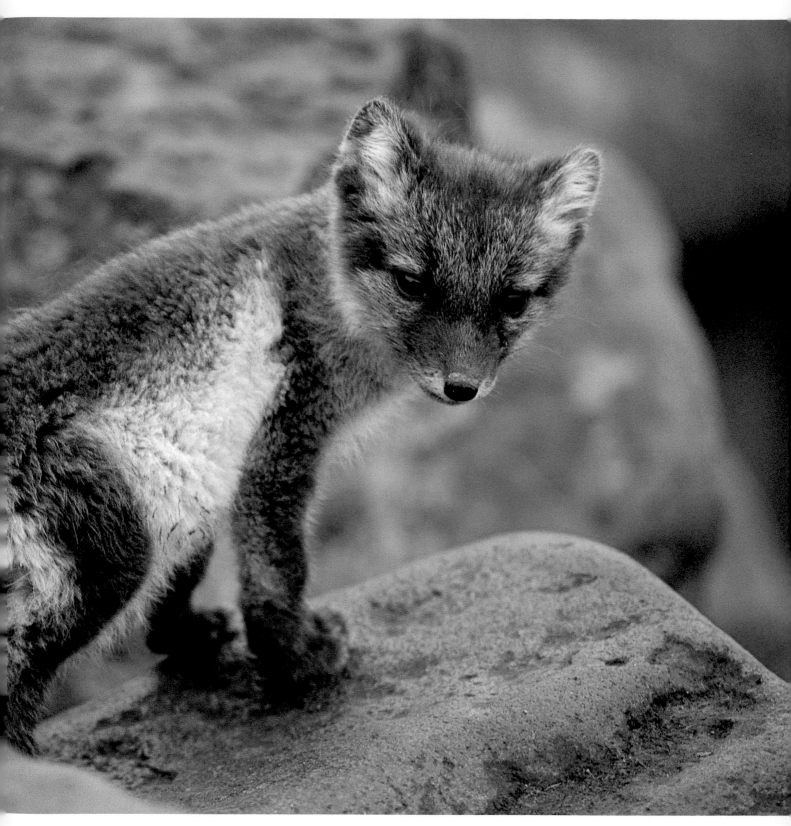

258–259 An arctic fox kit summits a boulder in a Pribilof fur seal colony to check out the whereabouts of his parents and playful siblings.

260–261 An Alaskan brown bear fishes for salmon at Brooks Falls in Katmai National Park on the Alaska Peninsula. Once thought to be a separate species from the grizzly bears of the Lower 48, these much larger bears simply have a higher protein diet from the lucrative salmon runs along the coast of Alaska.

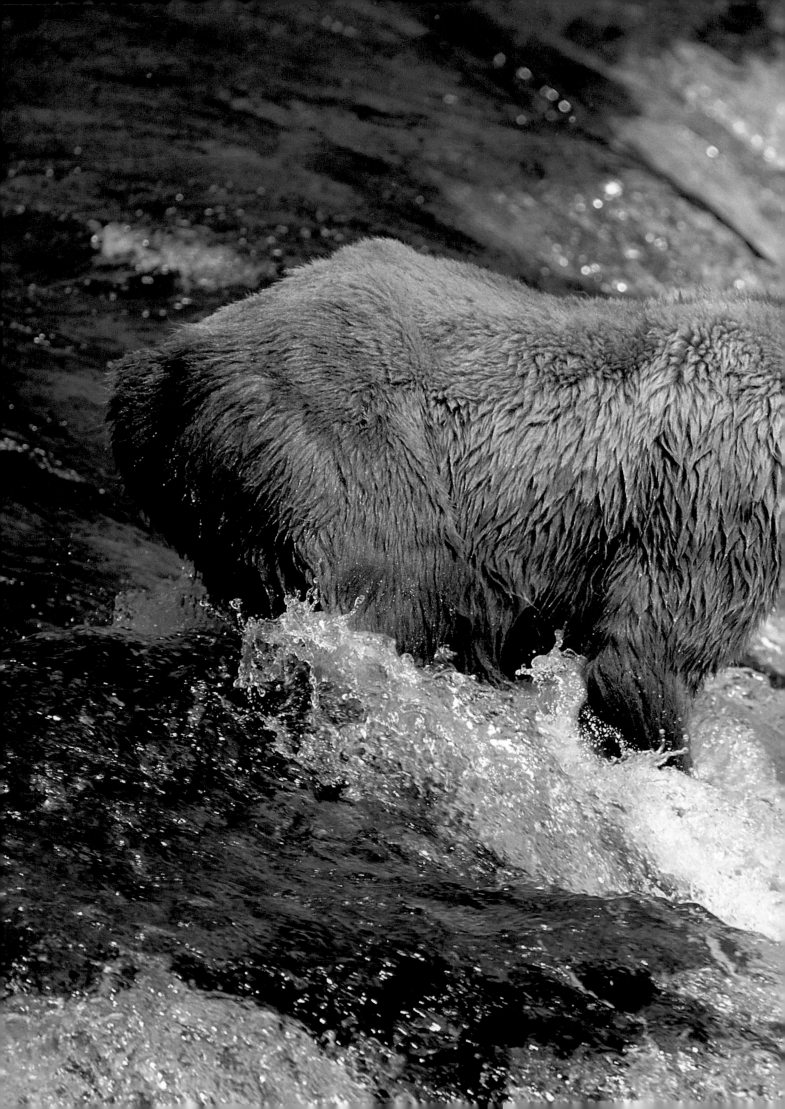

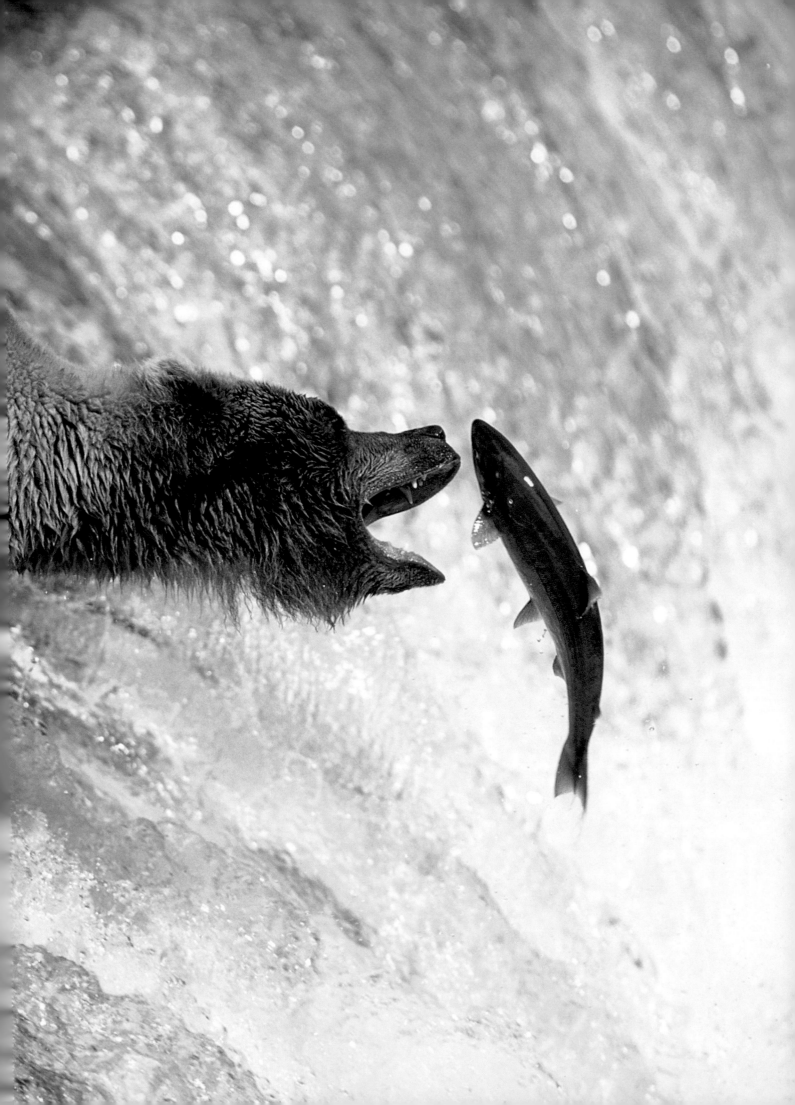

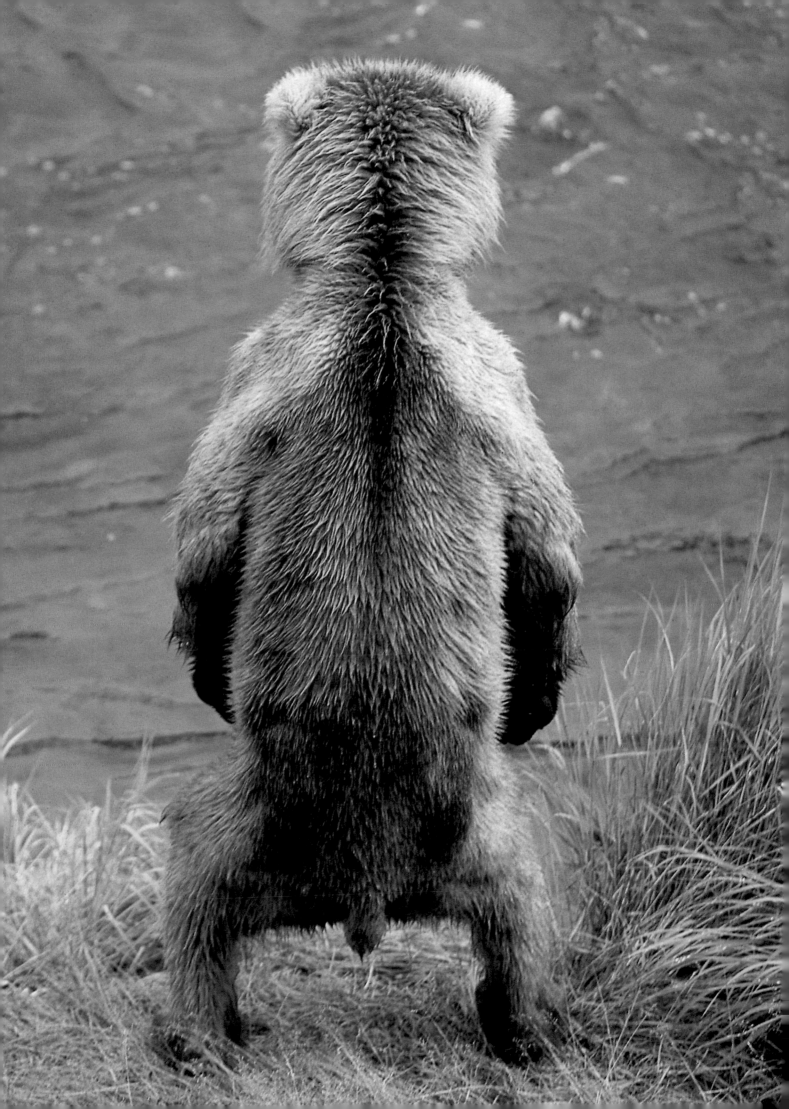

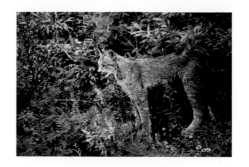

262 *An Alaskan brown bear standing on its hind legs strikes a hauntingly human profile, perhaps accounting for legendary "bigfoot" sightings.*

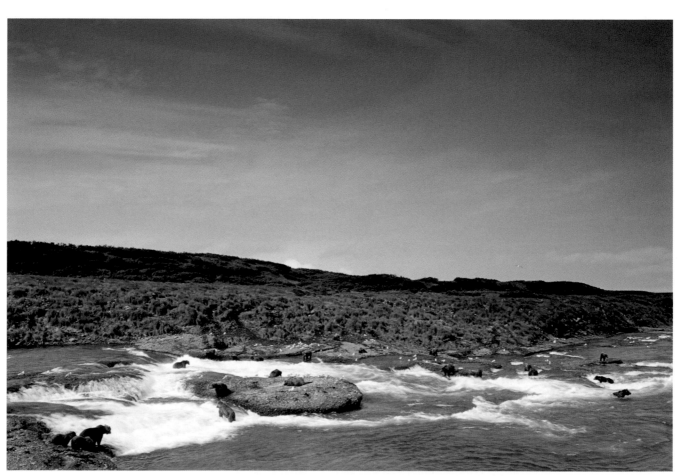

263 top *A Canada lynx stands tall in a bed of flowers moments before pouncing on a snowshoe hare beside the Teklanika River in Denali National Park.*

263 bottom *Twenty-two bears fish the waters below McNeil Falls on the Alaska Peninsula during the height of the summer salmon run.*

264 *A pair of red fox kits play outside their den beside Chenik Lagoon on the Alaska Peninsula. Foxes often follow brown bears to scavenge the remains of salmon.*

264–265 *A large male Alaskan brown bear peers out of deep foliage within sight of the den of the red foxes (left) beside Chenik Lagoon.*

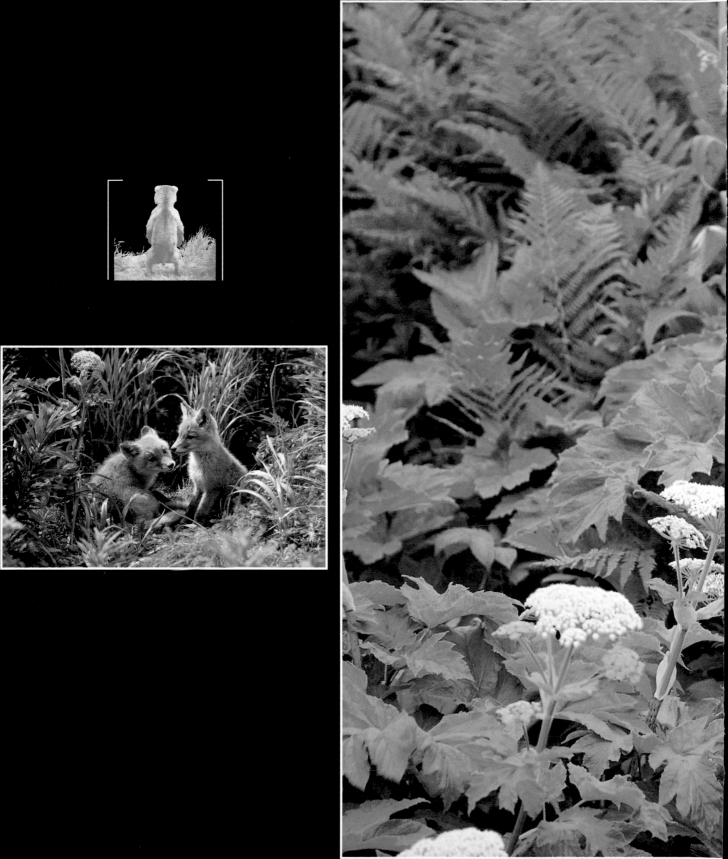

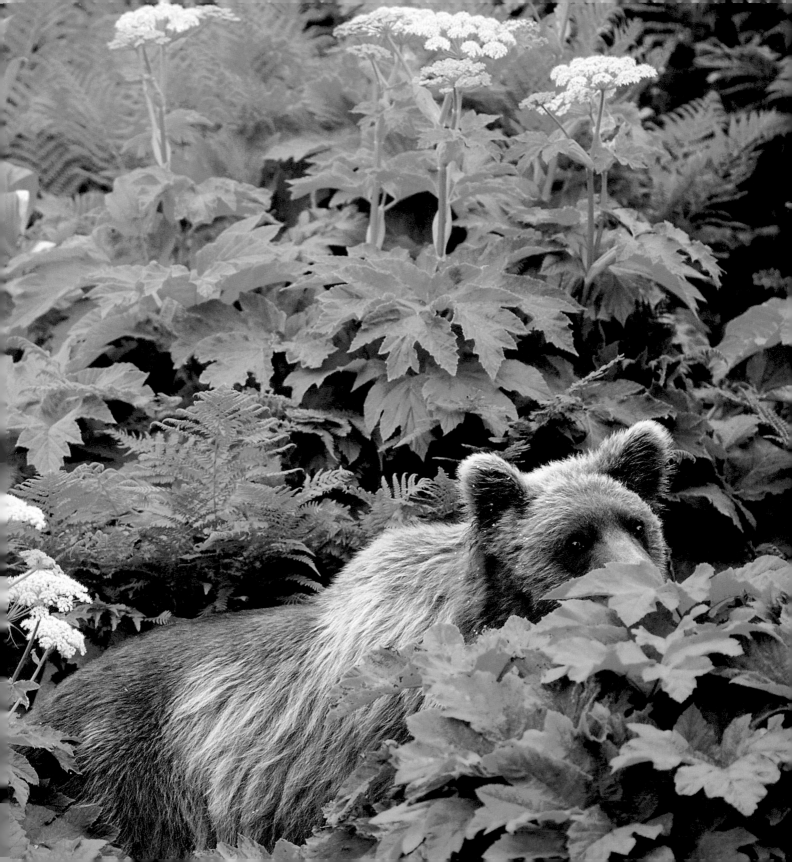

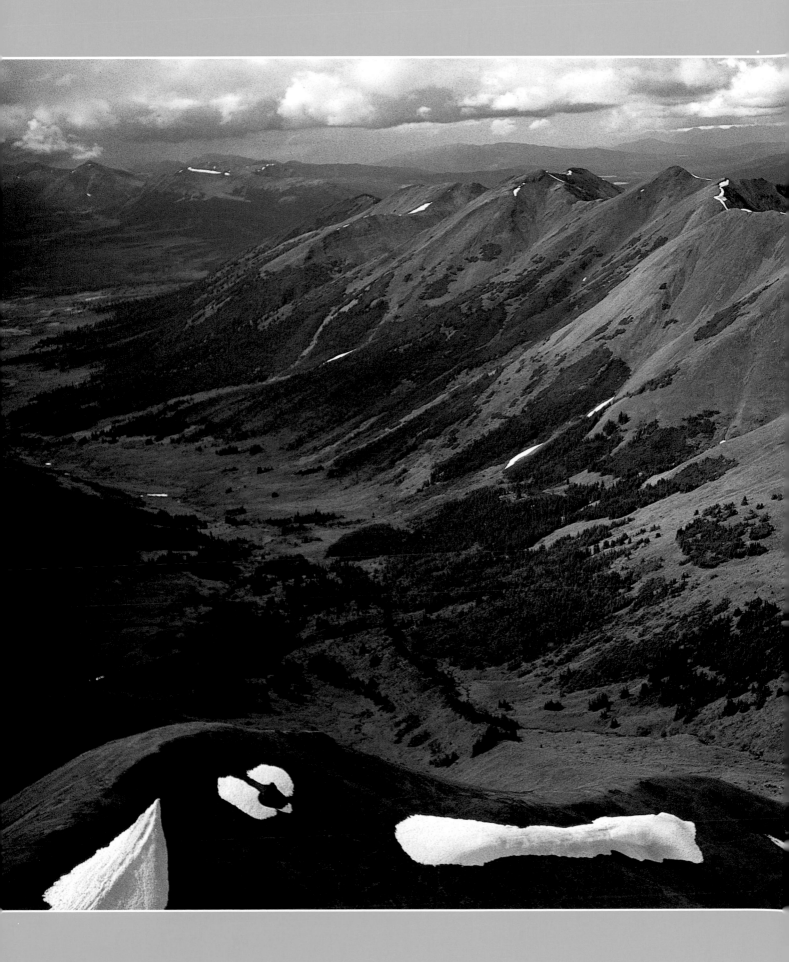

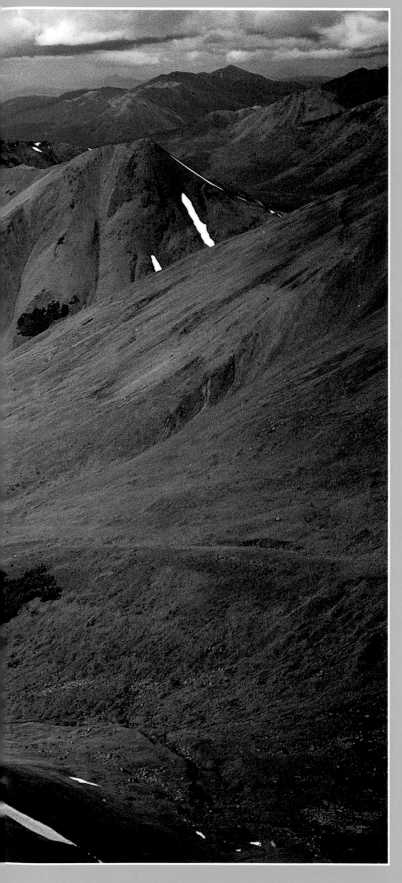

266–267 The wild and remote Mackenzie Mountains that straddle the Yukon-Northwest Territories border are a northern extension of the Rockies.

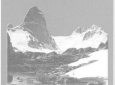

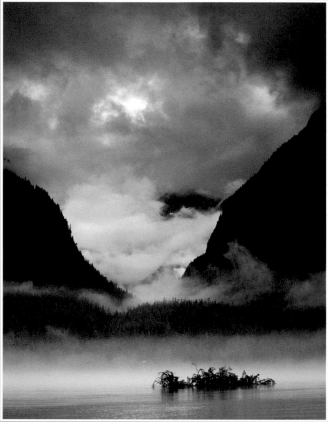

The Yukon and British Columbia

267 Temperate rainforest clings to mountains beside Portland Inlet, a major fjord along the central coast of British Columbia.

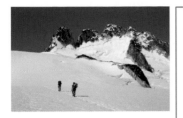

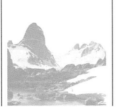

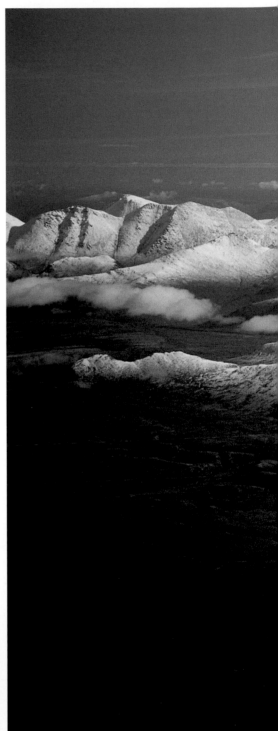

My own first visit to the Yukon came as a perceptual surprise. Everything was so much larger than in the pictures I'd seen. After I returned home, Canada's highest peak—Mount Logan—was enormous in my memory, yet quite unimpressive in my distant photograph. I knew then and there that words and photographs would have a hard time conveying how very much bigger and wilder the Canadian sector of the Pacific Northwest is, compared to its American counterpart.

Right afterwards, in the early 1970s with the first landing on the moon fresh in everyone's mind, I made the bold assertion in a published essay that in everything but measured distance, the climbers who made the first ascent of Mount Logan in 1925 were more remote than the lunar astronauts in 1969. Nine men had endured temperatures that dropped to –40°F on a mountain that only a handful of people had ever seen 150 miles from civilization with no contact with the outside world for 44 days.

At 19,850 feet, Mount Logan may be North America's second highest, but with an eleven-mile section above 16,000 feet, it is unquestionably the largest. It sits amidst thousands of square miles of the world's most glacier-covered terrain outside Greenland and Antarctica. Even today, an official road map of the Yukon lists "settlements" instead of cities—twenty-one in all, with others too small to mention.

To the south, the province of British Columbia remains very much a frontier, apart from the busy modernity of Vancouver and the corridor surrounding the Trans-Canada Highway that leads eastward above the United States border. Despite Vancouver's many attributes, it is no more British Columbia than New York City is North America. A better comparison might be to call Vancouver the Seattle of British Columbia: a cosmopolitan city built around a protected natural harbor backdropped by a skyline of verdant forest and snowy peaks. The majority of foreign visitors go no further than Vancouver or the ski resorts of Whistler, a hundred miles to the north. A lesser number pass through the spectacular Interior Ranges on their way to the pleasuring grounds of the Canadian Rockies: Lake Louise, Banff, and Jasper—subjects of another chapter.

The Trans-Canada Highway, opened in 1962, but not fully paved when I first drove it in 1964, has

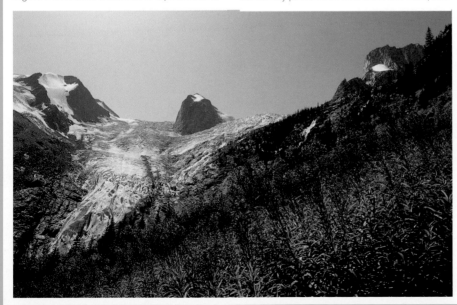

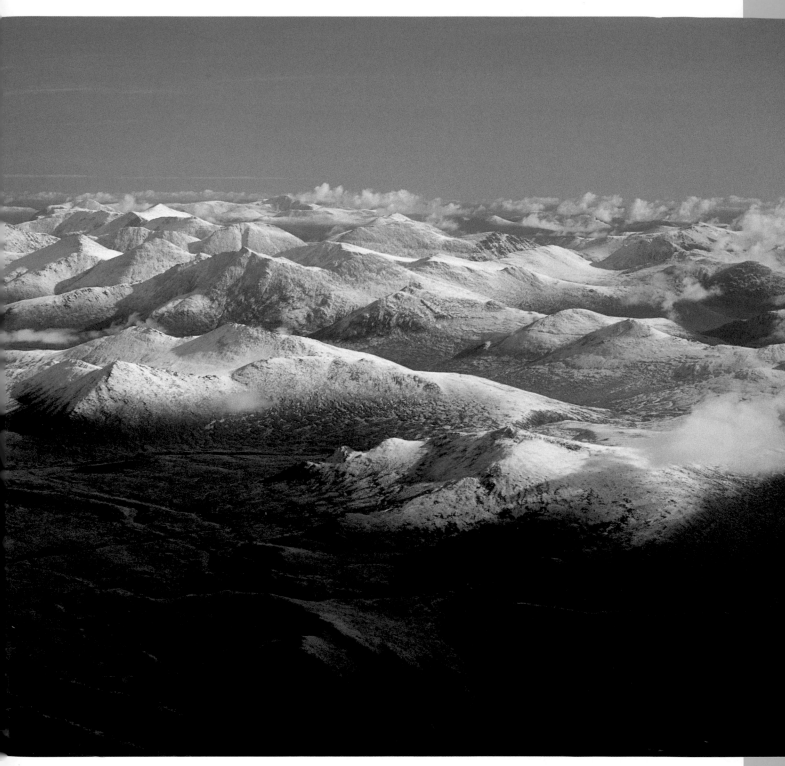

268 bottom Wild spires rising out of the glaciers of the Bugaboo Mountains in the Purcell Range of British Columbia attracted European alpinists in the early twentieth century. Now a provincial park, the mountains are best known for premier helicopter skiing.

268–269 Fresh August snow caps green tundra on the lower peaks of the Kluane Range in the Yukon. To the west is the world's most heavily glaciated terrain outside Greenland and Antarctica, culminating in 19,850 foot Mount Logan of the Saint Elias Range.

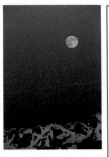

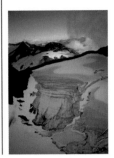

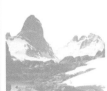

270 top left A full moon rises over the Bugaboo Mountains of southern British Columbia.

270 top right Farther north, a hanging glacier crowns Mount Vetter in lands deeded to the Nisga'a Indians.

made many of these mountain ranges far more accessible. A *National Geographic* map touts a side road to the summit of Mount Revelstoke in the national park of the same name "for those of limited stamina," yet fails to show the existence of the Bugaboo Glacier Provincial Park, sixty miles south of Glacier National Park well off the highway. The wildly shaped granite spires of the Bugaboos, reminiscent of Chamonix, erupt from icefields to offer some of the continent's best Alpine climbing in summer and helicopter skiing in winter.

In 1971, when I made the first ascent of the 3,300-foot West Face of North Howser Tower—the biggest face in the Bugaboos—I looked from the summit at a panorama with no roads, trails, or other evidence of the hand of man. By the early 1980s, astronauts were noticing one of the few artifacts visible from space in one of the other Interior Ranges. I later flew over the Bowron Valley beside the Cariboo Mountains to document the fresh 75-mile swath of world's largest clearcut forest.

As late as 1950, 85 percent of the interior of British Columbia was virgin evergreen forest owned

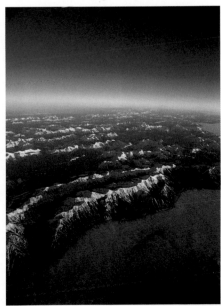

and managed by the government. The provincial forest service dedicated itself to the harvesting of timber for profit, rather than the protection of it for future generations. Much of the pristine landscape has been devastated in the past thirty years, thanks to the construction of public highways that made it economically feasible for private companies to build local roads to extract timber.

In 1974, when the Stewart-Cassiar Highway opened lengthwise through the northern province to connect with the Alaska Highway just over the Yukon border, I saw no clearcutting after the first few miles of the narrow dirt road beyond where it turned off from the older Yellowhead Highway. When I repeated the drive in 1992, all the prime forests had been cut near the road for hundreds of miles.

Years earlier and closer to the coast, logging companies had built roads and clearcut around the Nass River Valley on traditional Nisga'a tribal lands. The enterprising Nisga'a were aware of King George III's 1763 royal proclamation that the colonies were to leave indigenous people and their lands undisturbed. As early as 1913, a Nisga'a delegation went to London to confirm that their aboriginal rights had not been extinguished. Canadian politicians were told to negotiate their claim, but instead they passed a law making it illegal to raise funds in support of any Indian land claim.

The Nisga'a never gave up. In August 1998, I photographed *their* 800 square miles of lands, newly returned to them with full political and judicial authority, for *Time* magazine. News stories heralded the end of the pioneer ethic of conquering savages and exploiting natural resources to carve out homes in the wilderness.

Forest exploitation has finally begun to wind down while there are still forests left to preserve. Since 1991, over 200 new provincial parks have been created in British Columbia and more are on the drawing boards. Forest advocates continue to keep up the vigil, remembering their recent battles over the logging of Vancouver Island, where only a few areas, such as Pacific Rim National Park and the new Upper Carmanah Provincial Park, have

been saved. Even this degree of protection only happened after international outcry over "The Black Hole," a huge scar caused by clearcutting and burning in formerly pristine Clayoquot Sound.

An urban journalist once summed up Canada north of Vancouver as "moose, mines, and energy," but what's most conspicuously missing are virgin forests—until you get to the Yukon. Acquired from the Hudson's Bay Company as part of the "North-Western Territory" in 1870, the Yukon was made a separate territory in 1898 during the Klondike gold rush. At that time it had more residents than today.

Many tourists visit the Yukon by first traversing the "Inside Passage" by ferry to Haines or Skagway. From these Alaskan ports, roads lead just over a hundred miles inland to the white Dall sheep and glaciers of Kluane National Park or to Whitehorse. Not far out of Skagway is the start of the legendary Chilkoot Trail from the Klondike gold stampede, now maintained as a National Historical Site. It leads thirty-three miles from coastal Alaska over a steep pass into the vast interior plateau of the Yukon River in a corner of British Columbia close to the Yukon border.

The Yukon extends all the way to the Beaufort Sea, where half of its Arctic Coast is preserved in North Yukon National Park, grazed by hundreds of thousands of caribou which migrate back and forth from Alaska. In the central interior, Dawson City at the end of the Klondike Highway was Canada's largest west of Manitoba during the gold rush. After a newer rush for oil, a failed pipeline route became the wild Canol Heritage Trail, which I've followed into the Mackenzie Mountains as far as Macmillan Pass on the border of the Northwest Territories.

The Yukon's most important highway was not originally its own. Passing 630 miles through the province, the Alaska Highway was built in an amazing six months in 1942 after the Japanese attacked Pearl Harbor and the Aleutian Islands. Designed to connect Alaska with the lower forty-eight states, the highway has become the main arterial for a modern Yukon economy based on mining and tourism.

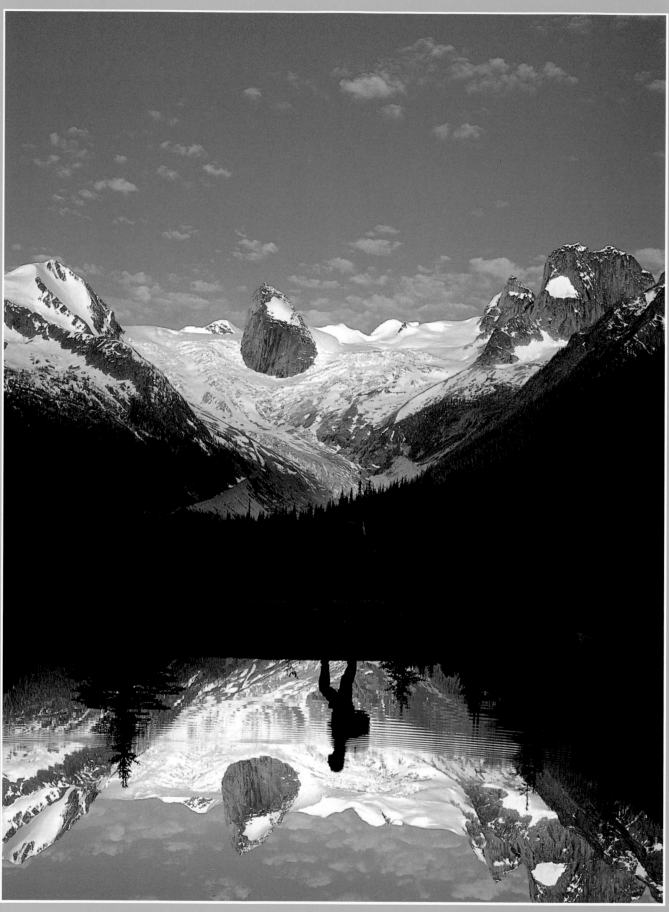

270 bottom From the air, repeating waves of the Interior Ranges of British Columbia recede toward the Canadian Rockies.

270–271 The granite spires of the Bugaboo Mountains line the horizon above a backpacker hidden in shadow, revealed only by a reflection that mirrors the lower point of view of the distant surface of the mountain pond. Absent from most road maps of Canada, the Bugaboos are approached by trail from the end of a series of dirt logging roads from the tiny settlement of Spillamacheen.

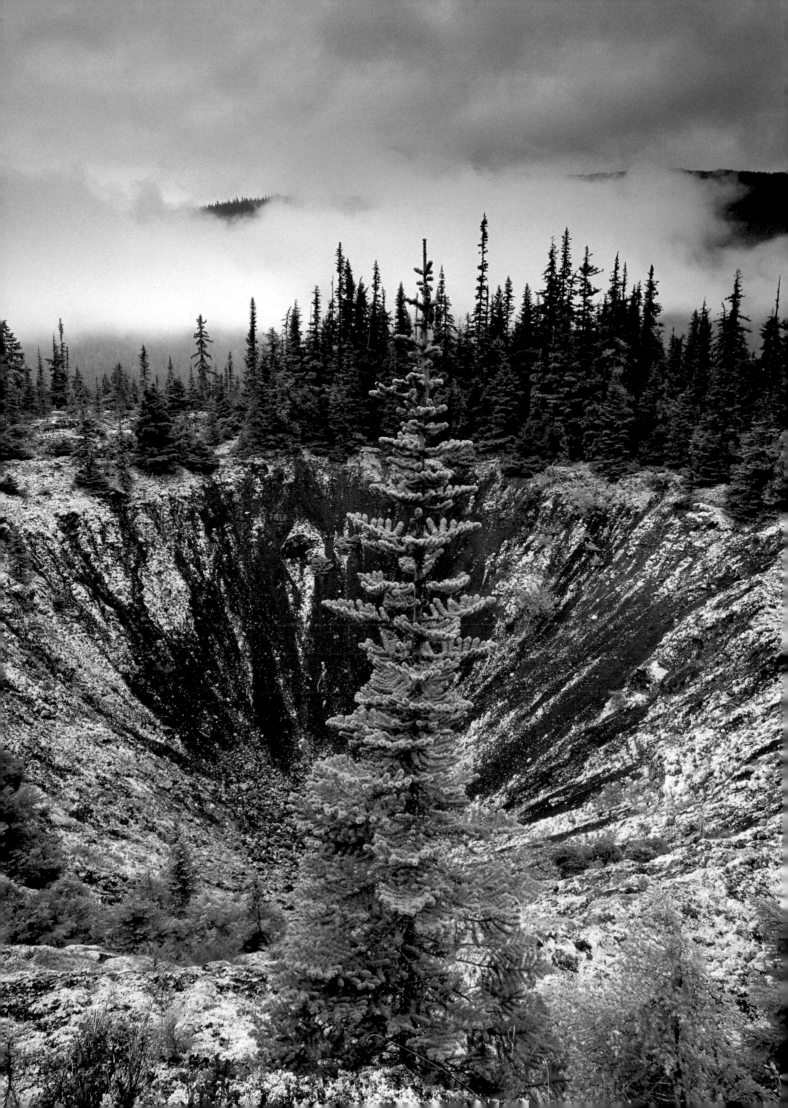

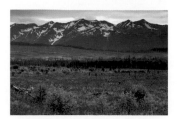

272 A young spruce sprouts on the rim of a volcanic crater that erupted about 250 years ago, killing hundreds of Nisga'a Indians in the Nass River Valley.

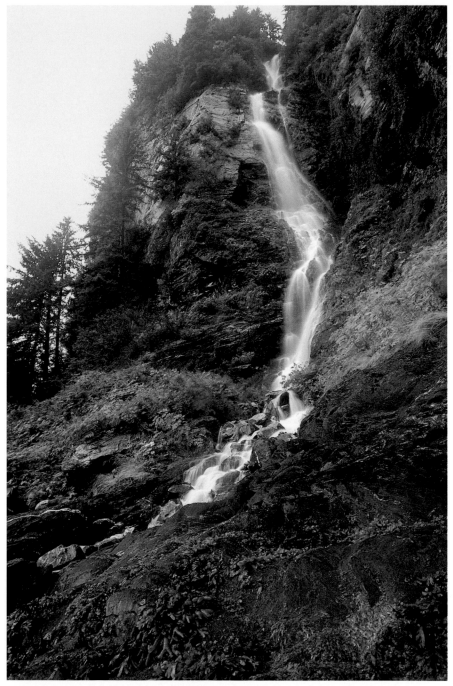

273 top Purple fireweed blankets the Irving Valley beside the narrow Cassiar Highway that traverses northern British Columbia.

273 bottom A tidewater waterfall plunges over high cliffs on Nisga'a tribal lands into Portland Inlet in northern British Columbia.

274 Red maple leaves, the symbol of Canada, sprout from young lava on lands ceded to the Nisga'a tribe in 1998 with full political jurisdiction.

274–275 Sunrise through morning mist casts a warm glow over the Skeena River near Smithers in northern British Columbia.

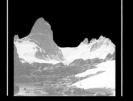

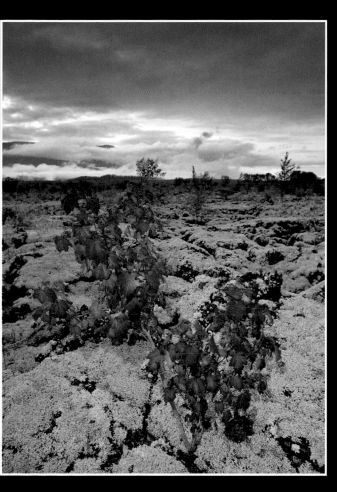

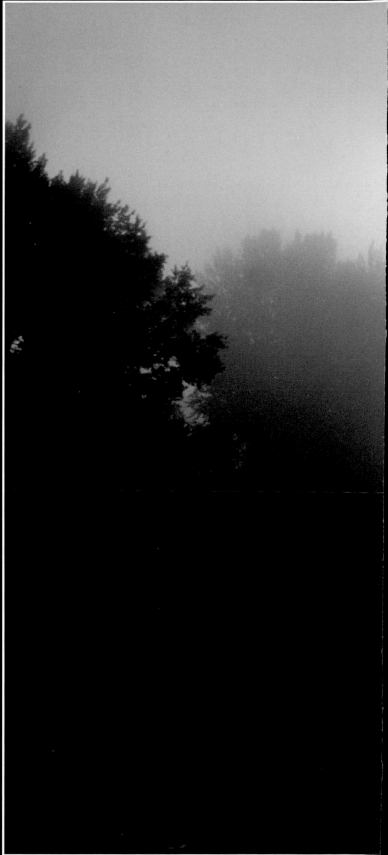

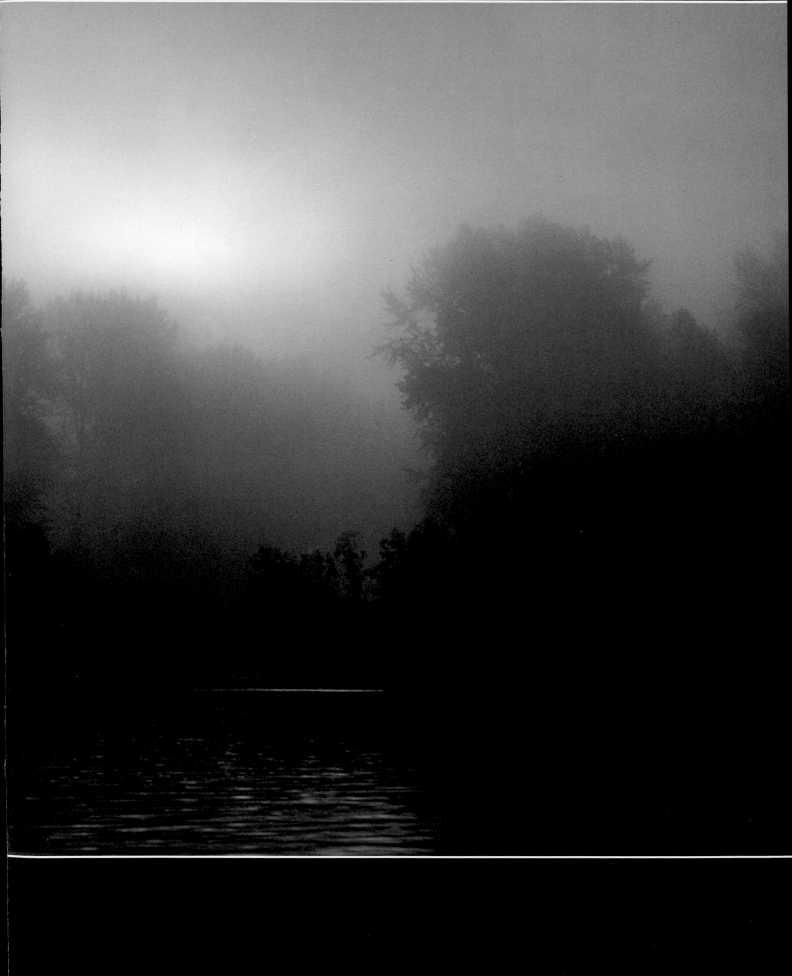

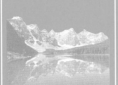

276 Spring break-up begins on one edge of frozen Peyto Lake in Jasper National Park.

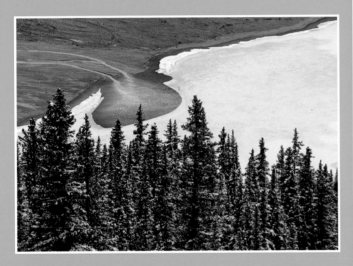

The Canadian Rockies

276–277 Fresh snow in July surrounds a pond in an alpine meadow near Lake O'Hara in Yoho National Park on the opposite side of the range from Lake Louise.

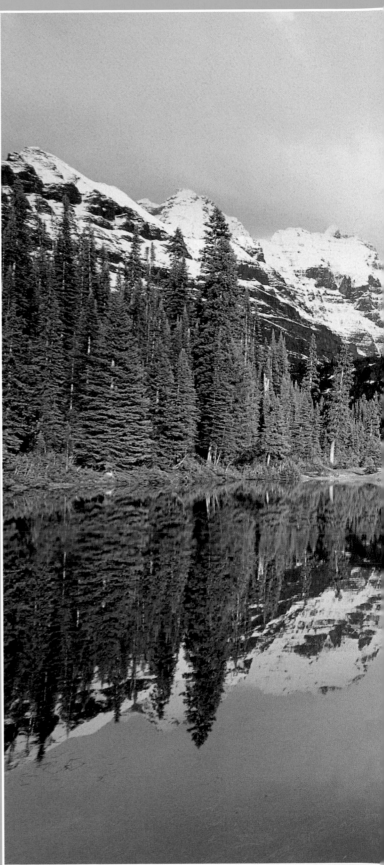

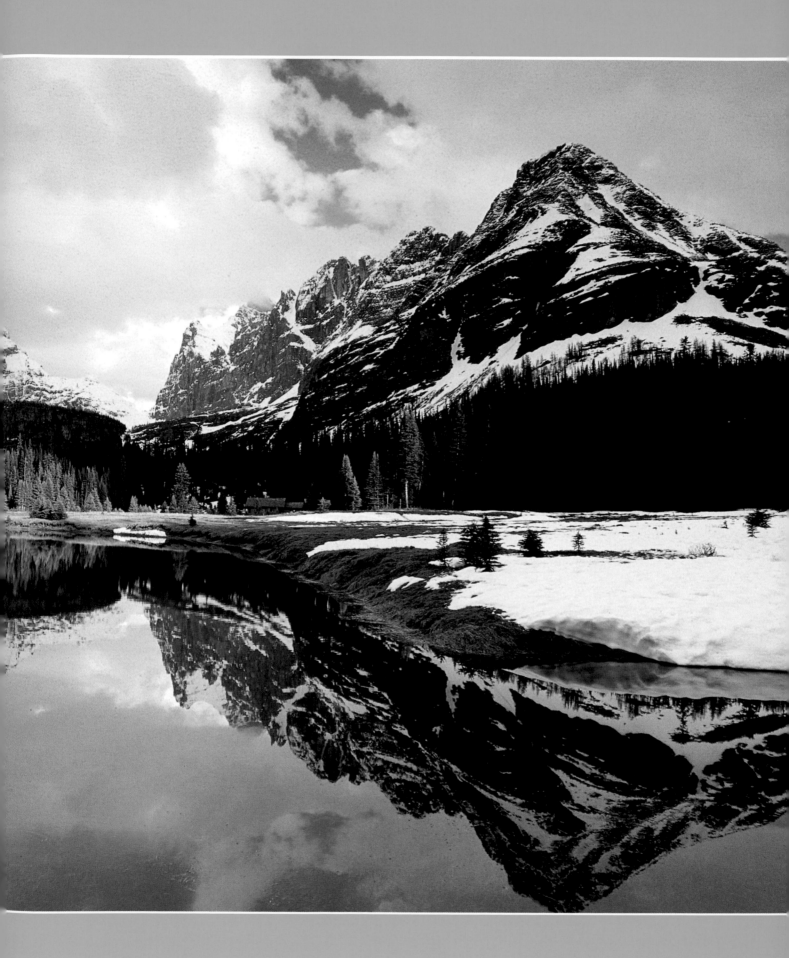

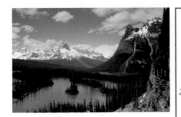

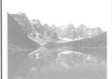

278 left The hidden valley of Lake O'Hara in Yoho National Park is seen from the Hanging Gardens of Babylon.

278 right Mount Robson, highest in the Canadian Rockies at 12,972 feet, rises 10,000 feet above the forests.

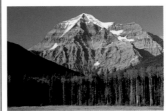

I first saw the Canadian Rockies as an apparition across the plains of Alberta on a clear summer morning in 1964. As I was driving north of Calgary on the new Trans–Canada Highway at dawn, a shadowy line on the horizon suddenly glowed crimson in the sunrise. A continuous wall of storybook mountains extended as far as I could see, blanketed in glaciers and permanent snowfields by the cool temperatures and long winters of its northerly latitudes.

My young family was bound for the first of many summer vacations in Banff National Park. By the end of the week we had also visited Jasper, Kootenay, and Yoho, the other national parks in a contiguous cluster that straddles the wildest and most scenic part of the Canadian Rockies.

The range stretches 400 miles north of the United States border before splintering into a series of lower sub-ranges—the Cassiar, Mackenzie, Olgilvie, Pelly, and Selwyn Mountains—which extend well into the Arctic. For 250 miles between Crowsnest Pass near the border and Jasper in the north, only the Trans–Canada Highway crosses the rugged range. However, the Icefields Parkway, one of the world's most scenic highways, traverses 142 miles of the heart of the Rockies. The parkway branches off thirty miles north of Banff at Lake Louise, where a classic 400-room chateau is perched on the edge of the legendary lake's green waters.

Where the parkway crosses the Continental Divide at Sunwapta Pass, the waters don't simply split toward the Atlantic or the Pacific, but instead diverge three ways within a few miles toward the Pacific Ocean, Hudson Bay, and the Beaufort Sea of the Arctic Ocean. Just beyond the pass is the 125-square-mile Columbia Icefield, formed where glaciers descending from a cluster of summits join together in a high basin. Though the main icefield cannot be seen from the road, an arm of the Athabaska Glacier reached so far down a side valley in 1964 that I could touch moving ice within a minute after getting out of my car. Since then, the glacier has retreated more than a mile up the canyon.

Before the Trans–Canada Highway, access to remote mountains and valleys along basically the same route was provided by the Canadian Pacific Railroad. As it was nearing completion in 1883, two workers fought over rights to charge admission to hot springs emanating from a cave in the hills above the tracks. The railroad settled the matter by getting the government to set aside ten square miles as a public spa "reserved from sale or settlement or squatting." In 1887, the area was expanded into "The Rocky Mountains Park of Canada," with an area of 260 square miles. Later renamed Banff National Park, this first national park in Canada is now larger than two Yosemite National Parks. Jasper National Park, created in 1907, is larger than three Yosemites.

American historians single out the Lewis and Clark Expedition as unique because it crossed the continent within the United States as early as 1805. They often fail to mention that Sir Alexander Mackenzie had already crossed from sea to sea over the Rockies through Canada in 1793. By 1811, David Thompson had traversed Athabaska Pass in winter, opening a fur trading route across Jasper National Park to the Pacific. North of the pass in 1827, a Scottish botanist named David Douglas made the first climb of an ice-covered mountain in North America. He touted Mount Brown as being the continent's highest point at 17,000 feet—well above Europe's Mont Blanc at 15,771 feet.

After generations of explorers and climbers failed to find the great peak, it became apparent that Douglas had climbed a mere 10,000-foot summit well north of the Canadian Rockies' highest peak, magnificent Mount Robson, which rises a full 10,000 feet above its icy reflection in Kinney Lake to 12,972 feet. Now within a provincial park of its own, Robson was first climbed in 1913 by an Alpine Club of Canada party led by the Austrian guide Conrad Kain.

Guides from Austria and Switzerland were lured to the Canadian Rockies by the Canadian Pacific Railroad just before the turn of the Twentieth Century. Soon after the route linking the two coasts of Canada was completed in 1885, it became apparent that travel to the remote mountain areas was not an economic success. The railroad began promoting the Rockies as "The Canadian Alps," called the range "an improvement on Switzerland," and brought over Edward Whymper, who had made the first ascent of the Matterhorn in 1865.

Though Whymper was too elderly to make first ascents, he was in Banff Park in 1901 when two Swiss guides accompanied the audacious young Reverend James Outram to the summit of Mount Assiniboine, still described today as "The Matterhorn of the Rockies." Many other major peaks were climbed within the decade, and the railroad built a string of plush resort hotels, culminating in the huge Banff Springs Hotel that holds more than a thousand guests.

The city of Banff was allowed to evolve into a national park anomaly, a private town of 7,500 people wholly within a public park. More than four million visitors come through each year to dine, drink, golf, fish, swim, and ski. Many of the businesses are now Japanese owned and operated. My preference is to pass through Banff and move farther afield to hike and climb in remote valleys, then return for a final night or two of comfort around Lake Louise, the Valley of the Ten Peaks, Lake O'Hara in Yoho, or Jasper, to name a few of the less urban, yet easily accessible areas in the heart of the Rockies.

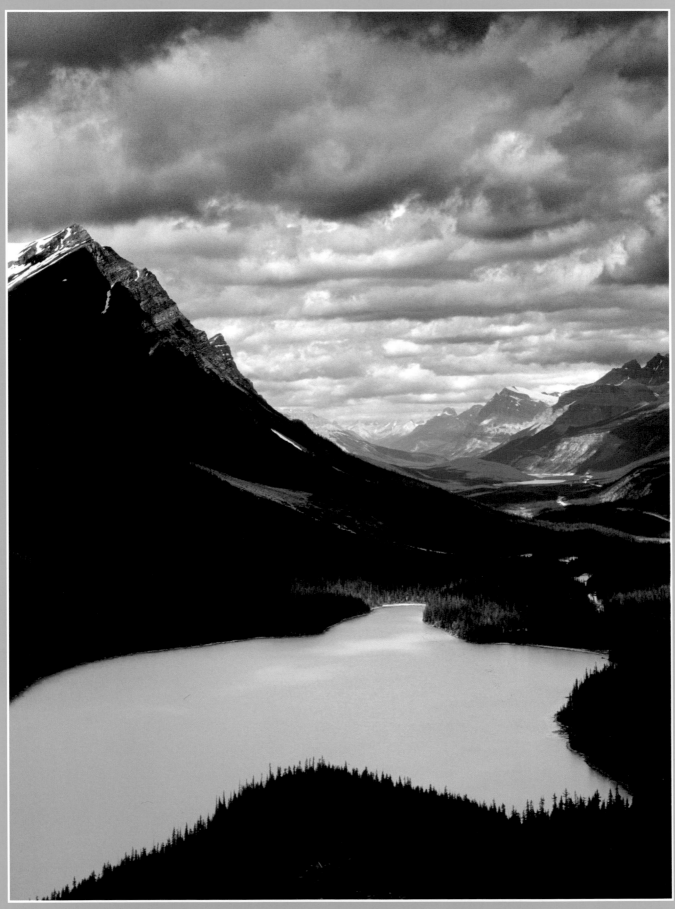

279 Summer storm clouds hang over the green glacial waters of Peyto Lake at the head of the Mistaya Valley in Jasper National Park. The intense greeen color is due to the close proximity of the active Peyto Glacier, which grinds away stone at its base into fine glacial silt. The ice once advanced far down the valley, carving its U shape, and when it last retreated, it deposited the terminal moraine of rock debris that has dammed off the lake. Glacial silt is gradually filling the lake, and within a few centuries it may begin to become a mountain meadow.

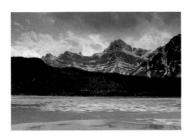

280 top Howse Peak rises high over the glacial green waters of Waterfowl Lake, still partly frozen in midsummer in the highlands of Banff National Park.

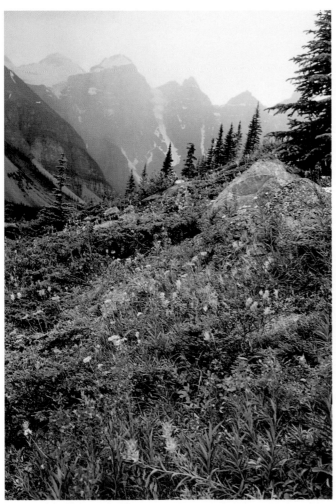

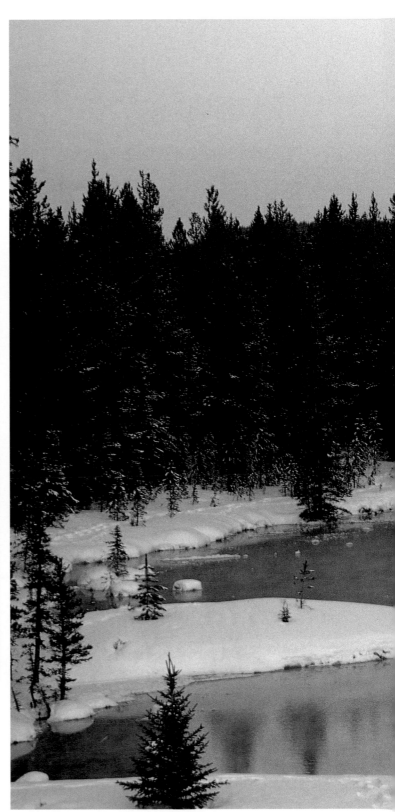

280 bottom Wetted by a passing thunderstorm, a profusion of August wildflowers stand out against the Valley of the Ten Peaks in Banff National Park.

280–281 The Bow River reflects the warm glow of the predawn twilight of a subzero January morning in Banff National Park.

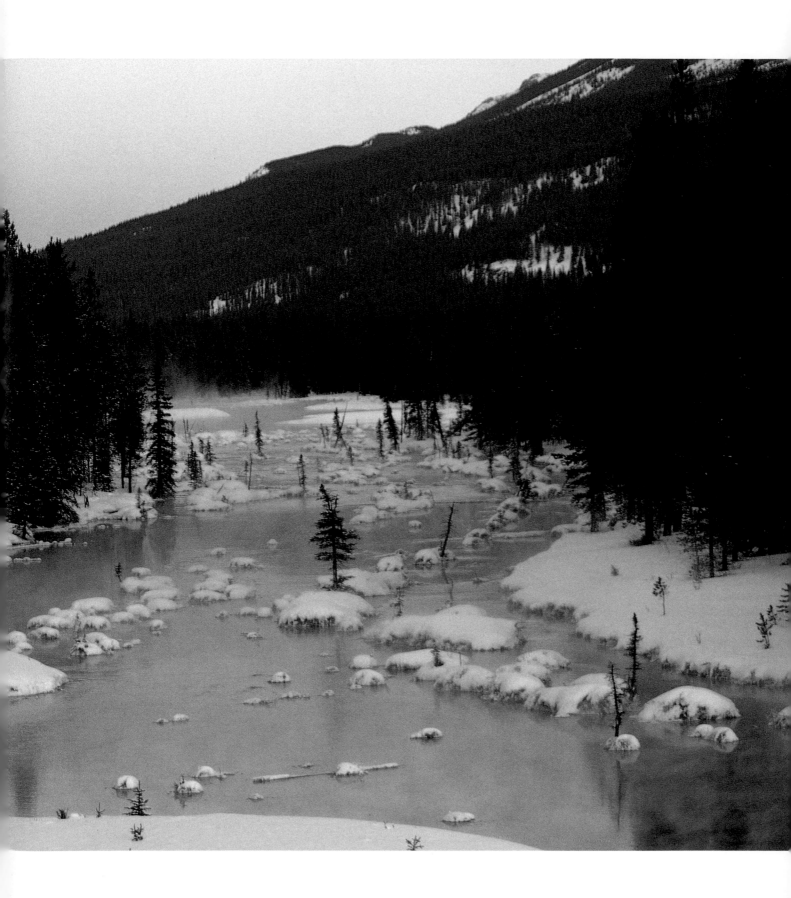

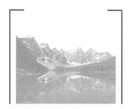

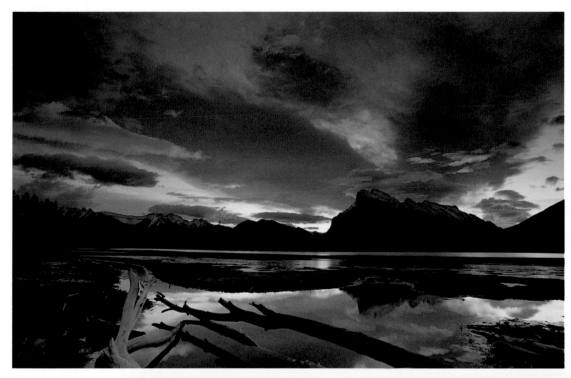

284–285 Meltwater atop frozen Vermilion Lake reflects evening light on peaks and clouds during a midwinter period of warm Chinook winds.

285 Also in Banff Park, a full moon sets over the glacier-draped east face of Mount Victoria above Lake Louise, the birthplace of recreational hiking in the Canadian Rockies in the 1890s.

282 top A fiery sunrise over the Bow River Valley near Banff reflects in Vermilion Lake.

282 bottom A hiker watches dawn break high over the Bow River Valley in Banff National Park.

283 Alpenglow colors the Valley of the Ten Peaks beyond a stream crossing in Larch Valley on the Sentinel Pass Trail.

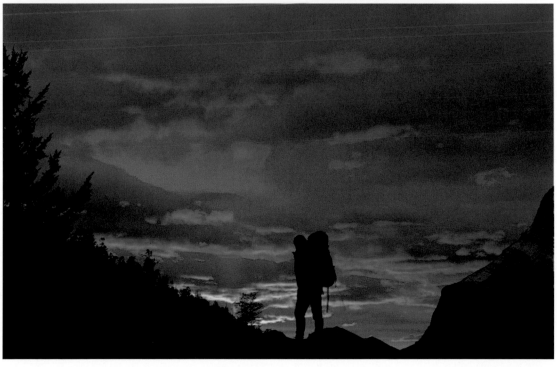

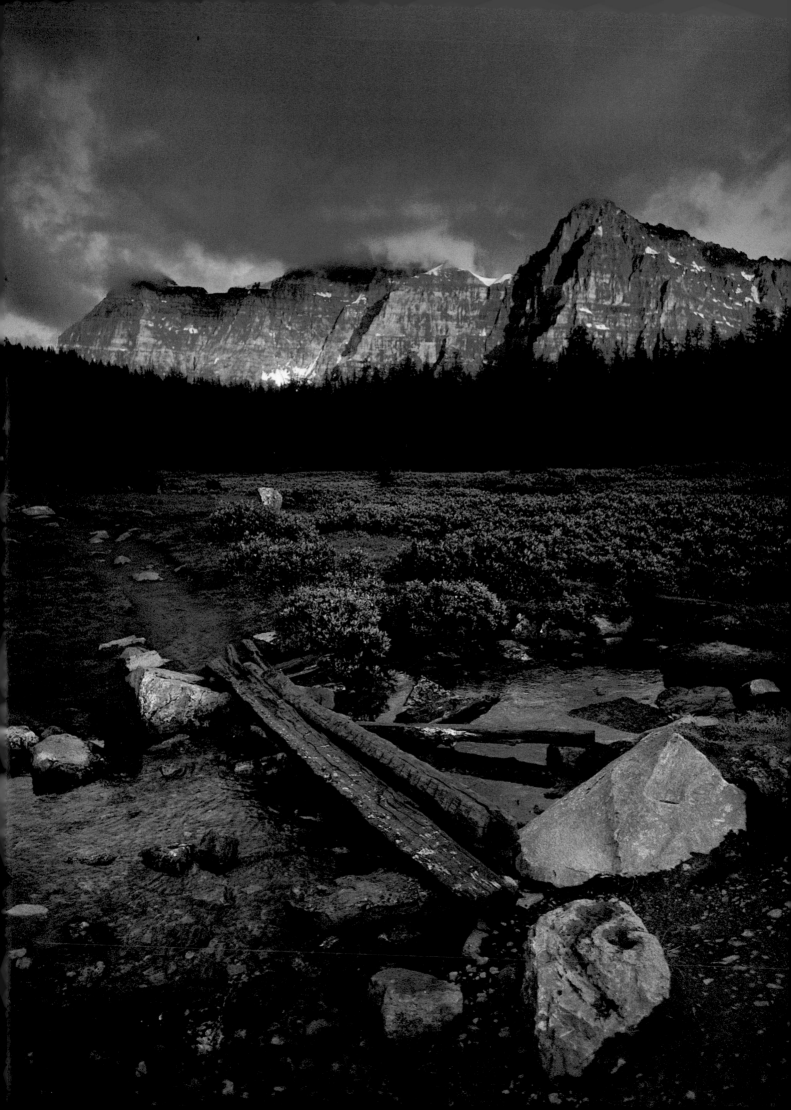

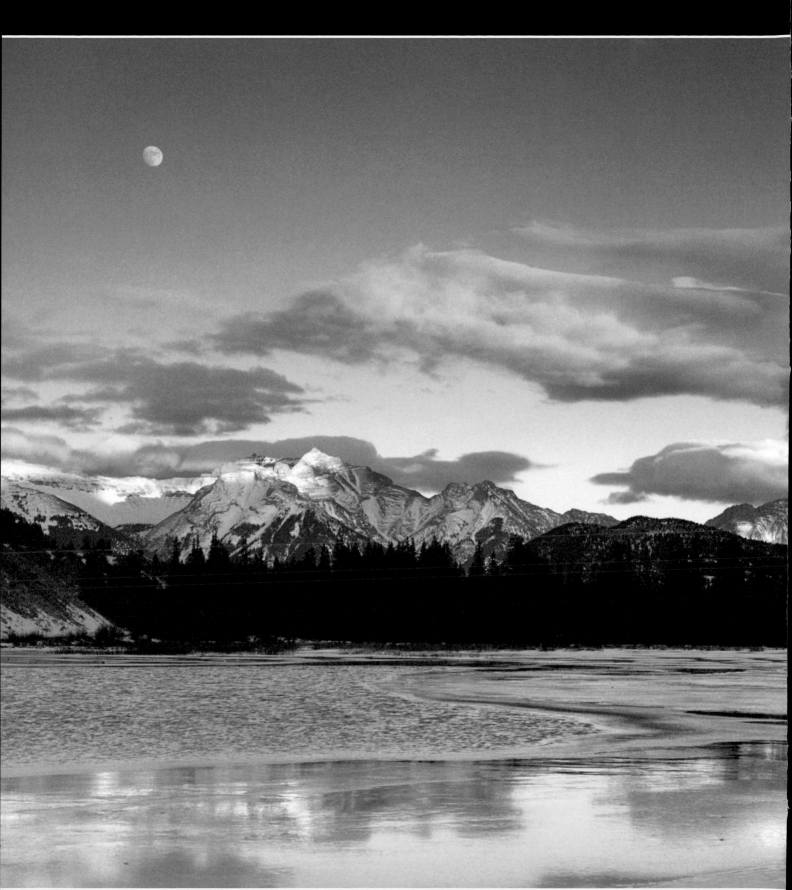

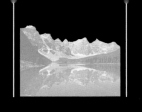
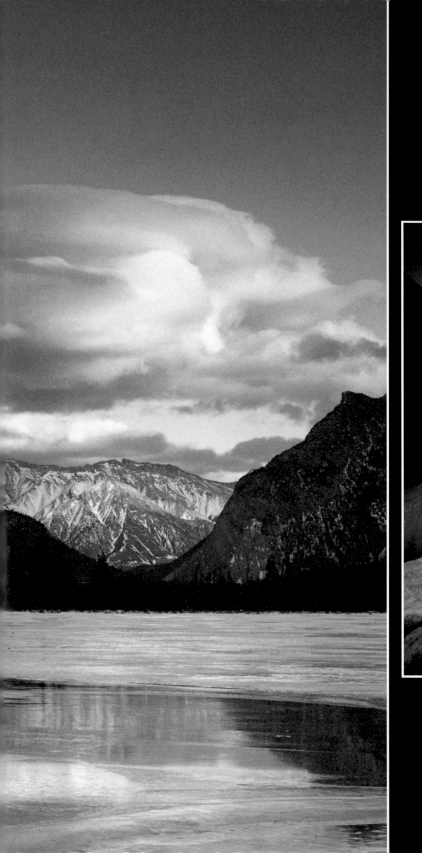
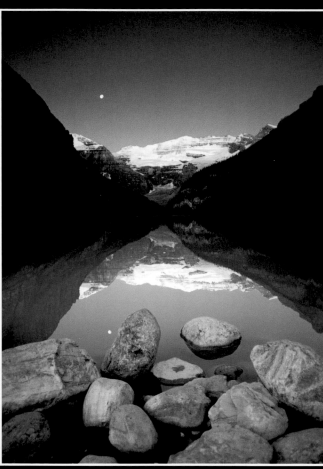

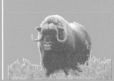

286 *The 2,000-foot face of Mount Proboscis in the Cirque of the Unclimbables is reflected in an unnamed lake.*

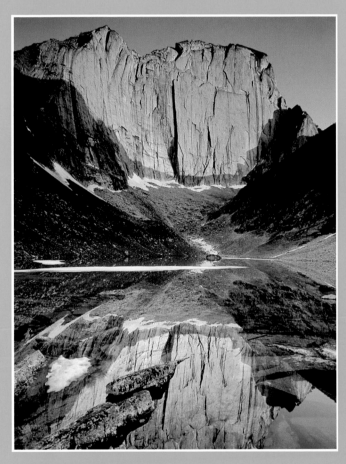

Canada's Northwest Territories

286–287 *A caribou crosses the Barrenlands beneath a pink summer sky at 11:00 P.M. in Canada's Western Arctic.*

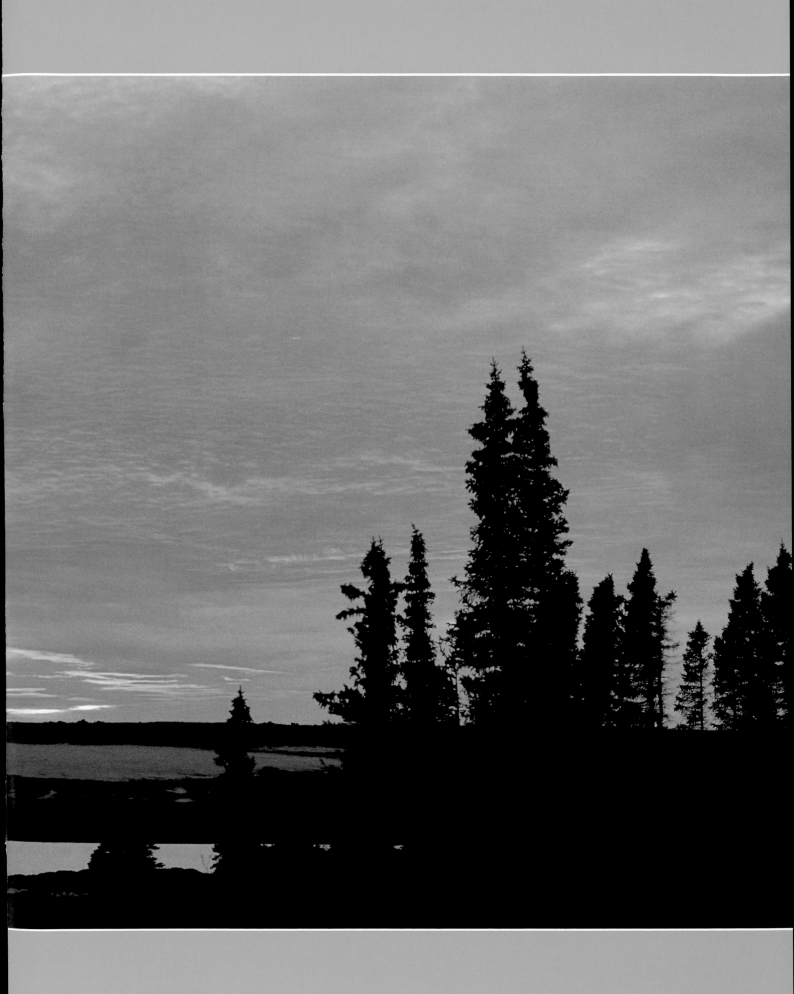

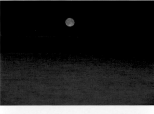

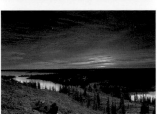

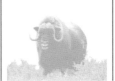

288 top A full moon rises over Whitefish Lake, 200 miles from the nearest road.

288 center The sun sets above an esker near the headwaters of the Thelon River.

During my last summer vacation in 1972, just before becoming a full-time photographer and writer, I joined a friend for several weeks in a place he said was the most beautiful on Earth. Officially unnamed, it was called the Cirque of the Unclimbables by the climbers who had discovered it a few years earlier. Fewer than twenty-five people had seen the Cirque when we camped in a paradise of alpine meadows surrounded with granite spires called Lotus Flower Tower and Parrot Beak Peak. Among other climbs, we made the first ascent of the face of the only officially named peak, 9062-foot Mount Sir James McBrien, the highest point in the Northwest Territories.

The largest roadless areas of habitable wildlands in North America are in the Canadian North, where we traveled by small plane, helicopter, and foot on my first two visits. Only when I later drove from California did I appreciate how the Far North gradually reveals itself through a progression of changes. Days became longer, sun angles lower, and vegetation less complex as species drop away with each passing mile into a more simplified landscape of elegant natural design.

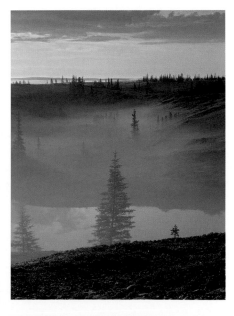

The northern treeline means far more than the end of trees and the beginning of tundra. It closely follows the isotherm drawn by scientists to demark Arctic and Subarctic life zones where average July temperatures fall below 50°F. The Inuit stayed north of the line; Athapaskan Indians to the south. The Inuit arrived from Siberia as coastal hunters of Arctic sea mammals long after loosely knit bands of Athapaskans had fanned out south of treeline to become nomadic hunters of caribou and bison. The two groups became fierce traditional enemies and rarely occupied the same lands.

On April 1, 1999 the Northwest Territories were split into two. The larger eastern sector was named Nunavut, while the remaining land to the northwest kept its name. The dividing line followed the classic boundary between forest and tundra, Arctic and Subarctic, Inuit and Indian, except where it verged north to reach the Arctic Coast. Thus the Inuit ended up as a large majority in Nunavut, but not in the NWT, where the Dene—encompassing many Athapaskan tribes with seven separate dialects—are presently negotiating massive land claims.

The capital of the NWT, Yellowknife, is a modern town of 17,000 set upon glacier-polished granite beside Great Slave Lake. Larger than some of the great lakes in volume, the 200-mile wide, 2000-foot deep lake is the source of the Mackenzie River that flows to the Arctic Coast. Nearby mines have long produced hundreds of thousands of ounces of gold a year, but the recent discovery of diamonds has created a new rush, with cartels such as De Beers running roughshod over the sensitivities of environmentalists to do widespread exploration and drilling in the wilderness.

To the east are the Barrenlands, a misnomer for some of the most beautiful landscapes on the planet. My fascination with them began forty years ago as I read Farley Mowat's Canadian bestseller, Never Cry Wolf. His descriptions of summer plains "thronged with life and brilliant with the colors of countless plants in bloom" and of lakes "whose very blue depths are flanked by summer flowers and sweeping green meadows" instantly dispelled any notions of the Arctic as cold and empty.

The new boundary of Nunavut runs through the 26,000-square-mile Thelon Game Sanctuary, set aside in 1927. The Thelon came about at the dawn of concerns over aerial hunting to preserve the rare forest musk oxen, which frequent an unusual forest oasis that snakes over a hundred miles north of treeline along the meandering course of the Thelon River. Here the Beverly caribou herd of over 400,000 migrates, as the Dene say, "like the wind coming from nowhere, filling up the land, then disappearing."

Today, the sanctity of this largest refuge in the world created expressly to protect wildlife is threatened both by drilling for diamonds and a draft plan to let Inuit and Dene people hunt and fish within traditional use areas, specifically including the Thelon Game Sanctuary.

In 1998, I watched Thelon musk ox flee photographers at first sight, while the previous year, I'd approached the same herds far more closely. In between, aboriginal hunters who live in towns and drive new pick-ups to the supermarket had flown deep into the Barrenlands to slaughter musk ox by the hundreds for "subsistence" without even taking much of the meat.

Though ecotourism is in its infancy in the NWT, a few national parks do exist. Wood Buffalo National Park on the border of Alberta has Canada's largest herds of free-roaming bison. Nahanni National Park protects the wild gorges and waterfalls of the legendary river of the same name. Aulavik in the High Arctic protects scenic badlands and archaeological sites.

I think of the entire Northwest Territories—as large as France, Germany, and Spain put together—as one vast natural preserve, among the Earth's last great unspoiled wildernesses. Protected by isolation more than by law, its High Arctic coasts, seas, and islands are the place to see whales, seals, and polar bears. Its central Barrenlands are a haven for wildlife along the raised glacial eskers that snake for hundreds of miles through tundra, forest, lake, and river. Its southern reaches hold North America's most expansive and intact boreal forests. All of this comes together without intervening civilization into continental North America's largest tract of roadless wilderness.

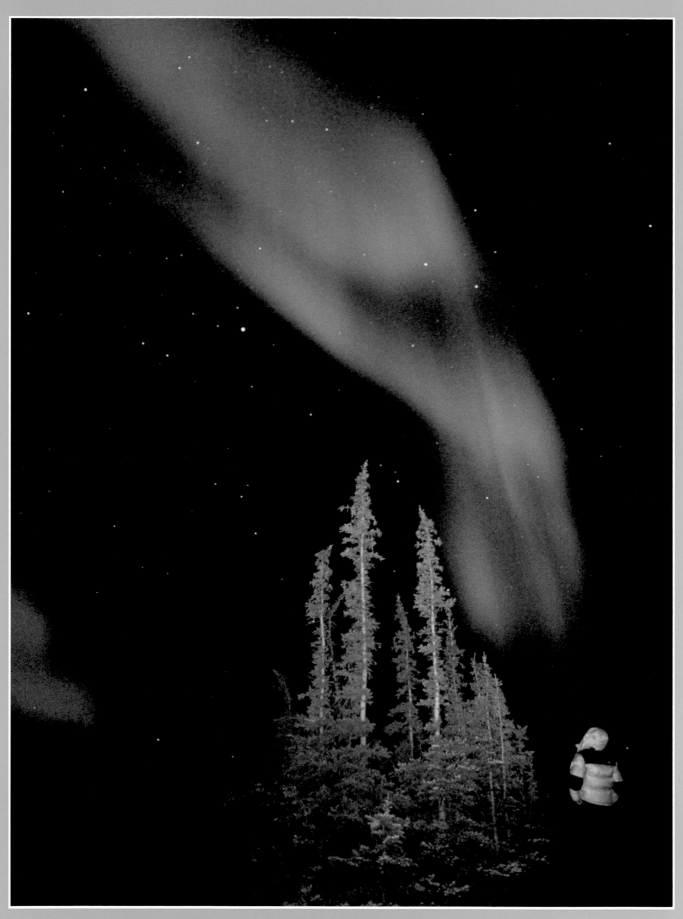

288 bottom Fall mists hover over the Barrenlands at the northern limit of treeline, where boreal forest ends and tundra begins.

289 At a remote camp near the headwaters of the Thelon River in the Barrenlands, the aurora borealis, better known as the northern lights, dances over a spruce forest in a starry sky on a September night. Here in the heart of the largest roadless wilderness on the continent that extends a thousand miles across northern Canada past Hudson Bay is the 26,000-square-mile Thelon Game Sanctuary.

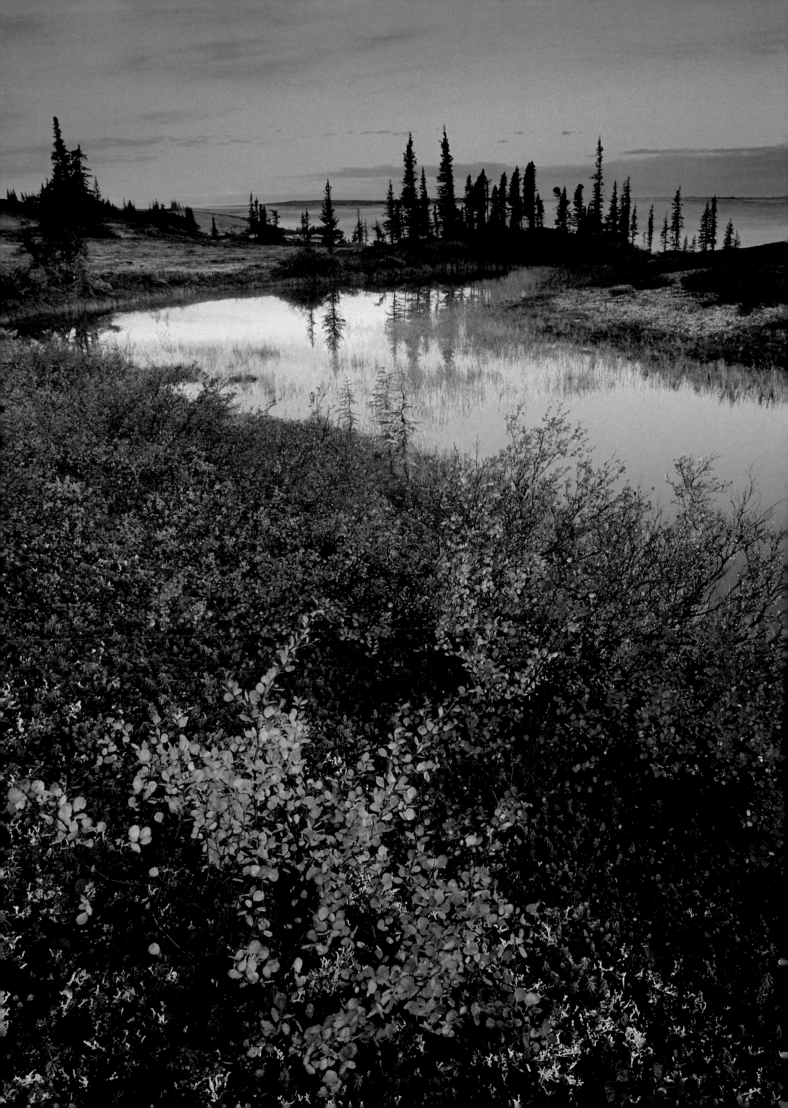

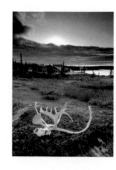
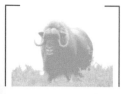

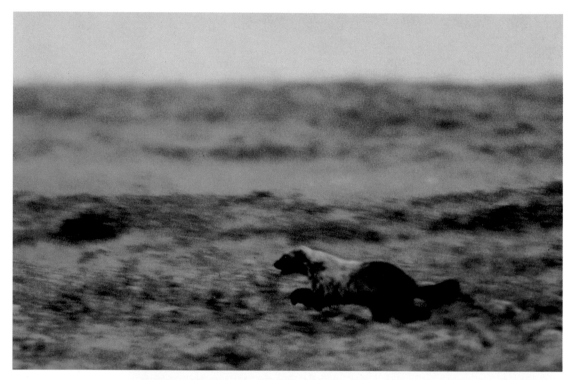

291 top A caribou skull near a wolf den marks a primeval struggle for survival near the headwaters of the Thelon River.

291 center A seldom-seen wolverine charges across open tundra in Barrenlands toward a herd of caribou.

291 bottom A caribou bull loses its "velvet" before shedding its antlers to save energy in winter. Blood flow cools the animal in the 24-hour summer sun and turns the antlers briefly blood red in fall.

290 Twilight over an Arctic pond near the headwaters of the Thelon River displays the full range of September colors on the tundra.

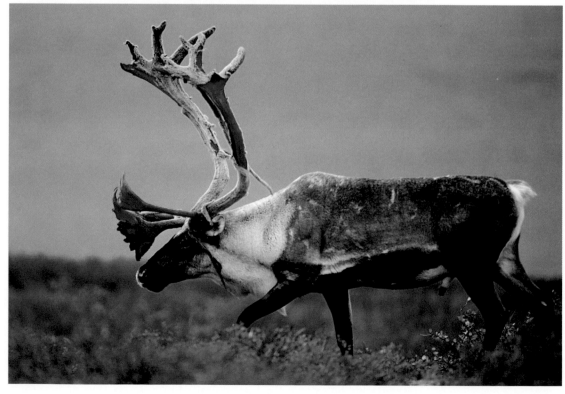

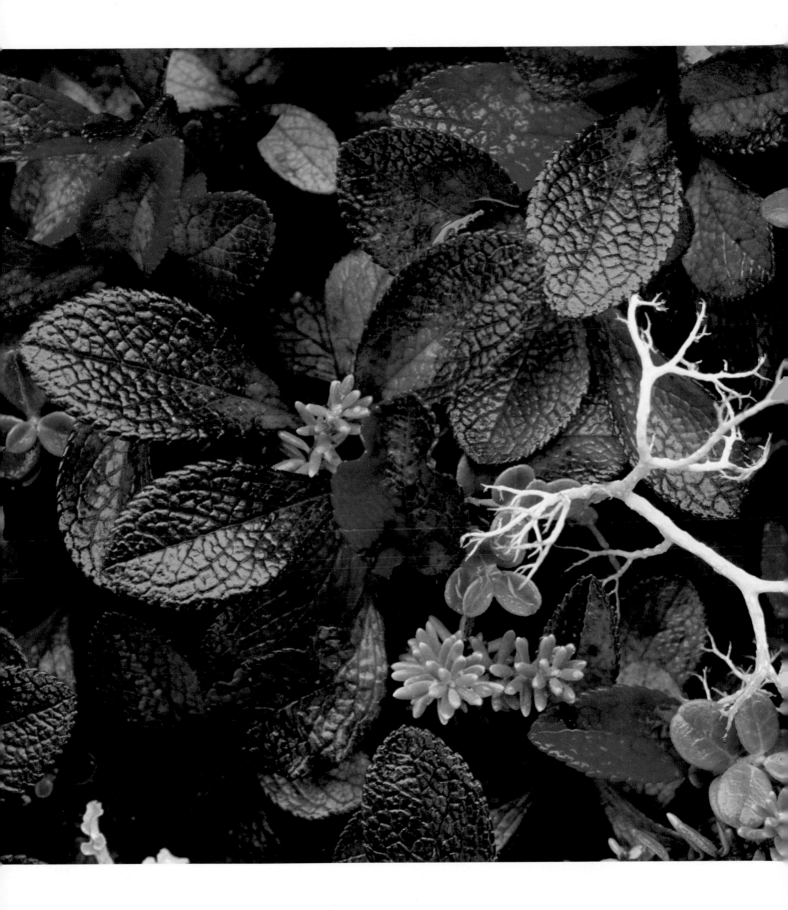

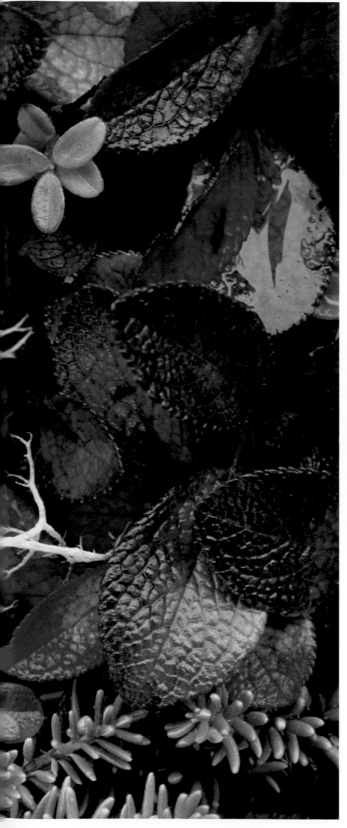

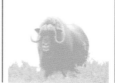

292–293 and 293
Caribou moss, actually
a lichen, sits amidst
bearberry leaves in the
Barrenlands, where
spruce boughs (below)
creep through on the
forest floor.

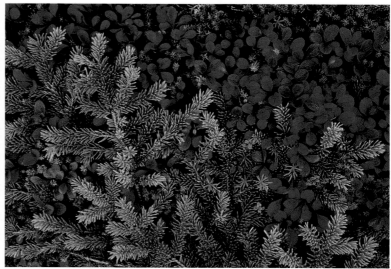

294 A mountain
goat climbs a sheer
cliff on Mount Harrison
Smith in the Cirque
of the Unclimbables.
The previous day,
climbers failed on
this mossy face with
ropes and pitons.

294–295 A rainstorm
veils unnamed peaks of
the Ragged Range of
the Mackenzie
Mountains above the
Nahanni River just
outside Nahanni National
Park, a UNESCO World
Heritage Site.

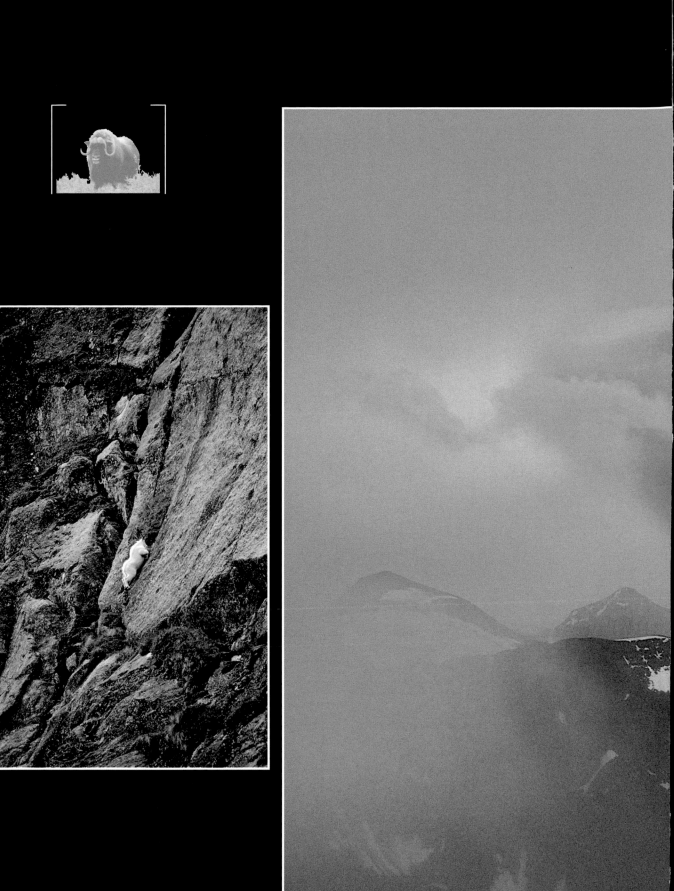

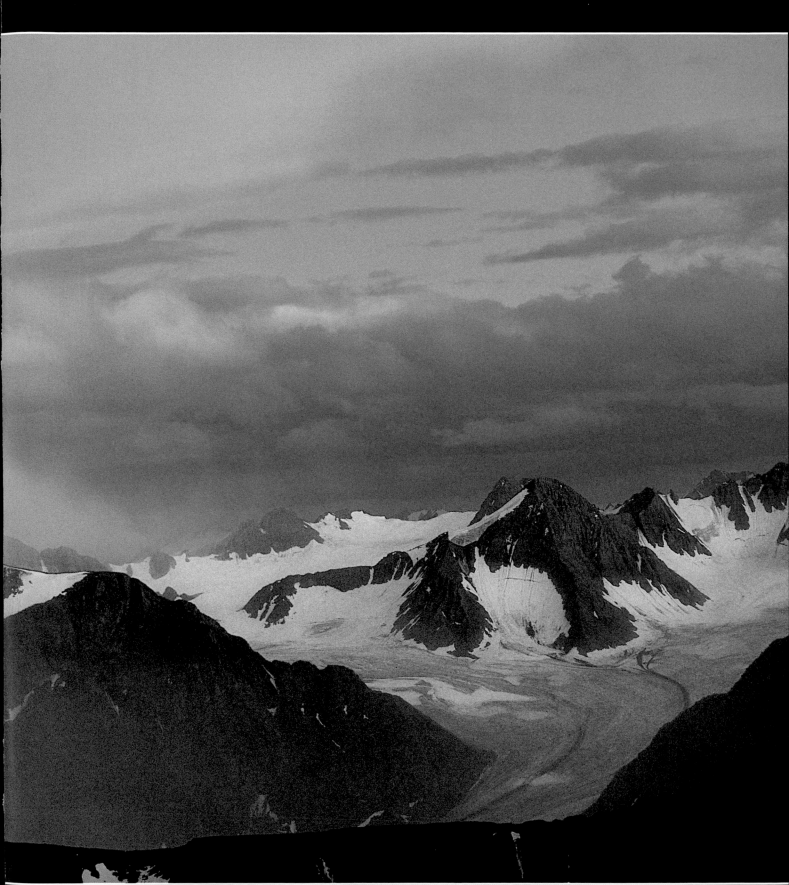

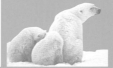

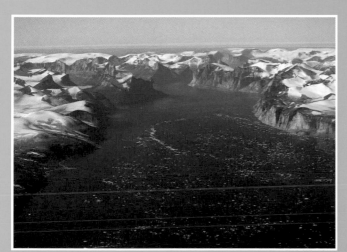

Canada's Eastern Arctic

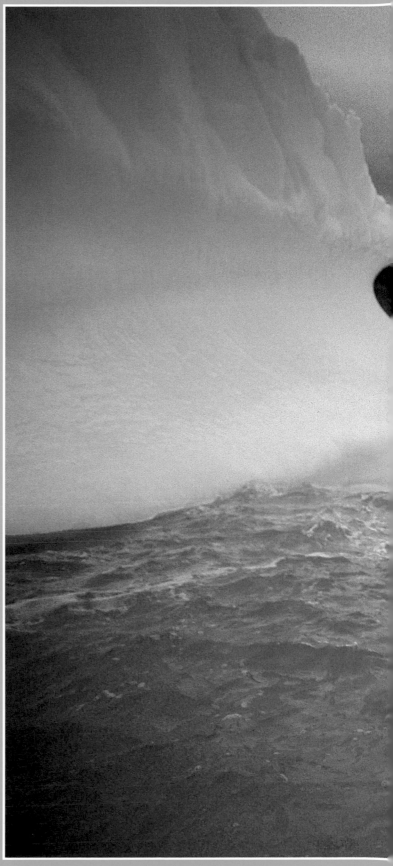

296–297 An iceberg looms large in Eclipse Sound between Baffin and Bylot Islands.

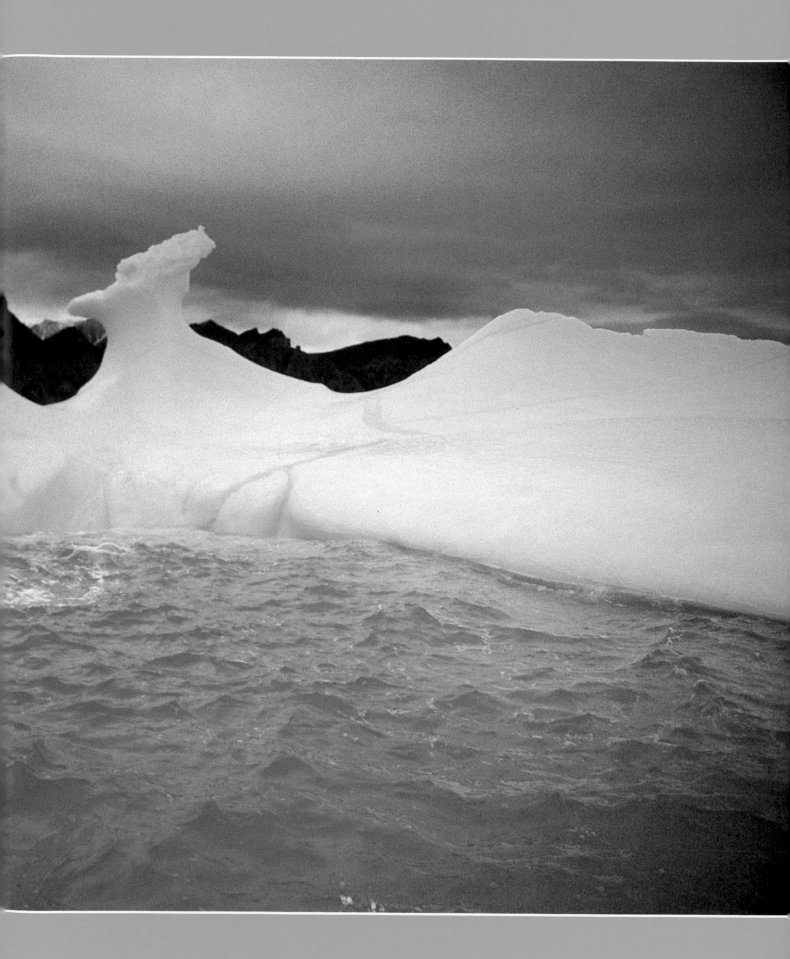

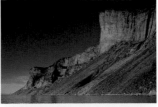

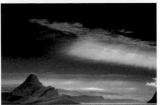

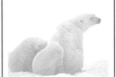

Canada's Eastern Arctic is a netherworld where the Barrenlands that touch Manitoba, Ontario, and Quebec roll northward until the continent splatters into islands before dropping off the edge of the earth into the Arctic Ocean. In many places glacier-scoured granites and gneisses expose the giant nucleus around which North America was formed—the vast 4-billion-year-old Canadian Shield. On April 1, 1999 all these lands became Nunavut, a new territory larger than any existing province.

Larger and farther north than Alaska, with a tenth the people and many more polar bears, Nunavut is truly the continent's "Last Frontier." The 85-percent Inuit majority has regained control of lands they inhabited long before Europeans claimed them without so much as a treaty. The name Inuit now refers to the native ethnic group of the entire circumpolar North, but in their Inuktitut language it originally meant "the people." Canadian Inuit object to being called Eskimo, while Alaskans do not. Their ancestors crossed the Bering Strait thousands of years ago, lured into the Canadian Arctic by the profusion of marine mammals, including polar bears.

Seeing large wild creatures is exciting for tourists, but for the Inuit these animals evoke the very embodiment of life and survival. To start the long winter night of Arctic darkness without enough stored meat meant slow death by starvation. Whales—bowhead, beluga, narwhal—made the difference in this most extreme inhabited environment on Earth.

Modern Inuit continue an economic, social, and artistic dependence on Arctic mammals. Their art conveys the abstract shapes of creatures that have long captured the fancy of more southerly cultures—bears, walrus, and whales, including the strange narwhal that gave rise to the legend of the unicorn when its spiraled, singular tusks were presented to medieval royalty.

Shortly before Nunavut became a territory, I explored parts of it with my son, Tony. We flew east from Yellowknife across the Barrenlands, a misnomer for the largest track of roadless wilderness in North America with more than a million lakes and caribou. Before crossing Hudson Bay, we passed over the Thelon Wildlife Sanctuary, the world's largest, where vast herds of caribou roam amidst musk oxen, wolves, and grizzly bears. Tony and I later explored some of this terrain on foot.

Our plane landed in Nunavut's capital, Iqaluit, formerly called Frobisher Bay after the British sailor who first landed there in 1576. The Hudson's Bay Company, established by royal decree in 1670, set up trading posts and controlled much of what is now Nunavut until selling their lands to the new Dominion of Canada in 1870.

To best explore and photograph the Arctic, Tony and I reversed our sleep patterns to stay up for August sunsets and sunrises two hours apart, then sleep by day with eye blinders. With the long hours of daylight, the weather was so mild that we went running at midnight in shorts without a shirt on a dirt street called the "Road to Nowhere," part of Nunavut's grand total of 12 miles of roads beyond city limits. It abruptly ended in tundra in just two miles.

Another flight took us north over wild cliffs and fjords to Pond Inlet on Baffin's north coast. We passed near Auyuittuq, Canada's first national park above the Arctic Circle, created in 1976 around the wild granite towers of Mounts Thor and Asgard. In Pond, we hired an Inuit guide and set out for a week in his open boat, wearing inflatable survival suits as we cruised fjords beneath Arctic Yosemites, while narwhals and seals surfaced out of the deeps.

At water's edge, three white spots below sheer cliffs caught my eye. As we neared shore, a polar bear family sprinted into a cul de sac surrounded by vertical walls. The mother bear turned with her two cubs and glowered down at us as our guide held his rifle to cover us as we leaped ashore to set up cameras.

Contrary to the myth that polar bears fear nothing, the rage in the mother bear's eyes spoke legions about Nunavut's growing conflict between ecotourism, sport hunting, and subsistence hunting involving the same wild creatures. Where animals are regularly hunted, wildlife viewing always suffers.

We had planned to sea kayak into Grise Fjord, Canada's northernmost town on Ellesmere Island, but our Inuit guides cancelled after a freak polar storm began to freeze the sea. Inuit were originally resettled into uninhabited Grise Fjord from the overfished Quebec side of Hudson Bay in 1953, but their later complaints about forced relocation helped fuel the creation of Nunavut.

Also south of Nunavut beside Hudson Bay is the world's polar bear capital of Churchill, Manitoba, where hundreds of these ultimate predators gather on the open tundra every fall on a thirty-mile peninsula around which the bay freezes first. They need sea ice to form before they can successfully hunt seals. In this area protected from hunting, they seem wholly unconcerned by fat-tired vehicles filled with camera-toting humans.

Though Churchill at 58° North is well south of the Arctic Circle, its climate is within a line biologists use to gauge the Arctic life zone. This "50°F summer isotherm" demarks where July temperatures fall below 50°F. It also roughly demarks some of the most compelling Arctic landscapes, where fingers of stunted boreal forest merge into open tundra.

Though I've climbed Arctic mountains and sailed iceberged seas, my fondest High Arctic memories are of camping on the tundra where the sky is big enough to see the sun set through a caribou's legs, then watch northern lights dance on the horizon. One such night, pierced by a wolf howl beneath a crescent moon, has become forever imprinted on my soul, though I found it impossible to capture in a single image on film.

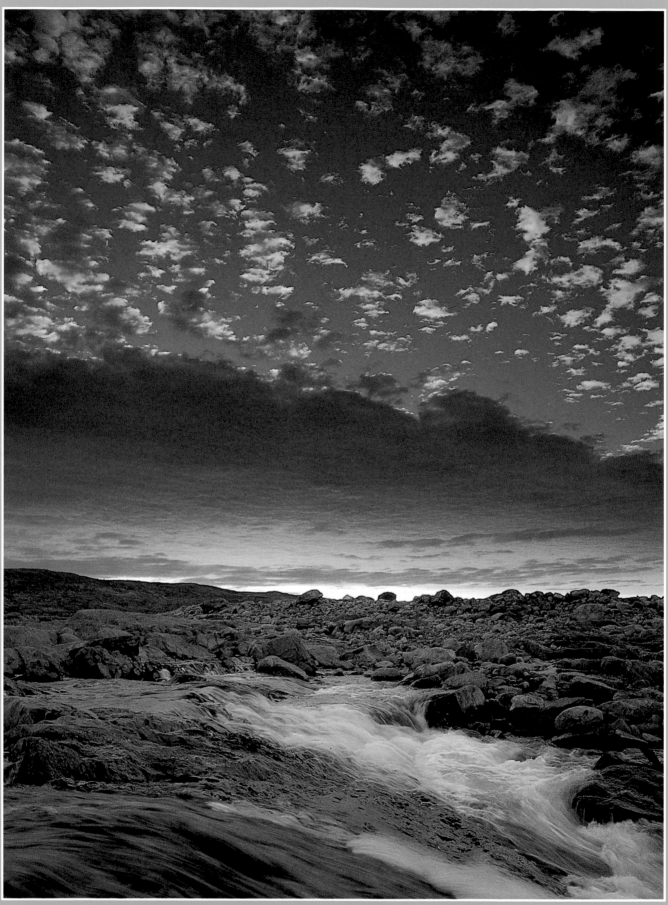

299 Freshwater cascades tumble through boulders atop the hard gneiss of the Canadian Shield in Sylvia Grinnell Territorial Park on Baffin Island. Located near Iqaluit, the capital of the brand new territory of Nunavut vetted on April 1, 1999, the park is at the head of Frobisher Bay, where the United States built and maintained a strategic airstrip, now used for basic air transportation in and out of remote Baffin Island. Inuit families spend the summer in tents beside these waters to fish during the brief Arctic summer.

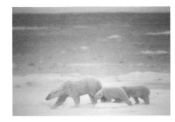

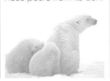

300 top A polar bear family walks through a blizzard with cubs hunkering downwind from their mother beside Hudson Bay on Cape Churchill.

300 center An arctic fox with a perfect star-shaped snowflake on its nose peers from its den.

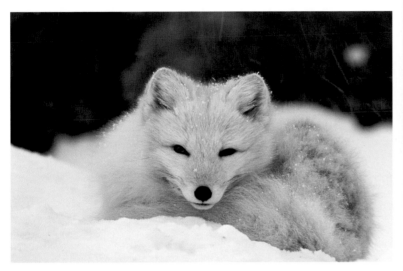

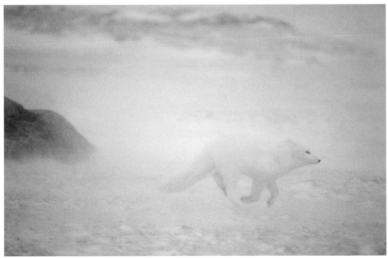

300 bottom An arctic fox appears almost invisible as it runs through a blizzard near Churchill, Manitoba. Brown or charcoal gray in summer, the foxes turn pure white in winter.

300–301 A polar bear mother with cubs-of-the-year hides from a blizzard near Cape Churchill, where the first ice forms on Hudson Bay. More than 300 bears gather each fall, waiting for the ice to form to hunt seals.

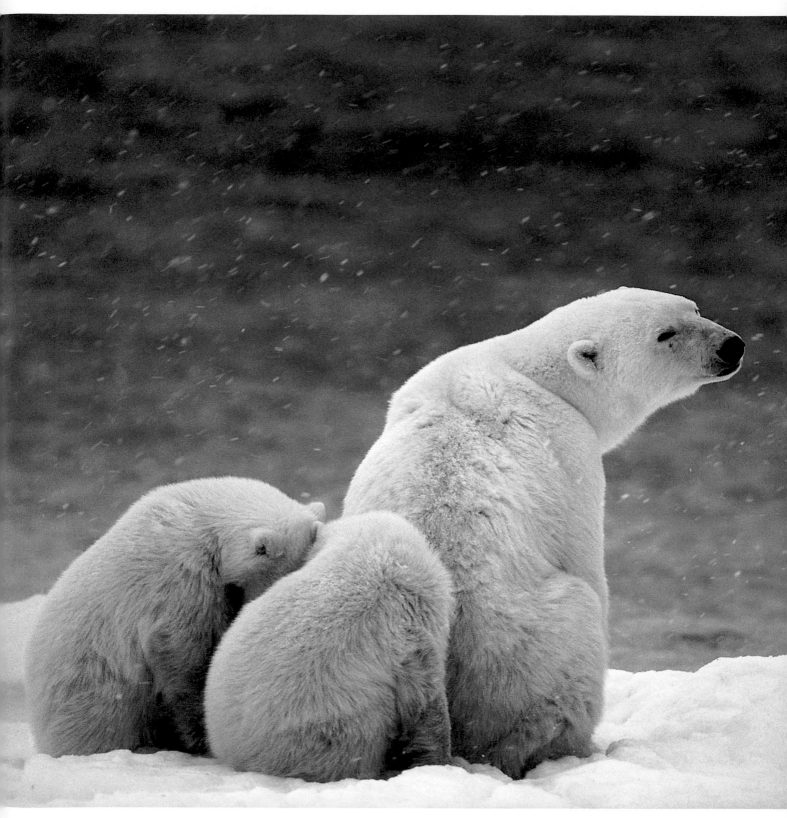

302–303 A polar bear cub cuddles against his mother beneath the evening sun on Cape Churchill.

303 A full moon rises over the "Land of Little Sticks" where the northernmost trees give way to tundra beside Hudson Bay.

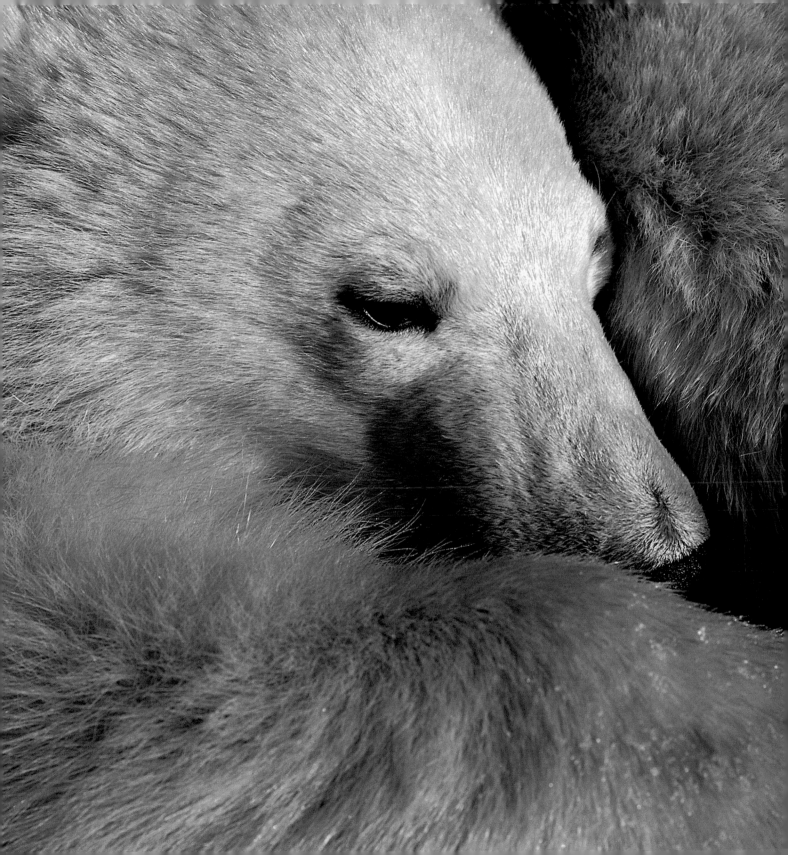

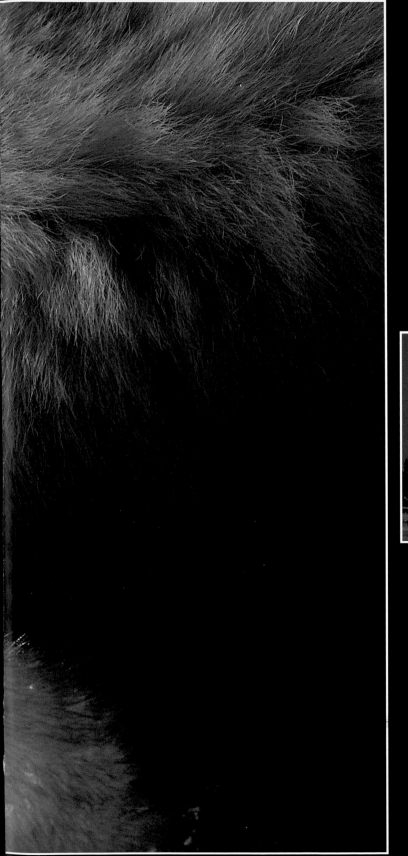
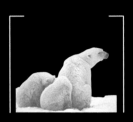
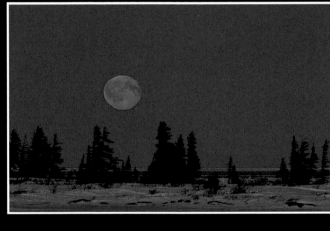

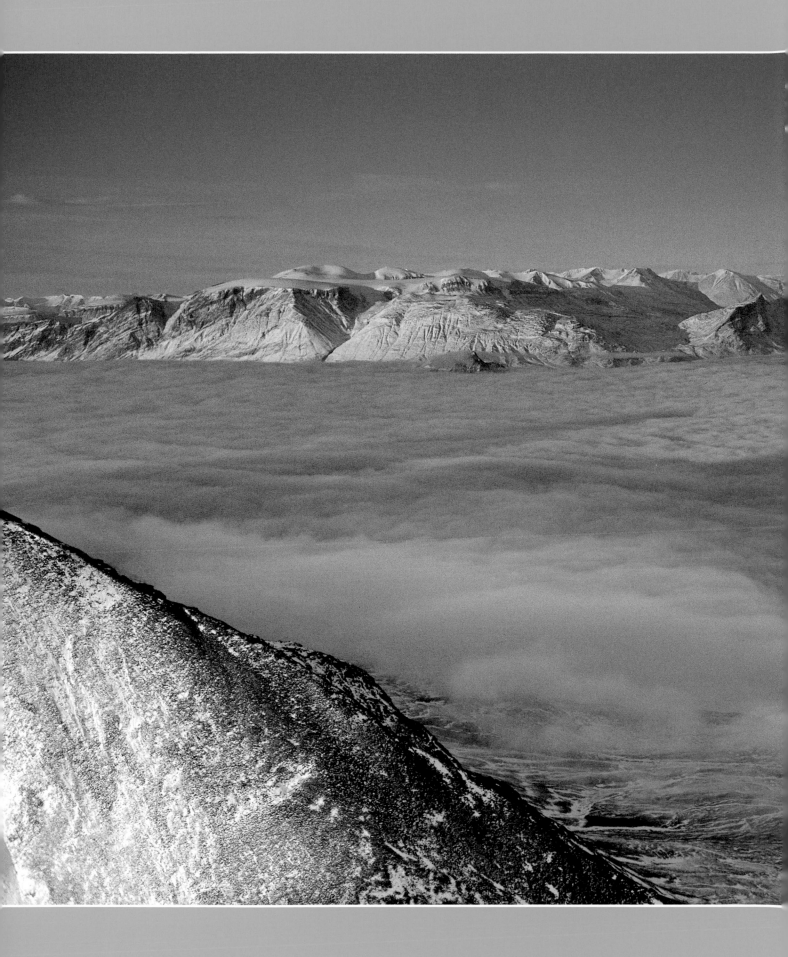

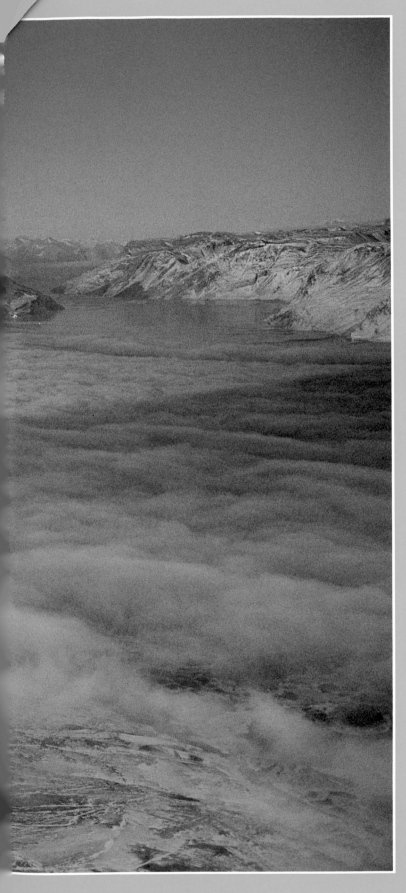

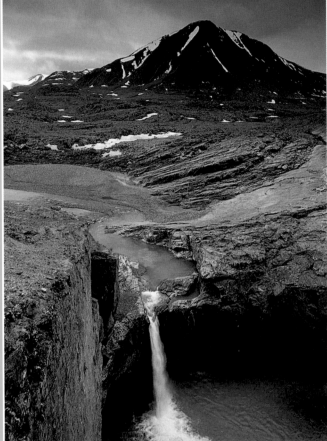

Greenland

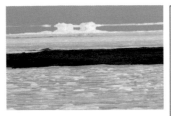

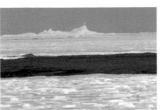

Despite what many Americans believe, Greenland is not a foreign, oceanic island far out in the North Atlantic, but a continental extension of North America. Beneath the 10,000 feet of ice that cover the vast interior of this largest island in the world is the bedrock of the Canadian Shield, the geological core of North America. In ice-free areas its coasts look for all the world like those beachless stretches of the Maine Coast where the same freshly glaciated granites and gneisses of the ancient shield roll into the sea. Were Greenland twenty miles off the coast of Maine, instead of being that brief distance from Ellesmere Island in the remote Canadian Arctic, it would be universally recognized as North American.

Artifacts indicate that ancient Inuit traveled eastward across Canada from Asia to arrive in Greenland at least 4,500 years ago. A renegade Norseman named Eric the Red sailed west from Iceland to make the first documented "discovery" of Greenland in 981 A.D. Five years later, he established the first colony, which vanished in the 15th century as a period of global warming ended and the ice began to advance again. His more famous son, Leif Ericson, sailed further west in 999 A.D. to land on the coast of Labrador and "discover" North America 492 years before Columbus.

Between 1817 and 1822, Scottish father-and-son whaling captains named Scoresby explored the apparently uninhabited east coast above the Arctic Circle and found 280-mile Scoresby Sound, the world's longest fjord. The following summer, Captain Clavering ventured 200 miles farther north and met 12 Inuit with tents, kayaks, and harpoons. They vanished in fright and no other living members of their separate Thule culture of Northeast Greenland have ever been seen again. The present 500 Inuit who inhabit the coast's most northerly village of Ittoqqortoormiit (formerly Scoresbysund) were transplanted from the south in 1925 by the Danish in a demonstration of sovereignty after Norway claimed the uninhabited Northeast Coast. In 1933, the World Court at the Hague confirmed Danish control based on centuries of presence so long as they displayed "the will to possess."

In 1979, Denmark relinquished "Home Rule" to the Inuit, who changed nearly every place name in the country. The capital of Godthab became Nuuk. Even the World War II American air base with the seemingly native name of Thule was rechristened "Pituffik." Denmark retained control of foreign policy, defense, currency, the judiciary, and visitation, with the tightest restrictions on the vast Northeast Greenland National Park, the world's largest. Half again as big as Texas, the park encompasses a third of all Greenland, including a surprising amount of ice-free land along the coasts and north of the ice cap.

The majority of ecotourism and mountaineering now takes place well south of the park in spectacular fjords, such as Tasiilaq and Tasermiut, where giant granite spires and cliffs erupt from the seas and surrounding glaciers. Though permits for summer climbing outside the park are not difficult to obtain, Reinhold Messner was denied one for a winter ski crossing of the island south of the park in the early 1990s.

My first ground visit to Greenland was a *Life* magazine assignment on the Sirius Sled Patrol, an elite Danish military corps. They patrol thousands of miles of this uninhabited coastline by dog sled and act as rangers for the national park. The Danes call the remote northeast coast the Arctic Riviera, a zone that has too little precipitation to breed glaciers, yet just enough to set wildflowers of all colors in bloom in the 24-hour summer sunlight. I camped there in autumn snows beneath northern lights after flying eye-to-eye beside Greenland's highest peaks in the Stauning Alps with the ice cap

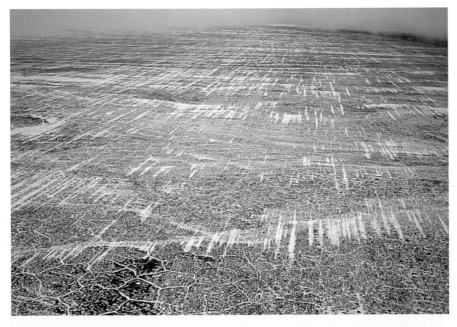

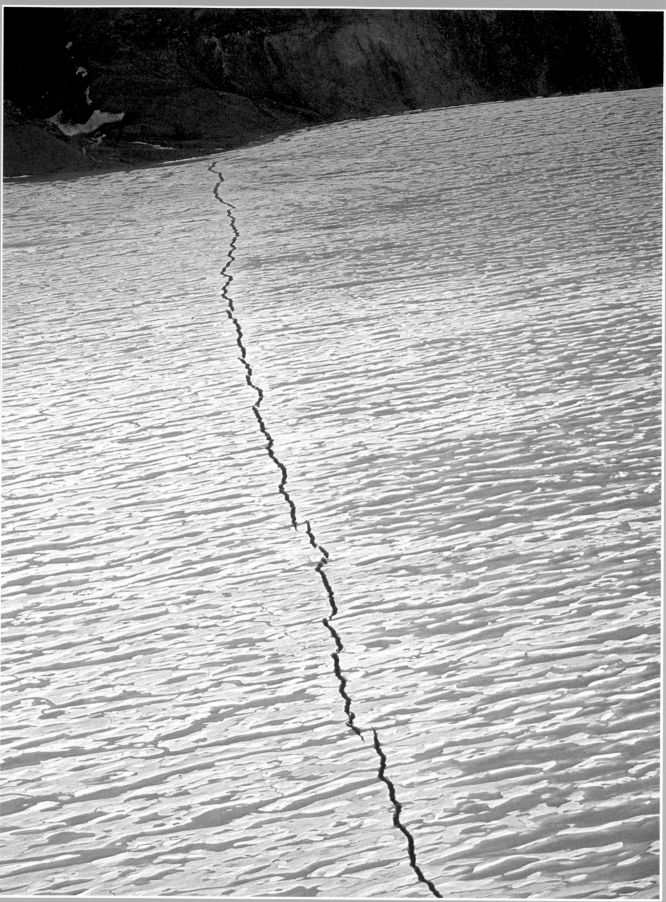

306 bottom Though the extreme northern tip of Greenland remains surprisingly ice free today, these great gouges were scoured by glaciers that receded back into the island's huge icecap only in the last few thousand years of warming since the most recent ice age.

307 Before summer break-up, a crack opens up in the ice of Frederick Hyde Fjord, which separates North and South Pearyland. Before the advent of the airplane, explorers traveled only in the spring and fall when fjords were all frozen.

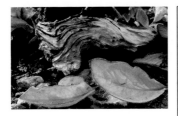

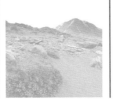

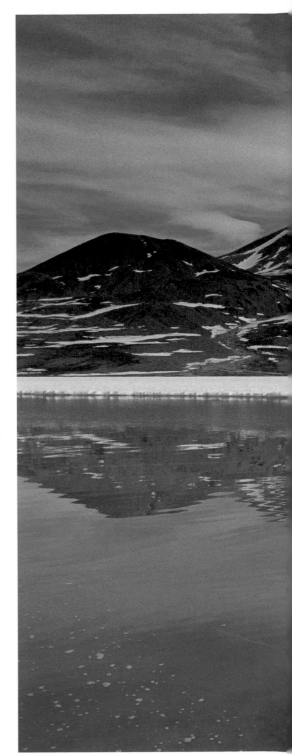

shimmering in the distance like a cloud. I was eager to return in summer to visit unexplored parts of this Arctic world that few people know.

The small expedition I joined in 1996 had spent over a decade garnering permission and funding to be able to explore the northern tip of Greenland within the park. The group's goals were to climb virgin peaks in the virtually unexplored H.H. Benedict Range, as well as to be the first to reach the northernmost point of land on Earth by self-propelled means.

In 1900, the famous American explorer, Robert E. Peary, had claimed nearby Cape Morris Jessup as the Earth's northernmost point of land and named it after the president of the American Museum of Natural History, who had given him $50,000. He further repaid Jessup by giving the museum a giant meteorite worshipped by Inuit whom he befriended to the extent of fathering children. He told them that he was only borrowing the stone to have experts examine it.

In 1921, Danish explorer Lauge Koch spotted an obvious island farther north, visible from Cape Jessup on a good day, but not until 1978 did the Danish Geodetic Institute confirm its coordinates. They landed a helicopter on the half-mile rocky edifice and gave it the insouciant name of Kaffeklubben—Coffee Club Island. When someone pointed to a dark spot nearly a mile farther north, they flew out to a 25-foot-wide chunk of graveled bedrock rising two feet above the water and named it Oodaaq Island after Peary's Inuit companion on his 1909 attempt to reach the North Pole, just 439 miles to the north.

The Danes have good reason to doubt Peary's claim to have reached the North Pole, based not only on his poor data to support that claim, but also on his dismal record of exploring and mapping northern Greenland. After failed expeditions into

Greenland's interior in 1884 and 1891, Peary claimed a huge independent island for the United States in 1900, naming it "Peary Land." As a direct result of his maps showing the island separated by a non-existent "Peary Channel," one of Denmark's legendary heroes of exploration, Mylius Erichsen, died in dead-end Independence Fjord. As American General A. W. Greely reported in the 1920s, "the coast as charted by Peary proved to be entirely erroneous."

In 1996, my expedition flew the entire Northeast Coast in a Twin Otter, stopping at Danish weather and patrol stations en route. As we finally stepped off the plane into Peary's footsteps, Kaffeklubben Island loomed large out of the sea ice, but Oodaq took days of searching to find. After crossing two miles of pack ice laced with open leads of water up to our thighs, we reached Kaffeklubben Island, where we found the most northerly flowering plants on Earth—purple saxifrage, arctic poppy, and alpine draba.

Oodaq had no flowering plants. When we reached it, feet soaked and numb, I laughed heartily as my partner, Bob Palais, tried to balance on the single rock breaking the surface. This was our island? Our great goal? Pack ice driven upward onto shore by polar storms had partially melted, creating a false sea level that obscured all but the island's highest point.

The remainder of the expedition included first ascents and ski descents of peaks, plus a long encounter with a herd of fearless musk oxen which spent the day eating wildflowers beside our tents. My most powerful memory of Greenland is recorded in my photograph of a dead musk ox receding into soft tundra, vanishing ever so gradually as grasses and flowers sprouted around it on the otherwise barren plain—an affirmation of the Arctic cycle of life.

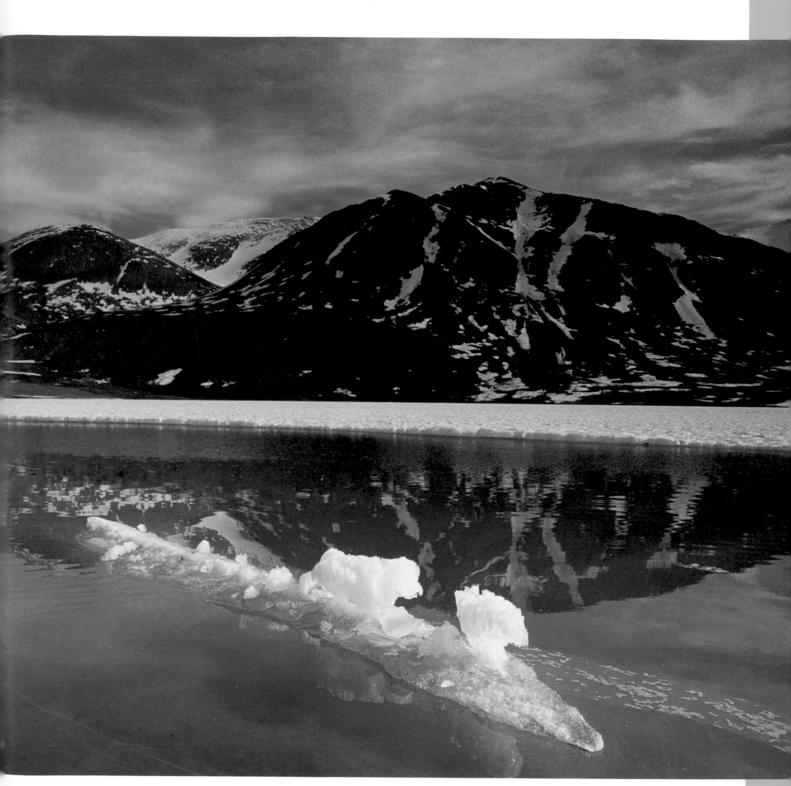

308–309 An iceberg floats in summer in a lake on the floor of Paradise Valley near Bliss Bay on the peaceful, uninhabited north coast of Greenland at 83° north in Northeast Greenland National Park. The background mountains of the H.H. Benedict Range all unclimbed until 1996, nearly a century after Robert E. Peary's first visit, when he named the area Pearyland in the false belief that it was a separate island from the rest of Greenland. He also claimed the wrong location for the northernmost point of land, further undermining his vaguely supported claim to have reached the North Pole in 1909.

310 top Eider ducks take flight over icebergs from their nesting grounds on the shores of Dove Bay at 79° north.

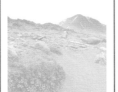

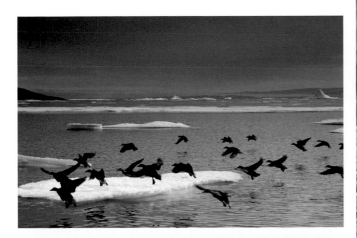

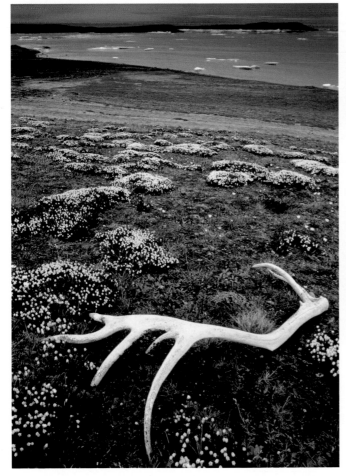

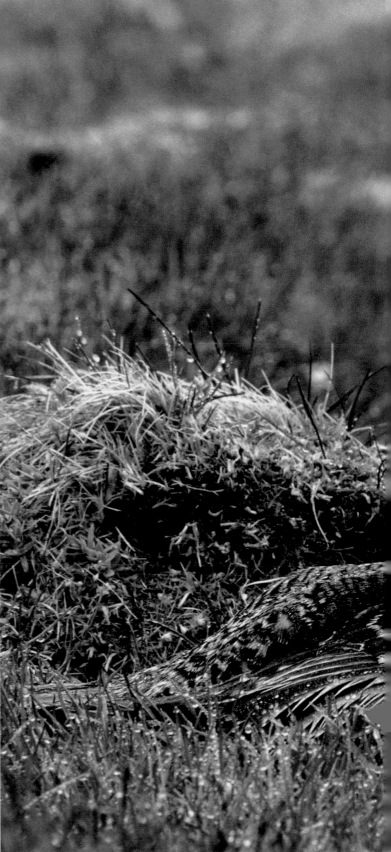

310 bottom Peary caribou, a rare species of tiny High Arctic caribou, vanished in a single season after the harsh winter of 1900 from all of the lands that are now Northeast Greenland National Park. On the open tundra of what Danish explorers call the "Arctic Riviera," a bleached antler lies beside purple saxifrage at Dove Bay.

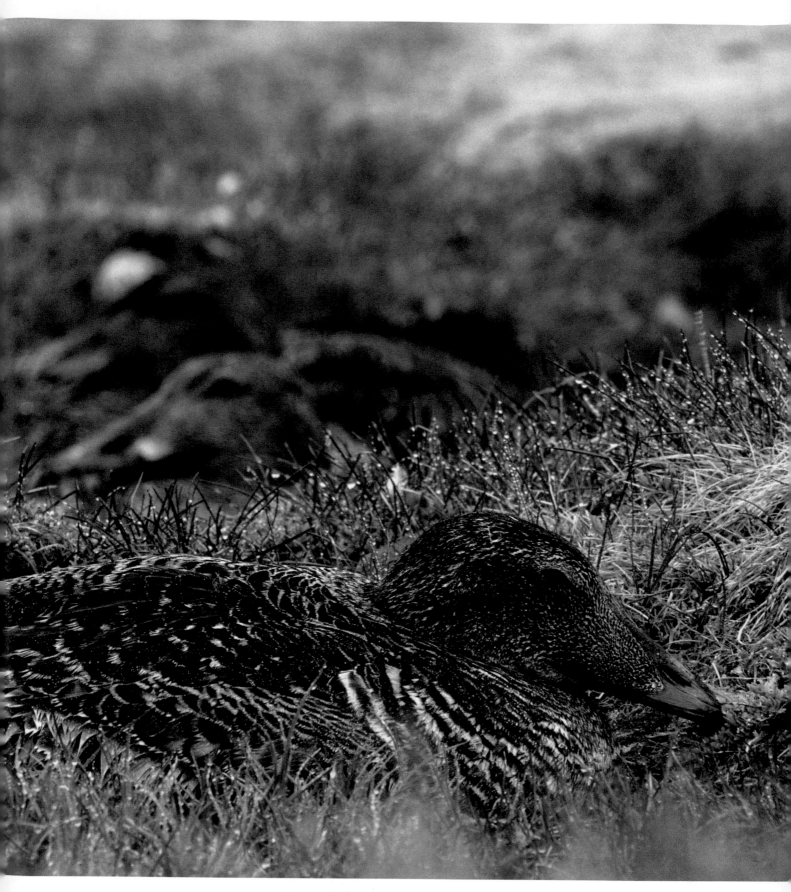

310–311 Eider ducks
nest in summer in the
soft tundra grasses of
the cape, seen beside
Dove Bay in the
photograph at left. The
famous Danish explorer
Mylius Erichsen named

the spot
Dansmarkshavn and
built a cabin shortly
before perishing as he
tried to follow Robert E.
Peary's "erroneous"
map through a non-
existent channel.

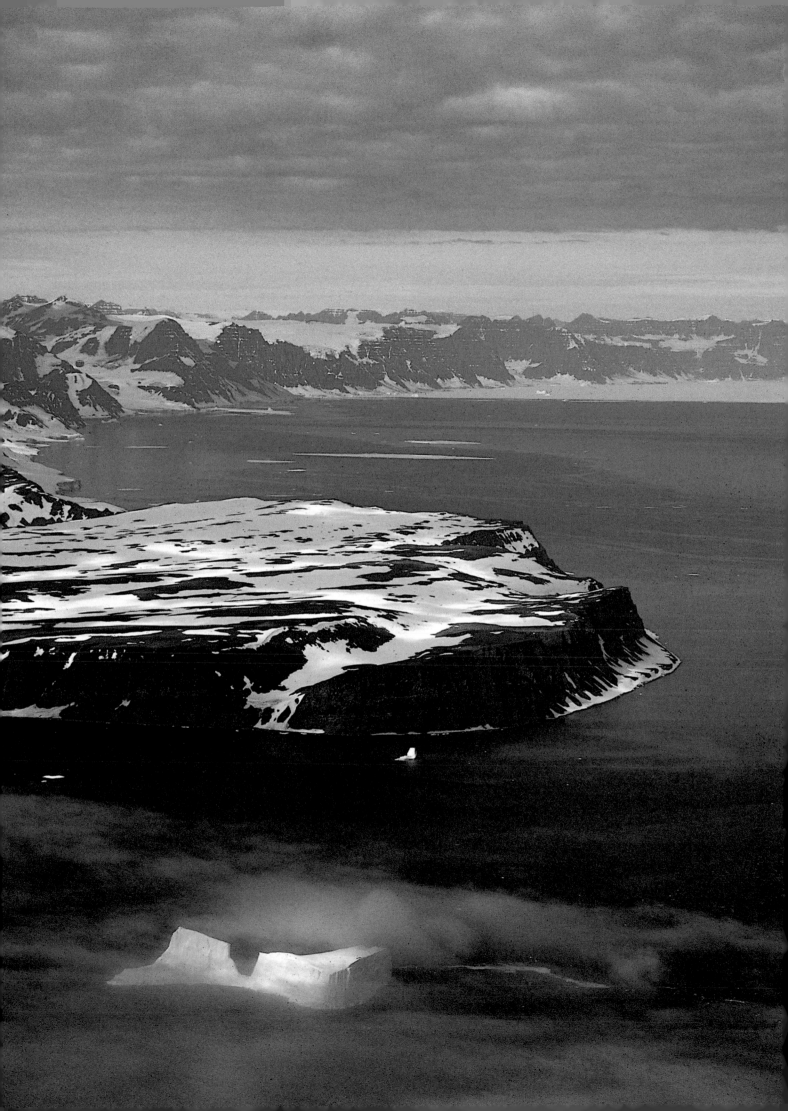

312 Icebergs veiled
in mist float out into
the Atlantic Ocean
from a bay south
of the Stauning Alps
in Northeast
Greenland National
Park.

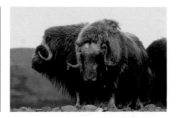

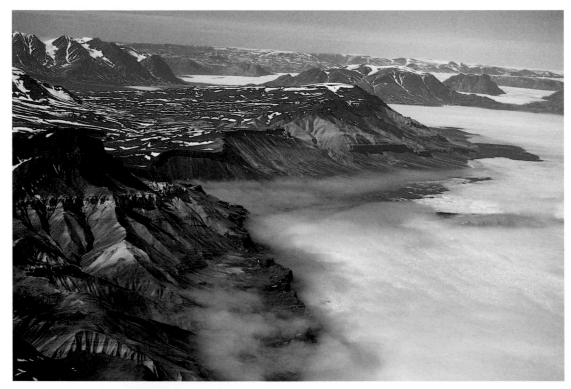

*313 top A herd of
musk oxen claim the
title of the northernmost
resident land mammal
as they browse the
tundra at 83°30" north
at the tip of North
Pearyland.*

*313 center The rugged
northeast coast rises
into the Stauning Alps
north of Mesters Vig.*

*313 bottom A glacier
called "The Elephant's
Foot" descends from
a tributary of the
Greenland Icecap
at 80° north.*

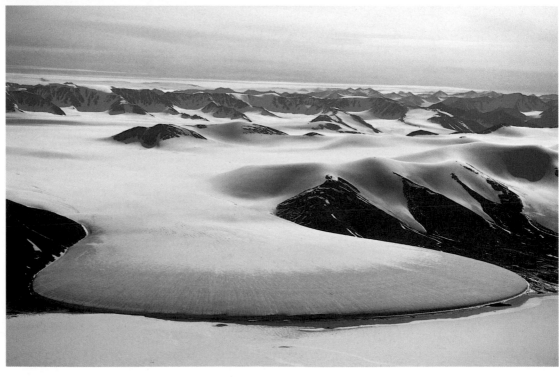

313

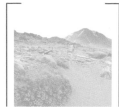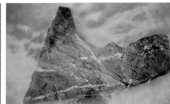

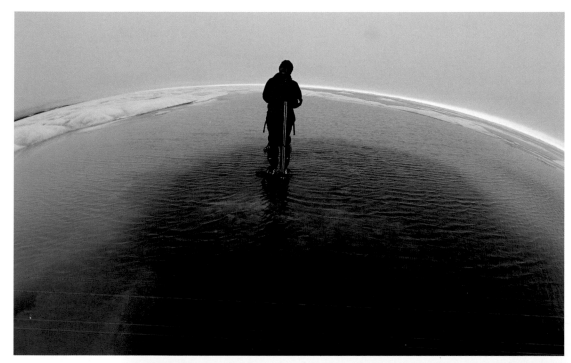

316 Mists creep inland over Bliss Bay toward the H.H. Benedict Range of North Pearyland.

316–317 Northern lights color a star-streaked sky over a dogsled camp in frozen Youngsund Fjord.

314 top and center Explorer Bob Palais balances atop the northernmost point of land on earth, a rock barely above the surface (top) of meltwater from pack ice driven aground by fierce arctic storms. During some years, Oodaq Island never appears above ice or water at 83°40" north; during others, a patch 50 feet long is above water.

314 bottom and 315 Sunrise flushes peaks of Northeast Greenland National Park at 74° north above frozen Youngsund Fjord.

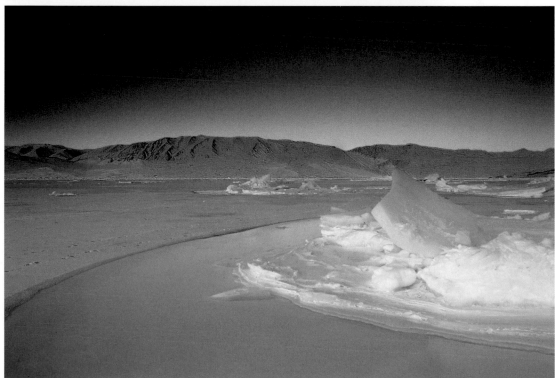

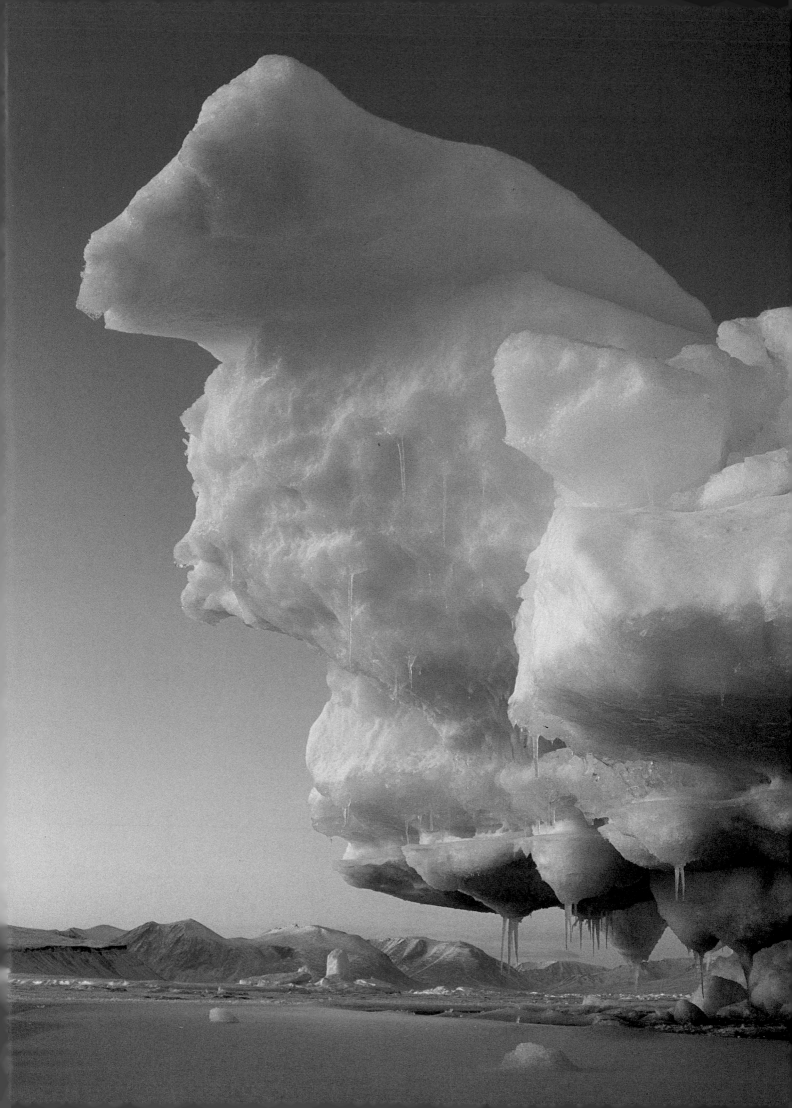

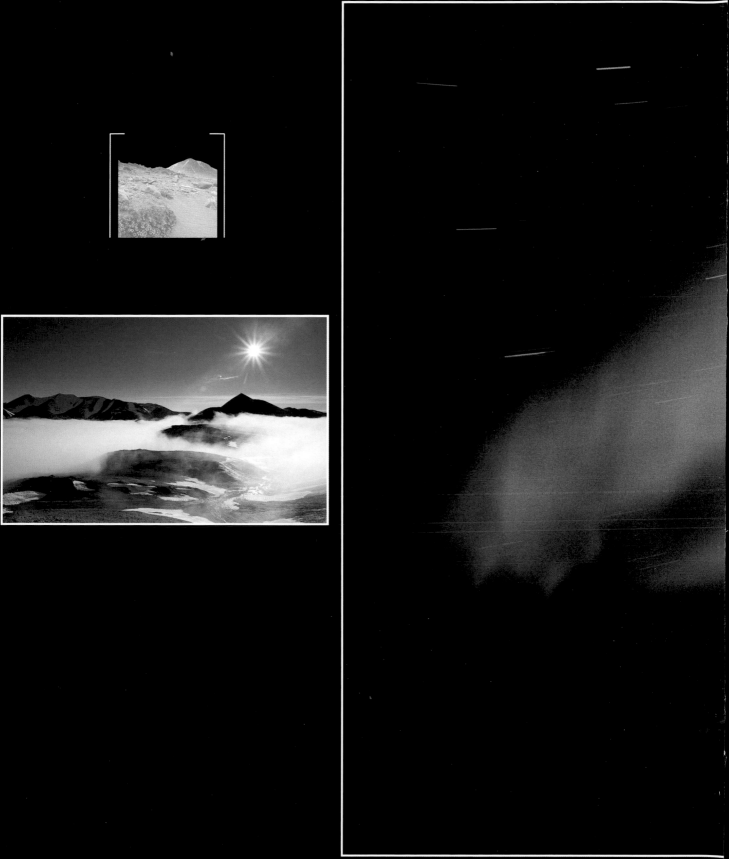

INDEX

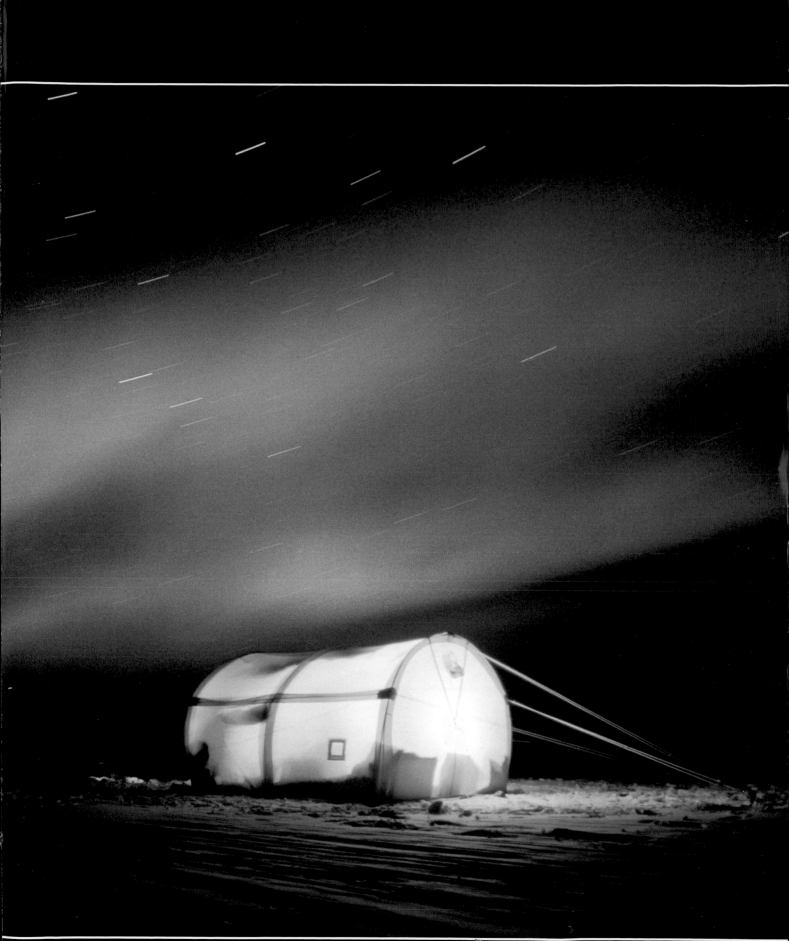

320 Wizard Island rises
out of Oregon's Crater
Lake, one of North
America's most famous
natural wonders created
6,500 years ago when
a volcano blew its top
and the resulting crater
filled to a depth of
1,900 feet.